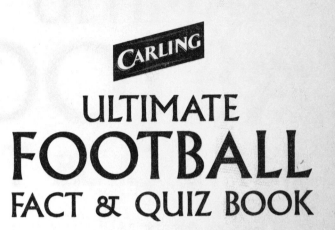

CARLING

ULTIMATE
FOOTBALL
FACT & QUIZ BOOK

ULTIMATE
FOOTBALL
FACT & QUIZ BOOK

Written and compiled by
HENRY RUSSELL

Cartoons by
PETER COUPE

STOPWATCH

First published in Great Britain by
Stopwatch Publishing Limited
First Floor
1-7 Shand Street
London
SE1 2ES

This edition published 1999

Printed and bound in Finland by WSOY

Cartoons by Peter Coupe
Written and compiled by Henry Russell

© Stopwatch Publishing Limited

ISBN 1 900032 98 8

CONTENTS

FOOTBALL QUIZZES

FOOTBALL QUIZ CONTENTS

AROUND THE WORLD

THE CARLING ULTIMATE FOOTBALL FACT AND QUIZ BOOK

Quiz 1
AROUND THE WORLD

1 During the 1950s, which Spanish team were known as 'The Club Kings of the World'?

2 During the build-up to the 1994 finals, which country inflicted Brazil's first ever defeat in World Cup qualifying matches?

3 In 1986, which team became the first from a Communist country to win the European Cup?

4 In which city do RWD Molenbeek play their home games?

5 What is the name of the football club in Boston, Massachusetts which was founded in 1862 and is the oldest outside Britain?

6 Which Argentine international was born on August 3, 1952 and played his first professional game for Huracan of Buenos Aires?

7 Which club has won the European Cup seven times, its own domestic League Championship 28 times and its Cup 16 times?

8 Which club was expelled from the 1995-96 Champions' League after being accused of trying to bribe a referee?

9 Which team plays its home games at the Karaiskaki Stadium, Piraeus, Athens?

10 Which team won the West German FA Cup in 1974, 1975, 1981 and 1988?

11 Who was the coach of Euro 96 winners Germany?

12 If Juventus is the Old Lady, who or what is the Old Man?

13 In which year was the Heysel disaster?

14 Which Bulgarian scored 19 goals in 50 games for his country before being killed in a road accident in 1971?

15 Which Italian international was born on February 18, 1967 in Caldogno and made his League debut for Vicenza at the age of only 15 before being transferred to Fiorentina, where he made his name, in 1985?

Answers

1 Real Madrid **2** Bolivia **3** Steaua Bucharest **4** Brussels **5** Oneida **6** Osvaldo Ardiles
7 Real Madrid **8** Dynamo Kiev **9** Olympiakos **10** Eintracht Frankfurt **11** Berti Vogts
12 AC Milan **13** 1985 **14** Georgi Asparoukhov **15** Roberto Baggio

THE CARLING ULTIMATE FOOTBALL FACT AND QUIZ BOOK

AROUND THE WORLD

1 Which King of Spain conferred the title 'Real' ('Royal') on Real Madrid?

2 Which Portuguese club won the 1987 European Cup, beating Bayern Munich in the Final in Vienna?

3 Which Spanish club plays its home matches at the Estadio Vicente Calderón?

4 Which team plays its home matches at Tolka Park, Dublin?

5 Who did Steaua Bucharest beat in the 1986 European Cup Final?

6 Who played in 21 World Cup finals matches in the 20th century, more than any other German?

7 Who scored the winning goal for the USA in their celebrated victory over England in the 1950 World Cup finals?

8 For which Buenos Aires club did Alfredo Di Stefano play before moving to Real Madrid?

9 In 1991, which Italian club failed to qualify for Europe for the first time in 28 years?

10 In 1994, against which country did Bulgaria record their first victory in the World Cup finals?

11 In the 1998 World Cup finals, who put Mexico ahead against Germany?

12 In which Spanish city do Rayo Vallecano play their home matches?

13 In which year was the Hillsborough disaster?

14 Which international was born on December 20, 1937 and first played for Chesterfield in 1955?

15 Which US club won the last Trans-Atlantic Challenge Cup in 1984?

Answers

1 Alfonso XIII **2** FC Porto **3** Atletico Madrid **4** Shamrock Rovers **5** Barcelona **6** Lothar Matthaus **7** Joe Gaetjens **8** River Plate **9** Juventus **10** Greece **11** Luis Hernandez **12** Madrid **13** 1989 **14** Gordon Banks **15** New York Cosmos

THE CARLING ULTIMATE FOOTBALL FACT AND QUIZ BOOK

Quiz 3
AROUND THE WORLD

1 Who scored seven goals for Yugoslavia in their 1998 World Cup qualifying play-off against Hungary?

2 Who scored the winner for Romania in their group match against England in the 1998 World Cup finals?

3 Who was the Polish goalkeeper in Porto's 1987 European Cup-winning side?

4 During the 1998 World Cup finals, Bulgarian coach Hristo Bonev resigned after his team had lost 6-1 to which other European country?

5 In which country are Nacional and Penarol the leading teams?

6 Under communism, which Moscow club was particularly associated with electrical trades workers?

7 Which Argentine formed a striking partnership with Welshman John Charles at Juventus?

8 Which Italian international was born on May 8, 1960 and joined AC Milan in 1974 a week after having been rejected by Inter?

9 Which Spanish League club plays its home matches at the San Mamés stadium?

10 Which two members of the Manchester United team that won the 1968 European Cup had survived the Munich air disaster?

11 Which was the first club to win all three major European trophies – the European Cup, the Cup Winners' Cup and the UEFA Cup?

12 Which Welsh team is known as 'The Exiles' because its ground is just over the border in England?

13 Who scored the first goal for Croatia in their 1998 World Cup quarter-final?

14 Who was the Algerian winger in Porto's 1987 European Cup-winning side?

15 For which Buenos Aires club did 1978 World Cup winners Mario Kempes, Leopoldo Luque and Daniel Passarella all play?

Answers

1 Predrag Mijatovic **2** Dan Petrescu **3** Mijnarczyk **4** Spain **5** Uruguay **6** Dynamo Moscow **7** Omar Sivori **8** Franco Baresi **9** Athletic Bilbao **10** Bobby Charlton and Bill Foulkes **11** Juventus **12** Newport **13** Robert Jarni **14** Rabah Madjer **15** River Plate

AROUND THE WORLD

1 In 1994 at the age of 42, who became the oldest player to appear in the World Cup finals?

2 In which Danish city do Brondby play their home games?

3 In which Dutch city do Feyenoord play their home games?

4 Players of which French League club were approached by Marseille in the 1993 match-fixing scandal?

5 Which manager led FC Porto to the 1987 European Cup and then took over the Portuguese national side?

6 Under communism, which Moscow club was particularly associated with car manufacturers?

7 Which club won the Portuguese League Championship for the first time in 1938 and retained the title the following year?

8 Which international was born on September 11, 1945 and signed full time for Bayern Munich in 1962?

9 Which was the second club to win all three major European trophies – the European Cup, the Cup Winners' Cup and the UEFA Cup?

10 Who are the Big Three Dutch football clubs?

11 Who managed the 1934 and 1938 World Cup winners and was known as 'The Father of Italian Football'?

12 For which Brazilian club did Pele play?

13 In 1966, which club was banned from the Inter-Cities Fairs Cup for three years after Chelsea players were stoned during their match against them in Italy?

14 In 1991, which club became the first Chilean team to win the South American Libertadores Cup?

15 In 1993, which Marseille midfielder offered Valenciennes players money to roll over in the League game between the two clubs?

THE CARLING ULTIMATE FOOTBALL FACT AND QUIZ BOOK

Quiz 5
AROUND THE WORLD

1 In which Spanish city do Hercules play their home games?

2 Under Communism, which Moscow club was particularly associated with the army?

3 Which Dutch club won the European Cup in 1970?

4 Which European city is home to Red Star 93?

5 Which European club used to play in the Campo da Constituçião but now has its home in the 76,000-capacity Estádio das Antas?

6 Which international – now his country's leading goalscorer – was born on May 10, 1969 and made his first appearance for Ajax in 1987?

7 Who scored the winning goal for Ajax in the 1987 European Cup Winners' Cup Final?

8 Dennis Bergkamp is named after Denis Law – how come they spell their first names differently?

9 In which Turkish city do Fenerbahçe play their home games?

10 Which Argentine team beat Celtic in the final of the 1967-68 World Club Championship?

11 Which Brazilian club plays its home matches at the Vila Belmiro stadium?

12 Which former Blackburn Rovers goalkeeper coached Anderlecht in the 1940s and 1950s?

13 Which French club was managed in the 1930s by three Englishmen – Peter Framer, Victor Gibson and Charlie Bell?

14 Which French League team plays its home games at La Beaujoire?

15 Which leading Chilean club is named after a wildcat?

THE CARLING ULTIMATE FOOTBALL FACT AND QUIZ BOOK

AROUND THE WORLD

1 Which nation won the first European Championship in 1960?

2 Who won the European Cup in 1971, 1972 and 1973?

3 In 1989, which club became the first team from Colombia to win the Libertadores Cup?

4 What relation are the Brazilians Rai and Socrates?

5 What was the pre-1991 name of Croatia Zagreb?

6 Which all-time great was born on May 22, 1946 and played 37 times for Northern Ireland between 1964 and 1978?

7 Which English manager led FC Porto to three successive Portuguese League Championships in the 1990s?

8 Which French League club plays its home matches at the Stade Vélodrome?

9 Which nation appeared in both the 1974 and 1978 World Cup Finals?

10 Which Soviet team won the European Cup Winners' Cup in 1975 and 1986?

11 Who became President of Marseille in 1985?

12 Who did Arsenal beat in the 1970 Fairs Cup Final?

13 Who scored his 1000th first class goal on November 20, 1969?

14 In the 1970s, which country was associated with 'Total Football'?

15 Which club did Swindon Town beat in the 1970 Anglo-Italian Cup Final?

Answers

1 The USSR **2** Ajax **3** Nacional Medellin **4** Brothers **5** Dinamo Zagreb **6** George Best **7** Bobby Robson **8** Olympique Marseille **9** Holland **10** Dynamo Kiev **11** Bernard Tapie **12** Anderlecht **13** Pele **14** Holland **15** Napoli

THE CARLING ULTIMATE FOOTBALL FACT AND QUIZ BOOK

Quiz 7
AROUND THE WORLD

1 Which club plays its home matches at the Vicente Calderón Stadium?

2 Which country beat Argentina 5-0 in the 1994 World Cup qualifiers?

3 Which French League club has the motto 'Droit au But', meaning 'straight for goal'?

4 Which future Prime Minister of Italy saved AC Milan from bankruptcy in 1986?

5 Which international was born on February 10, 1926 in Belfast, reached the quarter finals of the 1958 World Cup and led Spurs to the Double in 1961?

6 Which Soviet team won the European Cup Winners' Cup in 1981?

7 Who played for Chile in the 1998 World Cup finals and then went to West Ham United?

8 Who was the manager of Brazil at the World Cup finals of 1982 and 1986?

9 Who won the Dutch Double in 1965 and 1969?

10 In which year did Atletico Madrid win the Double?

11 Under what name did the countries of the rapidly disintegrating USSR participate in the 1992 European Championship finals?

12 What is the name of the leading football club in Gelsenkirchen, Germany?

13 Which Brazilian team plays its home matches at the world's largest club stadium, the 150,000-capacity Morumbi?

14 Which German League team plays its home matches at the Müngersdorfer Stadion?

15 Which international was born in Stirling on December 9, 1942, won 54 caps for his native country and died on December 7, 1997?

Answers

1 Atletico Madrid **2** Colombia **3** Olympique Marseille **4** Silvio Berlusconi **5** Danny Blanchflower **6** Dynamo Tbilisi **7** Javier Margas **8** Tele Santana **9** Feyenoord **10** 1996 **11** The Commonwealth of Independent States (CIS) **12** FC Schalke '04 **13** São Paulo **14** Cologne **15** Billy Bremner

THE CARLING ULTIMATE FOOTBALL FACT AND QUIZ BOOK

AROUND THE WORLD

1 Which Stoke City and England centre half left England just before the 1950 World Cup to seek fame and fortune with Millonarios in Colombia?

2 Which team did Johan Cruyff join on leaving Ajax in 1973-74?

3 Which was the first Dutch club to win a European trophy?

4 Who was the Colombia coach at the 1990 World Cup finals?

5 Who won the 1988 European Championship?

6 At the 1998 World Cup finals, which nation's team was coached by Miroslav Blazic?

7 For which club did Russian goalkeeper Lev Yashin play?

8 In 1993, which team became the first to retain the World Club Championship?

9 To what did Dynamo Berlin change its name in 1990?

10 Which Dutchman was sent off in the match against Belgium in the 1998 World Cup finals?

11 Which German League team plays its home matches at the Südstadion?

12 Which international was born in Paris on May 24, 1966 and became a legend in Yorkshire and Lancashire before retiring prematurely in 1997?

13 Which player was discovered in Haarlem, then went to Feyenoord, Ajax, PSV Eindhoven, Milan and Chelsea?

14 Which Spanish club sacked John Toshack as manager in November 1990?

15 Who is the President of Atletico Madrid?

THE CARLING ULTIMATE FOOTBALL FACT AND QUIZ BOOK

Quiz 9
AROUND THE WORLD

1 Who scored five goals for Russia against Cameroon in the 1994 World Cup finals?

2 Name either of the Dutchmen who failed to score in their 1998 World Cup semi-final penalty shoot-out against Brazil.

3 Six members of Austria's squad for the 1998 World Cup finals played for the same club – which?

4 What distinctive article of headwear was worn on the pitch by Spanish footballer Rafael 'Pichichi' Moreno in the 1910s?

5 What was the score in the first international football match, Scotland v England on November 30, 1872?

6 Which former Portuguese national coach succeeded Bobby Robson as manager of Sporting Lisbon?

7 Which German League team plays its home matches at the Westfalen-Stadion?

8 Which team was stripped of the French League Championship in 1994?

9 Which winner of 106 international caps was born on October 11, 1937 in Ashington, County Durham?

10 Who undertook a four-match tour of England in 1945, beating Cardiff City 10-1 and Arsenal 4-3 and drawing 3-3 with Chelsea and 2-2 with Rangers?

11 Who won the Golden Boot at the 1998 World Cup finals?

12 Who won the Spanish League Championship for four years in succession, 1991-94?

13 First played in 1871, what is the world's oldest surviving football tournament?

14 In which year were Celtic losing finalists in the European Cup?

15 Which Argentina-born centre forward was nicknamed 'White Arrow'?

Answers

1 Oleg Salenko **2** Philip Cocu and Ronald De Boer **3** FK Austria **4** A white skull cap **5** 0-0 **6** Carlos Queiros **7** Borussia Dortmund **8** Marseilles **9** Bobby Charlton **10** Dynamo Moscow **11** Davor Suker (Croatia) **12** Barcelona **13** The English FA Cup **14** 1970 **15** Alfredo di Stefano

THE CARLING ULTIMATE FOOTBALL FACT AND QUIZ BOOK

Quiz 10

AROUND THE WORLD

1 Which Brazilian star of the 1980s was known as 'The White Pele'?

2 Which Dutchman scored the goals for Inter Milan that knocked Norwich City out of the 1993-94 UEFA Cup?

3 Which Englishman preceded Louis Van Gaal as Barcelona coach?

4 Which German League team plays its home matches at the Volksparkstadion?

5 Which international was born on April 25, 1947, played for Ajax, Barcelona, Los Angeles Aztecs and Washington Diplomats, Levante, Ajax again and finally Feyenoord?

6 Which Moscow Dynamo goalkeeper later became a celebrated sports photographer?

7 Who came third in the 1966 World Cup?

8 Who was known as The Galloping Major?

9 For which Rio club did Zico play?

10 If all great teams are built around a great goalkeeper, a great defender and a great striker, who fulfilled each of those roles in the Bayern Munich side that won the 1967 Cup Winners' Cup?

11 In the 1966 World Cup, Portugal's back four of Morais, Batista, Jose Carlos and Hilario all played for the same club – which?

12 In which year did Rangers win the European Cup Winners' Cup?

13 Which Belgian club won the European Cup Winners' Cup in 1976?

14 Which Colombian international was shot dead in Bogota after returning from the 1994 World Cup finals?

15 Which German League team plays its home matches at the Wilhelm Koch Stadion?

Answers

1 Zico **2** Dennis Bergkamp **3** Bobby Robson **4** Hamburg **5** Johan Cruyff **6** Alexei Khomich **7** Portugal **8** Ferenc Puskas **9** Flamengo **10** Sepp Maier, Franz Beckenbauer and Gerd Muller **11** Sporting Lisbon **12** 1972 **13** Anderlecht **14** Andres Escobar **15** St Pauli

THE CARLING ULTIMATE FOOTBALL FACT AND QUIZ BOOK

Quiz 11
AROUND THE WORLD

1 Which international was born on March 4, 1951 and signed for Celtic at just about the time they won the European Cup?

2 Who won Olympic gold for football in 1908 and 1912?

3 Who won the first three Russian League Championships after the collapse of communism?

4 Who won the Italian Serie A title in 1990, 1995, 1997 and 1998?

5 Born in 1907, died in 1980, who is the only England player to have more international goals than caps to his credit?

6 Fans of which Brazilian club come to matches wearing white face powder?

7 For which Russian club did Nikita Simonian score a record 133 goals in the 1950s?

8 How many times in the 20th century did Scotland reach the World Cup finals?

9 Which club finished in the top four in Sweden every year in the 1980s?

10 Which Greek League club plays its home games at the Nikos Goumas stadium, Athens?

11 Which mainland European club – i.e. not Sunderland – plays its home matches at The Stadium of Light?

12 Who did Juventus beat in the 1996 European Cup Final?

13 Who kept goal for Steaua Bucharest in the 1986 European Cup Final, in which they beat Barcelona on penalties?

14 Who won Olympic gold for football in 1906?

15 Who, in 1995, became the first foreign player to win the Scottish Football Writers' Player of the Year Award?

Answers

1 Kenny Dalglish **2** Great Britain **3** Spartak Moscow **4** Juventus **5** William Ralph Dean **6** Fluminese **7** Spartak Moscow **8** Seven **9** IFK Gothenburg **10** AEK **11** Benfica **12** Ajax **13** Helmut Ducadam **14** Denmark **15** Brian Laudrup

AROUND THE WORLD

1 In 1963, a world record crowd of 177,656 attended a local derby between two Rio de Janeiro clubs – name either.

2 In 1994-95, which French team went 32 league matches without defeat?

3 In which year did Aberdeen win the European Cup Winners' Cup?

4 Which club made Pope John Paul II an honorary member during his visit to Spain in 1982?

5 Which famous club plays its home matches at the Bombonera Stadium, Buenos Aires?

6 Which French team reached two European Cup Finals in the 1950s, losing both times to Real Madrid?

7 Which Greek League club plays its home games at the Karaiskakis stadium, Athens?

8 Which international was born in Ashton, Lancashire on December 8, 1941 and achieved a unique feat in a World Cup Final?

9 Who beat Juventus in the 1997 European Cup Final?

10 Who won the Romanian League Championship five times running, 1994-98?

11 Who won the Russian League Championship in 1992, 1993, 1994, 1996, 1997 and 1998?

12 How many times in the 20th century did Argentina win the World Cup?

13 Which club played in the De Meer Stadium from 1934 to 1998?

14 Which international was born in Hayes on October 27, 1957 and played 53 times for his country, which he later managed?

15 Which is the oldest football club in Greece?

Answers

1 Flamengo and Fluminese **2** Nantes **3** 1983 **4** Barcelona **5** Boca Juniors **6** Stade de Reims **7** Olympiakos **8** Geoff Hurst **9** Borussia Dortmund **10** Steaua Bucharest **11** Spartak Moscow **12** Twice **13** Ajax Amsterdam **14** Glenn Hoddle **15** Olympiakos

THE CARLING ULTIMATE FOOTBALL FACT AND QUIZ BOOK

Quiz 13
AROUND THE WORLD

1 Which leading Argentine club was founded by Irish immigrant Patrick MacCarthy?

2 Which Romanian was the first player to win the European Cup with two different clubs (Steaua Bucharest in 1986 and Red Star Belgrade in 1991)?

3 Which Scottish club were the beaten finalists in the 1987 UEFA Cup?

4 Which three-lettered Brazilian coached Peru at the 1978 World Cup finals?

5 Who beat Juventus in the 1998 European Cup Final?

6 Who scored a record 13 goals for France in the 1958 World Cup finals?

7 Whose goal for Nacional gave the Uruguayans victory over Nottingham Forest in the 1980 World Club Championship?

8 For which club did Carlos Alberto, the 1970 World Cup-winning captain of Brazil, play in his native country?

9 How many Boca Juniors players were in Argentina's 1978 World Cup winning squad?

10 How many French clubs won the European Cup in the 20th century?

11 In which Brazilian city do Vasco Da Gama play their home matches?

12 In which year did Argentina first win the World Cup?

13 In which year did Spain win the European Championship?

14 Which club plays its home games at Windsor Park, Belfast?

15 Which club won the Uruguayan League Championship for five years in succession, 1939-43?

Answers

1 Boca Juniors **2** Belodedici **3** Dundee United **4** Tim **5** Real Madrid **6** Just Fontaine **7** Waldemar Victorino **8** Fluminese **9** None **10** None (Marseille won the 1993 Final but were stripped of the title because of a match-fixing scandal) **11** Rio de Janeiro **12** 1978 **13** 1964 **14** Linfield **15** Nacional

AROUND THE WORLD

1 Which international was born on February 5, 1965 in Constanta and played in the 1990, 1994 and 1998 World Cup finals?

2 Which international was born on October 17, 1934, played throughout his career for Fulham and was the first English professional to earn £100 a week?

3 Which Italian club won the European Cup Winners' Cup in 1993 and the UEFA Cup in 1995?

4 Which two Irish League clubs play their home matches at Tolka Park, Dublin?

5 For which club did 1966 West German captain Uwe Seeler play?

6 For which Italian club did Spanish international Luis Suarez play during the 1960s?

7 In which year did Argentina win the World Cup for the second time?

8 Which Argentine scored 464 goals in 435 games for Nacional of Uruguay in the late 1930s and 1940s?

9 Which country's national stadium is called Ulleval?

10 Which English club knocked Eintracht Frankfurt out of the 1975-76 European Cup Winners' Cup?

11 Which international was born in Augsburg on July 21, 1939 and scored in the 1966 World Cup Final?

12 Which international was born on September 1, 1962 in Surinam and became the first foreign manager to win the English FA Cup?

13 Which Irish League club plays its home games at Dalymount Park?

14 Which was the first West German club to win a European trophy?

15 Who scored Italy's goal in the home leg of their play-off against Russia for a place in the 1998 World Cup finals?

Answers

1 Gheorge Hagi **2** Johnny Haynes **3** Parma **4** Shamrock Rovers and Shelbourne **5** Hamburg **6** Internazionale **7** 1986 **8** Atilio Garcia **9** Norway **10** West Ham United **11** Helmut Haller **12** Ruud Gullit **13** Bohemians **14** Borussia Dortmund (1966 Cup Winners' Cup) **15** Pierluigi Casiraghi

THE CARLING ULTIMATE FOOTBALL FACT AND QUIZ BOOK

Quiz 15
AROUND THE WORLD

1 Who was the disgraced President of Marseille?

2 Apart from Athens and Thessaloniki, which is the only other city in Greece to have been home to winners of the Greek League Championship?

3 From which club did Borussia Dortmund buy sweeper Matthias Sammer in 1993?

4 Which electrical company has given its name to the Eindhoven Stadium in Holland?

5 Which famous club plays its home matches at the Cordero Stadium in Avellaneda, Argentina?

6 Which international – born in Edinburgh on September 11, 1942 – played club football for Rangers throughout his career and later managed the club?

7 Which Italian league club plays its home games at the Stadio Comunale Artemio Franchi in the Campo di Marte?

8 Which member of Argentina's 1978 World Cup winning team lost a brother in a road accident during the tournament?

9 Which Uruguayan club beat Aston Villa in the 1982 World Club Championship?

10 Who did Spain beat in the 1964 European Championship Final?

11 Who scored Italy's goal against Norway in the 1998 World Cup finals?

12 Who was manager of France in the 1998 World Cup finals?

13 In the 1998 World Cup finals, which Frenchman was sent off in the game against Saudi Arabia?

14 In which Austrian city do FC Tirol play their home games?

15 In which year did Celtic become the first British club to win the European Cup?

Answers

1 Bernard Tapie **2** Larissa **3** Inter Milan **4** Phillips **5** Independiente **6** John Greig **7** Fiorentina **8** Leopoldo Luque **9** Peñarol **10** The USSR **11** Christian Vieri **12** Aime Jacquet **13** Zinedine Zidane **14** Innsbruck **15** 1967

THE CARLING ULTIMATE FOOTBALL FACT AND QUIZ BOOK

Quiz 16
AROUND THE WORLD

1 What nationality was 1980s Real Madrid striker Hugo Sanchez?

2 Which French club plays home matches at the Stade Geoffroy Guichard?

3 Which great Paraguayan centre forward scored a record 37 League goals for Independiente (Argentina) in 1937?

4 Which international was born in London on February 20, 1940, played first for Chelsea and scored 44 goals in 57 matches for his country?

5 Which leading Montevideo club was founded in 1891 as the Central Uruguayan Railway Cricket Club?

6 Which two Italian clubs share the Stadio delle Alpi?

7 Who scored six goals for Argentina in the 1978 World Cup finals?

8 Who scored the winning goal for Real Madrid in the 1998 European Cup Final against Juventus?

9 In 1998, which country became the first to win a World Cup finals game by the Golden Goal?

10 Which Argentine team is nicknamed The Red Devils?

11 Which Austrian striker has scored in European Cup Winners' Cup finals for both Barcelona and Rapid Vienna?

12 Which Dutch football team was started in 1913 as the sports club of the Philips electronics company?

13 Which German club moved in 1974 from the Red Earth Stadium to the Westfalenstadion?

14 Which international was born on May 27, 1967 in Gateshead and made his first team debut for Newcastle United in 1985?

15 Which Mexican goalkeeper played in all five World Cup finals tournaments from 1950 to 1966?

Answers

1 Mexican **2** St Etienne **3** Arsenio Erico **4** Jimmy Greaves **5** Peñarol **6** Juventus and Torino **7** Mario Kempes **8** Predrag Mijatovic **9** France **10** Independiente **11** Hans Krankl **12** PSV Eindhoven **13** Borussia Dortmund **14** Paul Gascoigne **15** Antonio Carbajal

THE CARLING ULTIMATE FOOTBALL FACT AND QUIZ BOOK

Quiz 17
AROUND THE WORLD

1 Which two Italian clubs share the Stadio Luigi Ferraris?

2 Who kept goal for Celtic in the 1967 European Cup Final?

3 Who was Real Madrid's German coach in 1998?

4 Who was the captain of Argentina when they won the World Cup in 1978?

5 In the 1930s under the Fascists, which great Italian club changed its name to Ambrosiana, after the patron saint of its home city?

6 In which city do GAIS, IFK and Orgryte play their home games?

7 Which club from Madeira plays in the Portuguese League?

8 Which Dutchman scored the goal that finally put Argentina out of the 1998 World Cup?

9 Which German club plays its home matches at the Neckar Stadium?

10 Which international was born on August 18, 1933 in Marrakesh, Morocco and scored 27 goals in 20 games for his country, including 13 in the 1958 World Cup finals?

11 Which Italian League club plays its home games at the San Paolo stadium?

12 Which Nigerian international played for Ajax and Internazionale before joining Arsenal in 1999?

13 Which Roman Catholic former Celtic star did Graeme Souness bring to Rangers in 1988?

14 Who did Celtic beat in the 1967 European Cup Winners' Cup Final?

15 Who scored France's Golden Goal in the match against Paraguay in the 1998 World Cup finals?

THE CARLING ULTIMATE FOOTBALL FACT AND QUIZ BOOK

Quiz 18
AROUND THE WORLD

1 After England v Scotland, which is the world's second oldest international fixture (first played in 1902)?

2 In which city do AIK and Djurgardens play their home games?

3 In which Norwegian city do Rosenborg play their home games?

4 To date, only four clubs have ever won the Portuguese League. Three are Benfica, Sporting Lisbon and Porto – who are the fourth?

5 Who was the captain of Uruguay when they won the 1950 World Cup?

6 Which Greek club is nicknamed 'The Harem Girls'?

7 Which international was born in Preston on April 5, 1922 and was knighted in 1998?

8 Which Italian club adopted their colours in imitation of Notts County?

9 Who is Rangers' record goalscorer?

10 Who knocked holders Celtic out of the European Cup in 1967-68?

11 Who missed the last penalty as Italy went out to France in the 1998 World Cup quarter-finals?

12 In the 1940s, by what nickname were Milan's Swedish forwards Gunnar Gren, Gunnar Nordahl and Nils Liedholm collectively known?

13 In which Norwegian city do Valerenga play their home games?

14 Who scored twice for France in the 1998 World Cup Final?

15 Which club has won the Chilean League title most often?

Answers

1 Austria v Hungary **2** Stockholm (Sweden) **3** Trondheim **4** Belenenses **5** Obdulio Varela **6** AEK Athens **7** Tom Finney **8** Juventus **9** Ally McCoist **10** Dynamo Kiev **11** Di Biagio **12** Gre-No-Li **13** Oslo **14** Zinedine Zidane **15** Colo Colo

THE CARLING ULTIMATE FOOTBALL FACT AND QUIZ BOOK

AROUND THE WORLD

1 Which international captain was born on July 18, 1942 in Treviglio and played for Inter Milan throughout his career?

2 Which Italian club won the Italian Championship for five years running in the 1930s?

3 Which Italian team has an all-violet strip?

4 Who scored twice for France in the 1998 World Cup semi-final against Croatia?

5 Who was the captain of Austria's so-called Wunderteam (1931-34)?

6 Whose Rangers' goalscoring record of 233 goals did Ally McCoist overtake?

7 For which club did Italy's 1934 World Cup-winning goalkeeper Gianpiero Combi play?

8 In which country was Eusebio born?

9 Which Portuguese club plays home games at the José Alvalade Stadium?

10 Which Italian team was all but wiped out by the 1949 Superga air crash?

11 Which Swiss League club plays its home games at the Hardturm stadium?

12 Which team won the Austrian league Championship eight times between 1912 and 1923?

13 Who kept goal for Belgium in the 1980 European Championship Final against West Germany?

14 In which year did Belenenses win their first – and so far their only – Portuguese League Championship?

15 Who were the first losing European Cup finalists in 1960?

Answers

1 Giacinto Facchetti **2** Juventus **3** Fiorentina **4** Lilian Thuram **5** Matthias Sindelar **6** Bob McPhail **7** Juventus **8** Mozambique **9** Sporting Lisbon **10** Torino **11** Grasshoppers, Zurich **12** Rapid Vienna **13** Jean-Marie Pfaff **14** 1948 **15** Eintracht Frankfurt

AROUND THE WORLD

1 Who won 115 international caps for Sweden between 1963 and 1978?

2 Whose name links Czechoslovakia, Slovakia, Aston Villa and Celtic?

3 For which club did Italy's 1934 World Cup-winning goalkeeper Dino Zoff play?

4 In 1884, which was the first English club to win the Welsh Cup?

5 In 1938, which Austrian team won the German Cup?

6 In 1954, who was the coach of World Cup winners West Germany?

7 Name the Yugoslav coach who walked out on Eintracht Frankfurt in the middle of the 1992-93 season.

8 Which international was born in Dudley, Worcestershire on October 1, 1936 and died two weeks after the Munich Air Disaster in 1958?

9 Which international, surname Ferreira, was born in Lourenco Marques, Mozambique on January 25, 1942?

10 Which Swedish club reached the European Cup Final in 1979?

11 Which Turkish League club plays its home games at the Ali Sami Yen Stadium, Istanbul?

12 Who kept goal for Belgium in the 1986 World Cup semi-final against Argentina?

13 Which country's most capped player is goalkeeper Thomas Ravelli?

14 Which Belgian club plays its home games at the Constant Vanden Stock stadium?

15 Which club won the Portuguese League Championship four years running, 1995-98?

THE CARLING ULTIMATE FOOTBALL FACT AND QUIZ BOOK

Quiz 21
AROUND THE WORLD

1 Which Italian team won the League and Cup double in 1995?

2 Which Rio de Janeiro team is nicknamed 'The People's Club'?

3 Which Swedish club won the UEFA Cup in 1982 and 1987?

4 Which team won the Italian League Championship in 1976, its first title since 1949?

5 Who scored all four goals for Rapid Vienna in their 4-3 victory over Schalke '04 in the 1938 German Cup Final?

6 Who scored England's last-minute goal against Belgium in the 1990 World Cup finals?

7 Who succeeded Dragoslav Stepanovic as coach of Eintracht Frankfurt?

8 Who was born in Barracas on July 4, 1926 and played international football for three countries – his native Argentina, Colombia and Spain?

9 Who won the European Cup in 1974, 1975 and 1976?

10 If you were a Fleming who shouted 'Allez les mauves', which team would you support?

11 In which year did Eintracht Frankfurt win the UEFA Cup?

12 Which architect played for Rapid Vienna and then designed their stadium?

13 Which country reached the semi-finals of the 1992 European Championships and the 1994 World Cup?

14 Which great Brazilian club team plays in black shirts with a white diagonal stripe?

15 Which international was born on October 15, 1968 and made his League debut for Nantes in 1986 before moving to Marseille and then Juventus?

Answers

1 Juventus **2** Flamengo **3** IFK Gothenburg **4** Torino **5** Franz Binder **6** David Platt **7** Jupp Heynckes **8** Alfredo Di Stefano **9** Bayern Munich **10** Anderlecht **11** 1980 **12** Gerhard Hanappi **13** Sweden **14** Vasco da Gama **15** Didier Deschamps

THE CARLING ULTIMATE FOOTBALL FACT AND QUIZ BOOK

Quiz 22
AROUND THE WORLD

1 Which Russian club were known as 'The Policemen'?

2 Which was the Romanian army team?

3 Which West German scored 68 goals in 62 internationals?

4 Who was captain of Juventus when they won the 1996 European Cup?

5 Which two countries will host Euro 2000?

6 By what name was the Stade du Roi Baudouin previously known?

7 How many times in the 20th century did Brazil win the World Cup?

8 In 1961, which club became the first from outside Moscow to win the League Championship of the USSR?

9 Which city is home to the Nacional and Peñarol clubs?

10 Which club plays its home games at the 105,000-seater Santiago Bernabeu Stadium?

11 Which international was born on May 15, 1970 in Hoorn and joined Ajax in 1982 with his brother Ronald?

12 Which other West German team did Eintracht Frankfurt beat in the 1980 UEFA Cup Final?

13 Which country hosted Euro 96?

14 Which was the Romanian police team?

15 Who scored both Germany's goals in the Euro 96 Final against the Czech Republic?

Answers

1 Dynamo Moscow 2 Steaua Bucharest 3 Gerd Muller 4 Gianluca Vialli 5 Belgium and Holland 6 Heysel 7 Four 8 Dynamo Kiev 9 Montevideo (Uruguay) 10 Real Madrid 11 Frank de Boer 12 Borussia Moenchengladbach 13 England 14 Dinamo Bucharest 15 Oliver Bierhoff

GREAT CLUBS OF ENGLAND

THE CARLING ULTIMATE FOOTBALL FACT AND QUIZ BOOK

Quiz 1
GREAT CLUBS OF ENGLAND

1 Apart from Charlton Athletic, which other English League club is nicknamed The Valiants?

2 In which South American country is there a football club called Everton?

3 In which year did Manchester City first win the League Championship?

4 In which year did Oldham Athletic first reach the semi-final of the FA Cup?

5 Which English League club is nicknamed The Pirates?

6 Which great club was originally known as Dial Square?

7 Which team entered the Football League for the first time in 1987?

8 Which team first came into the Football League in 1977?

9 Which team's ground has the postcode L4 0TH?

10 Who scored 178 goals for Newcastle United between 1946 and 1957?

11 At which League club did both William 'Dixie' Dean and Tom 'Pongo' Waring begin their distinguished careers?

12 In 1957-58, which club scored 104 goals, conceded 100 and finished fifth in the First Division?

13 In which year did Newcastle United win the European Fairs Cup?

14 What was the name of Wimbledon's original ground?

15 Which English League club is named after the house in which the founders met to inaugurate the team?

Answers

1 Port Vale **2** Chile **3** 1937 **4** 1913 **5** Bristol Rovers **6** Arsenal **7** Scarborough **8** Wimbledon **9** Liverpool **10** Jackie Milburn **11** Tranmere Rovers **12** Manchester City **13** 1969 **14** Plough Lane **15** Port Vale

GREAT CLUBS OF ENGLAND

1 Which English League club plays its home matches at Boothferry Park?

2 Which team are also known as The Moonlight Dribblers?

3 Which team has a fanzine called 'Goodbye Horse'?

4 Which is the most successful League club in English football history?

5 Who beat Oldham Athletic in the 1990 FA Cup semi-final?

6 With which other London club did Arsenal nearly merge in 1913?

7 In the 1930s, who transformed Charlton Athletic from also-rans into one of the leading sides in England?

8 In which season did Manchester City win the League Championship for the second time in their history?

9 In which year did Hull City make their only appearance to date in the semi-final of the FA Cup?

10 Supporters of which team may be heard singing: 'Don't be mistaken, don't be misled, We're not Scousers, we're from Birkenhead'?

11 What was the original, intended name of Liverpool Football Club?

12 Which Cheshire team dropped out of the Football League in 1896, returning in 1926?

13 Which English League club has a fanzine called 'The Oatcake'?

14 Which English League team was formerly known as Eastville Rovers?

15 Which team entered the First Division in 1919 without having won promotion and remained there into the 21st century?

Answers

1 Hull City **2** Everton **3** Charlton Athletic **4** Liverpool **5** Manchester United **6** Fulham **7** Jimmy Seed **8** 1967-68 **9** 1930 **10** Tranmere Rovers **11** Everton (yes, really) **12** Crewe Alexandra **13** Stoke City **14** Bristol Rovers **15** Arsenal

THE CARLING ULTIMATE FOOTBALL FACT AND QUIZ BOOK

Quiz 3
GREAT CLUBS OF ENGLAND

1 Which team has a fanzine called 'When Skies Are Grey'?

2 Who beat Oldham Athletic in the 1994 FA Cup semi-final?

3 Who scored 27 goals for Division Four Scarborough in the 1992-93 season?

4 Who scored two goals for Newcastle United in the first leg of the 1969 European Fairs Cup Final against Ujpest Dozsa?

5 Who was manager of Wimbledon during their first season in the Football League?

6 Who won the FA Cup in 1953, the year of Queen Elizabeth II's coronation?

7 From which club did Liverpool buy Rob Jones in October 1991?

8 In 1893, the first ever Liverpool team contained ten Scots – who was the token Englishman in goal?

9 In 1919, which club replaced Leeds City in the Football League?

10 In which year did Arsenal win their first Championship?

11 In which year did Manchester City win the FA Cup for the second time?

12 In which year did Stoke City – a founder member of the Football League – win their first major trophy, the League Cup?

13 In which year were Charlton Athletic runners-up in the League?

14 Which English club plays in a tangerine strip?

15 Which English League club has a fanzine called 'Give Us An R'?

Answers

1 Everton **2** Manchester United **3** Darren Foreman **4** Bobby Moncur **5** Allen Batsford **6** Blackpool **7** Crewe Alexandra **8** Bill McOwen **9** Port Vale **10** 1931 **11** 1934 **12** 1972 **13** 1937 **14** Blackpool **15** Tranmere Rovers

THE CARLING ULTIMATE FOOTBALL FACT AND QUIZ BOOK

Quiz 4

GREAT CLUBS OF ENGLAND

1 Which English League team was formerly known as The Purdown Poachers?

2 Which team has a fanzine called 'Satis?'?

3 Who did Oldham Athletic beat 6-3 on aggregate in the 1990 League Cup semi-final?

4 Who has made more League appearances for Scarborough than any other player?

5 Who has played more League games and scored more goals than anyone else for Wimbledon?

6 Who knocked Hull City out in the 1930 FA Cup semi-final?

7 Who scored the third goal for Newcastle United in the first leg of the 1969 European Fairs Cup Final against Ujpest Dozsa?

8 In which year did Arsenal first win the League and FA Cup Double?

9 In which year did Liverpool win the League Championship for the first time?

10 In which year did Manchester City win the FA Cup for the third time?

11 In which year did Oldham Athletic finish second in the old First Division?

12 In which year did Wimbledon win the FA Cup?

13 In which year was Bristol Rovers' Eastville ground severely damaged by fire?

14 In which year were Charlton Athletic beaten finalists in the FA Cup?

15 The purchase of which Colombian from Parma during the 1995-96 season is widely believed to have disrupted the balance of the Newcastle United side and cost them the Premiership title?

Answers

1 Bristol Rovers **2** Everton **3** West Ham United **4** Ian Ironside **5** Alan Cork **6** Arsenal **7** Jim Scott **8** 1971 **9** 1901 **10** 1956 **11** 1915 **12** 1988 **13** 1980 **14** 1946 **15** Faustino Asprilla

GREAT CLUBS OF ENGLAND

1 Which Blackpool player was voted the best right back in the world after the 1962 World Cup finals in Chile?

2 Which Cheshire team reached the FA Cup semi-final in 1888?

3 Which club has a fanzine called 'Tiger Rag'?

4 Which team has a fanzine called 'Speke From The Harbour'?

5 Which Third Division club reached the semi-final of the FA Cup in 1954?

6 Who did Stoke City beat in the 1972 League Cup Final?

7 Who was appointed manager of Scarborough in June 1996?

8 Who was manager of Tranmere Rovers from 1987 to 1996?

9 In which year did Charlton Athletic win the FA Cup?

10 In which year did Liverpool win the FA Cup for the first time?

11 In which year did Manchester City win the FA Cup for the fourth time?

12 Who knocked Port Vale out of the 1954 FA Cup in the semi-final?

13 Which England international began his professional career by making 189 appearances for Crewe Alexandra before moving to Aston Villa?

14 Which English League team plays its home games at Glanford Park?

15 Which Oldham Athletic left back was suspended for a year for refusing to leave the field after having been sent off against Middlesbrough in the 1914-15 season?

Answers

1 Jimmy Armfield **2** Crewe Alexandra **3** Hull City **4** Everton **5** Port Vale **6** Chelsea **7** Mick Wadsworth **8** John King **9** 1947 **10** 1965 **11** 1969 **12** West Bromwich Albion **13** David Platt **14** Scunthorpe United **15** Billy Cook

THE CARLING ULTIMATE FOOTBALL FACT AND QUIZ BOOK

GREAT CLUBS OF ENGLAND

1 Which team's motto – Nil Satis Nisi Optimum – is widely parodied as Nil-Nil Satis?

2 Which Tranmere Rovers player was appointed manager of the club in April 1996?

3 Who did Blackpool sell to Queen's Park Rangers for £750,000 in August 1993?

4 Who did Wimbledon beat in the 1988 FA Cup Final?

5 Who has made the most League appearances for Arsenal – 558 matches between 1975 and 1993?

6 Which club has a fanzine called 'Amber Nectar'?

7 Who made 92 League appearances and scored 21 goals for Newcastle United between 1984 and 1988?

8 Who scored Stoke City's first goal in the 1972 League Cup Final?

9 With which Rugby Union team did Bristol Rovers share a ground from 1986 to 1996?

10 How many times in the 20th century did Liverpool win the European Cup?

11 In 1947, who dropped the FA Cup, breaking the top off its lid?

12 In 1991, who succeeded Jim Smith as manager of Newcastle United?

13 In the 1954 FA Cup semi-final, which former Port Vale player scored for the winning goal for their opponents, West Bromwich Albion?

14 In which year did Arsenal first win the FA Cup?

15 What was the nickname of Alan Lawson, the Oldham Athletic star of the 1960s?

Answers

1 Everton **2** John Aldridge **3** Trevor Sinclair **4** Liverpool **5** David O'Leary **6** Hull City **7** Paul Gascoigne **8** Terry Conroy **9** Bath **10** Four **11** Charlton manager Jimmy Seed **12** Osvaldo Ardiles **13** Ronnie Allen **14** 1930 **15** Iron Man

THE CARLING ULTIMATE FOOTBALL FACT AND QUIZ BOOK

GREAT CLUBS OF ENGLAND

1 Where do Bristol Rovers now play their home matches?

2 Which English League team has a fanzine called 'Fe' (the chemical symbol for Iron)?

3 Which team did Terry Neill manage before succeeding Bill Nicholson at Tottenham Hotspur in 1974?

4 Who did Blackpool buy from Stoke City for £11,500 in 1947?

5 Who kept goal for Everton in the 1968 FA Cup Final?

6 Which Lancashire club knocked Crewe Alexandra out in the semi-final of the 1888 FA Cup?

7 Who scored Stoke City's second goal in the 1972 League Cup Final?

8 Who scored the winner for Manchester City in the 1904 FA Cup Final?

9 Who scored the winning goal for Wimbledon in the 1988 FA Cup Final?

10 For which Yorkshire club did former Football League Secretary Alan Hardaker play as an amateur?

11 From which Italian club did Arsenal buy Dennis Bergkamp in June 1995?

12 In 1953-54, which Third Division North club went 30 League games without conceding a goal?

13 In 1971, who knocked Stoke City out in the semi-final of the FA Cup?

14 In which year did Liverpool first win the UEFA Cup?

15 In which year did Tranmere Rovers reach the semi-final of the League Cup?

THE CARLING ULTIMATE FOOTBALL FACT AND QUIZ BOOK

Quiz 8
GREAT CLUBS OF ENGLAND

1 In which year did Wimbledon reach the semi-finals of both the FA Cup and the League Cup?

2 On a 1967 tour of which country were Oldham Athletic cursed by a witch doctor?

3 On New Year's Day 1991, which Newcastle United player became the first player to be sent off in a League match broadcast live on television?

4 Supporters of which English League club sing 'Goodnight Irene'?

5 Which Charlton Athletic player was widely known as 'the finest keeper England never had'?

6 Which club plays home games at Bloomfield Road?

7 Which English League club has a fanzine called 'Son Of A Referee'?

8 Which Evertonian played 99 times for Wales?

9 Who became manager of Crewe Alexandra in June 1983?

10 Who scored both goals for Manchester City in the 1934 FA Cup Final?

11 From which club did Oldham Athletic buy Ian Olney in June 1992?

12 In 1959, which club was almost renamed London Athletic?

13 In 1968, which team was expelled from the League over illegal payments but soon re-elected?

14 In 1972, who knocked Stoke City out in the semi-final of the FA Cup?

15 In 1997, who broke Cliff Bastin's record for the greatest number of goals scored for Arsenal?

Answers

1 1997 **2** Rhodesia **3** Paul Gascoigne **4** Bristol Rovers **5** Sam Bartram **6** Blackpool **7** Scunthorpe United **8** Neville Southall **9** Dario Gradi **10** Fred Tilson **11** Aston Villa **12** Charlton Athletic **13** Port Vale **14** Arsenal **15** Ian Wright

THE CARLING ULTIMATE FOOTBALL FACT AND QUIZ BOOK

GREAT CLUBS OF ENGLAND

1 In the 1956-57 season, which side finished bottom of the Third Division North after a run of 30 games without a win?

2 Until 1988, which English League team played its home games at The Old Showground?

3 Which great left winger left Derby County and joined Third Division Hull City as player manager at the start of the 1948-49 season?

4 Which trophy did Blackpool win in 1971?

5 Which World Heavyweight Boxing Champion signed for Liverpool in 1944 – although he never played a match?

6 Who beat Tranmere Rovers on penalties in the 1994 League Cup semi-final?

7 Who joined the board of Newcastle United on April 18, 1990?

8 Who knocked Wimbledon out of the 1997 League Cup in the semi-final?

9 Who managed Everton from 1977 to 1981?

10 Who scored the first goal for Manchester City in the 1956 FA Cup Final?

11 For which goalkeeper did Newcastle United pay £850,000 in 1988, less than a month after he had won the FA Cup with Wimbledon?

12 In which season did Blackpool finish second in the old First Division, their highest ever League position?

13 In which year did Bill Shankly become manager of Liverpool?

14 In which year did Charlton Athletic leave The Valley?

15 On January 30, 1960, Crewe Alexandra met Tottenham Hotspur in the Fourth Round of the FA Cup in front of a record crowd of 20,000. The score was also a record – Crewe scored two goals; how many did Spurs get?

THE CARLING ULTIMATE FOOTBALL FACT AND QUIZ BOOK

Quiz 10
GREAT CLUBS OF ENGLAND

1 Which Arsenal player was sent off at Sheffield Wednesday in the 1998-99 season during the fracas in which Paolo Di Canio was also shown red after he pushed over the referee?

2 Which England goalkeeper is Stoke City's most capped international?

3 Which footballing knight was general manager of Port Vale from 1965 to 1968?

4 Who is the Carlo celebrated by Bristol Rovers' fans in a song about their January 1991 victory over Bristol City?

5 Who is the highest scorer in Everton's history?

6 Who knocked Hull City out in the quarter finals of the the 1948-49 FA Cup?

7 Who knocked Wimbledon out of the 1997 FA Cup in the semi-final?

8 Who played 595 matches for Tranmere Rovers between 1946 and 1964?

9 Who scored the winner for Manchester City in the 1969 FA Cup Final?

10 Who was manager of Oldham Athletic from 1970 to 1982?

11 With which League team did both Ray Clemence and Kevin Keegan begin their illustrious careers?

12 At which two grounds did Charlton Athletic play their home games during their absence from The Valley?

13 In 1934, 84,569 people watched a Sixth Round FA Cup tie at Maine Road – the highest ever British attendance outside London or Glasgow. Who were Manchester City's opponents?

14 In which year did Bill Shankly retire as manager of Liverpool?

15 In which year were Blackpool last in the old First Division?

GREAT CLUBS OF ENGLAND

1 On October 17, 1995, Crewe Alexandra recorded a club record victory over Hartlepool United in the Auto Windscreens Shield – what was the score?

2 Supporters of which team used to throw Weetabix around at away matches?

3 Which English League team is nicknamed The Grecians?

4 Which French team beat Arsenal in the 1998-99 Champions' League?

5 Who made 78 League appearances and scored 48 goals for Newcastle United between 1982 and 1984?

6 Who scored 141 goals for Tranmere Rovers between 1985 and 1995?

7 Who scored 195 goals for Hull City in a career that began in 1960 and ended in 1971?

8 Who took the penalty saved by Gordon Banks in the second leg of Stoke City's 1972 League Cup semi-final against West Ham United?

9 Who was appointed manager of Oldham Athletic in February 1997?

10 Who was appointed manager of Scunthorpe United in February 1997?

11 Who was manager of Port Vale from March 1984 to February 1999?

12 Who was manager of Wimbledon when they won the FA Cup?

13 What colours do Crewe Alexandra play in?

14 Which Arsenal great began his career with Exeter City in 1927?

15 Which English League club has a fanzine called 'Bert Trautmann's Head'?

Answers

1 8-0 **2** Bristol Rovers **3** Exeter City **4** Lens **5** Kevin Keegan **6** Ian Muir **7** Chris Chilton **8** Geoff Hurst **9** Neil Warnock **10** Brian Laws **11** John Rudge **12** Johnny Summers **13** Red and white **14** Cliff Bastin **15** Manchester City

THE CARLING ULTIMATE FOOTBALL FACT AND QUIZ BOOK

Quiz 12
GREAT CLUBS OF ENGLAND

1 Which English League club is nicknamed The Saddlers?

2 Which former England international was appointed manager of Hull City in July 1997?

3 Which English League club is nicknamed The Lilywhites?

4 Which former Leyton Orient stalwart was manager of Bristol Rovers in 1992?

5 Who had two spells as manager of Scunthorpe United, first from 1987 to 1991 and then from 1996 to 1997?

6 Who is the only man to have managed both Stoke City and West Ham United?

7 Who saved a penalty for Wimbledon in the 1988 FA Cup Final?

8 Who scored 36 League goals for Newcastle United in the 1926-27 season?

9 Who succeeded Bill Shankly as manager of Liverpool?

10 Who was Blackpool's leading scorer in the 1996-97 season?

11 Who was manager of Oldham Athletic from 1982 to 1994?

12 Who was the captain of the 1971 double-winning Arsenal side?

13 In a version of The Kinks' 'Lola', supporters of which team claim to be 'the world's most passionate fans'?

14 In which season did Hull City win the Third Division Championship?

15 In which year did Charlton Athletic return to The Valley?

Answers

1 Walsall **2** Mark Hateley **3** Preston North End **4** Dennis Rofe **5** Mick Buxton **6** Lou Macari **7** Dave Beasant **8** Hughie Gallacher **9** Bob Paisley **10** Tony Ellis **11** Joe Royle **12** Frank McLintock **13** Newcastle United **14** 1965-66 **15** 1992

Quiz 13
GREAT CLUBS OF ENGLAND

1 In which year were Scunthorpe United elected to the Football League?

2 Name the Crewe Alexandra goalkeeper who was sent off after only 19 seconds of their match against Darlington in 1993-94.

3 On Preston North End shirts, what do the initials 'PP' stand for?

4 Where do Wimbledon currently play their home games?

5 Which English League club plays its home games at The Bescot Stadium?

6 Which former Leeds United and England full back was manager of Exeter City from 1988 to 1991 and again from 1994 to 1995?

7 Which Oldham Athletic player scored 26 goals in 38 matches in the 1909-10 season?

8 Who managed Bristol Rovers twice – once from 1981-83 and then again from 1985-87?

9 Who was appointed manager of Blackpool in July 1997?

10 Who was the manager of Stoke City when they won the League Cup in 1972?

11 For which country did Arsenal's Bob Wilson keep goal?

12 Who was the only English-born player in the Liverpool team that won the 1986 FA Cup?

13 At the end of the 1994-95 season, Bristol Rovers achieved their highest League position. Where did they finish in Division Two?

14 For which West Country club did Arnold Mitchell make 495 League appearances between 1952 and 1966?

15 In the 20th century, for which two Luton Town players did Arsenal pay over a million pounds each?

THE CARLING ULTIMATE FOOTBALL FACT AND QUIZ BOOK

Quiz 14

GREAT CLUBS OF ENGLAND

1 On October 6, 1923, which Oldham Athletic player scored twice for his own team and twice for the opposition as Latics beat Manchester United 3-2?

2 To which club did Hull City sell Andy Payton for £750,000 in November 1991?

3 Which manager of Crewe Alexandra sacked himself on October 15, 1970, so that a younger man could take his place?

4 Which English League club has a fanzine called 'Hoof The Ball Up!'?

5 Which English League club has a fanzine called 'Moving Swiftly On'?

6 Which team were known in the 19th century as The Old Invincibles?

7 Who did Charlton Athletic sell to Leeds United for £2.8 million in July 1996?

8 Who did Newcastle United sell to Sunderland for £20,500 in February 1948?

9 Who played 640 games for Liverpool between 1960 and 1978?

10 Who was appointed manager of Stoke City in July 1997?

11 Who was manager of Blackpool from 1935 to 1958?

12 Who was manager of Scunthorpe United from 1915 to 1953?

13 Who was Manchester City's captain when they won the League in 1968?

14 Before moving stadium in 1990, which English League club was based at Fellows Park?

15 In which year did Bristol Rovers win the Third Division Championship?

THE CARLING ULTIMATE FOOTBALL FACT AND QUIZ BOOK

Quiz 15

GREAT CLUBS OF ENGLAND

1 Which club has a fanzine called 'One Nil Down Two One Up'?

2 Which England cricket captain played football for Scunthorpe United?

3 Which English League team has a fanzine called 'Raising The Coffin'?

4 Which legendary Newcastle United centre forward seldom headed the ball because of fibrositis?

5 Which team lost 1-0 at Crewe Alexandra in their last League match on March 2, 1962?

6 Which West Country team won the Fourth Division Championship in 1990, its only major honour to date?

7 Who did Charlton Athletic buy from Barnsley in 1998?

8 Who did Manchester City sell to West Ham United in 1997?

9 Who is currently the most prominent director of Wimbledon?

10 Who played 506 times for Stoke City between 1958 and 1976?

11 Who scored 39 goals for Hull City in the 1932-33 season?

12 Who scored 245 goals for Liverpool in a career that began in 1959 and ended in 1969?

13 Who scored six of Oldham Athletic's seven goals in their 1989-90 League Cup defeat of Scarborough?

14 Who were runners-up in the FA Cup finals of 1948 and 1951?

15 In 1996, which former Liverpool player became player manager of Swansea City?

Answers

1 Arsenal 2 Ian Botham 3 Preston North End 4 Jackie Milburn 5 Accrington Stanley 6 Exeter City 7 Neil Redfearn 8 Steve Lomas 9 Sam Hammam 10 Eric Skeels 11 Bill McNaughton 12 Roger Hunt 13 Frank Bunn 14 Blackpool 15 Jan Molby

THE CARLING ULTIMATE FOOTBALL FACT AND QUIZ BOOK

GREAT CLUBS OF ENGLAND

1 In a bid to change their luck, which team changed its strip from the traditional red shirts and white shorts to cherry and white hoops for a Second Division relegation match against Millwall in 1934?

2 In which year did Burnley first win the League Championship?

3 In which year did Walsall win the Fourth Division Championship?

4 What is the name of Wolverhampton Wanderers' ground?

5 Which club plays its home games at Craven Cottage?

6 Which English League team is nicknamed The Blades?

7 Which English League team is nicknamed The Cobblers?

8 Which English League team plays its home games at The Manor?

9 Which London club is nicknamed The Eagles?

10 Which team plays its home matches at Portman Road?

11 Who was appointed manager of Sunderland in March 1995?

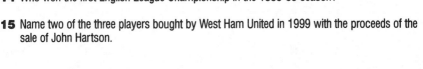

12 Who was the last Englishman to manage Chelsea?

13 Who were the first English League Champions of the 20th century?

14 Who won the first English League Championship in the 1888-89 season?

15 Name two of the three players bought by West Ham United in 1999 with the proceeds of the sale of John Hartson.

Answers

1 Manchester United **2** 1921 **3** 1960 **4** Molineux **5** Fulham **6** Sheffield United **7** Northampton Town **8** Oxford United **9** Crystal Palace **10** Ipswich Town **11** Peter Reid **12** Glenn Hoddle **13** Aston Villa **14** Preston North End **15** Paolo Di Canio, Marc-Vivien Foé and Scott Minto

THE CARLING ULTIMATE FOOTBALL FACT AND QUIZ BOOK

GREAT CLUBS OF ENGLAND

1 In which year did Burnley win the FA Cup?

2 Since 1994, which English League team has played its home matches at Sixfields Stadium?

3 Which Aston Villa winger of the late 19th and early 20th centuries is reputed to have played one game in the rain carrying an umbrella?

4 Which club was once frequently – but is now only occasionally – known as The Glaziers?

5 Which English League club has fanzines called 'Rage On' and 'Yellow Fever'?

6 Which English League team plays its home matches at Bramall Lane?

7 Which former Liverpool manager died on February 14, 1996?

8 Which team has a fanzine called 'Without A Care In The World'?

9 Which club won its first League Championship in 1908?

10 Which Third Division side knocked mighty Arsenal out of the FA Cup in the Third Round in 1933?

11 Who are known as The Trotters?

12 Who beat Fulham 10-0 in the League Cup Second Round First Leg in 1986?

13 Who has been the Chairman of Chelsea since 1982?

14 Who is the President of Wolverhampton Wanderers?

15 Who was manager of Sunderland when they won the FA Cup in 1973?

THE CARLING ULTIMATE FOOTBALL FACT AND QUIZ BOOK

GREAT CLUBS OF ENGLAND

1 Who was the captain of the Preston North End side that won the first English League Championship?

2 From 1898 to 1997, which English League team played its home matches at Roker Park?

3 In 1961, which team became the first winners of the League Cup?

4 In which year did Burnley last win the League?

5 In which year did Chelsea first win the FA Cup?

6 In which year did Manchester United first win the FA Cup?

7 In which year did Oxford United enter the Football League?

8 What colour scheme did Bolton Wanderers wear in the 1880s to make their players look bigger than they really were?

9 What was the name of the ground at which Northampton Town played their home matches until 1994?

10 Which club flew The Nest in 1924?

11 Which Danish team knocked Liverpool out of the 1995-96 UEFA Cup?

12 Which English League club has a fanzine called 'Greasy Chip Buttie'?

13 Which English League club plays its home games at Deepdale?

14 Which future England manager ran Ipswich Town from 1955 to 1963?

15 Which player won the most England caps while playing for Fulham?

GREAT CLUBS OF ENGLAND

1 Who has scored more goals for Wolverhampton Wanderers than any other player?

2 Who scored the first goal for Walsall against Arsenal in the FA Cup Third Round match in 1933?

3 At the end of which season was the Kop at Anfield demolished?

4 Fulham returned to the First Division in 1959 – when were they relegated again?

5 In which season did Northampton Town play in the old First Division?

6 In which year did Ipswich Town win the Third Division Championship?

7 In which year did Sheffield United win the League Championship?

8 In which year were Crystal Palace first promoted to the old First Division?

9 Name the three former Derby County players who managed Bolton Wanderers consecutively from 1992.

10 Which club plays its home games at Turf Moor?

11 Who captained Oxford United to the Third Division Championship in 1968?

12 Which English League club has a fanzine called 'Sex & Chocolate'?

13 Which team did Oxford United replace in the Football League?

14 Which was the first team to do the Double?

15 Who scored five goals for Chelsea in their 13-0 victory over Jeunesse Hautcharage in the 1971-72 European Cup Winners' Cup?

Answers

1 Steve Bull **2** Gilbert Alsop **3** 1993-94 **4** 1968 **5** 1965-66 **6** 1957 **7** 1898 **8** 1969
9 Bruce Rioch, Roy McFarland and Colin Todd **10** Burnley **11** Ron Atkinson **12** Sunderland
13 Accrington Stanley **14** Preston North End **15** Peter Osgood

THE CARLING ULTIMATE FOOTBALL FACT AND QUIZ BOOK

Quiz 20
GREAT CLUBS OF ENGLAND

1 Who scored the second goal – a penalty – for Walsall against Arsenal in the FA Cup Third Round match in 1933?

2 Who scored the winner for Manchester United in the 1909 FA Cup Final?

3 Who was Aston Villa manager in 1982 when they won the European Cup?

4 In which year did Burnley finish third from bottom of the Fourth Division, the lowest position in their history?

5 In which year did Fulham reach the FA Cup Final?

6 In which year did Sunderland win the last of their six League Championships?

7 In which year did Walsall reach the semi-final of the League Cup?

8 Which club won all three of its English League Championships in the 1950s?

9 Which former Blackpool hero managed Bolton Wanderers from 1971 to 1974?

10 Which team won the Second Division Championship in 1961 and 1968?

11 Which English League club has a fanzine called 'A Load Of Bull'?

12 Who did Manchester United beat in the 1948 FA Cup Final?

13 Who did Preston North End beat in the 1938 FA Cup Final?

14 Who has scored more goals for Chelsea than any other player?

15 Who played 571 games for Crystal Palace between 1973 and 1988?

THE CARLING ULTIMATE FOOTBALL FACT AND QUIZ BOOK

Quiz 21

GREAT CLUBS OF ENGLAND

1 Who scored the only goal of the 1982 European Cup Final, in which Aston Villa beat Bayern Munich?

2 Whose defeat of Liverpool in the 1994 FA Cup prompted the resignation of manager Graeme Souness?

3 At the end of the 19th century and the beginning of the 20th, who were known as The Team of all the Talents?

4 Between the establishment of modern football and the Millennium, how many times did Sheffield United win the FA Cup?

5 How many times did Bolton Wanderers win the FA Cup in the 20th century?

6 In which year did Chelsea win the First Division Championship?

7 In which year did Ipswich Town win the League Championship?

8 In which year did Northampton Town win the Third Division Championship?

9 What was Ron Atkinson's nickname during his playing days at Oxford United?

10 Which club has a fanzine called 'Bob Lord's Sausage'?

11 Which English League club plays in old gold shirts?

12 Which former Crystal Palace player won 19 caps for Wales while on the books at Selhurst Park between 1991 and 1994?

13 Who kept goal for Fulham in the 1975 FA Cup Final?

14 Which England manager once played for Queen's Park Rangers?

15 Who scored all five Liverpool goals as they beat Fulham in the 1993-94 League Cup?

Answers

1 Peter Withe **2** Bristol City **3** Sunderland **4** Four times **5** Four times **6** 1955 **7** 1962 **8** 1963 **9** The Tank **10** Burnley **11** Wolverhampton Wanderers **12** Eric Young **13** Peter Mellor **14** Terry Venables **15** Robbie Fowler

THE CARLING ULTIMATE FOOTBALL FACT AND QUIZ BOOK

GREAT CLUBS OF ENGLAND

1 Who scored the winner for Preston North End from the penalty spot in extra time in the 1938 FA Cup Final?

2 Who scored twice for Manchester United in the 1948 FA Cup Final?

3 Who was the captain of Aston Villa who lifted the European Cup in 1982?

4 During the 1972-73 season, Walsall used a record number of goalkeepers in their League programme – how many?

5 For the youth team of which English League club did comedian and entertainer Des O'Connor play during the Second World War?

6 In which year did Crystal Palace finish third in the old First Division at the end of their best ever season?

7 In which year did Wolverhampton Wanderers last win the FA Cup?

8 in which year did Oxford United win the Second Division Championship and thus gain promotion to the top flight of English League football for the first time in their history?

9 What was the name of Bolton Wanderers' ground from 1895 to 1997?

10 What was the score in the 1963 FA Cup Final, in which Manchester United beat Leicester City?

11 Which great Preston North End and England winger subsequently became President of his old club?

12 Which team has a fanzine called 'Cockney Rebel'?

13 Which two former England captains played together in Fulham's 1975 FA Cup Final side?

14 Who kept goal for Sunderland's Team of all the Talents?

15 Who managed Aston Villa from 1894-1926?

THE CARLING ULTIMATE FOOTBALL FACT AND QUIZ BOOK

Quiz 23
GREAT CLUBS OF ENGLAND

1 On October 18, 1992, who overtook Roger Hunt as Liverpool's leading scorer?

2 Who scored Sheffield United's first goal in the 1915 FA Cup Final?

3 Who succeeded Alf Ramsey as manager of Ipswich Town?

4 Who was the last Championship-winning manager of Burnley?

5 At which ground have Bolton Wanderers played home games since 1997?

6 In which year did Ipswich Town win the FA Cup?

7 Which Fulham player won a World Cup Winner's medal in 1966?

8 Which goalkeeper played 522 League games for Burnley between 1907 and 1928?

9 Which great figure in the history of Aston Villa founded the Football League in 1888 and became its first President?

10 Which Irishman is Walsall's most capped international?

11 Who did Liverpool beat in a penalty shoot-out in the semi-final of the 1992 FA Cup?

12 Who did Wolverhampton Wanderers beat in the 1960 FA Cup Final?

13 Who scored 30 League goals for Oxford United in Division Two in 1984-85?

14 Who scored 135 League goals for Northampton Town between 1947 and 1960?

15 Who scored Sheffield United's second goal in the 1915 FA Cup Final?

THE CARLING ULTIMATE FOOTBALL FACT AND QUIZ BOOK

Quiz 24
GREAT CLUBS OF ENGLAND

1 Who scored twice for Crystal Palace in the 1990 FA Cup Final?

2 Who scored twice for Manchester United in the 1963 FA Cup Final?

3 Who was centre forward in Sunderland's Team of all the Talents?

4 Who, in 1965, became the first London club to win the League Cup?

5 With a slightly superior goal average (1.51 against 1.41), who pipped Preston North End to the 1953 League title?

6 For which Italian club did Gianluca Vialli play before moving to Chelsea?

7 From which club did Liverpool buy Mark Walters in the 1990-91 season?

8 In which season did Bolton Wanderers play in the old Fourth Division?

9 What is the title of Fulham's leading fanzine?

10 Which Dane became manager of Walsall in June 1997?

11 Which team has a fanzine called 'Witton Wisdom'?

12 Who did Ipswich Town beat in the 1978 FA Cup Final?

13 Who did Sunderland beat in the 1973 FA Cup Final?

14 Who made 447 League appearances for Preston North End between 1961 and 1975 and then managed the club from 1983 to 1985?

15 Who scored 28 League and Cup goals for Northampton Town between 1927 and 1929?

Answers

1 Ian Wright 2 David Herd 3 Johnny Campbell 4 Chelsea 5 Arsenal 6 Juventus 7 Rangers
8 1987-88 9 'One F in Fulham' 10 Jan Sorensen 11 Aston Villa 12 Arsenal 13 Leeds United
14 Alan Kelly 15 Harry Loasby

Quiz 25

GREAT CLUBS OF ENGLAND

1 Who scored 77 League goals for Oxford United between 1962 and 1973?

2 Who scored Crystal Palace's first goal in the 1990 FA Cup Final?

3 Who scored Sheffield United's third goal in the 1915 FA Cup Final?

4 Who scored the first goal for Manchester United in the 1963 FA Cup Final?

5 Who scored the only goal of the 1914 FA Cup Final, in which Burnley beat Liverpool 1-0?

6 Who scored two goals for Wolverhampton Wanderers in the 1960 FA Cup Final?

7 From which club did Crystal Palace buy Nigel Martyn – the first £1 million goalkeeper – in 1990?

8 In 1964, which club became the first from the Fourth Division to reach the Sixth Round of the FA Cup?

9 Which Blackburn player in the 1960 FA Cup Final went on to become a Wolves' legend?

10 Which England international goalkeeper made more appearances for Bolton Wanderers than any other player?

11 Which English League club is nicknamed The Clarets?

12 Which former Fulham player led the consortium that took over the club in 1987?

13 Which manager walked out on Aston Villa in February 1982, just three months before they won the European Cup?

14 Which Preston North End player won 76 England caps?

15 Who did Chelsea sell to Leeds United straight after he had played well in the 1998 European Cup Winners' Cup Final?

THE CARLING ULTIMATE FOOTBALL FACT AND QUIZ BOOK

GREAT CLUBS OF ENGLAND

1 Who did Sheffield United beat in the 1915 FA Cup Final?

2 Who kept goal for Manchester United in the 1968 European Cup Final?

3 Who managed Northampton Town from 1969 to 1972 then remained at the club as General Manager before joining the board in 1985?

4 Who scored the winning goal for Ipswich Town in the 1978 FA Cup Final?

5 Who refereed the 1981 League Cup Final between Liverpool and West Ham United?

6 Who was manager of Walsall from 1957 to 1964 and then again from 1969 to 1972?

7 Why is April 19, 1991 a significant date in the history of Liverpool FC?

8 How many times did Manchester United win the FA Cup under Ron Atkinson?

9 In 1994-95, which London team finished in the last four of all three major tournaments – the FA Cup, the League Cup and (worst of all) the Premiership?

10 In which European capital city was Bolton's Gudni Bergsson born?

11 In which year did Oxford United win the League Cup?

12 What was the score in the FA Cup Fifth Round Merseyside derby in February 1991 after which Kenny Dalglish resigned as Liverpool manager?

13 Which Aston Villa player had to leave the field after only eight minutes of the 1982 European Cup Final?

14 Which Australian former Liverpool player named his daughter Chelsea after the London club?

15 Which English League club plays its home games at Vicarage Road?

THE CARLING ULTIMATE FOOTBALL FACT AND QUIZ BOOK

GREAT CLUBS OF ENGLAND

1 Which future England manager ran Ipswich Town from 1969 to 1982?

2 Which Welsh international later ran a sweetshop close to the Burnley ground at which he made his name?

3 Who did Sheffield United beat in the 1925 FA Cup Final?

4 Who did Wolverhampton Wanderers beat in the 1949 FA Cup Final?

5 Who had a heroic game in goal for Sunderland in the 1973 FA Cup Final?

6 Who was appointed manager of Northampton Town in January 1995?

7 Who was appointed manager of Preston North End in December 1994?

8 With which of their London neighbours did Fulham nearly merge in 1987?

9 In 1927-28, Northampton Town were runners up in the Third Division South – which London club won the Championship of that division?

10 Where did Martin Dobson go on leaving Burnley?

11 Which '70s Bolton Wanderers defender ended his playing days with Tampa in Florida and then returned to manage his old club?

12 Which English League team is nicknamed The Hornets?

13 Which Manchester United legend managed Preston North End from 1973 to 1975?

14 Which prodigal son returned to Anfield from Italy on August 18, 1988?

15 Who beat Sunderland 8-0 in 1968?

Answers

*1 Bobby Robson **2** Leighton James **3** Cardiff City **4** Leicester City **5** Jim Montgomery **6** Ian Atkins **7** Gary Peters **8** Queen's Park Rangers **9** Millwall **10** Everton **11** Sam Allardyce **12** Watford **13** Bobby Charlton **14** Ian Rush **15** West Ham United*

THE CARLING ULTIMATE FOOTBALL FACT AND QUIZ BOOK

GREAT CLUBS OF ENGLAND

1 Who did Oxford United beat in the 1986 League Cup Final?

2 Who has scored more League goals for Fulham than any other player?

3 Who managed Crystal Palace for four days in 1984?

4 Who scored 74 goals in 198 appearances for Chelsea in the 1970s?

5 Who scored the winner for Sheffield United in the 1925 FA Cup Final?

6 Who scored two goals for Manchester United in the 1983 FA Cup Final replay?

7 Who scored two goals for Wolverhampton Wanderers in the 1949 FA Cup Final?

8 Who took Jimmy Rimmer's place in the Aston Villa goal after only eight minutes of the 1982 European Cup Final?

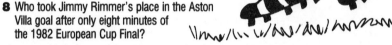

9 Who was Ipswich Town's England full back and captain of the 1970s and 1980s?

10 Fans of which club are particularly associated with the song 'One Man Went To Mow'?

11 How many players did Aston Villa use during their Championship-winning season 1980-81?

12 From 1961-62, how many seasons did it take Northampton Town to rise from the Fourth Division to the First?

13 In December 1892, which English League club became the first to score 10 goals away from home?

14 In the 1975-76 season, which Crystal Palace player became the first representative of the Third Division to play for his country in 15 years?

15 In which year did Ipswich Town win the UEFA Cup?

THE CARLING ULTIMATE FOOTBALL FACT AND QUIZ BOOK

Quiz 29
GREAT CLUBS OF ENGLAND

1 In which year did Watford gain promotion to the old First Division?

2 Which Manchester United legend managed Preston North End from 1977 to 1981?

3 Which Scottish international goalkeeper was a member of Burnley's 1960 Championship-winning squad?

4 Who beat Sunderland 8-0 in 1982?

5 Who failed to score for Liverpool from the penalty spot in the 1988 FA Cup Final?

6 Which former Manchester United, Everton and Northern Ireland player is now a podiatrist?

7 Who scored Oxford United's first goal in the 1986 League Cup Final?

8 Who scored the first goal for Wolverhampton Wanderers in the 1974 League Cup Final?

9 Who was Fulham's first choice goalkeeper for much of the 1960s?

10 Who went from Lion of Vienna to President of Bolton Wanderers?

11 According to the Ipswich Town song, what does everyone call Edward Ebenezer Jeremiah Brown?

12 Before joining Preston North End, which goalkeeper had previously played for Rotherham United, Everton, Notts County, Sunderland, Blackburn Rovers, Manchester City, Tottenham Hotspur, Aberdeen and Crystal Palace?

13 How many years did it take Northampton Town to go from the First Division to the Fourth?

14 In which European capital city was Bolton's Nathan Blake born?

15 In which year were Watford runners-up in the old First Division?

THE CARLING ULTIMATE FOOTBALL FACT AND QUIZ BOOK

GREAT CLUBS OF ENGLAND

1 Which Anfield star began his playing career at South Liverpool, then went to Newport County and Oxford United before signing for Liverpool proper?

2 Which Crystal Palace player won an England cap in 1962, while his club were in the Third Division?

3 Which future England manager played for Fulham in the 1960s?

4 Which successful team of the 1930s was nicknamed The Bank of England?

5 Who began his career with Burnley in 1962 and later became the club groundsman?

6 Who preceded Brian Little as manager of Aston Villa?

7 Who scored 205 League goals for Sheffield United between 1919 and 1930?

8 Who scored Oxford United's second goal in the 1986 League Cup Final?

9 Who scored the second goal for Wolverhampton Wanderers in the 1974 League Cup Final?

10 Who was manager of Chelsea when they first won the FA Cup?

11 Who were the first Champions of the Premier League in 1993?

12 At the end of which season were Preston North End last relegated from the top flight of English League football?

13 By what nickname were Rokermen Charlie Buchan, Frank Cuggy and Jackie Mordue collectively known?

14 How many goals did Ian Rush score for Liverpool before he moved to Juventus?

15 In the 1971-72 season, which Crystal Palace player's effort was given as a goal but then rubbed out almost immediately when the scorer told the referee that his shot against Nottingham Forest had not crossed the line?

Answers

1 John Aldridge **2** Johnny Byrne **3** Bobby Robson **4** Sunderland **5** Arthur Bellamy **6** Ron Atkinson **7** Harry Johnson **8** Ray Houghton **9** John Richards **10** Dave Sexton **11** Manchester United **12** 1960-61 **13** The Sunderland Triangle **14** 207 **15** Steve Kember

THE CARLING ULTIMATE FOOTBALL FACT AND QUIZ BOOK

Quiz 31
GREAT CLUBS OF ENGLAND

1 In which year did Watford reach the Final of the FA Cup?

2 Robert Maxwell planned to merge Oxford United with Reading. What was his proposed name for the new club?

3 What nationality is Aston Villa goalkeeper Mark Bosnich?

4 Where did Ipswich Town get Paul Mariner?

5 Which 1966 World Cup winner managed Sheffield United in 1981?

6 Which Chelsea player of the 1970s is remembered more for his long throw-ins than for the 43 goals he scored in his 112 League appearances?

7 Which England international made 214 appearances for Burnley before moving to Tottenham Hotspur in 1971?

8 Which Wolverhampton Wanderers full back of the 1960s and 1970s had the same name as a great English playwright?

9 Who did Bolton Wanderers borrow from West Bromwich Albion during their fight to avoid relegation from the Premiership in the 1997-98 season?

10 Who managed Northampton Town from 1907 to 1912 before going on to win the League with two other clubs?

11 Who scored 32 League goals for Manchester United in the 1959-60 season?

12 Who scored within two minutes of making his debut for Fulham on September 4, 1976?

13 In which year did AFC Bournemouth adopt their present name?

14 In which year did Barnet enter the Football League?

15 In which year did Wrexham join the English Football League?

THE CARLING ULTIMATE FOOTBALL FACT AND QUIZ BOOK

Quiz 32

GREAT CLUBS OF ENGLAND

1 Which club has fanzines called 'One More Point' and 'Eastern Eagle'?

2 Which club has always played its home games at the Priestfield Stadium?

3 Which English League club is nicknamed The Cestrians?

4 Which English League club plays its home games at Elland Road?

5 Which English League team is nicknamed The Canaries?

6 Which English League team is nicknamed The Owls?

7 Which English League team were a Town until 1970 but have since been a City?

8 Which English League team are nicknamed The Stags?

9 Which English League club plays its home games at Loftus Road?

10 Which team are known as The Shakers?

11 Who beat Watford in the 1984 FA Cup Final?

12 Who played 478 games for Oxford United between 1962 and 1977?

13 Who scored two goals for Liverpool in the Merseyside FA Cup Final in 1986?

14 As what had AFC Bournemouth previously been known?

15 In which year were Watford relegated from the old First Division?

Answers

1 Crystal Palace **2** Gillingham **3** Chester City **4** Leeds United **5** Norwich City **6** Sheffield Wednesday **7** Swansea City **8** Mansfield Town **9** Queen's Park Rangers **10** Bury **11** Everton **12** John Shuker **13** Ian Rush **14** Bournemouth and Boscombe Athletic **15** 1988

THE CARLING ULTIMATE FOOTBALL FACT AND QUIZ BOOK

GREAT CLUBS OF ENGLAND

1 Which English Football League team plays its home games at the Underhill Stadium?

2 Which English League club has a fanzine called 'A Kick Up The Rs'?

3 Which English League club has a fanzine called 'Cheep Shot'?

4 Which English League club has a fanzine called 'Jackanory'?

5 Which English League club plays its home matches at the Field Mill Ground, Quarry Lane?

6 Which English League club plays its home matches at The Racecourse Ground?

7 Which English League team has a fanzine called 'Cheat!'?

8 Which English League team is nicknamed The Quakers?

9 Which former Manchester City star managed Chester City from 1976 to 1982?

10 Which Lancashire team won the FA Cup in 1900 and 1903?

11 Which team's only major honour to date is the Fourth Division Championship in 1964?

12 Who did Liverpool beat in the 1984 European Cup Final?

13 Who succeeded George Graham as manager of Leeds United in 1998?

14 Who was sacked in 1988 when he complained about the sale of Dean Saunders?

15 From which club did Chester City acquire former England international Cyrille Regis?

THE CARLING ULTIMATE FOOTBALL FACT AND QUIZ BOOK

GREAT CLUBS OF ENGLAND

1 In which year did Mansfield Town reach the Sixth Round of the FA Cup?

2 In which year did Norwich City first gain promotion to the top flight of English football?

3 Of which club was Stan Flashman once Chairman?

4 To which club did Oxford United sell Dean Saunders in 1988?

5 What is the name of AFC Bournemouth's ground?

6 Which English League club has a fanzine called 'In The Loft'?

7 Which English League club has won the Welsh Cup a record number of times?

8 Which English League club plays its home games at Feethams?

9 Which English League club plays its home games at The Vetch Field?

10 Which English League team has a fanzine called 'Boddle'?

11 Which former Liverpool player scored the winning goal for Brighton and Hove Albion that knocked his old team out of the 1983 FA Cup in the Fifth Round?

12 Which future England manager led Watford to their greatest successes?

13 Which team hold the record for the greatest margin of victory in an FA Cup Final, beating Derby County 6-0 in 1903?

14 Which team won promotion from Division Three in 1996 after conceding only 20 League goals in the season?

15 Who were the last Champions of the old First Division?

THE CARLING ULTIMATE FOOTBALL FACT AND QUIZ BOOK

GREAT CLUBS OF ENGLAND

1 In 1971, which team considered changing its name to Manchester North End?

2 In 1995-96, which Gillingham goalkeeper equalled the League record of 29 clean sheets in a season?

3 In which year did Liverpool first win the League Cup?

4 In which year did Swansea City first win promotion to the old First Division?

5 in which year did Mansfield Town win the Freight Rover Trophy at Wembley?

6 Two London clubs are nicknamed The Bees – one is Brentford; what is the other?

7 Which club plays its home games at The Deva Stadium, Bumpers Lane?

8 Which club will move to a ground called Minchery Farm when it is completed?

9 Which comedian and television game show host was a director of AFC Bournemouth?

10 Which English League club has a fanzine called 'Beat About The Bush'?

11 Which English League club now plays in all white but is still nicknamed The Peacocks?

12 Which English League team has a fanzine called 'Spitting Feathers'?

13 Which goalkeeper won 28 caps for Wales while playing for Wrexham?

14 Which rock star is Chairman of Watford?

15 Which team has a fanzine called 'Where's The Money Gone'?

THE CARLING ULTIMATE FOOTBALL FACT AND QUIZ BOOK

GREAT CLUBS OF ENGLAND

1 Who was manager of Norwich City when they won promotion to the old First Division?

2 By what religious name were Mansfield Town known until 1910?

3 In January 1981, who inflicted Liverpool's first home defeat in 86 matches?

4 In which year did Leeds United do the double of League Cup and European Fairs Cup?

5 In which year did Norwich City first win the League Cup?

6 Since the demise of Maidstone United in 1992, which has been the only Football League club in Kent?

7 What relation is Roy Dwight, who scored for Nottingham Forest in the 1959 FA Cup Final, to rock star football fan Elton John?

8 Which club has a fanzine called 'Two Together'?

9 Which English League club has a fanzine called 'All Quiet On The Western Avenue'?

10 Which English League team has a fanzine called 'Where Were You At The Shay'?

11 Which team has a fanzine called 'Mission Impossible'?

12 Who did Fourth Division Oxford United beat 3-1 in the Fifth Round of the 1964 FA Cup?

13 Who established an FA Cup goalscoring record with nine goals for Bournemouth against Margate in 1971?

14 Who made 592 League appearances for Wrexham between 1959 and 1979?

15 Who managed Swansea City when they won promotion to the old First Division?

---

1 Ron Saunders 2 Mansfield Wesleyans 3 Leicester City 4 1968 5 1962 6 Gillingham 7 Uncle 8 Barnet 9 Queen's Park Rangers 10 Bury 11 Darlington 12 Blackburn Rovers 13 Ted McDougall 14 Arfon Griffiths 15 John Toshack

Answers

Quiz 37

GREAT CLUBS OF ENGLAND

1 Who played their home games at Sealand Road between 1906 and 1990?

2 Who won the FA Cup in 1896, 1907 and 1935?

3 In which year did Norwich City win the League Cup for the second time?

4 In which year did Swansea first reach the semi-final of the FA Cup?

5 Which director of AFC Bournemouth was killed in a road accident during Italia '90?

6 Which English League club has had 18 homes and four different team colours?

7 Which English League team has a fanzine called 'The Hatchet'?

8 Which English League club has a fanzine called 'Clap Your Hands, Stamp Your Feet'?

9 Which Gillingham player was the Football League's leading scorer in 1973-74, with 31 goals?

10 Which League club played at Macclesfield's Moss Rose Ground from 1990 to 1992?

11 Which London club was founded in 1888 but did not turn professional until 1965?

12 Which team has a fanzine called 'Darlo, It's Just Like Watching Brazil'?

13 Who did Sheffield Wednesday beat in the 1991 League Cup Final?

14 Who knocked Fourth Division Oxford United out of the 1964 FA Cup in the Sixth Round?

15 Who managed Leeds United for 44 days in 1974?

Answers

1 Chester City **2** Sheffield Wednesday **3** 1985 **4** 1926 **5** Brian Tiler **6** Queen's Park Rangers **7** Bury **8** Watford **9** Brian Yeo **10** Chester City **11** Barnet **12** Darlington **13** Manchester United **14** Preston North End **15** Brian Clough

THE CARLING ULTIMATE FOOTBALL FACT AND QUIZ BOOK

Quiz 38
GREAT CLUBS OF ENGLAND

1 Who scored 55 goals for Mansfield Town in the Third Division (North) in 1936-37?

2 Who was Liverpool's so-called 'Super Sub' of the late 1970s and early 1980s?

3 Wrexham have had more than a hundred Joneses playing for them. Which one did they buy from Liverpool in 1978?

4 From which club did Liverpool buy Graeme Souness on January 10, 1978?

5 In 1926, who knocked Swansea Town out of the FA Cup in the semi-final?

6 In which year did Queen's Park Rangers first make it into the First Division?

7 Of which League club is the Duke of Westminster the Patron?

8 Supporters of which team are particularly associated with the song 'Marching On Together'?

9 Which club has fanzines called 'Community Service' and 'Exiled!'?

10 Which former England goalkeeper managed Barnet from 1994-96?

11 Which Lancashire team won promotion to the First Division in 1894, its first year in the League?

12 Who became chairman of Oxford United during the 1981-82 season?

13 Who did Norwich City beat in the 1962 League Cup Final?

14 Who has played more games and scored more goals for Watford than any other player?

15 Who is Gillingham's most capped international, having made three of his 70 appearances for Ireland while at Priestfield?

THE CARLING ULTIMATE FOOTBALL FACT AND QUIZ BOOK

Quiz 39
GREAT CLUBS OF ENGLAND

1 Who managed Mansfield Town from 1983 to 1989?

2 Who scored 44 goals for Wrexham in the 1933-34 season?

3 Who scored the winner for Sheffield Wednesday in the 1991 League Cup Final?

4 Who was appointed manager of Darlington in November 1996?

5 In which year did Chester change its name to Chester City?

6 In which year did Queen's Park Rangers – then of the Third Division – win the League Cup?

7 In which year did Sheffield Wednesday win the last of their four League titles?

8 In which year did Swansea last reach the semi-final of the FA Cup?

9 Which club has a fanzine called 'To Ell And Back'?

10 Which club joined the League in 1920, dropped out of it in 1938, and was re-elected in 1950?

11 Which former England player was Director of Football at Barnet in the 1996-97 season?

12 Which former Middlesbrough and Northern Ireland goalkeeper preceded David Hodgson as manager of Darlington?

13 Which former West Ham United winger became manager of AFC Bournemouth in 1983?

14 Which London team won the Second Division Championship in 1996-97?

15 Which Watford player won 31 caps for Wales?

Answers

1 Ian Greaves **2** Tom Bamford **3** Sheridan **4** David Hodgson **5** 1983 **6** 1967 **7** 1930 **8** 1964
9 Leeds United **10** Gillingham **11** Alan Mullery **12** Jim Platt **13** Harry Redknapp **14** Bury
15 Kenny Jackett

THE CARLING ULTIMATE FOOTBALL FACT AND QUIZ BOOK

GREAT CLUBS OF ENGLAND

1 Who did Norwich City beat in the 1985 League Cup Final?

2 Who scored Liverpool's first goal in the 1976 UEFA Cup Final against Bruges?

3 Who was appointed manager of Mansfield Town in October 1996?

4 Who was appointed manager of Wrexham in November 1989?

5 Who won 18 of his 36 Northern Ireland caps while playing for Oxford United?

6 In 1974-75, who did Liverpool beat in the First Round of the European Cup Winners' Cup?

7 The last two players to score for Oxford United in the Southern League were also the first two players to score for them in League Division Four – name either.

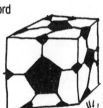

8 To which club did manager Barry Fry go immediately after leaving Barnet in 1993?

9 Which club has a fanzine called 'The Square Ball'?

10 Which English League team has a fanzine called 'Follow The Yellow Brick Road'?

11 Which former Chelsea player was manager of Bournemouth between 1980 and 1982?

12 Which former Tottenham Hotspur player managed Darlington from 1983-87?

13 Which player won 31 England caps while playing for Watford?

14 Which Sunderland player scored the own goal that gave Norwich City victory in the 1985 League Cup Final?

15 Which Wrexham player was sent off after only 20 seconds of the match at Hull on Christmas Day 1936?

THE CARLING ULTIMATE FOOTBALL FACT AND QUIZ BOOK

GREAT CLUBS OF ENGLAND

1 Who beat Sheffield Wednesday in two Cup Finals in 1993?

2 Who did Chester sell to Liverpool for £300,000 in May 1980?

3 Who did Queen's Park Rangers beat in the 1967 League Cup Final?

4 Who knocked Swansea out of the FA Cup in the 1964 semi-final?

5 Who played 571 matches for Gillingham between 1957 and 1972?

6 With which team did Colin Bell, later of Manchester City and England, begin his League career?

7 How wide in inches are the black stripes on AFC Bournemouth shirts?

8 In 1925-26, which Lancashire team had a Christmas run of eight League games without defeat, including victory at Anfield, home and away wins over Manchester City, and an 8-1 thrashing of Burnley?

9 In 1978, who did Wrexham beat 4-1 in front of a crowd of 42,000 at St James' Park?

10 In 1996-97, which uncle and nephew played together for Leeds United?

11 In which year did Chester reach the semi-final of the League Cup?

12 In which year did Watford reach the semi-final of the League Cup?

13 Which brothers were swapped between Sheffield Wednesday and Queen's Park Rangers?

14 Which English League team is nicknamed The Rams?

15 Which Liverpool player was sent off in the 1974 Charity Shield?

THE CARLING ULTIMATE FOOTBALL FACT AND QUIZ BOOK

GREAT CLUBS OF ENGLAND

1 Who beat Barnet 9-1 at Underhill in 1998-99?

2 Who beat Norwich City in the 1959 FA Cup semi-final?

3 Who beat Norwich City in the 1989 FA Cup semi-final?

4 Who beat Swansea City 8-0 in the Third Round of the 1990 FA Cup?

5 Who did Gillingham sell to Tottenham Hotspur for £350,000 in June 1992?

6 Who made 440 League appearances for Mansfield Town between 1970 and 1983?

7 Who scored Queen's Park Rangers' first goal in the 1967 League Cup Final?

8 Who was appointed manager of Oxford United in September 1993?

9 From which Italian club did Sheffield Wednesday sign Benito Carbone in October 1996?

10 In which year did Mansfield Town win the Third Division Championship?

11 In which year did Queen's Park Rangers reach the FA Cup Final?

12 To which club did Billy Bremner go on leaving Leeds United?

13 Which club was the longest-serving member of the Third Division, from 1923 to 1970?

14 Which First Division club did Wycombe Wanderers hold to a goalless draw at home in the Third Round of the 1975 FA Cup?

15 Which goalkeeper made his debut for Barnet in their 5-2 defeat at Peterborough in February 1999?

THE CARLING ULTIMATE FOOTBALL FACT AND QUIZ BOOK

GREAT CLUBS OF ENGLAND

1 Which manager led Bury to the Second Division Championship in 1996-97?

2 Which team appeared in the semi-finals of the FA Cup 13 times between 1895 and 1909 but did not win the competition until 1946?

3 Who knocked Chester out of the 1975 League Cup in the semi-final, 5-4 on aggregate?

4 Who knocked Watford out of the 1979 League Cup in the semi-final?

5 Who scored 35 goals for Swansea Town in the 1931-32 season?

6 Who scored Liverpool's last goal in their 3-0 defeat of Newcastle United in the 1974 FA Cup Final?

7 Who was appointed manager of Gillingham in June 1995?

8 Who was manager of Oxford United when they entered the Football League in 1962?

9 In which year did Bournemouth have their best-ever FA Cup run, reaching the Sixth Round?

10 In which year did Mansfield Town win the Fourth Division Championship?

11 In which year did Wycombe Wanderers enter the Football League?

12 Which 16-year-old scored for Watford against Blackpool on November 30, 1996?

13 Which club won the English League Championship for the first time in 1972?

14 Which English League club won the Welsh Cup in 1908, 1933 and 1947?

15 Which English team did Liverpool beat in the semi-final of the 1972-73 UEFA Cup?

Answers

1 Stan Ternent **2** Derby County **3** Aston Villa **4** Nottingham Forest **5** Cyril Pearce **6** Steve Heighway **7** Tony Pulis **8** Arthur Turner **9** 1957 **10** 1975 **11** 1993 **12** Gifton Noel-Williams **13** Derby County **14** Chester **15** Tottenham Hotspur

THE CARLING ULTIMATE FOOTBALL FACT AND QUIZ BOOK

Quiz 44
GREAT CLUBS OF ENGLAND

1 Which former England international forward ended his playing days at Barnet?

2 Which legendary Welsh international scored 42 goals for Leeds United in the 1953-54 season?

3 Which Oxford United player was transferred to West Ham United but had to leave because he felt homesick?

4 Who beat Norwich City in the 1992 FA Cup semi-final?

5 Who became manager of Sheffield Wednesday in June 1995?

6 Who did Nottingham Forest buy from Swansea City for £375,000 in July 1993?

7 Who has managed both Gillingham and Wycombe Wanderers?

8 Who is Bury's longest-serving postwar manager (1953-61)?

9 Who scored for Queen's Park Rangers in the 1982 FA Cup Final?

10 from 1895 to 1997, which English League team played its home games at the Baseball Ground?

11 In 1995, which former Norwich City player managed the club for six months between the departure of John Deehan and the arrival of Gary Megson?

12 Name either of the First Division sides Bournemouth knocked out during their 1957 FA Cup run.

13 Name the Swansea City chairman who, in 1983, called the Welsh FA 'bumbling amateurs'?

14 What was the name of the ground at which Wycombe Wanderers played their home matches from 1901 to 1990?

15 Which club has a fanzine called 'Hello Albert'?

Answers

1 Jimmy Greaves **2** John Charles **3** Joey Beauchamp **4** Sunderland **5** David Pleat **6** Des Lyttle **7** Neil Smillie **8** Dave Russell **9** Terry Fenwick **10** Derby County **11** Martin O'Neill **12** Wolverhampton Wanderers and Tottenham Hotspur **13** Malcolm Struel **14** Loakes Park **15** Chester City

THE CARLING ULTIMATE FOOTBALL FACT AND QUIZ BOOK

GREAT CLUBS OF ENGLAND

1 Which English League club is nicknamed The Posh?

2 Which English League team plays its home matches at Gigg Lane?

3 Which former Spurs player managed QPR in the 1982 FA Cup Final against his old club?

4 Which modern League club won the FA Amateur Cup in 1946?

5 Which Sheffield Wednesday centre forward lost a leg after an on-field accident at Deepdale in 1953?

6 Which team has been managed by both Billy Bingham and Raich Carter?

7 Who has scored more goals than anyone else for Leeds United?

8 Who is the only Gillingham player to have played for England?

9 Who succeeded Graham Taylor as Watford manager in 1987?

10 Who were Arsenal's opponents in September 1972 when Jimmy Hill took over from an injured linesman?

11 Against which club does Mansfield Town play the most local of its local derbies?

12 From which club did Liverpool buy Kevin Keegan for £33,000 in 1971?

13 From which London club did Crystal Palace buy Dougie Freedman in September 1995?

14 In 1957, which Bournemouth player famously collided with a post and brought the whole goal down?

15 In which year did Queen's Park Rangers finish second in the old First Division?

THE CARLING ULTIMATE FOOTBALL FACT AND QUIZ BOOK

GREAT CLUBS OF ENGLAND

1 In which year did Sheffield Wednesday come within a point of relegation to the Fourth Division?

2 What is the name of Derby County's current stadium?

3 What is the name of the ground on which Wycombe Wanderers now play their home matches?

4 Which club has a fanzine called 'The Onion Bag'?

5 Which famous cook is a director of Norwich City?

6 Which team plays home matches at London Road?

7 Who has scored more goals than anyone else for Bury, in a career that ran from 1978-86?

8 Who preceded Graham Taylor the first time he became manager of Watford?

9 Who resigned as Swansea City manager in October 1983 but was reappointed in December?

10 Who scored for Leeds United in both the FA Cup Final and the FA Cup Final replay of 1970?

11 Who was manager of Gillingham when they won the Fourth Division Championship in 1964?

12 After their meteoric rise to the old First Division, in which year did Swansea City find themselves back in Division Four?

13 In April 1995, which former Evertonian succeeded Derek Mann as manager of Chester City?

14 In which year did Peterborough United join the Football League?

15 In which year were Bury last in the top division of the English League?

Answers

1 1976 **2** Pride Park **3** Adams Park **4** Chester City **5** Delia Smith **6** Peterborough United
7 Craig Madden **8** Mike Keen **9** John Toshack **10** Mick Jones **11** Freddie Cox **12** 1986
13 Kevin Ratcliffe **14** 1960 **15** 1929

THE CARLING ULTIMATE FOOTBALL FACT AND QUIZ BOOK

Quiz 47
GREAT CLUBS OF ENGLAND

1 Which English League club has been managed by Harry Catterick, Jack Charlton, Trevor Francis and Ron Atkinson?

2 Which modern League club was formerly known as New Brompton?

3 Which Queen's Park Rangers midfielder became England captain during the 1975-76 season?

4 Who became manager of Derby County in 1967?

5 Who made 13 appearances for Bournemouth before being transferred to Liverpool?

6 Who played for Mansfield Town from 1931 to 1936 and scored more goals for the club (104) than any other player in its history?

7 Who preceded Graham Taylor the second time he became manager of Watford in 1997?

8 Who scored Liverpool's goal in the 1971 FA Cup Final?

9 Who scored the fastest goal in the history of Wycombe Wanderers?

10 Who was appointed manager of Norwich City for the second time in June 1996?

11 Who was Leeds United's Welsh international goalkeeper of the 1960s?

12 Who was player manager of Barnet in 1993-94?

13 From which club did Liverpool buy Emlyn Hughes in March 1967?

14 Name the former youth team boss of Wycombe Wanderers who took over the manager's job when John Gregory left in 1998.

15 Which English football club is nicknamed The Bantams?

Quiz 48

GREAT CLUBS OF ENGLAND

1 Which English League club nicknamed The Robins plays its home games at The County Ground?

2 Which English League club plays its home matches at the City Ground?

3 Which English League team is sometimes known by the nickname Salop?

4 Which team is nicknamed, variously, The Tykes, The Colliers and The Reds?

5 Which team was known as Abbey United until 1949, when it turned professional?

6 Who began his second stint as manager of Grimsby Town in May 1997?

7 Who was Brian Clough's assistant at Derby County?

8 Who, in 1961, became the first club to win the Fourth Division Championship in its first year in the Football League?

9 In which year did Nottingham Forest first win the FA Cup?

10 On which Spanish island were Derby County players holidaying when they learned that they had won the 1972 League Championship?

11 Which Battling team won the FA Cup in 1912?

12 Which club plays its home games at Valley Parade?

13 Which English League club has a fanzine called 'Heaven 11'?

14 Which English League club is nicknamed The Mariners?

15 Which English League club plays home matches at Filbert Street?

Answers

1 Swindon Town **2** *Nottingham Forest* **3** *Shrewsbury Town* **4** *Barnsley* **5** *Cambridge United* **6** *Alan Buckley* **7** *Peter Taylor* **8** *Peterborough United* **9** *1898* **10** *Majorca* **11** *Barnsley* **12** *Bradford City* **13** *Reading* **14** *Grimsby Town* **15** *Leicester City*

THE CARLING ULTIMATE FOOTBALL FACT AND QUIZ BOOK

Quiz 49
GREAT CLUBS OF ENGLAND

1 Which English League club plays its home games at Gay Meadow?

2 Which English League club plays its home games at The Hawthorns?

3 Which former Swindon player managed the club from 1980 to 1983?

4 Which former Tottenham Hotspur and Scotland forward has twice been manager of Chesterfield?

5 Which team was first elected to the Fourth Division of the Football League in 1970?

6 Who has made more League appearances for Wycombe Wanderers than any other player?

7 Who scored 134 goals in 46 games for Peterborough United during the 1960-61 season?

8 Who were Liverpool's wingers in the mid-1960s?

9 Who won the Second Division Championship in 1927, 1929 and 1974?

10 From which club did Liverpool buy Dean Saunders in July 1991?

11 In which year did Nottingham Forest last win the FA Cup?

12 In which year did Swindon Town win promotion to the Premiership?

13 In which year were Middlesbrough runners-up in both the FA and League Cups?

14 In which year were Shrewsbury Town elected to the Third Division North of the Football League?

15 Which club was relegated from the Third Division in 1968 after having been docked 19 points for financial irregularities?

THE CARLING ULTIMATE FOOTBALL FACT AND QUIZ BOOK

GREAT CLUBS OF ENGLAND

1 Which club won the first of its five FA Cups (to the end of the millennium) in 1888 and the last in 1968?

2 Which club won the Second Division in 1925, 1937, 1954, 1957, 1971 and 1980?

3 Which English League club has a fanzine called 'Taking The Biscuit'?

4 Which English League club plays in claret and amber shirts, black shorts and black stockings?

5 Which English League club plays its home matches at Blundell Park?

6 Which English League club plays its home matches at the Recreation Ground?

7 Which team plays its home matches at the Abbey Stadium?

8 Which Yorkshire team has a fanzine called 'Better Red Than Dead'?

9 Who scored 18 League goals for Wycombe Wanderers in the 1995-96 season?

10 Who scored the winning goal for Liverpool against Celtic at Anfield in the semi-final of the 1965-66 European Cup Winners' Cup?

11 From which club did Cambridge United buy Steve Claridge in November 1992?

12 From which club did Liverpool buy Peter Thompson for £40,000 in August 1963?

13 In which year did Peterborough United reach the semi-final of the League Cup?

14 In which year did Shrewsbury Town reach the Sixth Round of the FA Cup?

15 In which year did West Bromwich Albion win their only League Championship?

Answers

1 West Bromwich Albion 2 Leicester City 3 Reading 4 Bradford City 5 Grimsby Town 6 Chesterfield 7 Cambridge United 8 Barnsley 9 Miguel De Souza 10 Geoff Strong 11 Luton Town 12 Preston North End 13 1966 14 1979 15 1920

THE CARLING ULTIMATE FOOTBALL FACT AND QUIZ BOOK

Quiz 51

GREAT CLUBS OF ENGLAND

1 Which club has a fanzine called 'City Gent'?

2 Which club, founded in 1871, is the oldest League football team south of the Trent?

3 Which English League club are nicknamed The Minstermen?

4 Which former England international striker had two spells as manager of Barnsley – 1978-80 and 1985-89?

5 Which former Grimsby star has a street in the town named after him?

6 Which League club has a fanzine called 'Foxed Off'?

7 Which Second Division club reached the FA Cup semi-final in 1997?

8 Who did Nottingham Forest beat in the 1959 FA Cup Final?

9 Who scored Middlesbrough's goal in the 1997 League Cup Final?

10 Who won the Fourth Division Championship in 1986 with a record number of points (102 out of a possible 138)?

11 Whose shares in Derby County did Brian Fearn buy for £5.6 million on July 31, 1990?

12 By how many points did Liverpool win the Second Division Championship in 1962?

13 From 1896 to 1998, which English League team played home matches at Elm Park?

14 In which year did Shrewsbury Town reach the semi-final of the League Cup?

15 Of which English League club is the Duke of Devonshire the President?

THE CARLING ULTIMATE FOOTBALL FACT AND QUIZ BOOK

Quiz 52
GREAT CLUBS OF ENGLAND

1 To which club did Cambridge United sell Dion Dublin for £1 million in August 1992?

2 What was the score when Barnsley went to Old Trafford in the Premiership in 1997-98?

3 Which Brazilian played 20 games for Bradford City in the 1996-97 season?

4 Which club has a mascot called Harry the Haddock?

5 Which English League club plays its home matches at Bootham Crescent?

6 Which Middlesbrough player scored 59 goals in the Second Division in the 1927-28 season?

7 Which striker did Derby County buy from Charlton Athletic for £280,000 in 1976-77?

8 Who beat Peterborough United in the 1966 League Cup semi-final?

9 Who did West Bromwich Albion beat in the the 1968 FA Cup Final?

10 Who reached the semi-finals of the FA Cup in 1910 and 1912?

11 Who scored Nottingham Forest's first goal in the 1959 FA Cup Final?

12 Who was appointed manager of Leicester City in December 1995?

13 For which club did Cec Podd make a record number of League appearances – 502 – between 1970 and 1984?

14 In which year did Reading reach the semi-final of the FA Cup?

15 In which year did Third Division York City reach the semi-final of the FA Cup?

Answers

1 Manchester United **2** Manchester 7 Barnsley 0 **3** Edinho **4** Grimsby Town **5** York City
6 George Camsell **7** Derek Hales **8** West Bromwich Albion **9** Everton **10** Swindon Town **11** Roy Dwight
12 Martin O'Neill **13** Bradford City **14** 1927 **15** 1955

THE CARLING ULTIMATE FOOTBALL FACT AND QUIZ BOOK

GREAT CLUBS OF ENGLAND

1 Which England goalkeeper began his career at Chesterfield in 1958?

2 Which English League club is based in Cleethorpes?

3 Which Leicester City player scored in 16 consecutive games in the 1924-25 season?

4 Which Middlesbrough player won 26 England caps between 1947 and 1952?

5 Which team has a fanzine called 'All Day And All Of The Night'?

6 Which team has a fanzine called 'The Abbey Rabbit'?

7 Which Third Division team knocked Arsenal out of the FA Cup in 1965?

8 Who beat Swindon Town in the 1910 FA Cup semi-final?

9 Who knocked Shrewsbury Town in the semi-final of the 1961 League Cup?

10 Who scored Nottingham Forest's second goal in the 1959 FA Cup Final?

11 Who scored the winner for Barnsley in their 1997-98 Premiership match at Anfield?

12 Who scored the winner for West Bromwich Albion in the 1968 FA Cup Final?

13 Who was Derby County's Championship-winning captain?

14 Complete the missing team name in this fanzine title: 'Another Vintage --------- Performance'.

15 From which club did Leicester City buy Matt Elliott in January 1997?

THE CARLING ULTIMATE FOOTBALL FACT AND QUIZ BOOK

Quiz 54

GREAT CLUBS OF ENGLAND

1 What nationality is Middlesbrough goalkeeper Mark Schwarzer?

2 Which English Fourth Division club won the Anglo-Scottish Cup in 1981?

3 Which now defunct League club was nicknamed The Stans or The Avenuites?

4 Which prewar Grimsby Town player is both their leading aggregate scorer and their most capped international, with seven appearances for Wales?

5 Which team's mascot is known as Martin The Moose?

6 Who beat Reading in the 1927 FA Cup semi-final?

7 Who beat Swindon Town in the 1912 FA Cup semi-final?

8 Who did West Bromwich Albion beat in the the 1954 FA Cup Final?

9 Who joined Derby County from Tottenham Hotspur in July 1968?

10 Who knocked York City out in the semi-final of the 1955 FA Cup?

11 Who scored 38 goals for Shrewsbury Town in Division Four in 1958-59?

12 Who scored twice for Barnsley as they knocked Manchester United out of the 1997-98 FA Cup in a Fifth Round replay at Oakwell?

13 Who supplied the cross from which Roy Dwight scored Nottingham Forest's first goal in the 1959 FA Cup Final?

14 Who was appointed manager of Peterborough United in May 1996?

15 How many Barnsley players were sent off in their Premiership home game against Liverpool in 1997-98?

Answers

1 Australian **2** Chesterfield **3** Bradford Park Avenue **4** Pat Glover **5** Cambridge United **6** Cardiff City **7** Barnsley **8** Preston North End **9** Dave Mackay **10** Newcastle United **11** Arthur Rowley **12** Scott Jones **13** Stewart Imlach **14** Barry Fry **15** Three

GREAT CLUBS OF ENGLAND

1 In 1920, which club's first League game was a 9-1 victory over Luton Town?

2 In which English city was Michael Owen born?

3 Which club reached the semi-finals of the FA Cup in 1936 and 1939?

4 Which club were beaten finalists in the FA Cup in 1949, 1961, 1963 and 1969?

5 Which English League club has a fanzine called 'A Large Scotch'?

6 Which English League club has a fanzine called 'The Boys from Brazil'?

7 Which former Republic of Ireland international was manager of Peterborough United in 1989-90?

8 Which is the only team to have won the European Cup more often than its own domestic League Championship?

9 Which team dropped out of the English Football League in 1974?

10 Which Third Division side began the 1985-86 season with a record 13 consecutive League wins?

11 Who came fourth in the Second Division in 1947, their highest ever League position?

12 Who made 481 League appearances for York City between 1958 and 1970?

13 Who scored twice for West Bromwich Albion in the 1954 FA Cup Final?

14 Who was the Derby County Chairman who signed Brian Clough as manager in 1966-67?

15 Who was the first manager of Cambridge United?

Answers

1 Swindon Town **2** Chester **3** Grimsby Town **4** Leicester City **5** Shrewsbury Town **6** Middlesbrough **7** Mark Lawrenson **8** Nottingham Forest **9** Bradford Park Avenue **10** Reading **11** Chesterfield **12** Barry Jackson **13** Ronnie Allen **14** Sam Longson **15** Bill Whittaker

THE CARLING ULTIMATE FOOTBALL FACT AND QUIZ BOOK

Quiz 56

GREAT CLUBS OF ENGLAND

1 In which year did Grimsby Town finish fifth in the First Division, their highest League position?

2 What nationality are Liverpool's Stig Inge Bjornebye and Bjorn Kvarme?

3 What was the name of the goalkeeper brought on as substitute by Leicester City in their 1996 First Division play-off final against Crystal Palace?

4 Which English League club began as Strollers but are now Albion?

5 Which future England manager played for Bradford Park Avenue in 1945?

6 Which striker did Peterborough Unite manager Barry Fry buy from Wycombe Wanderers?

7 Who broke the British transfer record in March 1949 when they signed Johnny Morris from Manchester United for £24,500?

8 Who did Nottingham Forest buy from Stoke City in September 1977?

9 Who managed Middlesbrough from 1973 to 1977?

10 Who scored 125 goals for York City between 1954 and 1966?

11 Who scored 158 League goals for Reading between 1947 and 1954?

12 Who scored a spectacular own goal for Barnsley against Leeds United at Elland Road in the 1997-98 Premiership?

13 Who was appointed manager of Shrewsbury Town in May 1997?

14 Who was manager of Swindon Town when they won promotion from Division Three in 1963?

15 Which team won the Fourth Division Championship in 1970 and 1985?

Answers

1 1935 **2** Norwegian **3** Zeljko Kalac **4** West Bromwich **5** Ron Greenwood **6** Miguel De Souza **7** Derby County **8** Peter Shilton **9** Jack Charlton **10** Norman Wilkinson **11** Ronnie Blackman **12** Adrian Moses **13** Jake King **14** Bert Head **15** Chesterfield

THE CARLING ULTIMATE FOOTBALL FACT AND QUIZ BOOK

GREAT CLUBS OF ENGLAND

1 Who won the Manager of the Year award while in charge of Cambridge United in 1991?

2 For which team did David James make 89 League appearances before transferring to Liverpool?

3 For which team did Jim Fryatt score the fastest ever League goal, after only four seconds of the match against Tranmere Rovers in 1964?

4 In the 1997-98 Premiership season, which overseas player scored for Barnsley at Elland Road and was then sent off for two bookable offences in less than a minute?

5 In which season did Cambridge United win the old Third Division Championship?

6 In which year did Swindon Town win the League Cup?

7 Which 18-year-old replaced the Cup-tied Peter Shilton in the Nottingham Forest goal in the 1978 League Cup Final?

8 Which English club broke the British transfer record in 1946-47 when they signed Scottish international inside forward Billy Steel of Morton for £15,500?

9 Which English League club plays its home games at The Dell?

10 Which goalkeeper did Reading sell to Newcastle United in August 1995 for £1.575 million?

11 Which player, sacked by Leyton Orient, was signed by Peterborough United?

12 Who made 448 League appearances for Grimsby Town between 1953 and 1969?

13 Who scored 39 First Division goals for West Bromwich Albion in the 1935-36 season?

14 Who was appointed manager of York City in March 1993?

15 Who was appointed Middlesbrough manager in May 1994?

---

13 William 'Ginger' Richardson **14** Alan Little **15** Bryan Robson
8 Derby County **9** Southampton **10** Shaka Hislop **11** Roger Stanislaus **12** Keith Jobling
1 John Beck **2** Watford **3** Bradford Park Avenue **4** Georgi Hristov **5** 1990-91 **6** 1969 **7** Chris Woods

Answers

THE CARLING ULTIMATE FOOTBALL FACT AND QUIZ BOOK

GREAT CLUBS OF ENGLAND

1 Whose mishit shot against Crystal Palace in the 1996 First Division play-off final took Leicester City back to the Premiership?

2 At which club's ground is there a Pontoon Stand?

3 Bradford Park Avenue was revived in 1988 – at which Rugby League ground did they play their home matches?

4 In which season did Reading finish second in the First Division?

5 In which year did Southampton first reach the FA Cup Final?

6 Where did Ashley Ward go when he left Barnsley during the 1998-99 season?

7 Which Chesterfield player had what looked like a good goal disallowed in their 1997 FA Cup semi-final against Middlesbrough?

8 Which former Manchester United boss was manager of York City from 1975 to 1977?

9 Which Middlesbrough goalkeeper of the 1970s won 22 caps for Northern Ireland?

10 Which team did Cambridge United pip for the Third Division Championship on the last day of the 1990-91 season?

11 Who did Leicester City buy from West Ham United in November 1998?

12 Who did Swindon Town beat in the 1969 League Cup Final?

13 Who has played more often and scored more goals for West Bromwich Albion than any other player?

14 Who played 482 League games for Peterborough United between 1968 and 1981?

15 Who preceded Bill Shankly as manager of Liverpool?

Answers

1 Steve Claridge 2 Grimsby Town 3 Bramley 4 1994-95 5 1900 6 Blackburn Rovers 7 Jonathan Howard 8 Wilf McGuinness 9 Jim Platt 10 Southend United 11 Andrew Impey 12 Arsenal 13 Tony Brown 14 Tommy Robson 15 Phil Taylor

GREAT CLUBS OF ENGLAND

1 Who scored the penalty in the 1978 League Cup Final replay that took the trophy to Nottingham Forest?

2 Who was the Derby County inside right and captain in the 1900s nicknamed 'Paleface'?

3 In 1997, who scored the first ever hat trick for Chesterfield in the FA Cup?

4 In which year did Southampton first win promotion to the old First Division?

5 In which year did West Bromwich Albion win the League Cup?

6 Supporters of which club perform a version of Juantanamera with the lyric: 'Sing when we're fishing, we only sing when we're fishing'?

7 Where did Danny Wilson go when he left Barnsley in 1998?

8 Which footballing legend applied for the manager's job at Bradford Park Avenue in 1953 but was rejected in favour of Norman Kirkman?

9 Which Middlesbrough star of the 1970s took over Willie Maddren's sports shop in Teesside Park?

10 Which team did Cambridge United beat 2-0 on the last day of the 1990-91 season to secure the Third Division Championship?

11 Who beat Reading in the 1995 First Division play-off final at Wembley?

12 Who did Derby County buy from Sunderland for £6000 in December 1945?

13 Who did Nottingham Forest beat in the 1978 League Cup Final?

14 Who did Wolverhampton Wanderers beat in the 1980 League Cup Final?

15 Who kept goal for Leicester City in the 1969 FA Cup Final?

---

12 Raich Carter 13 Liverpool 14 Nottingham Forest 15 Peter Shilton
7 Sheffield Wednesday 8 Bill Shankly 9 John Craggs 10 Swansea City 11 Bolton Wanderers
1 John Robertson 2 Steve Bloomer 3 Kevin Davies 4 1966 5 1966 6 Grimsby Town

Answers

THE CARLING ULTIMATE FOOTBALL FACT AND QUIZ BOOK

GREAT CLUBS OF ENGLAND

1 Who scored 122 League goals for Peterborough United between 1967 and 1975?

2 Who scored Liverpool's first goal in the 1965 FA Cup Final?

3 Who scored Swindon Town's first goal in the 1969 League Cup Final?

4 From which other seaside club did Grimsby Town buy Tommy Widdrington in July 1996?

5 In which year did Southampton finish second in the old First Division?

6 To which Premiership club did Chesterfield sell Kevin Davies?

7 West Ham United had (or have) a group of followers known as the Inter City Firm. Which team has a small band of away fans who call themselves The Inter-City Trickle?

8 Where did Middlesbrough play their home matches from 1903 to 1995?

9 Which Leicester City forward missed two great chances in the 1969 FA Cup Final against Manchester City?

10 Which player went to Reading after having previously played for Celtic and Legia Warsaw?

11 Who did Nottingham Forest beat in the 1979 League Cup Final when they retained the trophy?

12 Who is chairman of both the Pizza Express restaurant chain and Peterborough United FC?

13 Who preceded Danny Wilson as manager of Barnsley?

14 Who scored for Wolverhampton Wanderers in the 1980 League Cup Final?

15 Who scored Liverpool's second goal in the 1965 FA Cup Final?

Answers

1 Jim Hall **2** Roger Hunt **3** Roger Smart **4** Southampton **5** 1984 **6** Southampton **7** Cambridge United **8** Ayresome Park **9** Andy Lochhead **10** Dariusz Wdowczyk **11** Southampton **12** Peter Boizot **13** Viv Anderson **14** Andy Gray **15** Ian St John

THE CARLING ULTIMATE FOOTBALL FACT AND QUIZ BOOK

Quiz 61
GREAT CLUBS OF ENGLAND

1 Who scored twice for Swindon Town in the 1969 League Cup Final?

2 Who scored two goals for Derby County in the 1946 FA Cup Final?

3 Who scored West Bromwich Albion's goal in the first leg of the 1966 League Cup Final at West Ham?

4 Who won more of the Bradford local derbies – City or Park Avenue?

5 From which Scottish League club did Liverpool buy Ian St John?

6 In which year did Fourth Division Cambridge United reach the Sixth Round of the FA Cup?

7 In which year did Southampton win the FA Cup?

8 Which team lost its League status in 1910 but returned the following year?

9 Which team plays its home matches at the Cellnet Riverside Stadium?

10 Who became manager of Derby County in June 1995?

11 Who did Peterborough United sell to Walsall in July 1996 and then buy back from Birmingham City in November?

12 Who made 613 League appearances for Chesterfield between 1948 and 1967?

13 Who managed Reading from 1991 to 1994?

14 Who managed West Bromwich Albion when they last won the FA Cup in 1968?

15 Who scored the winning goal for Barnsley in the 1912 FA Cup Final?

THE CARLING ULTIMATE FOOTBALL FACT AND QUIZ BOOK

Quiz 62

GREAT CLUBS OF ENGLAND

1 Who scored two goals for Nottingham Forest in the 1979 League Cup Final against Southampton?

2 Who walked out on Wolverhampton Wanderers in 1969 to become a Jehovah's Witness?

3 Who was appointed manager of Bradford City in November 1995 and led the club straight to promotion from the Second Division?

4 Who was Leicester City's right back in the 1969 FA Cup Final?

5 Which club won the Anglo-Italian Cup in the first two years of the trophy's existence (1969 and 1970)?

6 From which club did Derby County buy Kevin Hector?

7 From which club did Leicester City acquire Steve Walsh?

8 In 1996, which English League team became the first to field three Brazilians?

9 In which year did Swindon Town win a play-off final but not promotion?

10 To which club did Ian St John go on leaving Liverpool?

11 Which former Arsenal and Republic of Ireland international player managed Bradford City from 1991 to 1994?

12 Which Liverpool great was manager of Grimsby Town from 1951 to 1953?

13 Which Wolverhampton Wanderer played 105 times for England?

14 Who did Barnsley beat after extra time in the 1912 FA Cup Final replay?

15 Who did Peterborough United beat 8-1 in the Fourth Division in 1969?

Answers

1 Garry Birtles **2** Peter Knowles **3** Chris Kamara **4** Peter Rodrigues **5** Swindon Town **6** Bradford Park Avenue **7** Wigan Athletic **8** Middlesbrough **9** 1990 **10** Coventry City **11** Frank Stapleton **12** Bill Shankly **13** Billy Wright **14** West Bromwich Albion **15** Oldham Athletic

Quiz 63

GREAT CLUBS OF ENGLAND

1 Who did Southampton beat in the 1976 FA Cup Final?

2 Who played 416 games for Cambridge United between 1975 and 1987?

3 Who scored Nottingham Forest's third goal in the 1979 League Cup Final against Southampton?

4 Who was appointed manager of Reading in June 1997?

5 Who was appointed manager of West Bromwich Albion in February 1997?

6 Who was manager of Chesterfield from 1991 to 1993?

7 Which club plays its home matches at Belle Vue?

8 Which English League club is nicknamed The Gulls?

9 Which English League club is nicknamed The Lions?

10 Which English League club is nicknamed The Pilgrims?

11 Which English League club plays home matches at Griffin Park?

12 Which English League club plays its home games at Kenilworth Road?

13 Which English League club plays its home games at Spotland?

14 Which English League club's home ground is at Brisbane Road?

15 Which League club is nicknamed The Bluebirds?

Answers

1 Manchester United 2 Steve Spriggs 3 Tony Woodcock 4 Terry Bullivant 5 Ray Harford 6 Paul Hart 7 Doncaster Rovers 8 Torquay United 9 Millwall 10 Plymouth Argyle 11 Brentford 12 Luton Town 13 Rochdale 14 Leyton Orient 15 Cardiff City

THE CARLING ULTIMATE FOOTBALL FACT AND QUIZ BOOK

Quiz 64
GREAT CLUBS OF ENGLAND

1 Which team has a fanzine called 'Monkey Business'?

2 Which team has a fanzine called 'The Penguin'?

3 Who became manager of Colchester United in January 1995?

4 Who did Nottingham Forest beat in the 1989 League Cup Final?

5 Who scored Southampton's winner in the 1976 FA Cup Final?

6 Who was appointed manager of West Ham United in August 1994?

7 By what name were Leyton Orient known from 1898 to 1946?

8 From 1910 to 1993, which club had its ground in Cold Blow Lane?

9 In which year did Colchester United lose their League status after finishing bottom of the Fourth Division?

10 In which year did Southampton reach the League Cup Final?

11 Which club has a fanzine called 'Keegan Was Crap Really'?

12 Which comedian is a director of Birmingham City?

13 Which English League club has a fanzine called 'Exceedingly Good Pies'?

14 Which English League club is nicknamed The Hatters?

15 Which English League club plays at Home Park?

Answers

1 Hartlepool United **2** Birmingham City **3** Steve Wignall **4** Luton Town **5** Bobby Stokes **6** Harry Redknapp **7** Clapton Orient **8** Millwall **9** 1990 **10** 1979 **11** Doncaster Rovers **12** Jasper Carrott **13** Rochdale **14** Luton Town **15** Plymouth Argyle

THE CARLING ULTIMATE FOOTBALL FACT AND QUIZ BOOK

GREAT CLUBS OF ENGLAND

1 Which English League club plays its home games at Plainmoor?

2 Which English League team lost one letter of its name in 1968?

3 Which League club was formerly known as Riverside and Riverside Albion?

4 Who scored six of West Ham's goals in their 8-0 victory over Sunderland in 1968?

5 Who scored two goals for Nottingham Forest in the 1989 League Cup Final against Luton Town?

6 With which other London club did Brentford nearly merge in the 1960s?

7 By what name were Birmingham City known until 1906?

8 By what name were Leyton Orient known from 1966 to 1987?

9 Fans of which team are particularly associated with a version of Rod Stewart's 'Sailing' which contains the words: 'No one likes us, we don't care'?

10 In what main colour do Rochdale play?

11 In which year did Colchester United regain their League status after winning the GM Vauxhall Conference?

12 Which club has a fanzine called 'No Smoking in the Main Stand'?

13 Which English League club has a fanzine called 'Bamber's Right Foot'?

14 Which English League club has a fanzine called 'Rub Of The Greens'?

15 Which English League club is sometimes known as The Strawplaiters?

THE CARLING ULTIMATE FOOTBALL FACT AND QUIZ BOOK

GREAT CLUBS OF ENGLAND

1 Which English League club plays its home matches at Victoria Park, Clarence Road?

2 Which is the only non-English team to have won the FA Cup?

3 Which rock star was once an apprentice footballer at Brentford?

4 Who beat Southampton in the 1979 League Cup Final?

5 Who did Nottingham Forest beat in the 1990 League Cup Final?

6 Who scored 298 goals for West Ham United between 1920 and 1935?

7 In which season did Hartlepool United win promotion from the old Fourth Division?

8 In which year did Cardiff City win the FA Cup?

9 In which year did Colchester United reach the Fifth Round of the FA Cup?

10 In which year did Luton Town win the Fourth Division Championship?

11 In which year did Rochdale reach the League Cup Final?

12 Which English club has a fanzine called 'Thorne In The Side'?

13 Which English League team has a fanzine called 'Tales From Senegal Fields'?

14 Which is the only English League side to play in green and white striped shirts, black shorts and white socks with green trim?

15 Which London club won the Third Division Championship in 1956 and 1970?

Answers

1 Hartlepool United **2** Cardiff City **3** Rod Stewart **4** Nottingham Forest **5** Oldham Athletic **6** Vic Watson **7** 1967-68 **8** 1927 **9** 1971 **10** 1968 **11** 1962 **12** Brentford **13** Millwall **14** Plymouth Argyle **15** Leyton Orient

Quiz 67
GREAT CLUBS OF ENGLAND

1 Which Torquay United player has been capped at international level by St Vincent?

2 Who beat Birmingham City in the 1975 FA Cup semi-final?

3 Who scored four goals for West Ham United as they beat Bury 10-0 in the 1983-84 League Cup?

4 Who scored Southampton's first goal in the 1979 League Cup Final?

5 Who scored the winner for Nottingham Forest in the 1990 League Cup Final against Oldham Athletic?

6 Who was manager of Doncaster Rovers during their greatest years (1950-58)?

7 How many Welshmen played for Cardiff City in the 1927 FA Cup Final?

8 In 1916, which English League ground was the first to be bombed by Germany?

9 In 1931-32, which club went a record 17 matches in a row and finished bottom of the Third Division North?

10 In which year did Luton Town win the Third Division (South) Championship?

11 Which 1960s West Ham goalkeeper played cricket for Worcestershire?

12 Which club does BBC anchorman Des Lynam support?

13 Which club has been in the top flight of English football for one season only – 1962-63?

14 Which club has been managed by Lawrie McMenemy, Dave Mackay and Billy Bremner?

15 Which is the largest English city never to have had a football club in the top flight of the League?

THE CARLING ULTIMATE FOOTBALL FACT AND QUIZ BOOK

Quiz 68
GREAT CLUBS OF ENGLAND

1 Which League club plays its home matches at Layer Road?

2 Which London club started as the works' team of Morton's Jam and Marmalade Company?

3 Who is the only man to have managed both Birmingham City and Swindon Town?

4 Who made 443 League appearances for Torquay United between 1947 and 1959?

5 Who retired as manager of Nottingham Forest on April 26, 1993?

6 Who scored Southampton's second goal in the 1979 League Cup Final?

7 After Hull, which is the second largest English city never to have had a football club in the top flight of the League?

8 From which club did Birmingham City buy Paul Furlong in July 1996?

9 From which Fourth Division club did West Ham United sign Alan Taylor during the 1974-75 season?

10 In November 1991, at which ground did police prepare to intervene to prevent a breach of the peace when visiting Doncaster Rovers supporters started chanting 'Would you like a piece of cake'?

11 To which club did Leyton Orient sell John Chiedozie for £600,000 in August 1981?

12 Which club became the first professional side south of Birmingham in 1885 when Wanderers merged with Excelsior?

13 Which club has applied for re-election more often than any other?

14 Which club has fanzines called 'Build A Bonfire' and 'Seaside Saga'?

15 Which former Ipswich star scored the first two goals for Colchester United in their 1971 FA Cup Fifth Round tie against Leeds United?

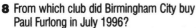

Answers

1 Colchester United 2 Millwall 3 Lou Macari 4 Dennis Lewis 5 Brian Clough 6 Nick Holmes 7 Plymouth 8 Chelsea 9 Rochdale 10 Turf Moor, Burnley 11 Notts County 12 Luton Town 13 Hartlepool United 14 Brighton and Hove Albion 15 Ray Crawford

THE CARLING ULTIMATE FOOTBALL FACT AND QUIZ BOOK

GREAT CLUBS OF ENGLAND

1 Which team did Cardiff City beat in the 1927 FA Cup Final?

2 Which West Ham player scored two goals in each of the final three rounds of the 1975 FA Cup?

3 Who knocked Millwall out of the FA Cup in the 1937 semi-finals?

4 Who scored 185 League goals for Southampton in his two spells at the club (1966-77 and 1979-82)?

5 Who scored 204 goals for Torquay United between 1948 and 1958?

6 Who succeeded Brian Clough as manager of Nottingham Forest?

7 After narrowly missing promotion for eight years running, which club finally won the Third Division South Championship in 1930?

8 To what did Hartlepool change its name in 1977?

9 In 1937, which was the first Third Division club to reach the semi-finals of the FA Cup?

10 In which year did Luton Town win the old Second Division Championship?

11 Where did Brighton play their home games between 1902 and 1997?

12 Which English team was runner-up in the European Fairs Cup in 1960 and 1961?

13 Which Fourth Division club won re-election by only one vote in 1980?

14 Which Southampton full back was offered the throne of Albania?

15 Who did Manchester United buy from Torquay United for £180,000 in May 1988?

GREAT CLUBS OF ENGLAND

1 Who did Nottingham Forest beat in the European Cup Final of 1979?

2 Who scored Colchester United's third goal in their 1971 FA Cup Fifth Round tie against Leeds United?

3 Who scored the winning goal for Cardiff City in the 1927 FA Cup Final?

4 Who scored three goals in three minutes for Leyton Orient against Shrewsbury Town in January 1955?

5 Who scored West Ham's first goal in the 1964 FA Cup Final?

6 For which country did Birmingham City's Malcolm Page make 22 international appearances between 1971 and 1979?

7 In which year did Luton Town reach the Final of the FA Cup?

8 In which year did Plymouth Argyle reach the semi-final of the FA Cup?

9 At which club have Brighton and Hove Albion played their home matches since their old ground was demolished?

10 Which English League club has a fanzine called 'My Eyes Have Seen The Glory'?

11 Which Manchester United goalkeeper began his distinguished career at Doncaster Rovers?

12 Which non-League club knocked Rochdale out of the FA Cup in 1984?

13 Who became manager of Leyton Orient in November 1996?

14 Who knocked Millwall out of the FA Cup in the 1900 semi-finals?

15 Who managed Southampton from 1955 to 1973?

GREAT CLUBS OF ENGLAND

1 Who scored the winning goal for Nottingham Forest in the 1979 European Cup Final?

2 Who scored West Ham's second goal in the 1964 FA Cup Final?

3 Who was manager of Hartlepool from 1965 to 1967?

4 Who was the Colchester United goalkeeper in their 1971 FA Cup Fifth Round tie against Leeds United?

5 Who was the FA Cup-winning captain of Cardiff City?

6 In which year did Birmingham City go down to the old Third Division for the first time in their history?

7 Name the Welshman who kept goal for Arsenal against Cardiff City in the 1927 FA Cup Final.

8 Which English League club has a fanzine called 'Into The O Zone'?

9 Which English League club plays its home matches at White Hart Lane?

10 Which former Chelsea star was appointed player manager of Doncaster Rovers in August 1996?

11 Which former Southampton manager resigned severed all remaining links with the club on the day Graeme Souness was sacked?

12 Which London club beat Rochdale 8-0 in 1987?

13 Who became manager of Hartlepool United in December 1996?

14 Who did Nottingham Forest beat in the 1980 European Cup Final?

15 Who knocked Millwall out of the FA Cup in the 1903 semi-finals?

Answers

1 Trevor Francis **2** Geoff Hurst **3** Brian Clough **4** Graham Smith **5** Fred Keenor **6** 1989 **7** Dan Lewis
8 Leyton Orient **9** Tottenham Hotspur **10** Kerry Dixon **11** Lawrie McMenemy **12** Leyton Orient
13 Mick Tait **14** Hamburg **15** Derby County

THE CARLING ULTIMATE FOOTBALL FACT AND QUIZ BOOK

Quiz 72
GREAT CLUBS OF ENGLAND

1 Who knocked Plymouth Argyle out of the FA Cup in the 1984 semi-final?

2 Who scored Luton Town's goal in the 1959 FA Cup Final?

3 Who scored West Ham's third goal in the 1964 FA Cup Final?

4 Who was the captain of Brighton and Hove Albion in the 1983 FA Cup Final?

5 With seven players over 30, which 1971 FA giantkillers were nicknamed Grandad's Army?

6 In which year did Luton Town win the League Cup?

7 In which year were Cardiff City losing finalists in the FA Cup?

8 Of which English League club is the Chairman snooker and boxing promoter Barry Hearn?

9 What was the popular nickname of Millwall's Harry Cripps?

10 Which comedian has been a director of Brighton and Hove Albion?

11 Which Third Division club reached the semi-final of the League Cup in 1974?

12 Which was the only non-League club to win the FA Cup in the 20th century?

13 Who became manager of Birmingham City in May 1996?

14 Who did West Ham United beat in the 1965 European Cup Winners' Cup Final?

15 Who made 447 League appearances for Hartlepool between 1948 and 1964?

THE CARLING ULTIMATE FOOTBALL FACT AND QUIZ BOOK

Quiz 73

GREAT CLUBS OF ENGLAND

1 Who played 317 League games for Rochdale between 1966 and 1974?

2 Who scored the winner for Nottingham Forest in the 1980 European Cup Final?

3 Who was appointed manager of Southampton in June 1997?

4 Who was the manager of Colchester United during their 1971 FA Cup run?

5 Whose fans sang, famously:
'And so this is Burnley,
And what have we done,
We've lost here already,
Would you like a cream bun'?

6 How many times have Tottenham Hotspur won the League Championship?

7 Supporters of which London club are most commonly associated with the chant:
'We're all mad, we're insane,
We eat Mars bars on the train'?

8 Which England international played against Nottingham Forest in the 1980 European Cup Final?

9 Which English League club is nicknamed The Seagulls?

10 Which English League team has a fanzine called 'The Ugly Inside'?

11 Which former Liverpool and Everton player was Birmingham City captain in 1997-98?

12 Which forward did Cardiff City sell to Sheffield United for £300,000 in February 1994?

13 Which future manager of Arsenal, Leeds United and Tottenham Hotspur was in charge of Millwall from 1982 to 1986?

14 Which Second Division side reached the semi-final of the League Cup in 1965?

15 Who did Luton Town beat in the 1988 League Cup Final?

THE CARLING ULTIMATE FOOTBALL FACT AND QUIZ BOOK

Quiz 74
GREAT CLUBS OF ENGLAND

1 Who pulled back two goals for Leeds United as they went out of the 1971 FA Cup to Colchester United?

2 Who scored 119 goals for Rochdale between 1964 and 1973?

3 Who scored both West Ham United's goals in the 1965 European Cup Winners' Cup Final?

4 With 98 goals between 1949 and 1964, who is Hartlepool's all-time leading scorer?

5 From which club did Millwall buy Paul Goddard in December 1989?

6 In 1996, which Southampton player had what looked like a good goal disallowed against Manchester United in the Sixth Round of the FA Cup?

7 In which year did Orient reach the semi-final of the FA Cup?

8 Name any one of the four clubs beaten by West Ham on their way to the 1965 European Cup Winners' Cup Final.

9 Where in the First Division did Brighton and Hove Albion finish in their best season, 1981-82?

10 Which Nottingham Forest player won 76 caps for England?

11 Which striker scored 17 goals in 136 appearances for Hartlepool and was then sold to deadly local rivals Darlington?

12 Which former Swedish international was on Birmingham City's books in 1997-98?

13 Which League team was originally formed in 1879 to play a game against the Yorkshire Institute for the Deaf?

14 Who did Tottenham Hotspur beat in the 1991 FA Cup Final?

15 Who scored 38 goals for Colchester United in 1961-62?

THE CARLING ULTIMATE FOOTBALL FACT AND QUIZ BOOK

GREAT CLUBS OF ENGLAND

1 Who scored 44 League goals for Rochdale in the Third Division North in the 1926-27 season?

2 Who scored two goals for Luton Town in the 1988 League Cup Final?

3 Who was manager of Plymouth Argyle from June 1995 to May 1997?

4 Who was the manager of Cardiff City in the year they won the FA Cup?

5 For which club did Clarrie Jordan score 42 goals in the Third Division North in 1946-47?

6 From which Italian club did Nottingham Forest buy Brian Roy in August 1994?

7 In 1992-93, which team set an English record when they went 13 League and Cup games without scoring a goal?

8 In which year were Luton Town beaten finalists in the League Cup?

9 Which striker left Colchester United for Birmingham in January 1994 and then went from St Andrews to Wycombe Wanderers in March 1995?

10 Which former England international goalkeeper was player manager of Plymouth Argyle from 1992 to 1995?

11 Which future manager of Everton ran Rochdale from 1953 to 1958?

12 Who became Britain's most expensive goalkeeper in November 1993 when he moved from Southampton to Blackburn Rovers for £2 million?

13 Who did Tottenham Hotspur beat in the 1981 FA Cup Final?

14 Who had a penalty saved at Birmingham City, a miss which cost Cardiff City the 1924 Championship?

15 Who has played more games than anyone else for West Ham United?

THE CARLING ULTIMATE FOOTBALL FACT AND QUIZ BOOK

Quiz 76
GREAT CLUBS OF ENGLAND

1 Who knocked Orient out of the FA Cup in the 1978 semi-final?

2 Who scored 93 goals for Millwall between 1984 and 1991?

3 Who scored Brighton and Hove Albion's first goal in the 1983 FA Cup Final?

4 Who was the first female Managing Director of Birmingham City?

5 For which club did Fred Emery play 417 times between 1925 and 1936?

6 Which club has a fanzine called 'The Blue Eagle'?

7 Which English League club are nicknamed The Terriers?

8 Which former Ipswich and England international full back was Birmingham City's first team coach in 1997-98?

9 Which future FA Cup-winning manager ran Rochdale from 1967 to 1968?

10 Which Nottingham Forest player went off with a broken leg during the 1959 FA Cup Final?

11 Which three brothers played in the same Southampton team in 1988?

12 Which Everton player was fined a week's wages for failing to leave the pitch for his half-time pep talk during the opening match of the 1990-91 season?

13 Who beat Brighton and Hove Albion in the 1991 play-off final for promotion to the First Division?

14 Who did Tottenham Hotspur beat in the 1967 FA Cup Final?

15 Who made 432 League appearances for Orient between 1965 and 1978?

Answers

1 Arsenal **2** Teddy Sheringham **3** Gordon Smith **4** Karren Brady **5** Doncaster Rovers **6** Colchester United **7** Huddersfield Town **8** Mick Mills **9** Bob Stokoe **10** Roy Dwight **11** Danny, Ray and Rodney Wallace **12** Neville Southall **13** Notts County **14** Chelsea **15** Peter Allen

THE CARLING ULTIMATE FOOTBALL FACT AND QUIZ BOOK

GREAT CLUBS OF ENGLAND

1 Who pipped Cardiff City to the 1924 Championship by 0.0241 of a goal?

2 Who scored 37 goals for Millwall in Third Division South during the 1926-27 season?

3 Who scored 180 League goals for Plymouth Argyle between 1924 and 1938?

4 Who scored for Luton Town as they lost 3-1 to Nottingham Forest in the 1989 League Cup Final?

5 During the 1988-89 season, which Southampton player had his jaw broken in an incident involving Paul Davis of Arsenal?

6 In 1996, which Millwall manager succeeded Jack Charlton as manager of the Republic of Ireland?

7 To which London club did Doncaster Rovers sell Rufus Brevett in February 1991?

8 Which 1930s Luton Town wing half was converted into a centre forward and earned the nickname 'Ten-Goal'?

9 Which English League club plays its home matches at The Alfred McAlpine Stadium?

10 Which former England international was Cardiff City's longest-serving postwar manager (1964-73)?

11 Which former Wolverhampton Wanderers manager was in charge of Birmingham City from 1965 to 1970?

12 Which Welsh star of the 1920s won 20 of his 23 international caps while playing for Plymouth Argyle?

13 Who began his career at Orient in 1974 and ended it at Leyton Orient in 1995, having played in the intervening period for QPR, Notts County, Newcastle and Watford?

14 Who did Tottenham Hotspur beat in the 1962 FA Cup Final?

15 Who did West Ham United buy for an initial £3.2 million in February 1997 and sell for £7.5 million in January 1999?

THE CARLING ULTIMATE FOOTBALL FACT AND QUIZ BOOK

GREAT CLUBS OF ENGLAND

1 Who knocked Colchester United out of the 1971 FA Cup in the Sixth Round?

2 Who succeeded Steve Gritt as manager of Brighton and Hove Albion?

3 Who was appointed manager of Rochdale in May 1996?

4 Why did Nottingham Forest play most of their home games during the 1968-69 season at Notts County's ground?

5 Against which team did Joe Payne of Luton Town score 10 goals in 1936?

6 Apart from Newcastle United, which other English League club is nicknamed The Magpies?

7 What is Bristol City's nickname?

8 Which 1998-99 Premiership club lost 1-0 to the Old Etonians in the 1882 FA Cup Final?

9 Which club has a fanzine called 'Peeping Tom'?

10 Which English League club has a fanzine called 'The Mag'?

11 Which English League club is nicknamed Pompey?

12 Which English League club is nicknamed The Merry Millers?

13 Which English League club is nicknamed The Shrimpers?

14 Which English League club plays its home games at Springfield Park?

15 Which League club has the post code L4 4EL?

1 Everton 2 Brian Horton 3 Graham Barrow 4 Because of damage caused by fire in their own Main Stand 5 Bristol Rovers 6 Notts County 7 The Robins 8 Blackburn Rovers 9 Coventry City 10 Newcastle United 11 Portsmouth 12 Rotherham United 13 Southend United 14 Wigan Athletic 15 Everton

Answers

THE CARLING ULTIMATE FOOTBALL FACT AND QUIZ BOOK

GREAT CLUBS OF ENGLAND

1 Which League team is nicknamed The Blues or The Cumbrians?

2 Which team plays home matches at Sincil Bank?

3 Who did Tottenham Hotspur beat in the 1961 FA Cup Final?

4 Who were Huddersfield Town's first League opponents at their new McAlpine Stadium?

5 How many times have Huddersfield Town won the League Championship?

6 In which year did Wigan Athletic win election to the Fourth Division?

7 Where do Bristol City play their home matches?

8 Which club has a fanzine called 'Gary Mabbutt's Knee'?

9 Which club previously played at South Byker and Chillingham Road, Heaton?

10 Which club was excluded from the League Cup in 1986 because of its ban on away supporters?

11 Which English League club has a fanzine called 'Blue And Wight'?

12 Which English League club has a fanzine called 'Moulin Rouge'?

13 Which English League club has a fanzine called 'No More Pie In The Sky'?

14 Which English League club plays its home games at Roots Hall?

15 Which English League team is nicknamed The Red Imps?

THE CARLING ULTIMATE FOOTBALL FACT AND QUIZ BOOK

Quiz 80
GREAT CLUBS OF ENGLAND

1 Which founder members of the Football League have since spent only four seasons outside the top division?

2 Which League team has a fanzine called 'Cumberland Sausage'?

3 Which team last won the FA Cup in 1928?

4 Who scored the first goal for Tottenham Hotspur in the 1967 FA Cup Final?

5 In which year did Everton first win the League Championship?

6 In which year did Huddersfield Town win the FA Cup?

7 In which year did Wigan Athletic reach the Sixth Round of the FA Cup?

8 In which year of the 1970s did Bristol City return to the First Division after an absence of 65 years?

9 Which club broke the League Cup during their post-match celebrations after the Final?

10 Which club has a fanzine called 'Lady Godiva Rides Again'?

11 Which English League club has a fanzine called 'January 3 '88'?

12 Which English League team has a fanzine called 'Deranged Ferret'?

13 Which English League club plays its home games at Millmoor?

14 Which is England's oldest League club, having been founded in 1862?

15 Which League team has a fanzine called 'What The Fox Going On'?

Answers

1 Everton *2* Carlisle United *3* Blackburn Rovers *4* Jimmy Robertson *5* 1891 *6* 1922 *7* 1987 *8* 1976 *9* Luton Town *10* Coventry City *11* Portsmouth *12* Lincoln City *13* Rotherham United *14* Notts County *15* Carlisle United

THE CARLING ULTIMATE FOOTBALL FACT AND QUIZ BOOK

GREAT CLUBS OF ENGLAND

1 Who played 451 League games for Southend United between 1950 and 1963?

2 Who scored 168 League goals for Blackburn Rovers between 1978 and 1992?

3 Who scored the second goal for Tottenham Hotspur in the 1967 FA Cup Final?

4 Who won the League Championship in 1905, 1907 and 1909?

5 At which ground did Huddersfield Town play their home matches until 1992?

6 Everton moved to Goodison Park in 1892 – where had they played before that?

7 In 1998, which Blackburn Rovers player jeopardised his international career by refusing to play for England B?

8 In which year did Notts County win the FA Cup?

9 In which year did Rotherham United miss out on promotion to the old First Division only through having a slightly inferior goal average to Luton Town?

10 Name the former West Ham United goalkeeper who managed Carlisle United.

11 Which English League club has a fanzine called 'Pisces'?

12 Which English League team has a fanzine called 'The Yellow Belly'?

13 Which team has a fanzine called 'Come in No 7 Your Time Is Up'?

14 Which team plays its home matches at Highfield Road?

15 Who did Southend United sell to Nottingham Forest for £2 million in June 1993?

GREAT CLUBS OF ENGLAND

1 Who scored 31 goals for Third Division Wigan Athletic in the 1996-97 season?

2 Who scored two goals for Tottenham Hotspur in the 1981 FA Cup Final replay?

3 Who was the chairman of Luton Town when the club banned away supporters in 1986-87?

4 Who won the FA Cup for the first time in 1910?

5 In 1987, which club became the first to be automatically relegated from the Fourth Division?

6 In 1999, who ousted Tim Flowers from between the Blackburn posts?

7 In which position did Bristol City's legendary Billy Wedlock play?

8 In which year did Coventry City win the Second Division Championship?

9 In which year did Everton first win the FA Cup?

10 In which year did Rotherham United reach the League Cup Final?

11 Supporters of which team rioted at Luton on March 13, 1985, prompting the home club to ban away fans?

12 Which English League club plays its home matches at Fratton Park?

13 Who captained Huddersfield Town to three consecutive League titles?

14 Who did Newcastle United beat in the 1910 FA Cup Final?

15 Who scored 62 goals for Wigan Athletic between 1978 and 1984?

THE CARLING ULTIMATE FOOTBALL FACT AND QUIZ BOOK

GREAT CLUBS OF ENGLAND

1 Who scored 122 goals for Southend United between 1953 and 1960?

2 Who scored the first goal for Tottenham Hotspur in the 1991 FA Cup Final?

3 Who was the Carlisle United chairman who sacked manager Mervyn Day in 1998?

4 Who were the first Second Division club to win the FA Cup?

5 What relation is West Ham United's Frank Lampard Junior to Liverpool's Jamie Redknapp?

6 Against whom did Ashley Ward score his first goal for Blackburn Rovers after his £4 million transfer from Barnsley?

7 In which season did Carlisle United first play in the old First Division?

8 In which year did Bristol City reach the FA Cup Final?

9 In which year did Coventry City win the FA Cup?

10 Which club won promotion to the First Division in 1927 and remained there until 1959?

11 Which England manager also managed Lincoln City?

12 Which English League club plays its home games at Edgeley Park?

13 Which English League club plays its home matches at Meadow Lane?

14 Which Northern Irishman became the first Wigan Athletic player to win an international cap?

15 Who made 520 League appearances for Huddersfield Town between 1914 and 1934?

THE CARLING ULTIMATE FOOTBALL FACT AND QUIZ BOOK

Quiz 84

GREAT CLUBS OF ENGLAND

1 Who scored both goals for Newcastle United in the 1910 FA Cup Final?

2 Who scored the first goal for Rotherham United in their League Cup Final first leg victory over Aston Villa?

3 Who was manager of Luton Town from 1978 to 1986?

4 Who was manager of Tottenham Hotspur when they won the Double in 1961?

5 From which club did Newcastle United buy Darren Huckerby in November 1995?

6 In which year did Bristol City finish second in the old First Division?

7 In which year did Tottenham Hotspur become a public company?

8 What was historic about Albert Shepherd's second goal for Newcastle United in the 1910 FA Cup Final?

9 Which club was unbeaten at home in the FA Cup from 1913 to 1932?

10 Which controversial player did Everton buy for £60,000 from Sheffield Wednesday in 1962-63?

11 In the 1998-99 season, who was captain of Chelsea?

12 Which English League club is nicknamed The Blues or The Hatters?

13 Which former Carlisle United player was their manager when they won promotion to the old First Division?

14 Which legendary Notts County goalkeeper made 564 League appearances for the club between 1904 and 1926?

15 Which team won the English League Championship in 1949 and 1950?

THE CARLING ULTIMATE FOOTBALL FACT AND QUIZ BOOK

GREAT CLUBS OF ENGLAND

1 Who played 317 League games for Wigan Athletic between 1981 and 1994?

2 Who scored the second goal for Rotherham United in their League Cup Final first leg victory over Aston Villa in 1961?

3 Who succeeded Roy Hodgson as manager of Blackburn Rovers?

4 Who was appointed manager of Luton Town in December 1995?

5 In 1910, which club was fined for fielding a weak team against Bristol Rovers, even though they won 3-0?

6 In 1928, which team won a League game on the same day as they had five players in the England v Scotland game at Wembley?

7 In the 1980s, which club dropped 86 League places in three years?

8 In which year did Wigan Athletic win the Third Division Championship?

9 Which club were held up in the fog and thus failed to arrive for their League game at Hartlepool on December 22, 1934?

10 Which English League side won the Anglo-Italian Cup in 1995, after having been runners-up in the previous year?

11 Which team plays its home matches at Brunton Park?

12 Who briefly managed Manchester City in 1973, between Malcolm Allison and Ron Saunders?

13 Who preceded Roy Hodgson as manager of Blackburn Rovers?

14 Who scored 220 goals for Tottenham Hotspur between 1961 and 1970?

15 Who scored Coventry City's first goal in the 1987 FA Cup Final?

THE CARLING ULTIMATE FOOTBALL FACT AND QUIZ BOOK

GREAT CLUBS OF ENGLAND

1 Who scored the winner for Everton in the 1995 FA Cup Final?

2 Who was appointed manager of Lincoln City in October 1995?

3 Who won the FA Cup in 1939?

4 Who won the inaugural Third Division North Championship in 1922?

5 At which ground did Manchester City play their home games before moving to Maine Road in 1923?

6 For poaching which manager were Everton fined £125,000 in 1994?

7 From which Scottish club did Blackburn Rovers buy Billy McKinlay?

8 In which season did Stockport County win the Fourth Division Championship?

9 What is the name of the new Lincoln City stand, built to replace the old Clanford End?

10 Which club has a fanzine called 'Hanging On The Telephone'?

11 Which Liverpool legend was manager of Carlisle United from 1949-51?

12 Which manager led Bristol City back into the First Division in 1976?

13 Who captained Newcastle United to the 1927 League Championship?

14 Who did Portsmouth beat in the 1939 FA Cup Final?

15 Who managed Notts County from 1969 to 1975, and then again from 1978 to 1982, after which he became the club's general manager?

Answers

1 Paul Rideout **2** John Beck **3** Portsmouth **4** Stockport County **5** Hyde Road **6** Mike Walker of Norwich City **7** Dundee United **8** 1966-67 **9** The Stacey West Stand **10** Huddersfield Town **11** Bill Shankly **12** Alan Dicks **13** Hughie Gallacher **14** Wolverhampton Wanderers **15** Jimmy Sirrel

THE CARLING ULTIMATE FOOTBALL FACT AND QUIZ BOOK

Quiz 87
GREAT CLUBS OF ENGLAND

1 Who scored 37 goals for Tottenham Hotspur in the 1962-63 season?

2 Who scored 130 goals for Rotherham United between 1946 and 1956?

3 Who scored Coventry City's second goal in the 1987 FA Cup Final?

4 Who was manager of Wigan Athletic during their first season in the Football League?

5 Give either of the years in which Stockport County reached the Fifth Round of the FA Cup.

6 In 1948, 82,930 people watched a match at Maine Road – the highest ever English League attendance. Who were Manchester City's opponents?

7 In 1988-89, which Everton chairman became the first League president ever to be voted out of office?

8 Name the Bermudian on Bristol City's books in 1997.

9 On August 24, 1976, which club became the first to go out of the League Cup on penalties?

10 To which club did Blackburn Rovers pay £5 million for Chris Sutton in July 1994?

11 Which Liverpool, Everton, Newcastle United and England player began his career at Carlisle United?

12 Which English League player scored Jamaica's first ever goal in the World Cup finals?

13 Which Tottenham Hotspur player scored an own goal in extra time to give Coventry City the 1987 FA Cup?

14 Who beat Tottenham Hotspur 7-0 in a League game in 1978?

15 Who managed Huddersfield Town to three League titles?

THE CARLING ULTIMATE FOOTBALL FACT AND QUIZ BOOK

Quiz 88
GREAT CLUBS OF ENGLAND

1 Who scored Newcastle United's second goal in the 1924 FA Cup Final against Aston Villa?

2 Which Bermudian played for West Ham United in the 1960s and 1970s?

3 Who was appointed manager of Notts County in January 1997?

4 Who was appointed Wigan Athletic manager in November 1995?

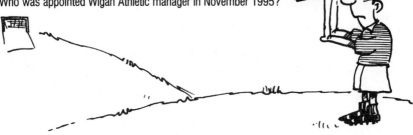

5 In 1979-80, which Fourth Division Championship-winning team scored 101 League goals in the season?

6 In which season did Lincoln City win the Fourth Division Championship?

7 In which year did Stockport County reach the semi-final of the League Cup?

8 On December 4, 1965, who became the first Tottenham Hotspur player to be sent off since 1925?

9 On February 7, 1987, which club became the first to complete 3,500 matches?

10 Which club has the largest pitch in the English League?

11 Which famous striker did Bristol City buy from Arsenal for £500,000 in July 1992 and sell to Newcastle United for £1.75 million in March 1993?

12 Who did Newcastle United beat in the 1932 FA Cup Final?

13 Who is Blackburn Rovers' multi-millionaire benefactor?

14 Who knocked Wigan Athletic out of the 1987 FA Cup in the Sixth Round?

15 Who made 459 League appearances for Rotherham United between 1946 and 1962?

Answers

1 Stan Seymour **2** Clyde Best **3** Sam Allardyce **4** John Deehan **5** Huddersfield Town **6** 1975-76 **7** 1997 **8** Frank Saul **9** Notts County **10** Manchester City **11** Andy Cole **12** Arsenal **13** Jack Walker **14** Leeds United **15** Danny Williams

THE CARLING ULTIMATE FOOTBALL FACT AND QUIZ BOOK

GREAT CLUBS OF ENGLAND

1 Who made 466 League appearances for Carlisle United between 1963 and 1969?

2 Who succeeded Howard Kendall as Everton manager in 1987?

3 Who was manager of Portsmouth when they won the FA Cup in 1939?

4 Who were joint managers of Coventry City at the 1987 FA Cup Final?

5 For what offence were seven Notts County players booked simultaneously in December 1983?

6 In 1970, Second Division Carlisle United reached the semi-final of the League Cup. Who knocked them out, 4-2 on aggregate?

7 In 1974, who succeeded Bill Nicholson as manager of Tottenham Hotspur?

8 In the big freeze of 1962-63, one of Lincoln City's fixtures was postponed 15 times – who were their opponents?

9 In which season did Everton finish second to Liverpool in both the League and the FA Cup?

10 What lucky items of clothing were worn for the 1939 FA Cup Final by Portsmouth manager Jack Tinn?

11 Which club are nicknamed The Citizens?

12 Which Lancashire club drew 5-5 with Accrington in their first ever League game in 1888?

13 Which GM Vauxhall Conference side knocked Coventry City out of the 1988-89 FA Cup in the Third Round?

14 Which English League club was formerly known as Bristol South End?

15 Who knocked Stockport County out in the semi-final of the 1997 League Cup?

THE CARLING ULTIMATE FOOTBALL FACT AND QUIZ BOOK

GREAT CLUBS OF ENGLAND

1 Who scored both goals for Newcastle United in the 1932 FA Cup Final?

2 Who scored five goals for Huddersfield Town as they beat Everton 8-2 in the 1952-53 season?

3 Who was appointed manager of Rotherham United in May 1997?

4 Whose place did Wigan Athletic take in the Football League?

5 Against which team did Coventry City keeper Steve Ogrizovic score with a long clearance on October 25, 1986?

6 In 1985, when Kevin Moran of Manchester United became the first player to be sent off in an FA Cup Final, which Everton player did he foul?

7 In which year did Blackburn Rovers win the Premiership?

8 In which year did Manchester City first win the FA Cup?

9 What was unique about Newcastle United's 0-0 draw with Portsmouth on December 5, 1931?

10 Which English club won the Welsh Cup in 1934?

11 Which English League club has a fanzine called 'Route One'?

12 Which English League club has a fanzine named 'The Tea Party'?

13 Which two former Nottingham Forest players were joint managers of Rotherham United from 1994 to 1996?

14 Which trophy did Carlisle United win in 1997?

15 Which two Lancashire teams are nicknamed The Latics?

Answers

1 Jack Allen **2** Jimmy Glazzard **3** Ronnie Moore **4** Southport **5** Sheffield Wednesday **6** Peter Reid
7 1995 **8** 1904 **9** It is the only first class match in which neither side conceded a corner **10** Bristol City
11 Wimbledon **12** Stockport County **13** Archie Gemmill and John McGovern
14 The Auto Windscreens Shield **15** Oldham Athletic and Wigan Athletic

Quiz 91

GREAT CLUBS OF ENGLAND

1 Who managed Portsmouth when they regained their First Division status in 1987?

2 Who scored from the penalty spot for Huddersfield Town in the 1922 FA Cup Final?

3 Who scored seven of Stoke City's goals in their 8-0 defeat of Lincoln City in 1957?

4 Who was appointed manager of Tottenham Hotspur in November 1994?

5 From which other Lancashire club did Everton buy Alan Ball in 1966?

6 How much did Blackburn Rovers get for Alan Shearer when they sold him to Newcastle United in 1996?

7 Which British Prime Minister was a Huddersfield Town fan?

8 Which Cup did Bristol City win in 1978?

9 Which English League club has a fanzine called 'City Til I Cry'?

10 Which English League team has a fanzine called 'Beyond The Boundary'?

11 Which former Newcastle United wing half managed the club from 1962 to 1975?

12 Which television pundit became managing director of Coventry City in April 1975?

13 Which Yorkshire team was managed by Emlyn Hughes from 1981 to 1983?

14 Who began and ended his career at Carlisle United, in the meantime going on to play for Sunderland, Manchester City and Newcastle United, winning 14 England caps between 1952 and 1954?

15 Who did Manchester City beat in the 1934 FA Cup Final?

Answers

1 Alan Ball 2 Billy Smith 3 Neville Coleman 4 Gerry Francis 5 Blackpool 6 £15 million 7 Harold Wilson 8 The Anglo-Scottish Cup 9 Manchester City 10 Oldham Athletic 11 Joe Harvey 12 Jimmy Hill 13 Rotherham United 14 Ivor Broadis 15 Portsmouth

THE CARLING ULTIMATE FOOTBALL FACT AND QUIZ BOOK

Quiz 92

GREAT CLUBS OF ENGLAND

1 Who did Tottenham Hotspur beat in the European Cup Winners' Cup Final of 1963?

2 Who played 764 games for Portsmouth between 1946 and 1965?

3 Who took Lincoln City's place in the Football League when they failed to gain re-election in 1920?

4 Who was appointed manager of Stockport County in July 1997?

5 For which club did John Atyeo make 314 appearances between 1951 and 1966?

6 From which club did Everton manager Harry Catterick buy Mike Trebilcock for £18,000 in 1965?

7 Who captained Manchester City to their 1934 FA Cup triumph?

8 Which club has a fanzine called 'Colin's Cheeky Bits'?

9 Which Coventry City player of the 1960s used to tee up free kicks by gripping the ball between his heels and flipping it into the air for a team mate to volley?

10 Which English League club was originally named Thornhill United?

11 Which team plays its home matches at Boundary Park?

12 Which was Denis Law's first League club?

13 Which was the first English club to rise from the Third Division and win the League Championship?

14 Which was the first English club to win a European trophy?

15 Who became player manager of Carlisle United in August 1946 at the age of 23?

Answers

1 Atletico Madrid **2** Jimmy Dickinson **3** Leeds United **4** Gary Megson **5** Bristol City **6** Plymouth Argyle **7** Matt Busby **8** Blackburn Rovers **9** Ernie Hunt **10** Rotherham United **11** Oldham Athletic **12** Huddersfield Town **13** Portsmouth **14** Tottenham Hotspur (The Cup Winners' Cup in 1963) **15** Ivor Broadis

THE CARLING ULTIMATE FOOTBALL FACT AND QUIZ BOOK

GREAT CLUBS OF ENGLAND

1 Who managed Newcastle United from 1992 to 1997?

2 At the end of the 1987-88 season, which club's entire squad was put on the transfer list by manager Dave Mackay?

3 At whose ground would you be if you sat in the Kippax?

4 In which year did Bradford City win the FA Cup?

5 In which year did Northampton Town win the Fourth Division Championship?

6 In which year did Sheffield United first win the FA Cup?

7 In which year did Tranmere Rovers reach the Fifth Round of the FA Cup?

8 To which ground in Bath did Bristol Rovers first move?

9 Which Doncaster Rovers defender was sent off against Brighton and Hove Albion during the last game at the Goldstone Ground?

10 Which English League club has a fanzine called 'The Black Arab'?

11 Which English League club has a fanzine called 'The Vale Park Beano'?

12 Which English League club is nicknamed The Baggies or The Throstles?

13 Which English League club is nicknamed The Foxes?

14 Which English League club is nicknamed The Ironsides?

15 Which English League club is nicknamed The Potters?

Answers

1 Kevin Keegan 2 Doncaster Rovers 3 Manchester City 4 1911 5 1987 6 1899 7 1968 8 Twerton Park 9 Darren Moore 10 Bristol Rovers 11 Port Vale 12 West Bromwich Albion 13 Leicester City 14 Middlesbrough 15 Stoke City

THE CARLING ULTIMATE FOOTBALL FACT AND QUIZ BOOK

GREAT CLUBS OF ENGLAND

1 Which English League club is nicknamed The Royals?

2 Which English League club is nicknamed The Spireites?

3 Which English League club is nicknamed The Tigers?

4 Which English League club plays its home games at Prenton Park?

5 Which English League club plays its home games at The Victoria Ground?

6 Which English League club plays its home games at the McCain Stadium?

7 Which English League team are nicknamed The Railwaymen?

8 Which is the nearest Underground station to Chelsea's ground?

9 Which English League team plays its home matches at The Valley?

10 Of which 1970s Queen's Park Rangers star was it said: 'If only he could pass a betting shop as well as he could pass a ball'?

11 Which team has fanzines called 'Do I Like Tangerine' and 'Another View From The Tower'?

12 Who made 402 League appearances for Lincoln City between 1946 and 1959?

13 Who scored 132 goals for Stockport County between 1951 and 1956?

14 Who was appointed manager of Wimbledon in January 1992?

15 In 1998, which Dutch international went on strike in protest at his English Premiership club's lack of ambition?

Answers

1 Reading 2 Chesterfield 3 Hull City 4 Tranmere Rovers 5 Stoke City 6 Scarborough 7 Crewe Alexandra 8 Fulham Broadway 9 Charlton Athletic 10 Stan Bowles 11 Blackpool 12 Tony Emery 13 Jack Connor 14 Joe Kinnear 15 Pierre Van Hooijdonk

THE CARLING ULTIMATE FOOTBALL FACT AND QUIZ BOOK

Quiz 1
FA CUP

1 Which club has won the English FA Cup most often?

2 Which team has appeared in four FA Cup finals and never won the trophy?

3 With which club did Don Revie win an FA Cup winners' medal in 1956?

4 To the end of the 20th century, how many different clubs have won the FA Cup?

5 Which club has appeared most often in English FA Cup finals?

6 Which Manchester United player began the 1957 FA Cup Final in goal, but was injured and had to leave the field, later returning to the wing?

7 Up to the end of the 20th century, which club had recorded eight FA Cup victories?

8 Which was the last team to win the FA Cup for the first time?

9 Who was the FA Cup-winning captain of Manchester United in 1957?

10 Which club has appeared most often in the semi-finals of the English FA Cup?

11 Which four survivors of the Munich air crash played for Manchester United in the 1958 FA Cup Final?

12 Who won the first FA Cup after the end of the First World War?

13 How many of the 50 eligible teams entered the first FA Cup in 1871-72?

14 Which team has appeared in five FA Cup Finals but won the trophy only once, in 1922?

15 Who won the FA Cup in 1898 and 1959?

Answers

1 Manchester United **2** Leicester City **3** Manchester City **4** Forty-two **5** Manchester United **6** Ray Wood **7** Tottenham Hotspur **8** Wimbledon in 1988 **9** Roger Byrne **10** Everton **11** Bobby Charlton, Harry Gregg, Bill Foulkes, Dennis Viollet **12** Aston Villa **13** Fifteen **14** Huddersfield Town **15** Nottingham Forest

THE CARLING ULTIMATE FOOTBALL FACT AND QUIZ BOOK

Quiz 2
FA CUP

1 Which team won the FA Cup three times in the 1920s?

2 Who beat Hyde United 26-0 in the First Round of the FA Cup in the 1887-88 season?

3 Who won the first FA Cup in 1872?

4 In which year did West Ham United win the FA Cup for the first time?

5 Which club won the FA Cup twice in the 1930s?

6 Who were the beaten finalists in the first FA Cup in 1872?

7 Where was the first FA Cup Final played?

8 Which club won the FA Cup three times in the 1950s?

9 Who played for Preston North End in the 1964 FA Cup Final at the age of 17 years 345 days?

10 Which club won the FA Cup three times in the 1960s?

11 Who scored the first FA Cup Final goal?

12 Who won the FA Cup for the first time in 1965?

13 Which club won the FA Cup twice in the 1970s?

14 Which now defunct club has won the English FA Cup five times?

15 Who scored two goals for Everton in the 1966 FA Cup Final?

Answers

1 Bolton Wanderers **2** Preston North End **3** Wanderers **4** 1964 **5** Arsenal **6** Royal Engineers **7** Kennington Oval **8** Newcastle United **9** Howard Kendall **10** Tottenham Hotspur **11** Morton Peto Betts **12** Liverpool **13** Arsenal **14** The Wanderers **15** Mike Trebilcock

FA CUP

1 In which year was the first all-London FA Cup Final?

2 Name two of the three clubs that won the FA Cup twice in the 1980s.

3 Under what pseudonym did Morton Peto Betts appear in the first FA Cup Final?

4 In which year was the first Merseyside FA Cup Final?

5 Which club won the FA Cup three times in the 1990s?

6 Which was the last amateur team to win the FA Cup?

7 Which was the first non-League club to win the FA Cup?

8 Who won the 1930 Graf Zeppelin FA Cup Final?

9 Who won the first all-London FA Cup Final in 1967?

10 In which year was the FA Cup Final first played at Wembley?

11 Who did Bolton Wanderers beat 2-0 in the White Horse Cup Final?

12 Who were runners-up in the first all-London FA Cup Final in 1967?

13 In 1931, West Bromwich Albion won the FA Cup and what else?

14 In which year was the last all-London FA Cup Final?

15 Who scored the winner for Manchester United against Everton in the 1985 FA Cup Final?

Answers

*1 1967 2 Liverpool, Manchester United and Tottenham Hotspur 3 A H Chequer 4 1989
5 Manchester United 6 Old Etonians (1882) 7 Tottenham Hotspur 8 Arsenal 9 Tottenham Hotspur
10 1923 11 West Ham United 12 Chelsea 13 Promotion from the Second Division 14 1982
15 Norman Whiteside*

THE CARLING ULTIMATE FOOTBALL FACT AND QUIZ BOOK

FA CUP

1 In which year was the 100th FA Cup Final?

2 Which club won the last all-London FA Cup Final in 1982?

3 Who scored Newcastle United's goal in their FA Cup Final victory over Arsenal in 1952?

4 In which FA Cup Final was there the controversial Over-The-Line-Goal?

5 Only two clubs have entered the FA Cup in every year since its inauguration; both are from the Thames Valley – name either.

6 Which club were beaten finalists in the last all-London FA Cup Final in 1982?

7 In 1901, which Tottenham Hotspur centre forward became the first man to score in every round of the FA Cup?

8 In which year did Middlesbrough first appear in an FA Cup Final?

9 Which club won the most recent of its five FA Cups in 1968?

10 In which year did the Wembley FA Cup Final first go to a replay?

11 Which Sheffield Wednesday player scored in every round of the 1935 FA Cup?

12 Who won the 1903 FA Cup Final by a record 6-0 margin?

13 To the end of the 20th century, two clubs had won the FA Cup three times – name either.

14 Which were the teams that drew the 1970 FA Cup Final at Wembley?

15 Who scored both Aston Villa's goals in their 1905 FA Cup Final victory over Newcastle United?

---

14 Chelsea and Leeds United **15** Harry Hampton
10 1970 **11** Ellis Rimmer **12** Bury **13** Sheffield Wednesday and West Ham United
5 Maidenhead and Marlow **6** Queen's Park Rangers **7** Alex Brown **8** 1997 **9** West Bromwich Albion
1 1981 **2** Tottenham Hotspur **3** George Robledo **4** Newcastle United v Arsenal 1932

Answers

THE CARLING ULTIMATE FOOTBALL FACT AND QUIZ BOOK

FA CUP

1 In which year did Manchester United win the FA Cup for the first time?

2 Where was the 1970 FA Cup Final replay held?

3 Who won the FA Cup in 1937 and 1973?

4 In which year did Everton win the first of their five 20th century FA Cups?

5 In which year did the Wembley FA Cup Final first go to extra time?

6 Who scored Arsenal's winner in the 1971 FA Cup Final against Liverpool?

7 What is the unique distinction of Wolverhampton Wanderers' Kenneth Hunt?

8 Who scored Arsenal's first goal in the 1971 FA Cup Final against Liverpool?

9 Who scored both goals for Wolverhampton Wanderers in the 1949 FA Cup Final?

10 In which year did Reg Lewis score two FA Cup Final goals for Arsenal?

11 West Bromwich Albion won the FA Cup in 1931 as a Second Division team – which was the next club from outside the top flight to win the trophy?

12 Who scored both Newcastle United's goals in the 1910 FA Cup Final replay against Barnsley?

13 Which Manchester United player became the first man to be sent off in an FA Cup Final?

14 Who scored the winning goal for Sunderland in the 1973 FA Cup Final?

15 Who won the FA Cup for the only time to date in 1911?

THE CARLING ULTIMATE FOOTBALL FACT AND QUIZ BOOK

FA CUP

1 Which was the first Second Division team to win the FA Cup?

2 Who kept goal for West Ham United in the 1975 FA Cup Final?

3 Who scored a hat trick in the 1953 FA Cup Final?

4 Which non-driver won a car for scoring Southampton's winner in the 1976 FA Cup Final?

5 Who scored for Bolton Wanderers in every round of the 1953 FA Cup?

6 Why was referee A Adams suspended for a month after the 1913 FA Cup Final between Aston Villa and Sunderland?

7 In 1914, which Lancashire team won the FA Cup for the only time in the 20th century?

8 Which club was fined £25 in 1895 for losing the FA Cup?

9 Which player of the 1950s holds the unique distinction of having won FA Cup winners' medals with clubs in England, Ireland and Scotland?

10 Between 1955 and 1997, who held the record for the fastest goal scored in an FA Cup Final?

11 What nickname was given to the original FA Cup trophy?

12 Which Sheffield team has won the FA Cup more often – United or Wednesday?

13 Tottenham Hotspur have won eight of the nine FA Cup Finals in which they have appeared – who beat them on the odd occasion?

14 What happened to Manchester City keeper Bert Trautmann during the 1956 FA Cup Final?

15 Which OUFC has won the FA Cup?

THE CARLING ULTIMATE FOOTBALL FACT AND QUIZ BOOK

MANAGERS

1 Which Englishman managed Padova from 1929-30 and Roma from 1930-32?

2 Which Englishman managed Napoli from 1929-35, Milan from 1936-37 and Genova from 1937-48?

3 Which Italian team was managed by George Aitken in the 1929-30 season?

4 Which Englishman was manager of Internazionale in the 1948-49 season?

5 Which Englishman managed seven Italian clubs, beginning at Juventus in 1949 and ending at Genova in 1960?

6 Which Englishman managed Juventus in the 1948-49 season?

7 Which Englishman managed Torino in the 1948-49 season?

8 Which Englishman managed Bologna in 1950-51 and Livorno in 1958-59?

9 Which Englishman managed Italian club Atalanta in the 1951-52 season?

10 Who was the British manager of Italian club Padova in the 1951-52 season?

11 Which Briton was manager of Lazio in the 1954-55 season?

12 Which former manager of Fulham ran Sampdoria in the 1957-58 season?

13 Which future manager of Fulham ran Roma in the 1957-58 season?

14 Which future manager of Blackburn Rovers ran Internazionale from 1995 to 1997?

15 Which former Scottish international was manager of Torino in 1997?

Answers

1 Herbert Burgess **2** William Garbutt **3** Juventus **4** David Astley **5** Jesse Carver **6** William Chalmers **7** Leslie Lievesley **8** Edmond Crawford **9** Denis Neville **10** Frank Soo **11** George Raynor **12** Bill Dodgin Snr **13** Alec Stock **14** Roy Hodgson **15** Graeme Souness

THE CARLING ULTIMATE FOOTBALL FACT AND QUIZ BOOK

Quiz 2
MANAGERS

1 Which former Crewe player managed Sampdoria for a brief and inglorious period in 1998-99?

2 Before moving to Southampton in 1997, of which club had Dave Jones previously been manager?

3 Which Dutchman was manager of Celtic when they won the Scottish League title in 1998?

4 Which Dutchman succeeded Walter Smith as Rangers manager in 1998?

5 Who preceded Arsène Wenger as manager of Arsenal?

6 Which Czech was manager of Aston Villa in 1990-91?

7 Who is the only man to have managed both Barnet and Birmingham City?

8 Which player succeeded Frank Clark as manager of Nottingham Forest in 1996?

9 Who succeeded Ron Greenwood as first team manager of West Ham United in 1975?

10 Who succeeded Dave Bassett as manager of Nottingham Forest in 1999?

11 Which former Stoke City centre half became manager of Oxford United in September 1993?

12 Which former Everton manager was at Preston North End from 1975-77?

13 Which 1966 World Cup hero was briefly manager of Sheffield United in 1981?

14 Who was sacked as manager of Port Vale in February 1999 after having managed them since 1984?

15 Who became manager of Wycombe Wanderers in 1998 after John Gregory returned to Aston Villa?

THE CARLING ULTIMATE FOOTBALL FACT AND QUIZ BOOK

Quiz 3
MANAGERS

1 Who succeeded Neil Smillie as manger of Wycombe Wanderers in February 1999?

2 Who was jailed for drink-driving in September 1991 and became manager of Portsmouth in February 1995?

3 Who managed both Swindon Town and West Ham United?

4 Which manager left Tottenham Hotspur in 1987 after tabloid revelations about his private life?

5 Of which club had Ossie Ardiles been manager before his triumphant return to Tottenham Hotspur in 1993?

6 Which former manager of Southampton was in charge of Sunderland in 1985-87?

7 In 1998-99, which former Leeds United and Scotland player was assistant to Lawrie McMenemy as manager of Northern Ireland?

8 In 1970, which manager led Huddersfield Town back to the First Division?

9 In 1996, Manchester City's 'Year of the Three Managers', who came between Alan Ball and Frank Clark?

10 Who was sacked as manager of Fulham to make way for Kevin Keegan?

11 Who has managed both West Ham United and Ipswich Town?

12 Who was the manager of Barnsley when they clinched promotion to the Premiership in 1997?

13 Who was the manager of Charlton Athletic when they clinched promotion to the Premiership in 1998?

14 Who were the joint managers of Charlton Athletic from 1991 to 1995?

15 Who was appointed manager of Crewe Alexandra in June 1983 and was still at the helm in 1999?

THE CARLING ULTIMATE FOOTBALL FACT AND QUIZ BOOK

Quiz 4
MANAGERS

1 Who was the first manager of Arsenal?

2 Who is the only man to have managed both Aston Villa and England?

3 Who was Arsenal manager when they won the Double in 1971?

4 Name the two men who have managed both Arsenal and Tottenham Hotspur?

5 Which manager claims to have had 'more clubs than Arnold Palmer'?

6 Who managed Crystal Palace from 1993 to 1995 and then Wycombe Wanderers in 1995-96?

7 Which manager led Brighton and Hove Albion to the 1983 FA Cup Final?

8 Which manager led Stoke City to their League Cup triumph in 1972?

9 Which manager led Everton to their FA Cup victory in 1966?

10 Who was General Manager of Queen's Park Rangers when they won the League Cup in 1967?

11 Who resigned in 1974 as manager of Tottenham Hotspur, saying 'players' have become impossible'?

12 Which manager led West Bromwich Albion to their FA Cup victory in 1968?

13 Who is the only man to have managed both Manchester City and England?

14 In 1955, whose 'Ducklings' won the First Division for the only time in their club's history?

15 Which manager of Bury took the reins at Crystal Palace in 1966, where he remained until 1972?

Answers

1 Sam Hollis **2** Graham Taylor **3** Bertie Mee **4** Terry Neill and George Graham **5** Tommy Docherty
6 Alan Smith **7** Jimmy Melia **8** Tony Waddington **9** Harry Catterick **10** Alec Stock **11** Bill Nicholson
12 Alan Ashman **13** Joe Mercer **14** Ted Drake, manager of Chelsea **15** Bert Head

THE CARLING ULTIMATE FOOTBALL FACT AND QUIZ BOOK

Quiz 5
MANAGERS

1 Which former manager of Chelsea was knighted in 1998?

2 Which former Chelsea manager was in charge at Swansea City in 1998-99?

3 Which club did Martin O'Neill manage in 1995, between Wycombe Wanderers and Leicester City?

4 Of which club was Arfon Griffiths the manager from 1977 to 1981?

5 Who was the last manager to lead Wolverhampton Wanderers to the League Championship?

6 Who was appointed manager of West Ham United in August 1994?

7 Which former taxi driver was twice manager of Tottenham Hotspur – 1984-86 and 1991-92?

8 Who was manager of Oxford United when they entered the Football League in 1962?

9 Who were the joint managers of Reading from 1994 to 1997?

10 Which 1966 World Cup hero was manager of Preston North End from 1977 to 1981?

11 Which 1966 World Cup hero was manager of Preston North End from 1973 to 1975?

12 Which London club was managed by Benny Fenton from 1966 to 1974?

13 In 1969, who succeeded Matt Busby as manager of Manchester United?

14 Which former Norwich City player managed the club from 1987 to 1992?

15 Which former Leyton Orient player became their manager in November 1996?

THE CARLING ULTIMATE FOOTBALL FACT AND QUIZ BOOK

Quiz 6
MANAGERS

1 Which great manager was born on May 26, 1909, played at wing half for Liverpool and Manchester City and won one cap for Scotland in 1933?

2 Which great manager was born on March 28, 1897, played club football for Waldhof and Mannheim and won three caps for Germany between 1921 and 1925?

3 Which great manager was born on February 9, 1928 and played for Holland in the early 1950s before developing the philosophy of 'total football' at Ajax?

4 Which great manager was born on March 12, 1885, and played for Torino before becoming manager and even psychologist of the Italian team that won the World Cup in 1934 and 1938?

5 Which great national manager was born on January 22, 1920, played for Southampton and Tottenham Hotspur and won 32 caps for England between 1949 and 1954?

6 Which great manager was born on July 25, 1933 and played outside right for Fluminese in the early 1950s?

7 Which great manager was born on September 15, 1915, played inside forward for Dresden and scored 17 goals in 16 games for Germany between 1937 and 1941?

8 Which great manager was born on June 21, 1906, played once for Hungary and then managed the great national team of the 1940s and 1950s?

9 Which great manager was born on September 2, 1913, played for Carlisle United and Preston North End and won five Scotland caps in 1938-39?

10 Which great manager was born in 1921 and played at centre half for Chelsea, Bradford Park Avenue, Brentford and Fulham before starting his backstage career at Eastbourne United in 1957?

11 Which great manager was born in 1933, played on the wing for Fulham and West Bromwich Albion and won 20 caps for England between 1958 and 1962?

12 Which great manager was born in 1944 and played for Lincoln City, a club he later managed?

13 Which great manager was born in 1913, played for Manchester United and Chelsea and was the first manager of his native country?

14 Which great manager was born in 1922 and played for Albion Rovers, Llanelli and Celtic, leading the last named to the double in 1954 before injury forced him into coaching?

15 Which great manager was born in 1916 in Argentina, brought up in Morocco, developed catenaccio at Inter Milan and was nicknamed 'The Slave Driver'?

Answers

1 Matt Busby **2** *Sepp Herberger* **3** *Rinus Michels* **4** *Vittorio Pozzo* **5** *Alf Ramsey* **6** *Tele Santana*
7 *Helmut Schoen* **8** *Gustav Sebes* **9** *Bill Shankly* **10** *Ron Greenwood* **11** *Bobby Robson*
12 *Graham Taylor* **13** *Walter Winterbottom* **14** *Jock Stein* **15** *Helenio Herrera*

MANAGERS

1 Who managed Argentina in the 1998 World Cup finals?

2 Who managed Austria in the 1998 World Cup finals?

3 Who managed Belgium in the 1998 World Cup finals?

4 Who managed Brazil in the 1998 World Cup finals?

5 Who managed Bulgaria in the 1998 World Cup finals?

6 Which 1998 World Cup finalists were managed by Claude Le Roy?

7 Which 1998 World Cup finalists were managed by Nelson Acosta?

8 Which 1998 World Cup finalists were managed by Hernan Gomez?

9 Which 1998 World Cup finalists were managed by Miroslav Blazevic?

10 Which 1998 World Cup finalists were managed by Bo Johannson?

11 Who was Glenn Hoddle's assistant manager at the 1998 World Cup finals?

12 Which manager led France to the 1998 World Cup in July and had his contract terminated in August?

13 Which 1998 World Cup finalists were managed by Berti Vogts?

14 Which 1998 World Cup finalists were managed by Jalal Talebi?

15 Who was the manager of Italy at the 1998 World Cup finals?

Answers

1 Daniel Passarella 2 Herbert Prohaska 3 George Leekens 4 Mario Zagallo 5 Hristo Bonev 6 Cameroon 7 Chile 8 Colombia 9 Croatia 10 Denmark 11 John Gorman 12 Aimé Jacquet 13 Germany 14 Iran 15 Cesare Maldini

THE CARLING ULTIMATE FOOTBALL FACT AND QUIZ BOOK

Quiz 8
MANAGERS

1 Which 1998 World Cup finalists were managed by Rene Simoes?

2 Who was the manager of 1998 World Cup finalists Japan?

3 Which 1998 World Cup finalists were managed by Manuel Lapuente?

4 Which former Northern Ireland international and current Premiership manager formed part of the BBC commentary team at the 1998 World Cup finals?

5 Which 1998 World Cup finalists were managed by Henri Michel?

6 Who was the manager of Holland at the 1998 World Cup finals?

7 Which of the 1998 World Cup finalists was managed by Bora Milutinovic?

8 Who was the manager of Norway at the 1998 World Cup finals?

9 Which country was managed by Paulo Carpeggiani at the 1998 World Cup finals?

10 Who was the manager of Romania at the 1998 World Cup finals?

11 Which former Brazilian international was manager of Saudi Arabia at the start of the 1998 World Cup finals?

12 Which nation was managed by Phillipe Troussier at the 1998 World Cup finals?

13 Who resigned as manager of Spain in September 1998 after a deeply disappointing World Cup?

14 Which nation was managed by Henri Kasperczak at the start of the 1998 World Cup finals?

15 Who was manager of the USA at the 1998 World Cup finals?

THE CARLING ULTIMATE FOOTBALL FACT AND QUIZ BOOK

Quiz 1
MIXED BAG

1 Which club won the League Championship in 1901, 1906, 1922, 1923, 1947, 1964, 1966, 1973, 1976, 1977, 1979, 1980, 1982, 1983, 1984, 1986, 1988 and 1990?

2 Which two strikers scored 42 goals for Millwall in the 1987-88 season?

3 Which club won the League Championship in 1931, 1933, 1934, 1935, 1938, 1948, 1953, 1971, 1989, 1991 and 1998?

4 Which two strikers scored 52 goals for Tottenham Hotspur in the 1994-95 season?

5 Which club won the League Championship in 1908, 1911, 1952, 1956, 1957, 1965, 1967, 1993, 1994, 1996 and 1997?

6 Which two strikers scored 40 goals for Coventry City in the 1977-78 season?

7 Which club won the League Championship in 1891, 1915, 1928, 1932, 1939, 1963, 1970, 1985 and 1987?

8 Which two strikers scored 28 goals for Nottingham Forest in the 1979-80 season?

9 Which club won the League Championship in 1894, 1896, 1897, 1899, 1900, 1910 and 1981?

10 Which two strikers scored 49 goals for Crystal Palace in the 1987-88 season?

11 Which club won the League Championship in 1892, 1893, 1895, 1902, 1913 and 1936?

12 Which two strikers scored 48 goals for Wolverhampton Wanderers in the 1972-73 season?

13 Which club won the League Championship in 1905, 1907, 1909 and 1927?

14 Which two strikers scored 70 goals for Ipswich Town in the 1960-61 season?

15 Which club won the League Championship in 1903, 1904, 1929 and 1930?

THE CARLING ULTIMATE FOOTBALL FACT AND QUIZ BOOK

MIXED BAG

1 Which two strikers scored 47 goals for Arsenal in the 1970-71 season?

2 Which club won the League Championship in 1924, 1925 and 1926?

3 Which two strikers scored 52 goals for Leeds United in the 1969-70 season?

4 Which club won the League Championship in 1969, 1974 and 1992?

5 Which two strikers scored 62 goals for Rangers in the 1991-92 season?

6 Which club won the League Championship in 1954, 1958 and 1959?

7 Which two strikers scored 53 goals for West Ham United in the 1985-86 season?

8 Which club won the League Championship in 1912, 1914 and 1995?

9 Which two strikers scored 41 goals for Aston Villa in the 1980-81 season?

10 Which club won the League Championship in 1949 and 1950?

11 Which two strikers scored 49 goals for Tottenham Hotspur in the 1963-64 season?

12 Which club won the League Championship in 1889 and 1890?

13 Which two strikers scored 65 goals for Newcastle United in the 1993-94 season?

14 Which club won the League Championship in 1921 and 1960?

15 Which two strikers scored 58 goals for Blackburn Rovers in the 1994-95 season?

THE CARLING ULTIMATE FOOTBALL FACT AND QUIZ BOOK

MIXED BAG

1 Which club won the League Championship in 1937 and 1968?

2 Which two strikers scored 39 goals for Liverpool in the 1975-76 season?

3 Which club won the League Championship in 1951 and 1961?

4 Which two strikers scored 50 goals for Liverpool in the 1982-83 season?

5 Which club won the League Championship in 1972 and 1975?

6 Which former Arsenal striker lost a thumb in a lawnmower accident?

7 In the 19th century, which team briefly wore white shirts with red spots because they thought this made them appear larger than life to the opposition?

8 Which club won its only League Championship in 1955?

9 Which club won its only League Championship in 1898?

10 Who bought Chelsea for £1 in 1982?

11 In 1986, which was the first League club to go into receivership twice?

12 Which club won its only League Championship in 1920?

13 Which club won its only League Championship in 1962?

14 With 12 goals in all competitions, who was Aston Villa's leading scorer in the 1997-98 season?

15 Which club won its only League Championship in 1978?

Answers

1 Manchester City **2** Kevin Keegan and John Toshack **3** Tottenham Hotspur **4** Kenny Dalglish and Ian Rush **5** Derby County **6** Charlie George **7** Bolton Wanderers **8** Chelsea **9** Sheffield United **10** Ken Bates **11** Wolverhampton Wanderers **12** West Bromwich Albion **13** Ipswich Town **14** Dwight Yorke **15** Nottingham Forest

THE CARLING ULTIMATE FOOTBALL FACT AND QUIZ BOOK

Quiz 4
MIXED BAG

1 With 12 goals in all competitions, who was Bolton Wanderers' leading scorer in the 1997-98 season?

2 Which player won the most England caps in the 1997-98 season?

3 With seven goals in all competitions, who was Crystal Palace's leading scorer in the 1997-98 season?

4 How many finalists will there be in Euro 2000?

5 With 11 goals in all competitions, who was Everton's leading scorer in the 1997-98 season?

6 Who went from Blackburn Rovers to Chelsea for £5 million in August 1997?

7 With 6 goals in all competitions, who was Newcastle United's leading scorer in the 1997-98 season?

8 Who went from Blackburn Rovers to Manchester United for £5 million in August 1997?

9 With 12 goals in all competitions, who was Sheffield Wednesday's leading scorer in the 1997-98 season?

10 From which Portuguese club did Tottenham Hotspur buy Jose Dominguez in August 1997?

11 Wimbledon had five joint leading scorers – Carl Cort, Efan Ekoku, Jason Euell, Michael Hughes and Carl Leaburn. How many goals did they each get?

12 From which German club did Blackburn Rovers buy Tore Pedersen in September 1997?

13 How many Premiership hat tricks were scored in the 1997-98 season – 15, 18 or 20?

14 Which controversial international goalkeeper moved from Oxford United to Sheffield Wednesday in September 1997?

15 Which Premiership referee sent most players off in the 1997-98 season?

Answers

1 Nathan Blake **2** Sol Campbell **3** Neil Shipperley **4** Sixteen **5** Duncan Ferguson **6** Graeme Le Saux **7** John Barnes **8** Henning Berg **9** Paolo Di Canio **10** Sporting Lisbon **11** Four **12** St Pauli **13** Fifteen **14** Bruce Grobbelaar **15** Graham Poll (11)

THE CARLING ULTIMATE FOOTBALL FACT AND QUIZ BOOK

Quiz 5
MIXED BAG

1 To which Dutch club did Arsenal sell Glenn Helder in October 1997?

2 From which Norwegian club did Everton buy Thomas Myhre in November 1997?

3 Where did Bolton Wanderers find Jussi Jaaskelainen?

4 Where did Coventry City get Viorel Moldovan in December 1997?

5 To which Portuguese club did Manchester United sell Karel Poborsky in December 1997?

6 To which club did Fulham pay £2.1 million for Chris Coleman in December 1997?

7 To which French club did Sheffield Wednesday sell Patrick Blondeau in January 1998?

8 To which Italian club did Derby County sell Aljosa Asanovic in January 1998?

9 Who came to Crystal Palace from Royal Antwerp in August 1997 and left them for Maccabi Haifa in January 1998?

10 Where did Blackburn Rovers get Callum Davidson in February 1998?

11 From which Austrian club did Leeds United buy Martin Hiden in February 1998?

12 Who went from Hartlepool to Liverpool to West Ham United to Sheffield United before becoming captain of Everton in 1998?

13 Who did Crystal Palace buy from Carlisle United in February 1998?

14 From which Greek club did Leicester City buy Theo Zagorakis in February 1998?

15 Name the goalkeeper bought by West Ham United from Rochdale in February 1998 for £300,000 down rising to £2.3 million, depending on appearances?

Answers

1 NAC Breda **2** Viking Stavanger **3** VPS (Finland) **4** Grasshopper Zurich **5** Benfica **6** Blackburn Rovers **7** Bordeaux **8** Napoli **9** Itzak Zohar **10** St Johnstone **11** Rapid Vienna **12** Don Hutchison **13** Matt Jansen **14** PAOK Salonika **15** Stephen Bywater

MIXED BAG

1 Who bought Nick Wright from Derby County in February 1998 for £35,000 payable only if they avoided relegation from the Nationwide Division Two (which they didn't)?

2 From which Greek club did Newcastle United buy Nikolaos Dabizas?

3 For which player did Manchester United pay York City £1 million in March 1998?

4 Who did West Ham United buy from Universidad (Chile) in March 1998?

5 Who joined Stoke City on a free transfer in March 1998 after a long and distinguished career at Everton?

6 From which Corsican club did West Ham United sign Mohamed Berthe in March 1998?

7 From which Dutch club did Leeds United buy Clyde Wijnhard in May 1998?

8 From which club did Blackburn Rovers buy Jimmy Corbett in May 1998?

9 Who bought Ben Thornley from Manchester United in May 1998?

10 How much did Blackburn Rovers pay for Southampton's Kevin Davies in June 1998?

11 From which French club did Newcastle United buy Stephane Guivarc'h?

12 Who did Liverpool buy from Karlsruhe in june 1998?

13 In the 1998-99 season, which two Premiership central defenders had ponytails?

14 Where did Aston Villa get Alan Thompson?

15 From which French club did Coventry City buy Jean-Gut Wallemme in June 1998?

Answers

1 Carlisle United **2** Olympiakos **3** Jonathan Greening **4** Javier Margas **5** Neville Southall **6** Gaz Ajaccio **7** Willem II **8** Gillingham **9** Huddersfield Town **10** £7.25 million **11** Auxerre **12** Sean Dundee **13** Darren Peacock (Blackburn Rovers) and Emmanuel Petit (Arsenal) **14** Bolton Wanderers **15** Lens

THE CARLING ULTIMATE FOOTBALL FACT AND QUIZ BOOK

Quiz 1

RECORDS

1 For which country did Karim Bagheri score seven goals in a World Cup match against The Maldives in 1997?

2 In 1957, which country won the first African Nations Cup?

3 Which club has won the FA Carling Premiership most often?

4 Which club lost only two of its 42 League games in the 1968-69 season?

5 Which German player was voted English Football Writers' Association Player of the Year in 1995?

6 Which Second Division Midlands club won all 17 of its home matches in the 1902-03 season?

7 Which team scored only 20 goals in 34 games in the 1966-67 season and finished bottom of the Scottish First Division?

8 Who beat Bon Accord 36-0 in the First Round of the Scottish FA Cup in 1885?

9 Who did Celtic beat 8-0 away in the Scottish Premier Division in March 1979?

10 Who scored 13 of Arbroath's 36 goals against Bon Accord in the 1885 Scottish FA Cup?

11 Who scored a hat trick for Chelsea against Portsmouth at the age of 17 years 10 months on Christmas day 1957?

12 Who was the fifth England player to be sent off in a full international, against Argentina in 1998?

13 In 1956, which country won the first Asian Cup?

14 In the 1963-64 season, which Second Division Yorkshire club was defeated only three times in 42 matches?

15 Which club did Manchester United beat 9-0 in the Premiership on March 4, 1995?

Quiz 2
RECORDS

1 Which First Division club went 85 games without defeat at home between January 1978 and January 1981?

2 Which Lancashire club beat Hyde United 26-0 in the FA Cup in 1887, a year before becoming founder members of the English Football League?

3 Which team finished next to bottom of the Scottish First Division in 1981 after managing only 18 goals in 39 League games?

4 Which Wolverhampton Wanderers and England defender was voted Football Writers' Association Player of the Year in 1952?

5 Who did Celtic beat 8-3 at home in January 1987?

6 Who scored five goals for Rangers against Stirling Albion in the 1966 Scottish League Cup?

7 Who scored six goals for Borussia Dortmund in their 1965 European Cup Winners' Cup match against Floriana (Malta)?

8 Who, in 1983 at the age of 18 years 18 days, became the youngest scorer in an FA Cup Final?

9 In 1960, which Uruguayan club became the first winners of the Copa Libertadores?

10 In the 1988-89 season, which Second Division London club was defeated only five times in 46 matches?

11 On January 31, 1978, which club ended Liverpool's run of 85 home games without defeat?

12 Which Blackburn Rovers player was voted English Football Writers' Association Player of the Year in 1994?

13 Which club did Blackburn Rovers beat 7-0 in the Premiership on November 18, 1995?

14 Which team finished bottom of the Scottish First Division in 1996 after managing only 23 goals in 36 League games?

15 Which three clubs have won the English League Championship three times in succession in the 20th century?

Answers

1 Liverpool **2** Preston North End **3** Stirling Albion **4** Billy Wright **5** Hamilton Academical **6** Jim Forrest **7** Lothar Emmerich **8** Norman Whiteside **9** Peñarol **10** Chelsea **11** Leicester City **12** Alan Shearer **13** Nottingham Forest **14** Dumbarton **15** Huddersfield Town, Arsenal and Liverpool

THE CARLING ULTIMATE FOOTBALL FACT AND QUIZ BOOK

Quiz 3
RECORDS

1 Who scored five Premiership goals for Manchester United in the match against Ipswich Town in March 1995?

2 Who scored 34 Premiership goals for Newcastle United in the 1993-94 season?

3 Who, in 1968 at the age of 21 years 212 days, became the youngest FA Cup Final captain?

4 Whose 10-0 defeat of Bury in 1983 is currently the joint holder of the record victory in the English League Cup?

5 In 1964, Oryx Douala became the first winners of the African Champions Cup. In which country do they play?

6 In the 1966-67 season, which Third Division London club lost only five of its 46 League matches?

7 In which years did Celtic win the Scottish League Championship nine times running?

8 Which Bolton Wanderers player was voted English Football Writers' Association Player of the Year in 1953?

9 Which club did Manchester United beat 7-0 in the Premiership on October 25, 1997?

10 Which team came bottom of the Scottish Second Division in the 1994-95 season after scoring only 22 goals in 36 games?

11 Which Third Division South club won all of its 21 home games in the 1929-30 season?

12 Who scored seven goals for Arsenal against Aston Villa in the old First Division on December 14, 1935?

13 Who scored 34 Premiership goals for Blackburn Rovers in the 1994-95 season? r

14 Who, in 1983, at the age of 17 years 324 days, became the youngest scorer in a League Cup Final?

15 Whose 10-0 defeat of Fulham in 1986 is currently the joint holder of the record victory in the English League Cup?

THE CARLING ULTIMATE FOOTBALL FACT AND QUIZ BOOK

Quiz 4
RECORDS

1 In 1975, Tonnerre Yaounde became the first winners of the African Cup Winners' Cup. In which country do they play?

2 In the 1989-90 season, which Third Division club lost only five of its 46 League matches?

3 In which years did Rangers win the Scottish League Championship nine times running?

4 Which club beat Wimbledon 7-1 in the Premiership on February 11, 1993?

5 Which London club was unbeaten at home for 59 matches from 1964 to 1967?

6 Which Sheffield Wednesday player was voted English Football Writers' Association Player of the Year in 1993?

7 Which team came next to bottom of the Scottish Third Division in 1996 after scoring only 26 goals in 36 League games?

8 Who beat Ipswich Town 9-0 in the Premiership in March 1995?

9 Who scored four goals for Oxford United against Luton Town in the First Division in the 1992-93 season?

10 Who scored 60 goals in 39 First Division games for Everton in the 1927-28 season?

11 Who, in 1985 at the age of 20 years 7 months 8 days, became the youngest League Cup Final captain?

12 On June 6, 1908, which became the first country outside the British Isles to play England?

13 Which club did Blackburn Rovers beat 7-1 in the Premiership on October 2, 1992?

14 Which Fourth Division club lost only four of its 46 League matches in the 1975-76 season?

15 Which now defunct Yorkshire club won a record 25 successive home games in 1926 and 1927?

Answers

1 Cameroon **2** Bristol Rovers **3** 1989-97 **4** Aston Villa **5** Millwall **6** Chris Waddle **7** Alloa Athletic **8** Manchester United **9** John Durnin **10** William Ralph Dean **11** Barry Venison (Sunderland) **12** Austria **13** Norwich City **14** Lincoln City **15** Bradford Park Avenue

THE CARLING ULTIMATE FOOTBALL FACT AND QUIZ BOOK

Quiz 5
RECORDS

1 Which Premiership team conceded 100 goals in 42 games in the 1993-94 season?

2 Which Preston North End player was voted English Football Writers' Association Player of the Year in 1954?

3 Which team scored 82 goals in 42 Premiership matches in the 1993-94 season and did not win the Championship?

4 Who played First Division football five days after his 50th birthday in 1965?

5

6 Which club did Everton beat 7-1 in the Premiership on December 28, 1996?

7 Who scored 42 goals for First Division Portsmouth in the 1992-93 season?

8 Who went to Nottingham Forest and won 8-1 in 1999?

Against which country did England play their last international before the outbreak of the Second World War?

9 Which club did Newcastle United beat 7-1 in the Premiership on March 12, 1994?

10 Which England striker was twice voted English Football Writers' Association Player of the Year in 1986 and 1992?

11 Which First Division Lancashire club won 21 home games in succession in 1971 and 1972?

12 Which First Division Lancashire team conceded 125 goals in 42 games in the 1930-31 season?

13 Which Fourth Division club lost only four of its 46 League matches in the 1981-82 season?

14 Which team scored 128 goals in 42 First Division matches in the 1930-31 season and did not win the Championship?

15 Who played for Newcastle United in the 1924 FA Cup Final at the age of 41 years 8 months?

Answers

1 Swindon Town **2** Tom Finney **3** Newcastle United **4** Stanley Matthews **5** Southampton **6** Guy Whittingham **7** Manchester United **8** Romania **9** Swindon Town **10** Gary Lineker **11** Liverpool **12** Blackpool **13** Sheffield United **14** Aston Villa **15** Walter Hampson

THE CARLING ULTIMATE FOOTBALL FACT AND QUIZ BOOK

Quiz 6
RECORDS

1 Who scored four goals for Sunderland against Millwall in the First Division in the 1995-96 season?

2 Who scored 59 goals in 37 matches for Second Division Middlesbrough in the 1926-27 season?

3 Who went to Newcastle in December 1908 and won 9-1?

4 Against which country did England play their first international after the Second World War (a match they won 7-2)?

5 Who scored four goals for Portsmouth against Bristol Rovers in the First Division in the 1992-93 season?

6 Which First Division Midlands club was unbeaten for the last 26 games of the 1977-78 season and the first 16 games of the 1978-79 season?

7 Which Fourth Division club conceded 109 goals in 46 games in the 1959-60 season?

8 Which Fourth Division club lost only four of its 46 League matches in the 1981-82 season?

9 Which Manchester City player – and future England manager – was voted English Football Writers' Association Player of the Year in 1955?

10 Which team won the Second Division Championship in 1927, scoring 122 goals in 42 matches?

11 Who beat Cardiff City 9-1 at Ninian Park in September 1955?

12 Who played for Manchester City in the 1924 FA Cup at the age of 49 years 8 months?

13 Who scored seven goals for Blackburn Rovers against Bristol Rovers in the Second Division in February 1955?

14 Who scored 35 goals in 46 Second Division matches for Reading in the 1993-94 season?

15 In the old Second Division, who won 8-0 at Halifax in September 1969?

Answers

1 Craig Russell **2** George Camsell **3** Sunderland **4** Northern Ireland **5** Southampton **6** Nottingham Forest **7** Hartlepool United **8** Bournemouth **9** Don Revie **10** Middlesbrough **11** Wolverhampton Wanderers **12** Billy Meredith **13** Tommy Briggs **14** Jimmy Quinn **15** Fulham

THE CARLING ULTIMATE FOOTBALL FACT AND QUIZ BOOK

Quiz 7 — RECORDS

1 On December 9, 1978, which club ended Nottingham Forest's run of 42 League matches without defeat?

2 On June 1, 1929, which became the first country outside the British Isles to play Scotland?

3 Which club did Newcastle United beat 7-1 in the Premiership on March 5, 1997?

4 Which Leeds United player was voted English Football Writers' Association Player of the Year in 1991?

5 Which Scottish Premier club twice conceded 100 goals in a season – the first time in 1984-85 and then again in 1987-88?

6 Which London team scored 127 goals in 42 games on its way to the 1928 Third Division South Championship?

7 Which two Premiership clubs drew 18 out of 42 matches in the 1993-94 season, a joint record?

8 Who is the only player ever to have been sent off in an FA Cup Final?

9 Who scored seven goals for Stoke City at Lincoln in the Second Division in 1957?

10 Who scored 52 goals in 46 Fourth Division games for Peterborough United in the 1960-61 season?

11 In 1878, which club became the first winners of the Welsh Cup?

12 In which season did Leith Athletic concede 137 goals in 38 Scottish First Division League games?

13 Which club did Blackburn Rovers beat 7-2 in the Premiership on August 28, 1997?

14 Which club went 25 Premiership games without defeat between February and November 1995?

15 Which Manchester City player was voted English Football Writers' Association Player of the Year in 1956?

Answers

1 Liverpool **2** Germany **3** Tottenham Hotspur **4** Gordon Strachan **5** Morton **6** Millwall **7** Manchester City and Sheffield United **8** Kevin Moran (Manchester United) **9** Neville Coleman **10** Terry Bly **11** Wrexham **12** 1931-32 **13** Sheffield Wednesday **14** Nottingham Forest **15** Bert Trautmann

THE CARLING ULTIMATE FOOTBALL FACT AND QUIZ BOOK

RECORDS

1 Which Premiership club drew 18 of its 42 matches in the 1994-95 season?

2 Which team scored 128 goals in 42 games on its way to the Third Division North Championship in 1929?

3 Who did Aberdeen beat 8-0 in March 1979?

4 Who scored five goals for Burnley against Stockport County in the Second Division in the 1996-97 season?

5 Who scored 31 goals in 40 Third Division games for Wigan Athletic in the 1996-97 season?

6 Who was sent off after 19 seconds of Crewe Alexandra's Third Division match at Darlington in 1994?

7 In 1978-79, which First Division club drew 23 of its 42 matches?

8 On May 25, 1933, which became the first country outside the British Isles to play Wales?

9 Where did Nottingham Forest win 7-1 on April 1, 1995?

10 Which Liverpool player was twice voted English Football Writers' Association Player of the Year in 1987 and 1990?

11 Which Scottish First Division side conceded 109 goals in 44 games in the 1992-93 season?

12 Which team scored 111 goals in 46 games in the 1961-62 season but did not even win promotion from the Third Division?

13 Who beat Nottingham Forest 7-0 in November 1995, to end their record Premiership run of 25 matches without defeat?

14 Who scored 10 goals for Luton Town against Bristol Rovers in the Third Division South on April 13, 1936?

15 Who scored 15 goals for Tottenham Hotspur in the 1901 FA Cup?

THE CARLING ULTIMATE FOOTBALL FACT AND QUIZ BOOK

Quiz 9
RECORDS

1 Who visited Airdrieonians in October 1950 and won 11-1?

2 Who was sent off after 75 seconds of the Premiership match between Blackburn Rovers and Leeds United on February 1, 1995?

3 In 1891, which club became the first League Champions of Northern Ireland?

4 In 1986-87, which Fourth Division club drew 23 of its 46 League matches?

5 Where did Manchester United win 6-0 on February 25, 1996?

6 Which club won the English League Championship in 1979, conceding only 16 goals in 42 matches?

7 Which First Division club went 29 League matches without defeat at the start of the 1973-74 season?

8 Which Preston North End player was voted English Football Writers' Association Player of the Year for the second time in 1957?

9 Which team scored 134 goals in 46 games in the on its way to becoming the Champions of Division Four in 1961?

10 Who scored nine goals for Tranmere Rovers against Oldham Athletic in the Third Division North on Boxing Day, 1935?

11 Who scored 12 goals for Tottenham Hotspur in the 1986-87 League Cup?

12 Who was sent off after 85 seconds of Manchester United's First Division match against Southampton on January 3, 1987?

13 Who won 10-0 at Alloa in March 1947?

14 On May 12, 1951, which became the first country outside the British Isles to play Northern Ireland?

15 Where did Liverpool win 6-1 in the Premiership on August 20, 1994?

Answers

1 Hibernian **2** Tim Flowers **3** Linfield **4** Exeter City **5** Bolton Wanderers **6** Liverpool **7** Leeds United **8** Tom Finney **9** Peterborough United **10** Bunny Bell **11** Clive Allen **12** Liam O'Brien **13** Dundee United **14** France **15** Crystal Palace

THE CARLING ULTIMATE FOOTBALL FACT AND QUIZ BOOK

RECORDS

1 Which club came second in the Second Division in 1991, conceding only 34 goals in 46 matches?

2 Which First Division club went 29 League matches without defeat at the start of the 1987-88 season?

3 Which Liverpool player was voted English Football Writers' Association Player of the year in 1989?

4 Which Scottish Premier Division club drew 21 of its 44 matches in the 1993-94 season?

5 Which two Scottish Premier Division sides scored 90 goals in 36 games in the 1982-83 season?

6 Who did England beat 9-0 in a European Championship qualifier in December 1982?

7 Who scored five goals for Fulham against Halifax Town in the Third Division in September 1969?

8 Who scored 35 goals for Celtic in the Scottish Premier Division in the 1986-87 season?

9 Who was sent off after 52 seconds of the FA Cup tie between Swindon Town and Everton on January 5, 1997?

10 Against which European country did the Republic of Ireland play its first international, on March 21, 1926?

11 For which Third Division club did Barrie Thomas score five goals against Luton Town in April 1965?

12 In the Scottish First Division, who scored 53 goals in 34 matches for Motherwell in the 1931-32 season?

13 Where did Chelsea win 6-1 in the Premiership on May 2, 1998?

14 Which Lancashire club won 30 consecutive First Division games between September 1920 and March 1921?

15 Which Scottish First Division club drew 21 of its 44 League games in the 1986-87 season?

THE CARLING ULTIMATE FOOTBALL FACT AND QUIZ BOOK

Quiz 11
RECORDS

1 Which side scored 132 goals in 34 games on its way to the 1958 Scottish Championship?

2 Which Tottenham Hotspur player was twice voted English Football Writers' Association Player of the Year in 1958 and 1961?

3 Which two clubs share the record for the number of Premiership wins in a season (27)?

4 Who did the Republic of Ireland beat 8-0 in a European Championship qualifier in November 1983?

5 Who was sent off after 90 seconds of Dynamo Moscow's UEFA Cup Third Round tie against Ghent in December 1991?

6 For which Third Division club did Keith East score five goals in the game against Mansfield Town in November 1965?

7 In the Scottish Second Division, who scored 66 goals in 38 matches for Ayr United in the 1927-28 season?

8 In which year did Wales last qualify for the World Cup finals?

9 Where did Tottenham Hotspur win 6-2 in the Premiership on December 6, 1997?

10 Which club has won the English League Championship most often?

11 Which First Division club won 31 of its 42 League matches in the 1960-61 season?

12 Which Lancashire club went eight home games without a win in the Third Division North in the 1931-32 season?

13 Which team scored 142 goals in 34 games on its way to the 1938 Scottish Second Division Championship?

14 Which Tottenham Hotspur striker was voted English Football Writers' Association Player of the Year in 1987?

15 Who beat England 7-1 in May 1954?

Answers

1 Heart of Midlothian **2** Danny Blanchflower **3** Blackburn Rovers and Manchester United **4** Malta **5** Sergei Dirkach **6** Swindon Town **7** Jim Smith **8** 1958 **9** Wimbledon **10** Liverpool **11** Tottenham Hotspur **12** Rochdale **13** Raith Rovers **14** Clive Allen **15** Hungary

THE CARLING ULTIMATE FOOTBALL FACT AND QUIZ BOOK

Quiz 12
RECORDS

1 Who was sent off after 55 seconds of the match between Uruguay and Scotland in the 1986 World Cup finals?

2 For which Third Division club did Alf Wood score five goals in the match against Blackburn Rovers in October 1971?

3 The world record for the fastest sending off in first class football belongs to Bologna's Giuseppe Lorenzo, who got his marching orders in the Serie A match against Parma on December 9, 1990 – how long did he last on the pitch?

4 Where did Liverpool win 5-0 in the Premiership on August 22, 1993?

5 Which club won the Premiership most often in the 20th century?

6 Which Luton Town player was voted English Football Writers' Association Player of the Year in 1959?

7 Which relegation-bound First Division club went 16 League games without a win in the 1958-59 season?

8 Which London Second Division club won 32 of its 42 matches in the 1919-20 season?

9 Which team scored 93 goals in 44 games in the 1993-94 season but was not promoted from the Scottish First Division?

10 Who beat the Republic of Ireland 7-0 in May 1982?

11 Who is Arsenal's all-time leading scorer?

12 Who scored 434 goals in a 619-match career from 1946 to 1965 with West Bromwich Albion, Fulham, Leicester City and Shrewsbury Town?

13 Name either of the clubs that has won the Second Division title six times.

14 Where did Leeds United win 5-0 in the Premiership on May 7, 1994?

15 Which club went 31 matches without a League win in the 1983-84 season and finished bottom of the Second Division?

Answers

1 Jose Batista **2** Shrewsbury Town **3** 10 seconds **4** Swindon Town **5** Manchester United **6** Syd Owen **7** Portsmouth **8** Tottenham Hotspur **9** Dunfermline Athletic **10** Brazil **11** Ian Wright **12** Arthur Rowley **13** Leicester City or Manchester City **14** Swindon Town **15** Cambridge United

THE CARLING ULTIMATE FOOTBALL FACT AND QUIZ BOOK

Quiz 13
RECORDS

1 Which Everton and Wales keeper was voted English Football Writers' Association Player of the Year in 1985?

2 Which player was sent off 21 times in his career with Rangers, West bromwich Albion, Vancouver Whitecaps, Heart of Midlothian and Scotland?

3 Which team won the Scottish First Division Championship in 1982, scoring 93 goals in 39 matches?

4 Which Third Division club won 32 of its 46 League matches in the 1971-72 season?

5 Who did Iran beat 17-0 in a World Cup qualifier in June 1997?

6 Who is Manchester United's all-time leading scorer?

7 Who scored 410 goals in a 408-match career from 1922 to 1938 with Celtic and Clydebank?

8 Who which Third Division club did Tony Caldwell score 5 goals in the match against Walsall in September 1983?

9 For which Third Division club did Andy Jones score five goals in the match against Newport County in May 1987?

10 In 1991, which German international became the first FIFA World Footballer of the Year?

11 Which club did Southampton beat 6-3 in the Premiership on October 26, 1996?

12 Which club won the Third Division title in 1962 and 1983?

13 Which Fourth Division club won 32 of its 46 matches in the 1975-76 season?

14 Which Second Division club suffered 15 consecutive League defeats in the 1988-89 season?

15 Which team scored 95 goals in 39 games on its way to the 1988 Scottish Second Division Championship?

Answers

1 Neville Southall **2** Willie Johnston **3** Motherwell **4** Aston Villa **5** The Maldives **6** Bobby Charlton **7** Jimmy McGrory **8** Bolton Wanderers **9** Port Vale **10** Lothar Matthaus **11** Manchester United **12** Portsmouth **13** Lincoln City **14** Walsall **15** Ayr United

THE CARLING ULTIMATE FOOTBALL FACT AND QUIZ BOOK

Quiz 14
RECORDS

1 Which Wolverhampton Wanderers player was voted English Football Writers' Association Player of the Year in 1960?

2 Who did Hungary beat 10-1 in the 1982 World Cup finals in Spain?

3 Who is Tottenham Hotspur's all-time leading scorer?

4 Who scored 349 goals for Everton between 1925 and 1937 – the all-time record?

5 For which Third Division club did Steve Wilkinson score five goals against Birmingham City in April 1990?

6 In 1992, which Dutch international was voted FIFA World Footballer of the Year?

7 In the 1970-71 season, which Fourth Division club went 25 League matches before recording its first win?

8 Which club won the Third Division title in 1968 and 1984?

9 Which Fourth Division club won 32 of its 46 matches in the 1985-86 season?

10 Which Liverpool striker was voted English Football Writers' Association Player of the Year in 1984?

11 Which two Midland teams drew 4-4 in the Premiership on February 22, 1995?

12 Who came second in the Scottish Third Division in 1997 after scoring 74 goals in 36 games?

13 Who did Hungary beat 9-0 in the 1954 World Cup finals in Switzerland?

14 Who has scored the most postwar goals in the FA Cup?

15 Who is Liverpool's all-time leading scorer?

THE CARLING ULTIMATE FOOTBALL FACT AND QUIZ BOOK

RECORDS

1 In 1993, which Italian international was voted FIFA World Footballer of the Year?

2 In the 1979-80 season, which Second Division club went 16 League games at the start of the season without a victory?

3 Which Burnley player was voted English Football Writers' Association Player of the Year in 1962?

4 Which Chelsea player scored in seven consecutive games between December 27, 1994 and February 5, 1995?

5 Which club won the Fourth Division title in 1970 and 1985?

6 Which English team scored only 28 goals in 38 games in the 1996-97 season but finished 11th in the Premiership?

7 Which Scottish Premier Division club won 27 of its 36 League matches in the 1995-96 season?

8 Who did Yugoslavia beat 9-0 in the 1974 World Cup finals in West Germany?

9 Who is West Ham United's all-time leading scorer?

10 Who scored 5 goals for Crewe Alexandra against Colchester United in the Third Division in the 1992-93 season?

11 With five goals to his credit, who has scored more goals in FA Cup Finals than any other player?

12 In 1994, which Brazilian international was voted FIFA World Footballer of the Year?

13 To which club did Sheffield Wednesday lose 7-1 at home in the Premiership on April Fool's Day 1995?

14 Which club won the Fourth Division title in 1966 and 1969?

15 Which Liverpool and Scotland forward was twice voted English Football Writers' Association Player of the Year in 1979 and 1983?

Answers

1 Roberto Baggio **2** Burnley **3** Jimmy Adamson **4** Mark Stein **5** Chesterfield **6** Leeds United **7** Rangers **8** Zaire **9** Vic Watson **10** Tony Naylor **11** Ian Rush **12** Romario **13** Nottingham Forest **14** Doncaster Rovers **15** Kenny Dalglish

THE CARLING ULTIMATE FOOTBALL FACT AND QUIZ BOOK

Quiz 16
RECORDS

1 Which Newcastle United player scored in seven consecutive games between September 14 and November 30, 1996?

2 Which Scottish Premier Division club won 27 of its 36 League matches in the 1984-85 season?

3 Which team scored only 24 goals in 42 matches in the 1984-85 season and finished bottom of Division One?

4 Who is Manchester City's all-time leading scorer?

5 Who made the worst ever start to a Premiership season, going 15 matches without a win in 1993-94?

6 Who scored five goals for Cambridge United against Exeter City in the Third Division in the 1993-94 season?

7 Who scored 13 penalties for Manchester City in the 1971-72 season?

8 For which Fourth Division club did Bert Lister score six goals against Southport on Boxing Day, 1962?

9 In 1995, which Liberian international was voted FIFA World Footballer of the Year?

10 Which club won the Fourth Division title in 1961 and 1974?

11 Which First Division Lancashire club lost its first 12 matches in the 1930-31 season?

12 Which Ipswich Town goalkeeper saved eight of the 10 penalties he faced in the 1979-80 season?

13 Which Scottish First Division club won 35 of its 42 League matches in the 1920-21 season?

14 Which Stoke City player was voted English Football Writers' Association Player of the Year for the second time in 1963?

15 Which team scored only 24 goals in 42 League games and finished bottom of Division Two in 1972?

Answers

1 Alan Shearer **2** Aberdeen **3** Stoke City **4** Tommy Johnson **5** Swindon Town **6** Steve Butler **7** Francis Lee **8** Oldham Athletic **9** George Weah **10** Peterborough United **11** Manchester United **12** Paul Cooper **13** Rangers **14** Stanley Matthews **15** Watford

Quiz 17
RECORDS

1 Who did Bolton Wanderers beat 7-0 in a First Division game in March 1997?

2 Who is Aston Villa's all-time leading scorer?

3 Who scored for Blackburn Rovers after only 13 seconds of their game againstt Everton on April 1, 1994?

4 In 1996, which Brazilian international was voted FIFA World Footballer of the Year?

5 Which club won the Third Division South three times?

6 Which Rangers goalkeeper went 1196 minutes from November 26, 1986 to January 31, 1987 without conceding a goal?

7 Which Scottish Second Division club won 33 of its 38 League matches in the 1966-67 season?

8 Which London team scored only 30 goals in 46 League games and finished bottom of Division Two in 1995?

9 Which Tottenham Hotspur midfielder was voted English Football Writers' Association Player of the Year in 1982?

10 Who did Newcastle United beat 13-0 in the old Second Division in October 1946?

11 Who is Blackburn Rovers' all-time leading scorer?

12 Who scored nine goals for Bournemouth against Margate in the First Round of the 1971-72 FA Cup?

13 Who scored for Chelsea after only 17 seconds of their game against Leicester City on October 8, 1994?

14 Who won 18 of their 21 away League matches in Division Three North in the 1946-47 season?

15 In 1948, who became the first English Football Writers' Association Player of the year?

Answers

1 Swindon Town **2** Pongo Waring **3** Chris Sutton **4** Ronaldo **5** Bristol City **6** Chris Woods **7** Morton
8 Leyton Orient **9** Steve Perryman **10** Newport County **11** Simon Garner **12** Ted MacDougall
13 John Spencer **14** Doncaster Rovers **15** Stanley Matthews

Quiz 18
RECORDS

1 On August 28, 1994, who scored a hat trick in four minutes 33 seconds for Liverpool against Arsenal?

2 To the end of the 20th century, how many players had scored hat tricks in the English FA Cup Final?

3 Which club has won the most Scottish League Championships?

4 Which Reading goalkeeper went 1103 minutes from March 24 to August 18, 1979 without conceding a goal?

5 Which Scottish First Division club won 26 of its 39 League matches in the 1981-82 season?

6 Which team scored only 33 goals in 42 games and finished bottom of the Third Division South in 1951?

7 Which West Ham United defender was voted English Football Writers' Association Player of the Year in 1964?

8 Who is Bolton Wanderers' all-time leading scorer?

9 Who lost 29 of their 42 Premiership matches in the 1994-95 season?

10 Who won 8-1 at Hartlepool in the Second Division in May 1994?

11 At the age of 17 years 3 days, who became the youngest player to appear in the Premiership when he turned out for West Ham United against Manchester City on New Year's Day 1996?

12 To the end of the 20th century, which club has won the English FA Cup most often?

13 Which Dutchman was voted English Football Writers' Association Player of the year in 1998?

14 Which Nottingham Forest defender was voted the English Football Writers' Association Player of the Year in 1978?

15 Which Premiership striker scored five hat tricks in the 1995-96 season?

Answers

1 Robbie Fowler **2** Three **3** Rangers **4** Steve Death **5** Motherwell **6** Crystal Palace **7** Bobby Moore **8** Nat Lofthouse **9** Ipswich Town **10** Plymouth Argyle **11** Neil Finn **12** Manchester United **13** Dennis Bergkamp **14** Kenny Burns **15** Alan Shearer (then of Blackburn Rovers)

THE CARLING ULTIMATE FOOTBALL FACT AND QUIZ BOOK

RECORDS

1 Which Scottish Second Division club won 27 of its 39 League matches in the 1983-84 season?

2 Which team scored only 32 goals in 42 games and finished third from bottom of the Third Division North in 1924?

3 Who did Gillingham beat 10-0 in the old Third Division in September 1987?

4 Who lost 31 of their 42 First Division matches in the 1984-85 season?

5 Who scored a hat trick for Blackburn Rovers in the 1890 FA Cup Final?

6 Who was the first England player to be sent off in a full international?

7 On September 5, 1992, at the age of 17 years 166 days, which Tottenham Hotspur player became the youngest Premiership scorer?

8 To the end of the 20th century, which club has won the Scottish FA Cup most often?

9 Which future manager of Nottingham Forest was voted English Football Writers' Association Player of the year while playing for Manchester United in 1949?

10 Which Leeds United player was voted English Football Writers' Association Player of the Year in 1965?

11 Which other coastal team did Brighton and Hove Albion beat 9-1 in the Third Division in November 1965?

12 Which Scottish Second Division club won 27 of its 39 League matches in the 1987-88 season?

13 Who came bottom of Division Three in 1970 after scoring only 27 goals in 46 League matches?

14 Who, to the end of the 1998-99 season, is the longest-serving Premiership manager?

15 Who lost 29 of their 36 matches in the Scottish Premier Division in the 1984-85 season?

RECORDS

1 Who scored 273 postwar goals for Celtic?

2 Who scored a hat trick for Notts County in the 1894 FA Cup Final?

3 Five English clubs have won the League Championship once – name them.

4 Which club won the English League Cup five times, in 1961, 1975, 1977, 1994 and 1996?

5 Which Italian was voted English Football Writers' Association Player of the Year in 1997?

6 Which left back played 478 League games for Oxford United between 1962 and 1977?

7 Which Liverpool defender was voted English Football Writers' Association Player of the Year in 1977?

8 Which Scottish Third Division club won 25 of its 36 League matches in the 1994-95 season?

9 Which Welsh club did Brentford beat 9-0 in the Third Division in October 1963?

10 Who finished bottom of Division Four in 1982 after having scored only 29 goals in 46 matches?

11 Who lost only four of their 42 Premiership matches in the 1993-94 season?

12 Who scored a hat trick for Blackpool in the 1953 FA Cup Final?

13 With a goal for Third Division Bristol City on March 3, 1928 at the age of 15 years 180 days, who was the youngest ever scorer in the English Football League?

14 Which Arsenal player – a future England manager – was voted English Football Writers' Association Player in 1950?

15 Which club won the English League Cup five times on the trot, from 1981 to 1985?

Answers

1 Bobby Lennox **2** Jimmy Logan **3** Chelsea, Sheffield United, Ipswich Town, Nottingham Forest and West Bromwich Albion **4** Aston Villa **5** Gianfranco Zola **6** John Shuker **7** Emlyn Hughes **8** Forfar Athletic **9** Wrexham **10** Crewe Alexandra **11** Manchester United **12** Stan Mortensen **13** Ronnie Dix **14** Joe Mercer **15** Liverpool

THE CARLING ULTIMATE FOOTBALL FACT AND QUIZ BOOK

Quiz 21
RECORDS

1 Which Lancashire club was undefeated in the League in the 1888-89 season?

2 Which Manchester United legend was voted English Football Writers' Association Player of the Year in 1966?

3 Which Second Division Lancashire club won all 14 of its home League matches in the 1893-94 season?

4 Who did Wrexham beat 10-1 in the Fourth Division in March 1962?

5 Who is the only goalkeeper to have scored in the FA Charity Shield?

6 Who played for First Division Sunderland at the age of 15 years 158 days on August 22, 1984?

7 Who scored six goals for Oldham Athletic against Scarborough in the League Cup in the 1989-90 season?

8 Who scored only 19 goals in 36 games in the 1988-89 season and finished bottom of the Scottish Premier Division?

9 Who was the second England player to be sent off in a full international, against Poland in 1973?

10 To the end of the 20th century, which club has won the Scottish League Cup most often?

11 Which Frenchman was voted English Football Writers' Association Player of the Year in 1996?

12 Which Ipswich Town player became the youngest First Division scorer at the age of 16 years 57 days on February 4, 1984?

13 Which Liverpool forward was voted English Football Writers' Association Player of the Year in 1976?

14 Which London club lost only one of its 38 First Division matches in the 1990-91 season?

15 Which Second Division Lancashire club won all 15 of its home League matches in the 1894-95 season?

Answers

1 Preston North End 2 Bobby Charlton 3 Liverpool 4 Hartlepool United 5 Pat Jennings 6 Derek Forster 7 Frankie Bunn 8 Hamilton Academical 9 Alan Ball 10 Rangers 11 Eric Cantona 12 Jason Dozzell 13 Kevin Keegan 14 Arsenal 15 Bury

THE CARLING ULTIMATE FOOTBALL FACT AND QUIZ BOOK

Quiz 22
RECORDS

1 Who scored five goals for Dundee United against Morton in the Scottish Premier Division in November 1984?

2 Which great player scored 1283 goals in 1365 first class football matches?

3 Who scored only 22 goals in 44 games in the 1991-92 season and finished bottom of the Scottish Premier Division?

4 Who was the third England player to be sent off in a full international, against Argentina in 1977?

5 Who won 8-1 at Crewe in September 1973?

6 For which country did Gary Cole score seven goals in a World Cup match against Fiji in 1981?

7 On March 9, 1988, at the age of 17 years 240 days, which Southampton player became the youngest scorer of a First Division hat trick?

8 Which Blackpool player was voted English Football Writers' Association Player of the Year in 1951?

9 Which Lancashire club lost only two of its 40 First Division matches in the 1987-88 season?

10 Which Leeds United defender was voted English Football Writers' Association Player of the Year in 1967?

11 Which Second Division Yorkshire club won all 17 of its home League matches in the 1899-1900 season?

12 Who did Rangers beat 8-1 away in the Scottish Premier Division in March 1979?

13 Who finished bottom of the Scottish First Division in 1994 after having scored only 30 goals in 44 League games?

14 Who scored eight goals for Celtic against Dunfermline Athletic in the Scottish First Division in September 1928?

15 Who was the first player to appear in 1000 English League games?

Answers

1 Paul Sturrock **2** Pele **3** Dunfermline Athletic **4** Trevor Cherry **5** Rotherham United **6** Australia **7** Alan Shearer **8** Harry Johnston **9** Liverpool **10** Jack Charlton **11** The Wednesday **12** Kilmarnock **13** Brechin City **14** Jimmy McGrory **15** Pat Jennings

SCOTTISH FOOTBALL

THE CARLING ULTIMATE FOOTBALL FACT AND QUIZ BOOK

Quiz 1
SCOTTISH FOOTBALL

1 In the 1998-99 season, who sponsored Stranraer's shirts?

2 Name the Manchester United goalkeeper signed by Celtic on loan in March 1998.

3 Which Celtic great was voted Scottish Footballer of the Year in 1965?

4 Which former Celtic player won 13 of his 21 Republic of Ireland caps while at Motherwell between 1994 and 1996?

5 Which Scottish League club plays its home games at Pittodrie?

6 Who moved from Lens to Hibernian in August 1997?

7 Who scored 31 League goals for Stenhousemuir in the 1936-37 season?

8 At the beginning of the 1998-99 season, who was manager of Aberdeen?

9 In March 1998, who moved from Chester City to Dundee United?

10 Where did Scotland play their home 1998 World Cup qualifier against Belarus?

11 Which Celtic player – formerly with Chelsea – was voted Scottish Footballer of the Year in 1998?

12 Which Scottish League club is nicknamed The Diamonds?

13 Who scored 52 League goals for Motherwell in the 1931-32 season?

14 At the beginning of the 1998-99 season, who was head coach of Celtic?

15 In March 1998, who moved from Preston North End to Dunfermline Athletic?

Answers

1 Stena Line **2** Kevin Pilkington **3** Billy McNeill **4** Tommy Coyne **5** Aberdeen **6** Jean Marc Boco **7** Robert Murray **8** Alex Miller **9** Julian Alsford **10** Pittodrie **11** Craig Burley **12** Airdrieonians **13** William McFadyen **14** Dr Jozef Venglos **15** Jamie Squires

THE CARLING ULTIMATE FOOTBALL FACT AND QUIZ BOOK

Quiz 2
SCOTTISH FOOTBALL

1 In the 1998-99 season, who sponsored Alloa Athletic's shirts?

2 In September 1997, who left Aberdeen for Inverness Caledonian Thistle?

3 In the 1998-99 season, who sponsored Arbroath's shirts?

4 Which Rangers great was twice voted Scottish Footballer of the Year, in 1966 and 1976?

5 Which Scottish League club plays its home matches at the Shyberry Excelsior Stadium?

6 Who beat Dundee United 12-1 in January 1954?

7 At the beginning of the 1998-99 season, who was manager of Dundee?

8 In March 1998, who moved to Hibernian from Bristol Rovers?

9 In the 1998-99 season, who sponsored Clyde's shirts?

10 Which country does Motherwell's Eliphas Shivute represent at international level?

11 Which of Rangers' overseas stars was twice voted Scottish Footballer of the Year, in 1995 and 1997?

12 Which Scottish League club is nicknamed The Wasps?

13 Who beat Rangers 10-2 in 1886?

14 At the beginning of the 1998-99 season, who was manager of Dundee United?

15 In the 1998-99 season, who sponsored East Fife's shirts?

Answers

1 Alloa Advertiser 2 Duncan Shearer 3 Perimax Diana 4 John Grieg 5 Airdrieonians 6 Motherwell 7 John Scott 8 Justin Skinner 9 OKI 10 Namibia 11 Brian Laudrup 12 Alloa Athletic 13 Airdrieonians 14 Paul Sturrock 15 R S Nicol & Sons

THE CARLING ULTIMATE FOOTBALL FACT AND QUIZ BOOK

Quiz 3
SCOTTISH FOOTBALL

1 What nationality is Rangers' Sebastian Rozental?

2 Which Celtic midfielder was voted 1998 Scottish PFA Player of the Year?

3 Which great goalkeeper was voted Scottish Footballer of the Year in 1967?

4 Which Scottish League club was formerly known as Excelsior FC?

5 With 58 internationals for Scotland between 1986 and 1996, who is Rangers' most capped player?

6 At the beginning of the 1998-99 season, who was manager of Dunfermline Athletic?

7 From which English Premiership club did Celtic sign Danish international defender Marc Rieper in September 1997?

8 In the 1998-99 season, who sponsored Forfar Athletic's shirts?

9 The ground of which Scottish League club has a Railway End and a Somerset Road end?

10 Which English midfielder was voted Scottish Footballer of the Year in 1996?

11 Which Heart of Midlothian full back was voted 1998 Scottish PFA Young Player of the Year?

12 Who scored 44 goals for Rangers in the 1931-32 season?

13 At the beginning of the 1998-99 season, who was coach of Heart of Midlothian?

14 In the 1998-99 season, who sponsored Inverness Caledonian Thistle's shirts?

15 Which Celtic midfielder was voted 1998 Scottish Football Writers' Player of the Year?

THE CARLING ULTIMATE FOOTBALL FACT AND QUIZ BOOK

Quiz 4
SCOTTISH FOOTBALL

1 Which Raith Rovers player was voted voted Scottish Footballer of the Year in 1968?

2 Which Scottish Premier League club almost bought Tomas Brolin in September 1997?

3 Which St Johnstone player won five Scotland caps between 1929 and 1933?

4 With which other Scottish League club did Clydebank share a ground in the 1998-99 season?

5 At the beginning of the 1998-99 season, who was manager of Kilmarnock?

6 In the 1998-99 season, who sponsored Livingston's shirts?

7 Which English forward was voted Scottish Footballer of the Year in 1994?

8 Which Scottish League club was formerly known as The Miners FC?

9 Who did Celtic beat 2-0 on the last day of the 1997-98 season to clinch their first League title for 10 years?

10 Who knocked Rangers out of the 1997-98 UEFA Cup?

11 Who scored 38 League goals for St Johnstone in the 1931-32 season?

12 At the beginning of the 1998-99 season, who was manager of Motherwell?

13 In the 1998-99 season, who sponsored Partick Thistle's shirts?

14 Which Celtic player was voted Scottish Footballer of the Year in 1969?

15 Which Scottish League club is nicknamed The Dark Blues?

Answers

1 Gordon Wallace **2** Heart of Midlothian **3** Sandy McLaren **4** Dumbarton **5** Robert Williamson **6** Motorola
7 Mark Hateley **8** Cowdenbeath **9** St Johnstone **10** Strasbourg **11** Jimmy Benson **12** Harri Kampman
13 Auto Windscreens **14** Bobby Murdoch **15** Dundee

THE CARLING ULTIMATE FOOTBALL FACT AND QUIZ BOOK

Quiz 5
SCOTTISH FOOTBALL

1 Who is Airdrieonians' most capped player, having made nine appearances for Scotland between 1929 and 1933?

2 Who knocked Celtic out of the 1997-98 UEFA Cup?

3 Who was sacked in May 1998 as manager of Partick Thistle?

4 At the beginning of the 1998-99 season, who was manager of Rangers?

5 In the 1998-99 season, who sponsored Queen of the South's shirts?

6 Which goalkeeper was voted Scottish Footballer of the Year in 1993?

7 Which Scottish League club has the post code DD3 7JY?

8 Who joined Raith Rovers from Millwall in September 1997?

9 Who scored 39 League goals for Airdrieonians in the 1916-17 season?

10 Who won the 1998 Scottish FA Cup?

11 At the beginning of the 1998-99 season, who was manager of St Johnstone?

12 In the 1998-99 season, who sponsored Stirling Albion's shirts?

13 Which Ayr United player won 3 caps for Scotland in 1929?

14 Which Hibernian player was voted Scottish Footballer of the Year in 1970?

15 Which Scottish League club was formerly known as Bainsford Britannia FC?

Answers

1 Jimmy Crapnell 2 Liverpool 3 John McVeigh 4 Dick Advocaat 5 Pizzeria Il Fiume
6 Andy Goram 7 Dundee 8 Jason Dair 9 Bert Yarnell 10 Heart of Midlothian 11 Alexander Clark
12 McKenzie Trailers 13 Jim Nisbett 14 Pat Stanton 15 East Stirlingshire

THE CARLING ULTIMATE FOOTBALL FACT AND QUIZ BOOK

Quiz 6
SCOTTISH FOOTBALL

1 Who joined Clydebank from Hull City in September 1997?

2 Who resigned as manager of Albion Rovers in May 1998?

3 At the beginning of the 1998-99 season, who was manager of Airdrieonians?

4 In June 1998, who left Rangers to become player-coach of Bradford City?

5 In the 1998-99 season, who sponsored Berwick Rangers' shirts?

6 Which French club knocked Kilmarnock out of the 1997-98 European Cup Winners' Cup?

7 Which Rangers forward was voted Scottish Footballer of the Year in 1992?

8 Which Scottish League club was formerly known as Dundee Hibernians FC?

9 Who scored 66 goals for Ayr United in the 1927-28 season?

10 At the beginning of the 1998-99 season, who was manager of Ayr United?

11 In October 1997, Richard Gough returned to Rangers after a brief spell with which US club?

12 In the 1998-99 season, who sponsored Brechin City's shirts?

13 Name Heart of Midlothian's all-time leading goalscorer, released by the club in June 1998?

14 Which Aberdeen defender was voted Scottish Footballer of the Year in 1971?

15 Which Scottish League club has the post code DD3 7JW?

Answers

1 Andy Brown **2** Vinnie Moore **3** Alexander MacDonald **4** Stuart McCall **5** Federation Brewery **6** Nice **7** Ally McCoist **8** Dundee United **9** Jimmy Smith **10** Gordon Dalziel **11** Kansas City Wiz **12** A P Jess Food Group **13** John Robertson **14** Martin Buchan **15** Dundee United

THE CARLING ULTIMATE FOOTBALL FACT AND QUIZ BOOK

Quiz 7
SCOTTISH FOOTBALL

1 Who scored 29 League goals for Clydebank in the 1990-91 season?

2 At the beginning of the 1998-99 season, who was player-manager of Clydebank?

3 In 1998, which former Scotland and West Ham United defender left his coaching job at Stirling Albion and then joined Livingston?

4 In October 1997, which former Scotland Under-21 midfielder joined Airdrieonians after a spell in prison?

5 In the 1998-99 season, who sponsored Cowdenbeath's shirts?

6 Which Dundee United player was voted Scottish Footballer of the Year in 1991?

7 Which Scottish League ground has a Hope Street End and a James Street End?

8 Who scored 43 goals for Falkirk in the 1928-29 season?

9 At the beginning of the 1998-99 season, who was manager of Falkirk?

10 In the 1998-99 season, who sponsored Dumbarton's shirts?

11 To which Spanish club did Rangers sell Joachim Bjorklund for £2.2 million in June 1998?

12 What nationality is Heart of Midlothian winger Jose Quitongo?

13 Which Greenock Morton player won 25 Scotland caps between 1948 and 1952?

14 Which Rangers player was voted Scottish Footballer of the Year in 1972?

15 Which Scottish League club are nicknamed The Loons?

Answers

1 Ken Eadie **2** Ian McCall **3** Ray Stewart **4** Sandy Robertson **5** Bernard Hunter Crane Hire
6 Maurice Malpas **7** Falkirk **8** Evelyn Morrison **9** Alexander Totten **10** Methode Electronics Europe
11 Valencia **12** Angolan **13** Jimmy Cowan **14** Dave Smith **15** Forfar Athletic

THE CARLING ULTIMATE FOOTBALL FACT AND QUIZ BOOK

Quiz 8
SCOTTISH FOOTBALL

1 At the beginning of the 1998-99 season, who was manager of Greenock Morton?

2 In November 1997, which Leicester City defender was named in the Scotland squad for the friendly against France in St Etienne?

3 In the 1998-99 season, who sponsored East Stirlingshire's shirts?

4 Which Aberdeen player was voted Scottish Footballer of the Year in 1990?

5 Which Scottish League club is nicknamed Ton?

6 Who scored 58 League goals for Greenock Morton in the 1963-64 season?

7 Who scored the first goal for Celtic in their 3-0 victory over Dundee United in the 1997 Coca-Cola Cup Final?

8 At the beginning of the 1998-99 season, who was player-manager of Hamilton Academical?

9 In 1998-99, which Scottish League club groundshared with Partick Thistle?

10 In the 1998-99 season, who sponsored Montrose's shirts?

11 Which Celtic player was voted Scottish Footballer of the Year in 1973?

12 Which Hamilton Academical defender has won 29 caps for Canada?

13 Which Scotland midfielder moved from Borussia Dortmund to Celtic in November 1997?

14 Who scored the second goal for Celtic in their 3-0 victory over Dundee United in the 1997 Coca-Cola Cup Final?

15 At the beginning of the 1998-99 season, who was manager of Hibernian?

Answers

1 William Stark 2 Matt Elliott 3 Richmond Park Hotel 4 Alex McLeish 5 Greenock Morton 6 Allan McGraw 7 Marc Rieper 8 Colin Miller 9 Hamilton Academical 10 The Bervie Chipper 11 George Connelly 12 Colin Miller 13 Paul Lambert 14 Henrik Larsson 15 Alexander McLeish

THE CARLING ULTIMATE FOOTBALL FACT AND QUIZ BOOK

Quiz 9
SCOTTISH FOOTBALL

1 In the 1998-99 season, who sponsored Queen's Park's shirts?

2 Which Rangers defender was voted Scottish Footballer of the Year in 1989?

3 Which Scottish League ground is in Gorgie Road, Edinburgh?

4 Who scored 34 League goals for Hamilton Academical in the 1936-37 season?

5 Who scored the only goal of Rangers' victory over Celtic in the first Old Firm game of the 1997-98 season?

6 Who scored the third goal for Celtic in their 3-0 victory over Dundee United in the 1997 Coca-Cola Cup Final?

7 At the beginning of the 1998-99 season, who was manager of Raith Rovers?

8 In the 1998-99 season, who sponsored Ross County's shirts?

9 Which player was twice voted Scottish Footballer of the Year – once in 1975, while at Rangers, and again in 1986, while with Heart of Midlothian?

10 Which Scottish League ground is in Albion Road, Edinburgh?

11 Who scored the first goal for Heart of Midlothian in their 2-1 defeat of Rangers in the 1998 Scottish FA Cup Final?

12 Who was sacked in November 1997 as manager of Aberdeen?

13 Who won 38 Scotland caps between 1949 and 1957 while playing for Hibernian?

14 At the beginning of the 1998-99 season, who was manager of St Mirren?

15 In the 1998-99 season, who sponsored Stenhousemuir's shirts?

Answers

1 Barr Irn Bru **2** Richard Gough **3** Heart of Midlothian **4** David Wilson **5** Richard Gough **6** M Andersson **7** James Nicholl **8** Maclean Electrical **9** Sandy Jardine **10** Hibernian **11** Colin Cameron **12** Roy Aitken **13** Lawrie Reilly **14** Tony Fitzpatrick **15** Four In One

THE CARLING ULTIMATE FOOTBALL FACT AND QUIZ BOOK

SCOTTISH FOOTBALL

1 Which Celtic player was voted Scottish Footballer of the Year in 1988?

2 Which Scottish League club plays its home matches at the Almondbank Stadium?

3 Who scored 42 League goals for Hibernian in the 1959-60 season?

4 Who scored the Scots' goal in their 2-1 defeat by France in a friendly in St Etienne in November 1997?

5 Who scored the second goal for Heart of Midlothian in their 2-1 defeat of Rangers in the 1998 Scottish FA Cup Final?

6 At the beginning of the 1998-99 season, who was manager of Stranraer?

7 In July 1997, from which Italian club did Rangers sign Jonas Thern?

8 Which Celtic full back was voted Scottish Footballer of the Year in 1977?

9 Which Raith Rovers player won six caps for Scotland between 1923 and 1925?

10 Which Scottish League club was formerly known as Ferranti Thistle and Meadowbank Thistle?

11 Who resigned as manager of Cowdenbeath in November 1997?

12 Who scored for Rangers in the 1998 Scottish FA Cup Final?

13 At the beginning of the 1998-99 season, who was manager of Alloa Athletic?

14 For which French club did Stephane Adam play before moving to Heart of Midlothian?

15 In July 1997, who did Rangers sign from Juventus?

THE CARLING ULTIMATE FOOTBALL FACT AND QUIZ BOOK

Quiz 11
SCOTTISH FOOTBALL

1 Which Dundee United player was voted Scottish Footballer of the Year in 1985?

2 Which Rangers player was sent off in the second Old Firm game of the 1997-98 season?

3 Which Scottish League ground has a D Cooper Stand?

4 Who scored 42 League goals for Raith Rovers in the 1937-38 season?

5 At the beginning of the 1998-99 season, who was manager of Arbroath?

6 In July 1997, who did Aberdeen buy from Celtic for £750,000?

7 In which Italian city was Rangers' Lorenzo Amoruso born on June 28, 1971?

8 Which Rangers player was voted Scottish Footballer of the Year in 1978?

9 Which Scottish League club is nicknamed The Doonhamers?

10 Which St Mirren player won seven Scotland caps between 1979 and 1980?

11 Who scored for Celtic as the second Old Firm game of the 1997-98 season ended 1-1?

12 At the beginning of the 1998-99 season, who was general manager of Clyde?

13 From which club did Celtic buy Darren Jackson for £1.5 million in July 1997?

14 In November 1997, Alex Miller replaced Roy Aitken as manager of Aberdeen. Where in England had Miller previously been Assistant Manager?

15 In which German city was Rangers' Jorg Albertz born on January 29, 1971?

Answers

1 Hamish McAlpine *2 Paul Gascoigne* *3 Motherwell* *4 Norman Heywood* *5 David Baikie* *6 Brian O'Neill* *7 Bari* *8 Derek Johnstone* *9 Queen of the South* *10 Iain Munro* *11 Alan Stubbs* *12 Ronnie MacDonald* *13 Hibernian* *14 Coventry City* *15 Moenchengladbach*

Quiz 12
SCOTTISH FOOTBALL

1 Which Aberdeen player was voted Scottish Footballer of the Year in 1984?

2 Which Scottish League ground is at Terregles Street, Dumfries?

3 Which St Mirren player won seven Scotland caps between 1980 and 1984?

4 At the beginning of the 1998-99 season, who was player-manager of East Fife?

5 In November 1997, who stepped down as Chairman of financially beleaguered Partick Thistle?

6 In which country was Celtic's Regi Blinker born on June 4, 1969?

7 Which Morton player was voted Scottish Footballer of the Year in 1979?

8 Who became manager of Celtic in July 1997?

9 Who play in black and white hoops and are known as the Spiders?

10 Who scored 45 League goals for St Mirren in the 1921-22 season?

11 At the beginning of the 1998-99 season, who was player-manager of Forfar Athletic?

12 Which Celtic striker was voted Scottish Footballer of the Year in 1983?

13 Which Rangers legend was born at Bellshill on September 24, 1962?

14 Which Scottish League club is based in Kirkcaldy?

15 Who rejoined Aberdeen from Coventry City in July 1997?

Answers

1 Willie Miller **2** Queen of the South **3** Billy Thomson **4** Stephen Kirk **5** Jim Oliver **6** Surinam
7 Andy Ritchie **8** Wim Jansen **9** Queen's Park **10** Dunky Walker **11** Ian McPhee **12** Charlie Nicholas
13 Ally McCoist **14** Raith Rovers **15** Eoin Jess

THE CARLING ULTIMATE FOOTBALL FACT AND QUIZ BOOK

Quiz 13
SCOTTISH FOOTBALL

1 Who scored 27 League goals for Stranraer in the 1977-78 season?

2 Who took over as Chairman of Partick Thistle in November 1997?

3 At the beginning of the 1998-99 season, who was manager of Inverness Caledonian Thistle?

4 From which club did Rangers buy Finnish international goalkeeper Antti Niemi?

5 In which city in Norway was Stale Stensaas born on July 7, 1971?

6 What was the name of the Icelandic international signed by Dundee United in November 1997?

7 Which Aberdeen midfielder was voted Scottish Footballer of the Year in 1980?

8 Which Scottish League club plays its home games at Victoria Park, Dingwall?

9 Who is the only Alloa Athletic player to have been capped by Scotland?

10 At the beginning of the 1998-99 season, who was player-coach of Livingston?

11 From which Italian club did Rangers sign Lorenzo Amoruso?

12 Name either of the players who scored twice for Scotland in their 4-1 defeat of Belarus in the World Cup qualifier at Pittodrie in September 1997.

13 Which Dundee United player was voted Scottish Footballer of the Year in 1982?

14 Which Scottish League ground is in Love Street, Paisley?

15 Who left Heart of Midlothian in November 1997 to become Alex Miller's assistant manager at Aberdeen?

Answers

1 Derrick Frye 2 Brown McMaster 3 Steven Paterson 4 Copenhagen 5 Trondheim 6 Siggi Jonsson 7 Gordon Strachan 8 Ross County 9 Jock Hepburn 10 John Robertson 11 Fiorentina 12 Kevin Gallacher and David Hopkin 13 Paul Sturrock 14 St Mirren 15 Paul Hegarty

THE CARLING ULTIMATE FOOTBALL FACT AND QUIZ BOOK

Quiz 14
SCOTTISH FOOTBALL

1 Who scored 49 League goals for Alloa Athletic in the 1921-22 season?

2 At the beginning of the 1998-99 season, who was manager of Partick Thistle?

3 In July 1997, which Scottish club bought Austrian midfielder Thomas Flogel from Austria Vienna?

4 Which Partick Thistle goalkeeper was voted Scottish Footballer of the Year in 1981?

5 Which Scottish League club was formerly known as Heather Rangers?

6 Who did Celtic beat 3-0 in the 1997 Coca-Cola Cup Final?

7 Who scored a penalty for Scotland against Brazil in the opening game of the 1998 World Cup finals?

8 Who won two of his five caps for Scotland between 1887 and 1889 while playing for Arbroath?

9 At the beginning of the 1998-99 season, who was manager of Queen of the South?

10 In November 1997, who moved from Carlisle United to Greenock Morton?

11 In which year were the Scottish World Cup squad joint winners of the country's Footballer of the Year award?

12 What nationality is Tony Rougier, Hibernian's 1997 signing from Raith Rovers?

13 Which Scottish League club are nicknamed Warriors?

14 Who scored 45 League goals in the 1958-59 season for Arbroath?

15 Who scored Scotland's goal in their 1-1 draw with Norway in the 1998 World Cup finals?

Answers

1 William Crilley **2** Tommy Bryce **3** Heart of Midlothian **4** Alan Rough **5** Stenhousemuir **6** Dundee United **7** John Collins **8** Ned Doig **9** Rowan Alexander **10** Owen Archdeacon **11** 1974 **12** Trinidadian **13** Stenhousemuir **14** David Easson **15** Craig Burley

THE CARLING ULTIMATE FOOTBALL FACT AND QUIZ BOOK

Quiz 15
SCOTTISH FOOTBALL

1 At the beginning of the 1998-99 season, who was player-coach of Stirling Albion?

2 From which English club did Hibernian sign Stephen Crawford in July 1997?

3 In December 1997, who signed a £3 million sponsorship deal with the Scotland international team?

4 Which Clyde player won 12 caps for Scotland between 1953 and 1958?

5 Which Highland League team is nicknamed The Cattachs?

6 At the beginning of the 1998-99 season, who was manager of Albion Rovers?

7 From which Norwegian club did Celtic sign Harald Brattbakk in December 1997?

8 Which Highland League team is nicknamed the Lilywhites?

9 Which Scottish club signed Icelandic goalkeeper Olle Gottskalksson in July 1997?

10 Who scored 32 League goals for Clyde in the 1956-57 season?

11 At the beginning of the 1998-99 season, who was player-manager of Berwick Rangers?

12 In July 1997, from which French club did Aberdeen re-sign Gary Smith?

13 In which city do Highland League club Cove Rangers play their home games?

14 Which East Fife player won five Scotland caps between 1949 and 1954?

15 Which Scotland international defender did Aberdeen sign from Middlesbrough in December 1997?

THE CARLING ULTIMATE FOOTBALL FACT AND QUIZ BOOK

Quiz 16
SCOTTISH FOOTBALL

1 At the beginning of the 1998-99 season, who was manager of Brechin City?

2 At the beginning of the 1998-99 season, who was manager of East Stirlingshire?

3 In July 1997, which Scottish Premier League club signed Jerome Vareille from Mulhouse?

4 Which Highland League side is nicknamed The Coasters?

5 Who scored 412 goals for East Fife in the 1947-48 season?

6 Who was sacked as manager of East Fife in December 1997?

7 From which English First Division club did St Johnstone sign Republic of Ireland defender Alan Kernaghan in December 1997?

8 In July 1997, which Scot was named as assistant to Wim Jansen at Celtic?

9 Which Highland League club is nicknamed Blue Toon?

10 Who scored 45 League goals for Forfar Athletic in the 1929-30 season?

11 At the beginning of the 1998-99 season, who was manager of Dumbarton?

12 Who resigned as manager of Greenock Morton in July 1997, only to return shortly afterwards as director of football?

13 Which Highland League team is known as The Speysiders?

14 Who moved from Stirling Albion to Dundee in December 1997?

15 Who scored 27 League goals for Inverness Caledonian Thistle in the 1996-97 season?

THE CARLING ULTIMATE FOOTBALL FACT AND QUIZ BOOK

Quiz 17
SCOTTISH FOOTBALL

1 At the beginning of the 1998-99 season, who was manager of Cowdenbeath?

2 In which year did Inverness Caledonian Thistle join the Scottish League?

3 Name the Yugoslav international goalkeeper who left Kilmarnock for Sporting Gijon in January 1998.

4 Where did Celtic get Henrik Larsson?

5 Which Highland League club is nicknamed The Scorries?

6 At the beginning of the 1998-99 season, who was manager of Montrose?

7 Where did Celtic get Craig Burley?

8 Which goalkeeper did Kilmarnock sign from Celtic in January 1998 to replace Dragoje Lekovic?

9 Who scored 21 League goals for Meadowbank Thistle in the 1986-87 season?

10 Who were the Highland League Champions in 1997-98?

11 At the beginning of the 1998-99 season, who was team coach of Queen's Park?

12 In January 1998, the manager of which Scottish club was fined £500 and banned from the touchline for six months after making remarks to an assistant referee?

13 Which goalkeeper won 53 caps for Scotland between 1976 and 1986 while playing for Partick Thistle?

14 Who moved from Stade Rennais to Celtic in July 1997?

15 Who scored for Heart of Midlothian from the penalty spot in the third minute of the 1998 Scottish FA Cup Final against Rangers?

Quiz 18
SCOTTISH FOOTBALL

1 At the beginning of the 1998-99 season, who was player-manager of Ross County?

2 In January 1998, which Cameroon international striker did Dundee United sign from Trabzonspor of Turkey?

3 In July 1997, Keith Knox moved from Clyde to which other Scottish club?

4 Who scored 41 League goals for Partick Thistle in the 1926-27 season?

5 Who scored the second goal for Heart of Midlothian in the 1998 Scottish FA Cup Final against Rangers?

6 At the beginning of the 1998-99 season, who was manager of Stenhousemuir?

7 In July 1997, Robert Scott moved from Ayr United to which other Scottish club?

8 In the 1998 Scottish FA Cup Final, who came on as a substitute for Rangers and scored?

9 To which German club did Celtic sell Andreas Thom?

10 Which Queen of the South player won three Scotland caps in 1949?

11 In July 1997, Craig McEwan moved from Clyde to which other Scottish club?

12 In the 1998-99 season, who sponsored Aberdeen's shirts?

13 To which club did Raith Rovers convincingly talk Twaddle in January 1998?

14 Who is Aberdeen's most capped player, having made 77 appearances for Scotland?

15 Who scored 37 League goals for Queen of the South in the 1927-28 season?

Answers

1 Neale Cooper **2** Jean Jacques Misse-Misse **3** Stranraer **4** Alec Hair **5** Stephane Adam **6** Terry Christie **7** Clyde **8** McCoist **9** Hertha Berlin **10** William Houliston **11** Raith Rovers **12** Atlantic Telecom **13** Greenock Morton **14** Alex McLeish **15** Alex Gray

THE CARLING ULTIMATE FOOTBALL FACT AND QUIZ BOOK

Quiz 19
SCOTTISH FOOTBALL

1 In July 1997, from which Scottish club did Ian Cameron move to Raith Rovers?

2 In the 1998-99 season, who sponsored Celtic's shirts?

3 Who is the Managing Director of Celtic?

4 Who left Heart of Midlothian for Tranmere Rovers in January 1998?

5 Who scored 26 League goals for Stirling Albion in the 1969-70 season?

6 In July 1997, which Scottish player moved from Alloa Athletic to Stenhousemuir?

7 In the 1998-99 season, who sponsored Dundee's shirts?

8 Who is the only Albion Rovers player ever to have been capped by Scotland?

THE SHIRTS HAVEN'T ARRIVED YET!

9 Who was sacked as manager of Hibernian in February 1998?

10 With 76 games for Scotland between 1984 and 1997, who is the most capped international in the history of Celtic?

11 In July 1997, to which other Scottish club did Lloyd Haddow move from Stenhousemuir?

12 In the 1998-99 season, who sponsored Dundee United's shirts?

13 Who beat Celtic 8-0 in April 1937?

14 Who scored 41 goals for Albion Rovers in the 1932-33 season?

15 Who was sacked as manager of Dundee in February 1998 when they led the Scottish First Division?

Answers

1 Hibernian 2 Umbro 3 Fergus McCann 4 Stephen Frail 5 Joe Hughes 6 Kevin Kane 7 Scottish Hydro-Electric 8 John White 9 Jim Duffy 10 Paul McStay 11 Alloa Athletic 12 Telewest Communications 13 Motherwell 14 John Renwick 15 John McCormack

SCOTTISH FOOTBALL

1 In the 1998-99 season, who sponsored Dunfermline Athletic's shirts?

2 Which defender was sold to Blackburn Rovers by St Johnstone in February 1998?

3 Which Dundee player won 24 Scotland caps between 1962 and 1966?

4 Who moved from Raith Rovers to Ayr United in July 1997?

5 Who scored 38 League goals for Berwick Rangers in the 1963-64 season?

6 In February 1997, which manager left Motherwell to take over at Hibernian?

7 In the 1998-99 season, who sponsored Heart of Midlothian's shirts?

8 To which other Scottish club did Euan Donaldson moved from St Johnstone in July 1997?

9 Who lost 11-0 to Celtic in October 1895?

10 Who scored 26 League goals for Brechin City in the 1959-60 season?

11 In the 1998-99 season, who sponsored Kilmarnock's shirts?

12 To which English League club did Colin Woodthorpe move from Aberdeen in July 1997?

13 To which US club did Richard Gough announce he would be going when he finally left Rangers at the end of the 1997-98 season?

14 Which Cowdenbeath player won three caps for Scotland in 1931?

15 Who scored 32 League goals for Dundee in the 1963-64 season?

Answers

1 Landmark Home Furnishing **2** Callum Davidson **3** Alex Hamilton **4** Paul Bonar **5** Ken Bowron
6 Alex McLeish **7** Strongbow **8** Clyde **9** Dundee **10** Ronald McIntosh **11** Sports Division
12 Stockport County **13** San Jose Clash **14** Jim Paterson **15** Alan Gilzean

THE CARLING ULTIMATE FOOTBALL FACT AND QUIZ BOOK

Quiz 21
SCOTTISH FOOTBALL

1 In the 1998-99 season, who sponsored Motherwell's shirts?

2 Which Scottish club signed former Norwich City goalkeeper Bryan Gunn in February 1998?

3 Who moved from Hamilton Academical to Albion Rovers in July 1997?

4 Who scored 40 League goals for Cowdenbeath in the 1925-26 season?

5 Who scored 50 League goals for Celtic in the 1935-36 season?

6 In the 1998-99 season, who sponsored Rangers' shirts?

7 Which Dumbarton player won eight Scotland caps between 1880 and 1886?

8 Who came to Celtic when Paolo Di Canio moved to Sheffield Wednesday?

9 Who did St Johnstone buy from Rangers for £150,000 in February 1998?

10 Who scored 38 League goals for Aberdeen in the 1929-30 season?

11 In the 1998-99 season, who sponsored St Johnstone's shirts?

12 What nationality is Motherwell coach Harri Kampman?

13 Which Dumbarton player won eight Scotland caps between 1882 and 1884?

14 Which Dundee United player won 55 caps for Scotland between 1984 and 1993?

15 Which former Scotland international did Kilmarnock sign from Tranmere Rovers in August 1997?

Answers

1 Motorola **2** Hibernian **3** John Campbell **4** Willie Devlin **5** Jimmy McGrory **6** McEwan's Lager
7 J Lindsay **8** Regi Blinker **9** Gary Bollan **10** Benny Yorston **11** Scottish Hydro-Electric **12** Finnish
13 J McAulay **14** Maurice Malpas **15** Pat Nevin

THE CARLING ULTIMATE FOOTBALL FACT AND QUIZ BOOK

Quiz 22
SCOTTISH FOOTBALL

1 In the 1998-99 season, who sponsored Airdrieonians' shirts?

2 To which English club did Tosh McKinlay go on loan in 1998?

3 Which player won five of his 14 caps for Wales while playing for East Stirlingshire between 1889 and 1890?

4 Who beat Celtic 2-1 on the opening day of the 1997-98 season?

5 Who scored 41 League goals for Dundee United in the 1955-56 season?

6 In the 1998-99 season, who sponsored Ayr United's shirts?

7 Where did Chic Charnley go on leaving Hibernian?

8 Who beat Kilmarnock 6-2 in the Third Round of the Scottish Coca-Cola Cup in August 1997?

9 Who scored 36 League goals for East Stirlingshire in the 1938-39 season?

10 Who won 13 of his 29 caps for Hungary while with Dunfermline Athletic?

11 In the 1998-99 season, who sponsored Clydebank's shirts?

12 What nationality is Rangers' winger Jonatan Johansson?

13 Who joined Albion Rovers from Ipswich Town in February 1998?

14 Who scored 53 League goals for Dunfermline Athletic in the 1925-26 season?

15 Who won two of his six Scotland caps while playing for Montrose in 1891 and 1892?

THE CARLING ULTIMATE FOOTBALL FACT AND QUIZ BOOK

Quiz 23
SCOTTISH FOOTBALL

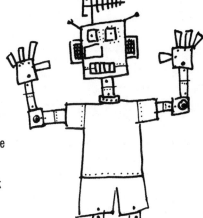

1 In the 1998-99 season, who sponsored Falkirk's shirts?

2 What was the score when Rangers met Liverpool in Walter Smith's testimonial match in March 1998?

3 Which Scottish club plays its home matches at East End Park?

4 Who refused to go back to Celtic at the start of the 1997-98 season and was then sold to Celta Vigo for £3.5 million?

5 Who won 14 caps for Scotland while playing for Queen's Park between 1883 and 1893?

6 In 1998, which Scottish club began toying with the idea of relocating to Dublin?

7 In the 1998-99 season, who sponsored Greenock Morton's shirts?

8 Which Hearts player won 29 caps for Scotland between 1900 and 1913?

9 Which Swedish club knocked Rangers out of the 1997-98 European Cup?

10 Who scored 30 League goals for Queen's Park in the 1937-38 season?

11 From which English club did Heart of Midlothian sign Lee Makel?

12 In the 1998-99 season, who sponsored Hamilton Academical's shirts?

13 Which Turkish side knocked Dundee United out of the 1997-98 UEFA Cup?

14 Who beat Queen's Park 9-0 in April 1930?

15 Who scored 44 League goals for Heart of Midlothian in the 1930-31 season?

Answers

1 John R Weir Mercedes-Benz Dealer **2** Rangers 1 Liverpool 0 **3** Dunfermline Athletic **4** Jorge Cadete
5 Walter Arnott **6** Clydebank **7** Sports Connection **8** Bobby Walker **9** IFK Gothenburg **10** William Martin
11 Huddersfield Town **12** M J Gleeson Group **13** Trabzonspor **14** Motherwell **15** Barney Battles

THE CARLING ULTIMATE FOOTBALL FACT AND QUIZ BOOK

Quiz 24
SCOTTISH FOOTBALL

1 In the 1998-99 season, who sponsored Hibernian's shirts?

2 In which year did Ross County first join the Scottish League?

3 To which English First Division club did Celtic's Peter Grant move in August 1997?

4 Which Kilmarnock player won 11 Scotland caps between 1929 and 1932?

5 Which Scot was manager of the Maldives for a week in 1998?

6 In the 1998-99 season, who sponsored Raith Rovers' shirts?

7 Which Rangers player scored for Denmark as they beat Scotland 1-0 at Ibrox in March 1998?

8 Who moved from Celtic to Swindon Town in August 1997?

9 Who scored 22 League goals for Ross County in the 1996-97 season?

10 Who scored 34 League goals for Kilmarnock in the 1960-61 season?

11 In the 1998-99 season, who sponsored St Mirren's shirts?

12 Who did Reading manager Tommy Burns sign from Kilmarnock for £400,000 in March 1998?

13 Who moved from Millwall to Raith Rovers in August 1997?

14 Who scored 31 League goals for Stenhousemuir in the 1927-28 season?

15 Who scored 34 League goals for Kilmarnock in the 1927-28 season?

THE CARLING ULTIMATE FOOTBALL FACT AND QUIZ BOOK

SEASON
1997-1998

THE CARLING ULTIMATE FOOTBALL FACT AND QUIZ BOOK

SEASON 1997-1998

May-August 1997

1 In May 1997, which Blackburn Rovers midfielder became the first player to reach 45 disciplinary points in a season?

2 Who was the English Premiership's first black referee?

3 Which club did Dave Jones manage before taking over at Southampton in June 1997?

4 In August 1997, which newly promoted club announced that they had sold all 17,000 of their season tickets?

5 Who scored a hat trick for Coventry City against Chelsea in the first match of the season?

6 Who scored two goals for Newcastle United in their opening day victory over Sheffield Wednesday?

7 Who returned to English football in August 1997 as manager of Blackburn Rovers?

8 Which Italian scored for Crystal Palace at Goodison Park on the opening day of the 1997-98 season?

9 Which Wimbledon player got his first yellow card of the season after just two minutes of the opening match against Liverpool?

10 Which former West Ham, Manchester United and England midfielder made his debut for Liverpool in August 1997?

11 Who were Barnsley's opponents in their first Premiership game?

12 Who scored Bolton Wanderers' opening day winner against Southampton?

13 Who missed a penalty for Manchester United on his return to his old club in the first Sunday game of the new season?

14 Who scored two goals for Arsenal in their opening game against Coventry City?

15 Who scored the winner for Barnsley at Crystal Palace?

Answers

1 Billy McKinlay **2** Uriah Rennie **3** Stockport County **4** Barnsley **5** Dion Dublin **6** Faustino Asprilla **7** Roy Hodgson **8** Attilio Lombardo **9** Vinnie Jones **10** Paul Ince **11** West Ham United **12** Nathan Blake **13** Teddy Sheringham **14** Ian Wright **15** Neil Redfearn

SEASON 1997-1998

1 Who scored a hat trick for Blackburn Rovers against Aston Villa in August 1997?

2 Who scored for Manchester United in their home victory over Southampton?

3 Which unfancied team won 2-1 at Anfield in August 1997?

4 Who were Derby County's opponents in the first match at their new stadium, Pride Park?

5 What was particularly memorable about Derby County's first match at Pride Park?

6 What was the score when the lights went out at Pride Park?

7 Which was the first English team to take part in the Champions' League without having won the Championship?

8 Who did Newcastle United beat 2-1 in their first Champions' League match?

9 Which two ex-Liverpool players did Newcastle United sign in August 1997?

10 Which Liverpool player was widely linked with a £12 million move to Barcelona?

11 Which Dutchman scored his first goal for Arsenal as they beat Southampton 3-1 at The Dell?

12 Which Newcastle United player was sent off in their Premiership game against Aston Villa?

13 Who scored four times for Chelsea in their 6-0 defeat of Barnsley?

14 Which team became the first to score seven goals in three Premiership matches?

15 Who scored a hat trick for Arsenal at Filbert Street in August 1997?

THE CARLING ULTIMATE FOOTBALL FACT AND QUIZ BOOK

Quiz 3

SEASON 1997-1998

September 1997

1 Who took the penalty that gave Sheffield Wednesday their first win of the season against Leicester City?

2 Who scored for Derby County with a twice-taken penalty against Barnsley?

3 Where did Barnsley get Ashley Ward?

4 Where did Sheffield Wednesday get Jim Magilton?

5 Which Blackburn player pulled a hamstring during his six minutes on the field for England against Moldova?

6 Which goalkeeper became the first player to make 200 Premiership appearances?

7 Against which club did Ian Wright score the hat trick he needed to take him past Cliff Bastin's record as Arsenal's all-time leading goalscorer?

8 Who put West Ham United ahead at Old Trafford (they eventually lost 2-1)?

9 Who scored a hat trick for Newcastle United in their 3-2 Champions' League victory over Barcelona?

10 Who scored for Everton on his debut against Barnsley?

11 Who scored a last-minute winner for Arsenal at Chelsea?

12 Who scored Bolton Wanderers' first goal at their new Reebok Stadium?

13 Who was sent off for Everton as they lost 1-0 to Newcastle?

14 Which Sheffield Wednesday player was sent off as they lost 5-2 at home to Derby County?

15 Who scored two goals for Derby County in their 5-2 win at Hillsborough?

Answers

1 Benito Carbone **2** Stefano Eranio **3** Derby County **4** Southampton **5** Stuart Ripley **6** Neville Southall **7** Bolton Wanderers **8** John Hartson **9** Faustino Asprilla **10** Danny Cadamarteri **11** Nigel Winterburn **12** Alan Thompson **13** Slaven Bilic **14** Patrick Blondeau **15** Francesco Baiano

THE CARLING ULTIMATE FOOTBALL FACT AND QUIZ BOOK

Quiz 4
SEASON 1997-1998

October 1997

1 Who scored the winner for Leeds United against Manchester United?

2 Who scored a hat-trick for West Ham United in the Second Round of the Coca-Cola Cup against Huddersfield Town?

3 Which Greek club knocked Arsenal out of the UEFA Cup?

4 Which former Middlesbrough player scored in both legs of Leicester City's UEFA Cup tie with Atletico Madrid?

5 Which Third Division club held Bolton Wanderers to a 4-4 draw in the Coca-Cola Cup?

6 Which Third Division side knocked Crystal Palace out of the Coca-Cola Cup?

7 Which Italian club scored after only 25 seconds of their Champions' League game at Old Trafford?

8 Who scored both goals for Newcastle in their draw at Dynamo Kiev?

9 Which Second Division side put Sheffield Wednesday out of the Coca-Cola Cup?

10 From which Norwegian club did Sheffield Wednesday sign Petter Rudi?

11 Who scored Arsenal's first two goals in their 5-0 defeat of Barnsley?

12 Who played his 488th match for Coventry City?

13 Which club inflicted Bolton Wanderers' first defeat at the Reebok Stadium?

14 Who scored a hat trick for Liverpool against Chelsea?

15 After 16 years at Everton, who asked for a transfer?

Answers

1 David Wetherall **2** John Hartson **3** PAOK Salonika **4** Juninho **5** Leyton Orient **6** Hull City **7** Juventus **8** John Beresford **9** Grimsby Town **10** Molde **11** Dennis Bergkamp **12** Steve Ogrizovic **13** Aston Villa **14** Patrik Berger **15** Neville Southall

THE CARLING ULTIMATE FOOTBALL FACT AND QUIZ BOOK

Quiz 5
SEASON 1997-1998

1 Which First Division side knocked Manchester United out of the Coca-Cola Cup?

2 Who made his debut for Birmingham City as a 90th-minute substitute in the Coca-Cola Cup against Arsenal and was sent off after only 30 seconds on the pitch?

3 Who knocked the holders, Leicester City, out of the Coca-Cola Cup?

4 Who scored twice for Derby County against Tottenham Hotspur in the Coca-Cola Cup?

5 Which Bolton Wanderers defender was sent off for crashing into West Ham goalkeeper Craig Forrest?

6 Who scored both Chelsea goals in their 3-2 defeat by Tromso in the first leg of their European Cup Winners' Cup tie?

7 Who scored a hat trick for Manchester United in their 7-0 defeat of Barnsley?

8 Who scored twice for Liverpool in their 4-0 win at home to Derby?

9 Who scored twice for Southampton in their 3-2 win over Tottenham Hotspur?

10 Which Arsenal player was sent off for grabbing the referee during his side's 0-0 draw with Aston Villa?

11 Who refereed the Arsenal v Aston Villa Premiership game?

12 Which West Ham player publicly criticised referee Mike Reed after defeat at Leicester?

13 Which £6 million Swede left Leeds United after having played only 19 League games?

14 Who scored his tenth goal of the season for Blackburn Rovers in the 1-1 draw with Newcastle United?

15 Who beat Liverpool 3-0 in the UEFA Cup Second Round first leg?

THE CARLING ULTIMATE FOOTBALL FACT AND QUIZ BOOK

SEASON 1997-1998

November 1997

1 Name two of the three players who each scored twice for Manchester United in their 6-1 defeat of Sheffield Wednesday.

2 Who scored two of Derby County's goals as they beat Arsenal?

3 Who missed a penalty for Arsenal against Derby County?

4 What was the score when the lights went out at West Ham during the game against Crystal Palace?

5 Who was sacked as manager of Sheffield Wednesday?

6 Who was booked for diving in Tottenham Hotspur's match with Leeds United?

7 Who scored Manchester United's first European hat trick for 19 years?

8 Who scored a hat trick in Chelsea's 7-1 defeat of Tromso in the second leg of their European Cup Winners' Cup tie?

9 Who scored a hat trick for Sheffield Wednesday in their 5-0 defeat of Bolton Wanderers?

10 Which visitors to Elland Road went three up in the first half and then lost?

11 Which West Ham United defender scored an own goal against Chelsea at Stamford Bridge?

12 Which two West Ham players had a little fight on the pitch at Stamford Bridge?

13 Who returned to Sheffield Wednesday as manager six years after he had left them?

14 Which was the first away team to win at Pride Park?

15 Who scored a hat trick as Liverpool knocked Grimsby Town out of the Coca-Cola Cup?

Answers

1 Teddy Sheringham, Andy Cole and Ole Gunnar Solskjaer **2** Paulo Wanchope **3** Ian Wright **4** 2-2
5 David Pleat **6** David Ginola **7** Andy Cole **8** Gianluca Vialli **9** Andy Booth **10** Derby County
11 Rio Ferdinand **12** Eyal Berkovic and John Moncur **13** Ron Atkinson **14** Newcastle United
15 Michael Owen

THE CARLING ULTIMATE FOOTBALL FACT AND QUIZ BOOK

SEASON 1997-1998

1 Who was sacked as manager of Tottenham Hotspur?

2 Who was appointed the new manager of Tottenham Hotspur?

3 Of which team had Spurs' new boss previously been coach?

4 Who scored two goals after coming on as a substitute for Manchester United in their 5-2 win at Wimbledon?

5 Who did Sheffield Wednesday beat in Ron Atkinson's first game in charge?

6 Who did Tottenham Hotspur lose to in Christian Gross's first game in charge?

7 Who scored Barnsley's winner at Anfield?

8 Which two Chelsea players scored from the penalty spot in their defeat of Everton?

9 Which Everton defender was sent off in the defeat at Chelsea?

10 Who beat Aston Villa 2-1 in the first leg of the UEFA Cup Third Round?

11 Who scored for Arsenal in extra time to put Coventry City out of the Coca-Cola Cup?

12 Which First Division club knocked Leeds United out of the Coca-Cola Cup?

13 Who scored for West Ham at Elland Road, as his father had before him?

14 Who scored Blackburn's winner against Chelsea?

15 Who did Manchester United beat 3-0 in their last home group match in the European Champions' League?

Answers

1 Gerry Francis 2 Christian Gross 3 Grasshopper Zurich 4 David Beckham 5 Arsenal 6 Crystal Palace 7 Ashley Ward 8 Dennis Wise and Gianfranco Zola 9 Slaven Bilic 10 Steaua Bucharest 11 Dennis Bergkamp 12 Reading 13 Frank Lampard 14 Gary Croft 15 Kosice

THE CARLING ULTIMATE FOOTBALL FACT AND QUIZ BOOK

SEASON 1997-1998

December 1997

1 Against Derby County, which Chelsea player scored the first hat trick of his professional career?

2 Which club inflicted Arsenal's first home defeat of the season?

3 What was the score when West Ham United and Crystal Palace replayed their Premiership fixture which had been abandoned when the floodlights failed?

4 Who scored a hat trick for Chelsea as they won 6-1 at Tottenham?

5 Who scored his first goal in two months for Arsenal at Newcastle?

6 Which two Coventry players were sent off in the Premiership game at Villa Park?

7 Who scored his first goal in 18 games in Aston Villa's 3-0 defeat of Coventry City?

8 Who beat Arsenal 3-1 at Highbury?

9 Who scored his first goal for Southampton against Leicester City after nine years with the club?

10 Who scored two goals for Coventry City in their 4-0 defeat of Tottenham Hotspur?

11 Which two Leeds players were sent off in their 0-0 draw with Chelsea at Stamford Bridge?

12 Who scored West Ham's winner against Sheffield Wednesday?

13 Against West Ham United, who scored his first goal for Blackburn Rovers since 1994?

14 Which 18-year-old scored the other two Blackburn goals in their defeat of West Ham United?

15 Which match at Selhurst Park became the third this season to be abandoned because of floodlight failure?

THE CARLING ULTIMATE FOOTBALL FACT AND QUIZ BOOK

SEASON 1997-1998

1 Which German international signed for Tottenham Hotspur for the second time?

2 Tottenham Hotspur rescued their German star from an unhappy spell at which Italian club?

3 Which former Sheffield Wednesday manager was appointed chief of youth and scouting at Tottenham Hotspur?

4 Which Premiership club bought Viorel Moldovan?

5 What nationality is Viorel Moldovan?

6 In the game against Everton, which Manchester United striker scored his 13th goal in 11 games?

7 Which former Newcastle United player scored the winner for his new club on his return to St James' Park?

8 Who scored two goals for Liverpool in their 3-1 defeat of Leeds United at Anfield?

9 Which Newcastle United midfielder was sent off in their defeat at Derby?

10 Which Coventry City player was sent off in their 1-0 defeat at West Ham?

11 From which Dutch club did Coventry sign George Boateng?

12 Who scored the winner for West Ham United against Coventry City?

13 Which Leicester City player scored an own goal against Arsenal at Highbury?

14 Who scored twice in Aston Villa's 4-1 defeat of Tottenham Hotspur?

15 Which Premiership club unveiled a £42 million plan to increase their capacity to 51,000?

THE CARLING ULTIMATE FOOTBALL FACT AND QUIZ BOOK

Quiz 10

SEASON 1997-1998

January 1998

1 Where did Manchester United lose for the first time in eight years?

2 Who scored a hat trick for Everton against Bolton Wanderers?

3 Who scored twice for Liverpool at St James' Park?

4 Which Wimbledon player was sent off after two minutes for elbowing West Ham United's Paul Kitson in the face?

5 Which Wimbledon player scored an own goal against West Ham United?

6 What was the name of Christian Gross's fitness coach, to whom the Department of Employment refused a work permit?

7 Which non-League side did West Ham United beat in the Third Round of the FA Cup?

8 In the Third Round of the FA Cup, which Premiership side won 3-1 at Anfield?

9 What was the final score in the FA Cup Third Round tie between Chelsea and Manchester United?

10 Who scored Newcastle United's FA Cup Third Round winner against Everton?

11 Which relegation-threatened Premiership club took on Tomas Brolin?

12 Who missed a penalty for West Ham in their Coca-Cola Cup defeat by Arsenal?

13 Who did Chelsea knock out of the Coca-Cola Cup on penalties?

14 Apart from Arsenal and Chelsea, who were the other two Coca-Cola Cup semi-finalists?

15 Where did Newcastle United not want to play their FA Cup Fourth Round tie?

---

1 Coventry City 2 Duncan Ferguson 3 Steve McManaman 4 Ben Thatcher 5 Alan Kimble 6 Fritz Schmidt 7 Emley 8 Coventry City 9 Chelsea 3 Manchester United 5 10 Ian Rush 11 Crystal Palace 12 John Hartson 13 Ipswich Town 14 Liverpool and Middlesbrough 15 Stevenage Borough

Answers

THE CARLING ULTIMATE FOOTBALL FACT AND QUIZ BOOK

Quiz 11
SEASON 1997-1998

1 Who came on as substitute and scored two goals for Chelsea against Coventry City?

2 Who scored two goals for West Ham United in their 6-0 defeat of Barnsley?

3 Who scored two goals for Wimbledon in their 3-2 FA Cup victory at Wrexham?

4 Who scored a hat trick for Blackburn Rovers in their 5-0 defeat of Aston Villa?

5 Which Aston Villa forward was put on the transfer list after allegedly spitting at a group of his club's fans?

6 Which referee did Coventry City manager Gordon Strachan describe as 'a disgrace'?

7 Who scored the only goal of the Tottenham Hotspur v West Ham United game?

8 Which West Ham United player was sent off after clashing with Ramon Vega of Tottenham Hotspur?

9 Who scored the winner for Southampton against Manchester United?

10 Who was charged by the FA with having taken a bung in 1989?

11 Who took over in goal for Arsenal when David Seaman was injured?

12 Who missed a penalty for Manchester City in their FA Cup Fourth Round defeat by West Ham United?

13 Which Manchester City old boy scored West Ham's winner in the FA Cup at Maine Road?

14 Which Liverpool forward was reported to have asked for £50,000 a week?

15 Who did West Ham United buy from Queen's Park Rangers?

13 Steve Lomas 14 Robbie Fowler 15 Trevor Sinclair
7 Jurgen Klinsmann 8 Samassi Abou 9 Kevin Davies 10 Brian Clough 11 Alex Manninger 12 Uwe Rosler
1 Mark Nicholls 2 Samassi Abou 3 Michael Hughes 4 Kevin Gallacher 5 Savo Milosevic 6 Steve Lodge

Answers

THE CARLING ULTIMATE FOOTBALL FACT AND QUIZ BOOK

Quiz 12

SEASON 1997-1998

February 1998

1 Who scored Leicester City's winner at Old Trafford?

2 Which Tottenham Hotspur player had his jaw broken at Oakwell in the FA Cup?

3 Who did Newcastle United buy from Everton?

4 Who scored a penalty for Leicester City against Leeds United?

5 Who missed a penalty for Leeds United against Leicester City?

6 Who scored twice for Arsenal in their Premiership defeat of Chelsea?

7 Who scored both goals for Chile in their friendly victory over England at Wembley?

8 Who was sacked as manager of Chelsea?

9 Who scored a hat trick for Liverpool to win them a point at Hillsborough?

10 Who scored Arsenal's winner against Crystal Palace at Highbury?

11 Which referee was dropped for a match after being criticised for his handling of the Chelsea v Arsenal Coca-Cola Cup semi-final?

12 Whose season was ended by an injury sustained in the Merseyside derby?

13 Who resigned as manager of Aston Villa?

14 Who scored the last penalty in the Fifth Round FA Cup shoot-out between Blackburn Rovers and West Ham United?

15 Who took over as manager of Aston Villa?

Quiz 13
SEASON 1997-1998

March 1998

1 Where did Manchester United's Philip Neville score the first goal of his professional career?

2 Who scored a hat trick for Blackburn Rovers against Leicester City?

3 Who scored twice for Aston Villa on his return to his previous club?

4 Which Southampton defender was sent off on his return to one of his previous clubs, Leeds United?

5 Who scored twice for Barnsley in their defeat of Wimbledon?

6 Who scored Tottenham Hotspur's winner against Bolton Wanderers?

7 What was the score in the first leg of the European Cup match between Monaco and Manchester United?

8 Whose goal for Leeds United beat Tottenham Hotspur in the Premiership?

9 Who scored twice for Chelsea in the European Cup Winners' Cup quarter-final first leg at Real Betis?

10 Which Everton defender was sent off for the third time this season at Southampton?

11 Who scored on his Arsenal debut against Wimbledon?

12 Who scored Arsenal's winner at Old Trafford?

13 Which two Newcastle United directors made disparaging remarks about the club's fans?

14 Who knocked Aston Villa out of the UEFA Cup on the away goals rule?

15 Who scored for West Ham United and then gave away a penalty as his team drew 1-1 draw at Highbury in the FA Cup Sixth Round?

THE CARLING ULTIMATE FOOTBALL FACT AND QUIZ BOOK

Quiz 14
SEASON 1997-1998

1 Which Arsenal player was sent off for elbowing West Ham United captain Steve Lomas in the face in the FA Cup Sixth Round replay?

2 What nationality is Arsenal reserve goalkeeper Alex Manninger?

3 Who knocked Coventry City out of the FA Cup in the Sixth Round on penalties?

4 Who scored the away goal in the second leg of the European Cup tie between Manchester United and Monaco?

5 Who equalised for Manchester United against Monaco?

6 Which Premiership club ended a run of eight consecutive defeats at Newcastle United?

7 What was the score in the second leg of Chelsea's European Cup Winners' Cup tie against Real Betis?

8 Who took over from Freddy Shepherd as chairman of Newcastle United?

9 Which Middlesbrough player scored in the Switzerland v England friendly international?

10 Which Tottenham Hotspur player scored in the Switzerland v England friendly international?

11 Whose goal enabled Everton to beat Blackburn Rovers?

12 Who scored a penalty for Bolton Wanderers in their 3-2 defeat of Sheffield Wednesday?

13 Who scored for Manchester United in their 1-1 draw at West Ham?

14 Which Barnsley player was sent off in the FA Cup tie at Newcastle United?

15 Who won 5-0 away at Pride Park?

THE CARLING ULTIMATE FOOTBALL FACT AND QUIZ BOOK

Quiz 15
SEASON 1997-1998

April 1998

1 Which Premiership club had Barnard, Morgan and Sheridan sent off in a single game?

2 Who scored Chelsea's first goal in the Coca-Cola Cup Final against Middlesbrough?

3 Who scored Chelsea's second goal in the Coca-Cola Cup Final against Middlesbrough?

4 From which airport were the Leeds United team booked to fly home after their match at West Ham United?

5 Who set a Premiership record by going eight consecutive matches without conceding a goal?

6 Who beat Chelsea 1-0 in the first leg of the European Cup Winners' Cup semi-final?

7 Who scored Arsenal's winner in the FA Cup semi-final against Wolverhampton Wanderers?

8 Who gave Manchester United the lead against Liverpool on Good Friday?

9 Who equalised for Liverpool against Manchester United and hen got himself sent off?

10 Which Newcastle United defender became the first player to score against Arsenal for 13 hours 43 minutes?

11 Who scored two goals for Arsenal against Newcastle United?

12 Who scored both goals for Leicester City in their 2-1 defeat of Crystal Palace?

13 Who scored his tenth goal of the season for Everton in their 2-0 win over Leeds United?

14 During the game at Everton, which Leeds United player was carried off and sent off simultaneously?

15 Which West Ham player ensured that he would miss him team's run-in by getting himself sent off against Derby County?

Answers

1 Barnsley **2** Frank Sinclair **3** Roberto Di Matteo **4** Stansted **5** Arsenal **6** Vicenza **7** Christopher Wreh **8** Ronnie Johnsen **9** Michael Owen **10** Warren Barton **11** Nicolas Anelka **12** Emile Heskey **13** Duncan Ferguson **14** Lucas Radebe **15** John Hartson

THE CARLING ULTIMATE FOOTBALL FACT AND QUIZ BOOK

Quiz 16
SEASON 1997-1998

1 Who scored Wimbledon's winner at Southampton?

2 Who scored two goals for Arsenal at Blackburn Rovers on Easter Monday?

3 Who scored his first goal for Liverpool against Crystal Palace?

4 Who scored Chelsea's first goal in the second leg of their European Cup Winners' Cup semi-final against Vicenza?

5 Who scored Chelsea's second goal in the second leg of their European Cup Winners' Cup semi-final against Vicenza?

6 Who scored Chelsea's third goal in the second leg of their European Cup Winners' Cup semi-final against Vicenza?

7 Who would Chelsea face in the European Cup Winners' Cup Final?

8 Which Manchester United player was sent off as they drew at home with Newcastle United?

9 Which Tottenham Hotspur player was sent off as they drew away at Barnsley?

10 Who did Crystal Palace beat to record their first home victory of the season?

11 Who scored with a penalty for Chelsea at Hillsborough?

12 Who scored a hat trick in the England B international against Russia?

13 What was the final score in the England B international against Russia?

14 Who scored twice for England against Portugal?

15 What was the final score in the England v Portugal friendly international?

Answers

1 Carl Leaburn **2** Ray Parlour **3** David Thompson **4** Gustavo Poyet **5** Gianfranco Zola
6 Mark Hughes **7** Stuttgart **8** Ole Gunnar Solskjaer **9** Ramon Vega **10** Derby County **11** Frank Leboeuf
12 Matthew Le Tissier **13** England 4 Russia 1 **14** Alan Shearer **15** England 3 Portugal 0

THE CARLING ULTIMATE FOOTBALL FACT AND QUIZ BOOK

Quiz 17
SEASON 1997-1998

May 1998

1 What was the nationality of both scorers for Arsenal in their 2-0 victory at Barnsley?

2 Who scored two goals for Leeds United in their 3-3 draw with Coventry City at Elland Road?

3 Who scored a hat trick for Coventry City in their 3-3 draw at Elland Road?

4 Who scored twice for Sheffield Wednesday in their 3-1 win at Everton?

5 Which team set a new Premiership record of nine consecutive victories?

6 Who won both the PFA and the Football Writers' Footballer of the Year awards?

7 Who scored four times for Tottenham Hotspur against Wimbledon?

8 Who scored two goals for Liverpool in their 5-0 defeat of West Ham United?

9 Against which club did Arsenal clinch the Championship?

10 Who scored two goals for Arsenal in this match?

11 Which Leeds United player was sent off in their 3-0 defeat at Old Trafford?

12 Which West ham United player was sent off in their 3-3 draw at Crystal Palace?

13 Who scored twice for West Ham United in their 3-3 draw at Crystal Palace?

14 Which two good and faithful servants of Tottenham Hotspur were given free transfers at the end of the season?

15 Who did Manchester United sign from PSV Eindhoven?

THE CARLING ULTIMATE FOOTBALL FACT AND QUIZ BOOK

Quiz 18
SEASON 1997-1998

1 Who scored a penalty for Aston Villa against Arsenal?

2 Who scored twice for Leicester City on his return to Upton Park?

3 Who scored the goal with which Derby County beat Liverpool?

4 Who scored on his debut for Crystal Palace against Sheffield Wednesday?

5 Who scored for Tottenham Hotspur in the 1-1 draw with Southampton?

6 Who scored for Southampton in the 1-1 draw with Tottenham Hotspur?

7 Whose penalty for Everton was saved in their last match of the season at home to Coventry City?

8 Who saved it?

9 Who put Everton ahead in this match?

10 Who equalised for Coventry City?

11 Where was the European Cup Winners' Cup Final held?

12 Who came on as substitute less than a minute before scoring the winner for Chelsea in the European Cup Winners' Cup Final?

13 Who did Arsenal beat in the FA Cup Final to complete the Double?

14 Charlton Athletic won the 1998 First Division play-off Final, beating Sunderland 7-6 on penalties after the match had been drawn 4-4 after extra time. Who scored a hat-trick for Charlton?

15 Which Sunderland player had his penalty saved in the 1998 First Division play-off Final?

Answers

1 Dwight Yorke **2** Tony Cottee **3** Paulo Wanchope **4** Clinton Morrison **5** Jurgen Klinsmann **6** Matthew Le Tissier **7** Nick Barmby **8** Magnus Hedman **9** Gareth Farrelly **10** Dion Dublin **11** Stockholm **12** Gianfranco Zola **13** Newcastle United **14** Clive Mendonca **15** Michael Gray

Quiz 19

SEASON 1997-1998

The Final Reckoning

1 Which two teams qualified for the 1998-99 Champions' League?

2 Which three teams were relegated from the Premiership?

3 Which club escaped relegation from the Premiership only on goal difference?

4 Which four teams qualified for the 1998-99 UEFA Cup?

5 Which club would represent England in the 1998-99 European Cup Winners' Cup?

6 Which Premiership club just missed out on a UEFA Cup place?

7 Which club won the First Division Championship?

8 Which club finished second in the First Division, thus winning automatic promotion to the Premiership?

9 Which three clubs were relegated from the First Division?

10 Which club won the Second Division Championship?

11 Which club won automatic promotion after finishing second in the Second Division?

12 Which club won the Second Division play-off final?

13 Which four teams were relegated from the Second Division?

14 Which club won the Third Division Championship?

15 Which two clubs also won automatic promotion from the Third Division?

Answers

1 Arsenal and Manchester United 2 Bolton Wanderers, Barnsley and Crystal Palace 3 Everton 4 Liverpool, Leeds United, Blackburn Rovers and Aston Villa 5 Chelsea 6 West Ham United 7 Nottingham Forest 8 Middlesbrough 9 Manchester City, Stoke City and Reading 10 Watford 11 Bristol City 12 Grimsby Town 13 Brentford, Plymouth Argyle, Carlisle United and Southend United 14 Notts County 15 Macclesfield Town and Lincoln City

THE CARLING ULTIMATE FOOTBALL FACT AND QUIZ BOOK

Quiz 20
SEASON 1997-1998

1 Which club won the Third Division play-off final?

2 Which club came bottom of the Third Division and were relegated to the GM Vauxhall Conference?

3 Which Third Division club had three League points deducted for fielding ineligible players?

4 Who was the Premiership's leading scorer, with 25 goals in all competitions?

5 Who was the Premiership's second leading scorer, with 24 goals in all competitions?

6 Who were the Premiership's joint third leading scorers, with 23 goals each in all competitions?

7 Who scored 22 goals in all competitions for Leeds United?

8 Who scored 22 goals in all competitions for Arsenal?

9 Who scored 21 goals in all competitions for Blackburn Rovers?

10 Who scored 20 goals in all competitions for Blackburn Rovers?

11 Who scored 19 goals in all competitions for Chelsea?

12 Who scored 17 goals in all competitions for Derby County?

13 Who became the all-time leading scorer in the Premiership?

14 Two players scored 11 goals for Southampton; one was Matthew Le Tissier – who was the other?

15 With 10 goals in all competitions, who was the leading scorer for relegated Barnsley?

Answers

1 Colchester United 2 Doncaster Rovers 3 Leyton Orient 4 Andy Cole 5 John Hartson 6 Dion Dublin and Michael Owen 7 Jimmy Floyd Hasselbaink 8 Dennis Bergkamp 9 Chris Sutton 10 Kevin Gallacher 11 Gianluca Vialli 12 Paulo Wanchope 13 Andy Cole 14 Egil Ostenstad 15 Neil Redfearn

SONGS AND CHANTS

THE CARLING ULTIMATE FOOTBALL FACT AND QUIZ BOOK

SONGS & CHANTS

1 According to the song, who do Everton supporters hate even more than Bill Shankly and St John?

2 Complete the missing name in the following Brighton and Hove Albion song to the tune 'The Quartermaster's Stores': *'He's shot, he's scored, It must be _____'.*

3 When Reading fans sang *'Trevor, Trevor, he's our man, If he can't do it, no one can'*, who was Trevor?

4 At Wycombe Wanderers, if Noel Ashford was God, who was Jesus?

5 Between 1991 and 1994, fans of which team described themselves as *'Peter Eustace's red, white and black / With a stupid yellow number on the back Army'*?

6 Fans of which team sing the following words to the tune of the Mary Hopkin hit: *'Those were the days my friend, / We thought they'd never end, / We won the League three times in a row…'*?

7 Whose fans sing the following – more in hope than expectation – to the tune of 'Halls of Montezuma': *'From the banks of the River Ouse, / To the shores of Sicily, / We'll fight, fight, fight for City, / 'Til we win the Football League'*?

8 Who are Manchester United fans referring to in their version of 'Lily The Pink' with the words: *'We'll drink a drink a drink To Denis the king, the king the king'*?

9 In 1983, to which unpopular manager were Preston North End fans referring when they sang this, to the tune of 'Save Your Kisses For Me': *'We've just lost eight on the bounce, / We've just lost eight on the bounce, / Bye bye Gordon, bye bye'*?

10 Fans of which team sing a version of 'The Twelve Days of Christmas' in which every present is a number of pints of Bass?

11 In the West Bromwich Albion version of 'One Man Went To Mow', which team do they recommend you visit when they sing: *'If you like kick and rush, / Played by dumb gorillas, / Don't waste your time at the Albion…'*?

12 In the 1986-87 season, when Yogi went to Scarborough (vandal, vandal), which team's colours was he wearing?

13 Identify the Wolverhampton players in the following song: *'Aye aye aye aye, Parkes is better than Yashin, / And Ernie is better than Eusebio, / And we'll give the Baggies a thrashin''.*

14 Fans of which club sing: *'I can't read, I can't write, / But that don't really matter, / 'Cause I come from the West Country / And I can drive a tractor'*?

15 Whose fans sing the following, to the tune of 'Dirty Old Town': *'I watch my team from the Crispin End, / Under the old Bushfield Stand'*?

---

13 Phil Parkes and Ernie Hunt **14** Exeter City **15** Wrexham
7 York City **8** Denis Law **9** Gordon Lee **10** Port Vale **11** Aston Villa **12** Wolverhampton Wanderers
1 Big Ron (Yeats) **2** Peter Ward **3** Trevor Senior **4** Dave Carroll **5** Leyton Orient **6** Huddersfield Town

Answers

THE CARLING ULTIMATE FOOTBALL FACT AND QUIZ BOOK

SONGS & CHANTS

1 To which tune do football fans sing *'You're supposed to be at home'*?

2 Which group had a 1980 hit with 'Oops Up Side Your Head', the tune to which *'Ooh aah Cantona'* and similar lyrics have been set?

3 To which tune, written by whom, do football fans sing: *'We hate Nottingham Forest, / We hate Liverpool too, / We hate West Ham United, / [fill in as applicable] we love you'*?

4 Give the title and composer of the tune to which football fans sing *''Ere we go, 'Ere we go, 'Ere we go'*, and *'Wember-ley Wember-ley Wember-ley'*?

5 To which tune do football fans sing *'You're not very good'*?

6 Which Scottish team are described in song as *'the heavenly dancers, Superb in attack and defence'*?

7 Supporters of which Scottish team sing 'The Soldier's Song'?

8 *'Sure you boast of your famous inventors, / And you sing of the land of the free, / But my song it concerns a centre, / Who played for the Celtic FC'* – who?

9 Which club's supporters particularly greet Cowdenbeath with the song: *'They come from near Lochgelly, / They have nae got a telly, \ They're dirty and they're smelly, \ The Cowden family'*?

10 Supporters of which club sing *'The sash my father wore'*?

11 Which group first had a hit with 'Daydream Believer', the song on which Sunderland's *'Cheer Up Peter Reid'* is based?

12 In the 1960s, which club's fans sang the following, to the tune 'Onward Christian Soldiers': *'Crawford is our leader, / Billy is our king, / Listen to the North Stand, \ Listen to them sing'*?

13 Complete the missing name in the Derby County song: *'The Villa fans will never mock, When they remember _____.*

14 Which former Nottingham Forest player's confidence was undermined by chants about his hairstyle which suggested he had *'a pineapple on his head'*?

15 Where do they go *'Boing!'*?

THE CARLING ULTIMATE FOOTBALL FACT AND QUIZ BOOK

Quiz 1
WHO SAID THAT?

1 Commenting on the 1998 World Cup finals, who said: 'The good news for Nigeria is that they're two-nil down very early in the game' – Ron Atkinson, Kevin Keegan or Brian Moore?

2 Commenting on the 1998 World Cup finals, who said: 'Batistuta gets most of his goals with the ball' – Jimmy Hill, Ian St John or Martin O'Neill ?

3 Commenting on the 1998 World Cup finals, who said: 'I wouldn't be surprised if this game went all the way to the finish' – Peter Drury, Ian St John or John Champion?

4 Commenting on the 1998 World Cup finals, which former England manager said: 'Apart from their goals, Norway haven't scored' – Bobby Robson, Graham Taylor or Terry Venables?

5 Commenting on the 1998 World Cup finals, which former England manager said: 'He never fails to hit the target. But that was a miss' – Bobby Robson, Graham Taylor or Terry Venables?

6 Commenting on the 1998 World Cup finals, which former Newcastle star said: 'Chile have three options – they could win or they could lose' – Kevin Keegan, Terry McDermott or Barry Venison?

7 Commenting on the 1998 World Cup finals, which former Newcastle United star said: 'That would have been a goal if the goalkeeper hadn't saved it' – Kevin Keegan, Malcolm Macdonald or Barry Venison?

8 Commenting on the 1998 World Cup finals, which cosmopolitan former England player said: 'I came to Nantes two years ago and it's much the same today, except that it's completely different' – Glenn Hoddle, Kevin Keegan or Ray Wilkins?

9 Commenting on the 1998 World Cup finals, which former Manchester United supremo said: 'They've picked their heads up off the ground and they now have a lot to carry on their shoulders' – Ron Atkinson, Tommy Docherty or Alex Ferguson?

10 Commenting on the 1998 World Cup finals, which philosopher with an Old Trafford connection said: 'Well, either side could win it, or it could be a draw' – Ron Atkinson, Eric Cantona or Lee Sharpe?

11 Commenting on the 1998 World Cup finals, which former Spurs manager said: 'Pires has got something about him – he can go both ways, depending on who's facing him' – Terry Neill, David Pleat or Terry Venables?

12 Commenting on the 1998 World Cup finals, which ex-footballer once famous for his hair style said: 'The Croatians don't play well without the ball' – Kevin Keegan, Chris Waddle or Barry Venison?

13 Commenting on the 1998 World Cup finals, which TV man said: 'It had to go in, but it didn't' – Peter Drury, Brian Moore or John Motson?

14 Commenting on the 1998 World Cup finals, which TV man said: 'That's lifted the crowd right up into the air' – Barry Davies, Brian Moore or John Motson?

15 Commenting on the 1998 World Cup Final in Paris, France, which Scotsman said: 'I've got a frog in my throat' – Graeme Souness, Ally McCoist or Alex Ferguson?

Answers

1 Kevin Keegan **2** Ian St John **3** Ian St John **4** Terry Venables **5** Bobby Robson **6** Kevin Keegan **7** Kevin Keegan **8** Kevin Keegan **9** Ron Atkinson **10** Ron Atkinson **11** David Pleat **12** Barry Venison **13** Peter Drury **14** Barry Davies **15** Ally McCoist

THE CARLING ULTIMATE FOOTBALL FACT AND QUIZ BOOK

Quiz 2
WHO SAID THAT?

1 Which footballing philosopher and theologian said: 'Okay, so we lost, but good things can come from it – negative and positive' – Glenn Hoddle, Kevin Keegan or Dave Sexton?

2 Which thinker of the commentary box said: 'I've had this sneaking feeling throughout the game that it's there to be won' – Ron Atkinson, Andy Gray or Trevor Brooking?

3 Which former England manager taught us: 'This game's about winning and losing – and if you win, that means you've beaten someone' – Bobby Robson, Glenn Hoddle or Graham Taylor?

4 Which great football administrator said: 'We have more non-English players in our League than any other country in the world' – David Davies, Graham Kelly or Gordon Taylor?

5 Which former Wales manager spoke of 'the most humiliating feeling you could ever wish for' – Bobby Gould, John Toshack or Terry Yorath?

6 Which commentator, with the carefully rehearsed spontaneity that has become his trademark, said: 'It's a one-man show, except there are two men involved – Hartson and Berkovic – and a third man, the goalkeeper?'

7 Which of Arsène Wenger's former acolytes praised the Gallic sage for giving him 'unbelievable belief' – Christopher Wreh, Paul Merson or Ian Wright?

8 Which former Southampton supremo said 'Kevin Keegan has now tasted the other side of the fence' – Ted Bates, Lawrie McMenemy or Dave Merrington?

9 Which great poet gave us: 'You wonder if the sands of time are catching up with them' – Omar Khayyam, Percy Bysshe Shelley or Kevin Keegan?

10 Which television commentator painted the dazzling picture evoked by the words: 'Seaman, like a falling oak, manages to change direction' – John Champion, John Motson or Gerald Sinstadt?

11 Who, according to Neil Webb, gave England's 1998 World Cup squad 'a shoulder to talk to'?

12 Who said, incredibly: 'There was only one team in the world I would have moved to after Benfica, and that team is West Ham'?

13 Who said: 'Eyal's a friend and a quality player'?

14 Which Premiership manager wrote in his 1998 autobiography: 'David Mellor is someone I'd happily take a swing at'?

15 Which Cottager said: 'You can't do better than go away from home and get a draw' – Mohamed Al Fayed, Kevin Keegan or Tommy Trinder?

Answers

1 Glenn Hoddle 2 Ron Atkinson 3 Graham Taylor 4 Gordon Taylor 5 Bobby Gould 6 John Motson 7 Ian Wright 8 Dave Merrington 9 Kevin Keegan 10 John Motson 11 Eileen Drewery 12 Scott Minto 13 John Hartson 14 Harry Redknapp 15 Kevin Keegan

THE CARLING ULTIMATE FOOTBALL FACT AND QUIZ BOOK

Quiz 3
WHO SAID THAT?

1 Which agent said: 'I have no morals when it comes to dealing with my clients'?

2 Who said to his team at the start of extra time in a European Cup Final, 'If you pass the ball to each other, you will beat them'?

3 Who, on being criticised by Matt Busby, told him: 'Make me captain and I'll be responsible'?

4 Who said, on leaving Manchester United: 'I have been sacked for falling in love'?

5 Who, on taking stick from Sunderland supporters for not agreeing to a proposed transfer from East Anglia to Wearside, said: 'Just because I'm a professional doesn't mean I'm not a human being'?

6 Who told Margaret Thatcher: 'These people are society's problems and we don't want your hooligans at our sport'?

7 Which footballer and supposed polymath said: 'An artist, in my eyes, is someone who can lighten up a darkened room'?

8 Who said: 'It meant more for the Scots to beat the English than it did for the English to beat the Scots'?

9 Who said: 'Football is not really about winning or goals or saves or supporters – it's about glory'?

10 Who said of Osvaldo Ardiles: 'It was like trying to tackle dust'?

11 Complete the missing name in this quotation from Hungarian International Ferenc Puskas: 'I remember that as a boy there was only one club for me – -------'.

12 Who said, after saving a penalty in an FA Cup Final: 'I was a bit disappointed. I should have caught it really'?

13 Which Bolton Wanderers defender allegedly told Chelsea winger Peter Brabrook: 'If thou tries to get past me, lad, thou will get gravel rash'?

14 Who said: 'No matter what I do in life I will never find anything to match scoring goals... Goals were like a drug'?

15 Who said: 'The Villa chairman, Doug Ellis, said he was right behind me. I told him I'd sooner have him in front of me where I could see him'?

Answers

1 Eric Hall 2 Matt Busby 3 George Best 4 Tommy Docherty 5 Mick Mills (Ipswich Town) 6 Ted Croker
7 Eric Cantona 8 Bobby Charlton 9 Danny Blanchflower 10 Joe Royle 11 Arsenal 12 Dave Beasant
13 Tommy Banks 14 Brian Clough 15 Tommy Docherty

THE CARLING ULTIMATE FOOTBALL FACT AND QUIZ BOOK

WHO SAID THAT?

1 When asked to agree to replaying his club's FA Cup tie with Sheffield United away at Bramall Lane, rather than at home, who said: 'We have a fair spirit but we're not stupid'?

2 Who said: 'We've had our first bad month for two years and suddenly the world's at an end, I'm no good at my job and everybody else is crap'?

3 Who said of his charges at Coventry: 'I love these players. I feel like going around each of them and tucking them in'?

4 On coming back from a trip to New York, which Aston Villa player said: 'No one has spoken to me since I returned and I don't need that'?

5 Who said: 'You and I have been given two hands, two legs and a half-decent brain. Some people have not been born like that for a reason'?

6 Which Scouser said: 'I hope the fans can see that I am only looking to improve myself'?

7 Which manager said: 'I don't know if the players lack confidence – they don't seem to lack it when they ask for a new contract'?

8 Who said of Kevin Keegan: 'He will not be able to leave us. He loves Fulham, he is married to Fulham and he will not be able to divorce us'?

9 Who explained his struggling team's victory at high-flying Bolton with the words: 'I always say we have a better chance of scoring when the ball is in the opposition box'?

10 Who said: 'Paolo is a big friend, a big player. But he had to go'?

11 Who said, on being appointed Southampton manager: 'I can always remember as a player and as a manager that I never used to like coming here much. That's what I want to carry on doing'?

12 When asked if he had any special pre-match rituals or superstitions, who replied: 'I always touch my right testicle 70 times'?

13 Who said: 'Andy should be hitting the target from those distances, but I'm not going to single anyone out'?

14 Who said: 'I have told the team that if we don't give away a goal, we don't lose'?

15 Who said: 'They raised their game because they were playing Manchester United – it's pathetic'?

WHO SAID THAT?

1 Who said: 'I'm not some crackpot who comes out with stupid remarks to cause controversy'?

2 Who said 'I am not a clown' and then, after Nottingham Forest lost 8-1 at home to Manchester United: 'I told you it was going to be a nine-goal thriller'?

3 Who said: 'I do not condone violence and wholeheartedly support the peace process in Northern Ireland' – Paul Gascoigne, Andy Goram or Marco Negri?

4 After four men had been caught trying to tamper with the floodlights at the Valley, which FA bigwig said: 'The integrity of the game is crucial to us all'?

5 After two of his players had been sent off against Bournemouth, which Second Division manager said: 'There must have been a rule change I missed. We had one player booked for aggressive walking'?

6 Of whom did Nicolas Anelka say: 'He plays only for himself and will never give me a ball I can score from'?

7 Which manager, sympathising with Glenn Hoddle, said: 'He was sacked for his beliefs. Still, 500 years ago, you could be burned at the stake for that'?

8 Which manager said of his trip to Highbury: 'It was the most bitter moment of my career. We felt cheated'?

9 Which FA bigwig said of Kevin Keegan's appointment as England manager: 'We have the nation's choice leading the country in some crucial matches'?

10 Which of the FA's former bigwigs said 'I don't want to say whether I resigned or was asked to resign. I'm certainly not going to skulk out of the back door'?

11 Who said: 'The existing four-yearly [World Cup] tournament is out of date. It dates from the 1930s when teams chugged from one continent to another on ships'?

12 Who was alledgedly described as 'a cannibal' by Trabozonspor chairman Mehmet Ali Yilmaz?

13 Who said: 'When you get used to caviare, it is difficult to come back to sausages'?

14 Who said: 'The referee was absolute bobbins'?

15 Who said: 'I'm being highlighted in an investigation I know nothing about. I want answers'?

Answers

1 Glenn Hoddle **2** Ron Atkinson **3** Andy Goram **4** David Davies **5** Joe Royle **6** Marc Overmars **7** Arsène Wenger **8** Steve Bruce (Sheffield United) **9** David Davies **10** Graham Kelly **11** Sepp Blatter **12** Kevin Campbell **13** Arsène Wenger **14** Southampton manager Dave Jones **15** Terry Venables

THE CARLING ULTIMATE FOOTBALL FACT AND QUIZ BOOK

Quiz 6
WHO SAID THAT?

1 Which manager said: 'It's easy to get to Ireland – it's just a straight walk across the Irish Sea as far as I'm concerned'?

2 Which Stoke City manager said: 'It is the unexpected that excites people, and players, not coaches, provide that'?

3 Who said: 'That's the story of my managerial life – buy in Woolworth's sell in Harrods'?

4 Who said: 'I am very strong-willed. People don't understand that. They think that, with that touch and flair, I'd have to be soft'?

5 Who said: 'Things are never as good as they seem when you are winning and never as bad as they seem when you are losing'?

6 Which manager said: 'I've never mastered the trick of pleasing the eight lads I have to leave out every Saturday'?

7 Who said: 'Look at Jesus. He was just an ordinary, run-of-the-mill sort of guy who had a genuine gift, just as Eileen has'?

8 Which Ranger told Willie Woodburn: 'The man who never made a mistake never made anything'?

9 Which Notts County boss said: 'The best team always wins. The rest is only gossip'?

10 Which coach said of his 1998 finalists: 'We are the Cinderellas of the World Cup. Our mission is to postpone midnight for as long as possible'?

11 Which Raith Rovers manager said of his team's 1994 victory in the Scottish League Cup Final: 'This would bring a tear to a glass eye'?

12 Which Tottenham Hotspur manager said: 'I prefer players not to be too clever at other things. It means they concentrate on football'?

13 Who said of Jason Lee: 'He's got to learn to take some stick. If he doesn't like it there are two ways to cure it. Either he gets his hair cut or he scores more goals'?

14 Which Oldham Athletic manager celebrated a draw at QPR with the words: 'Normally the only thing we get out of London is the train from Euston'?

15 Who said: 'I call myself Big 'Ead to remind myself not to be one'?

THE CARLING ULTIMATE FOOTBALL FACT AND QUIZ BOOK

Quiz 7
WHO SAID THAT?

1 Who said: 'Them discussions are the things that go on time and again in every dressing room'?

2 Who said of whom: 'He took about three or four steps before falling over in a rather strange way. To me it looked like someone who was acting'?

3 Who said: 'Wor kid was a much better player but I am a much better bloke'?

4 Who said: 'I always thought golf was a poof's game. Now I like it more than football'?

5 Which interested English club manager said of Ajax's Ronald de Boer said: 'If the tribunal allows him to break his contract, it is the beginning of the end. If the fans think all the players are interested in is the money they will lose heart and the clubs will lose identity'?

6 Who said: 'I'm not prepared to let my career go down the pan. Right now the team is not good enough to survive in the Premiership'?

7 During the 1998 World Cup finals in France, which Tory MP said: 'If you are tough looking and wearing an English flag, the police target you. That is a compliment to English martial spirit'?

8 During the 1998 World Cup finals in France, which great punster said: 'We're in Toulouse and both teams have got a lot to lose' – Kevin Keegan, Vic Reeves or Tom Stoppard?

9 In 1998, which Premiership manager correctly predicted that Israel would win the Eurovision Song Contest?

10 Who said, on being sacked as manager of Sheffield Wednesday: 'I have been let down savagely and sadly by weak men I feel should have been stronger'?

11 Who said: 'I though Christians were supposed to forgive people for their sins but that doesn't seem to be the case with me'?

12 Complete the following quotation: 'My name is Ally MacLeod and I am a born…'

13 Who described Manchester City as 'a massive club. It's just a little bit sickly'?

14 Who said, on turning down Dion Dublin's wage demands: 'The game is suffering from a form of diarrhoea where increasing amounts of money from television and larger crowds goes straight … into the players' pockets'?

15 Who said, on paying £2500 for a pair of boots: 'The problem is not just that I am flat-footed. I also have particularly wide feet'?

Answers

1 Glenn Hoddle **2** Paolo Di Canio of Paul Alcock **3** Jack Charlton **4** Julian Dicks **5** Arsène Wenger **6** Pierre van Hooijdonk of Nottingham Forest **7** Alan Clark **8** Kevin Keegan **9** Harry Redknapp (West Ham United) **10** Ron Atkinson **11** Chris Sutton **12** Winner **13** Joe Royle **14** Bryan Richardson **15** Stan Collymore

THE CARLING ULTIMATE FOOTBALL FACT AND QUIZ BOOK

WHO SAID THAT?

1 Which of his own team mates Manchester City manager said: 'I felt like the garrison commander at Rorke's Drift when the Zulus came pouring over the hill'?

2 Which Manchester City manager said: 'It won't be the end of the world if we lose, but it will be close to that'?

3 Which of the club's caretaker managers said: 'Watching Manchester City is the best laxative you can take'?

4 Which Manchester City manager said: 'Right now, if I robbed a bank I'd get mugged on the way out'?

5 Who said: 'The three toughest jobs are football management, lion taming and mountain rescue – in that order'?

6 Who said: 'I wanted to be England manager but I swear too much'?

7 Who said – although he subsequently denied it – 'I am looking forward to seeing some sexy football'?

8 Which Stockport County manager promised to give a referee 'what we got from him – a big fat zero'?

9 Which national coach said (in German): 'If I walked on water they would say it was only because I can't swim'?

10 Who did Liverpool fans call 'Agent Johnson'?

11 Who said: 'I have told my players never to believe what I say about them in the papers'?

12 Who said: 'I do a column for one of the Irish papers but I can't remember its name'?

13 Who said: 'I see Atletico Madrid just sacked another manager before the season started. He must have had a bad photocall'?

14 Who said that the British media 'make from a little mosquito a big elephant'?

15 Who said: 'If Everton were playing down the bottom of my garden I'd draw the curtains'?

THE CARLING ULTIMATE FOOTBALL FACT AND QUIZ BOOK

WHO THE HELL ARE YOU?

1 Which current Blackburn Rovers and former Bolton and Liverpool player was born in Birkenhead on June 18, 1971?

2 Which Liverpool player was born in Dumfries on April 28, 1974?

3 Which player was born in Gabona (Ivory Coast) on April 4, 1973 and joined West Ham from Cannes in 1997?

4 Which England captain was born in Romford, Essex on October 10, 1966 and given the forenames Anthony Alexander?

5 Which Liverpool defender was born in Drogheda on January 19, 1969?

6 Which Premiership goalkeeper was born in St Austell, Cornwall on August 11, 1966?

7 Which captain of Northern Ireland was born in Hannover on January 18, 1974?

8 Which current Premiership player was born in Bouillon (Belgium) on August 10, 1968?

9 Which Southampton player was born in Necare, Surinam on November 29, 1964?

10 Which Arsenal player was born in Versailles on March 14, 1970?

11 Which Derby County striker was born in Birmingham on July 27, 1973, and has the middle name Constantine?

12 Which Sheffield Wednesday player was born in Vessigebro on December 29, 1971?

13 Which Wimbledon player has the middle name Winston?

14 Which Premiership player was born in Guernsey on October 14, 1968?

15 Which Sheffield United and former Manchester United defender was born on June 30, 1965 in Ramsgate?

Answers

1 Jason McAteer *2 Dominic Matteo* *3 Samassi Abou* *4 Tony Adams* *5 Steve Staunton* *6 Nigel Martyn*
7 Steve Lomas *8 Philippe Albert* *9 Ken Monkou* *10 Nicolas Anelka* *11 Dean Sturridge*
12 Niclas Alexandersson *13 Carl Leaburn* *14 Matthew Le Tissier* *15 Gary Pallister*

THE CARLING ULTIMATE FOOTBALL FACT AND QUIZ BOOK

Quiz 2

WHO THE HELL ARE YOU?

1 Which Tottenham Hotspur and England player was born in Southampton on March 3, 1972?

2 Which Tottenham Hotspur player was born in Newcastle on June 19, 1971 and began his League career at Wrexham?

3 Which English Chelsea player has the middle name Pierre?

4 Which Premiership goalkeeper was born in Oldenzaal on March 24, 1963?

5 Which Sheffield Wednesday defender was born in Orrell on April 6, 1970?

6 Which Chelsea player was born in Guadeloupe on May 11, 1971?

7 Which Nottingham Forest and former England defender was born in Rowley Regis on December 5, 1965 and has the middle name Lloyd?

8 Which Tottenham Hotspur player was born in San Rafael, California on December 7, 1977?

9 Which Everton player was born in Hull on February 11, 1974 and given the forenames Nicholas Jonathan?

10 Which Premiership Italian was born in Cremona on July 9, 1964?

11 Which Slovak was born on March 4, 1969 and plays for Middlesbrough?

12 Which Arsenal player was born in Dieppe on September 22, 1970?

13 Which former England international was born in Jamaica on November 7, 1963 and given the forenames John Charles Bryan?

14 Which international defender was born in Oxford on July 24, 1966?

15 Which Blackburn Rovers defender was born in Dublin on August 27, 1970?

Answers

1 Darren Anderton 2 Chris Armstrong 3 Graeme Le Saux 4 Raimond Van Der Gouw 5 Peter Atherton 6 Bernard Lambourde 7 Carlton Palmer 8 Espen Baardsen 9 Nick Barmby 10 Gianluca Vialli 11 Vladimir Kinder 12 Emmanuel Petit 13 John Barnes 14 Martin Keown 15 Jeff Kenna

THE CARLING ULTIMATE FOOTBALL FACT AND QUIZ BOOK

Quiz 3
WHO THE HELL ARE YOU?

1 Which French international in the Premiership was born in Dakar (Senegal) on June 23, 1976?

2 Which Sheffield Wednesday defender – formerly with Manchester City, Oldham Athletic, Aston Villa and Everton – has the middle name Delisser?

3 Born on June 16, 1974 in Sierra Leone, this player has the forenames Christopher Gerald – what is his double-barrelled surname?

4 Which Manchester United player has the middle name Maurice?

5 Which Premiership player was born in Tallinn (Estonia) on February 3, 1972?

6 Which current Charlton Athletic player – formerly with Chelsea, Brentford and Southend United – has the middle name Aubrey?

7 Which Everton player was born in Middlesbrough and has the middle name Sydney?

8 Which former England international was born in Hackney (London) on November 26, 1965 and has the middle name Sinclair?

9 Which goalkeeper who played in the Premiership in the 1998-99 season was born in Willesden, London on March 20, 1959?

10 Which England international was born in Ilford on October 21, 1967 and has the middle names Emerson Carlyle?

11 Which Newcastle United player was born in Milan on July 27, 1975?

12 Which Derby County player has the middle name Cesar?

13 Which emerging Southampton star was born in Lancaster on February 27, 1978 and served his apprenticeship at Blackburn Rovers?

14 Which Leicester City player supports Arsenal, does not like being called by the shortened version of his first name and has the middle name Rodney?

15 Which Premiership midfielder was born in Larne on August 2, 1971 and has the middle name Eamonn?

Answers

1 Patrick Viera **2** Earl Barrett **3** Bart-Williams **4** Roy Keane **5** Mart Poom **6** Keith Jones **7** Peter Beagrie **8** Des Walker **9** Dave Beasant **10** Paul Ince **11** Alessandro Pistone **12** Paulo Wanchope **13** James Beattie **14** Andrew Impey **15** Michael Hughes

THE CARLING ULTIMATE FOOTBALL FACT AND QUIZ BOOK

WHO THE HELL ARE YOU?

1 Which West Ham United player was born in Hartford, Connecticut on May 5, 1967?

2 Who has a wife named Victoria and a son named Brooklyn?

3 Which Arsenal defender was born in Nuneaton on December 11, 1963?

4 Which current Premiership player was born on a kibbutz near Haifa on April 2, 1972?

5 Which of the few Englishmen currently at Chelsea has the middle name Joseph?

6 What was West Ham United goalkeeper Hislop's forename before he changed it to Shaka?

7 Which Chelsea player was born in Montevideo on November 15, 1967?

8 Which Tottenham Hotspur player was born at Salsomaggiore on April 14, 1967?

9 Which Coventry City player was born in Accra on September 5, 1975?

10 Which Scotland international was born in Keith on December 7, 1965 and has the forenames Edward Colin James?

11 Which Tottenham Hotspur player was born in Manchester on November 13, 1961 and has the middle names Euclid Aklana?

12 Which current Charlton player arrived at the Valley from West Ham by way of Shimizu (Japan)?

13 Which Premiership striker was born in Swansea on April 5, 1975?

14 Which Sheffield Wednesday player was born in Fareham, Hampshire, on November 6, 1967?

15 Which international striker was born on November 3, 1963 at Woolwich (London) and has the middle name Edward?

THE CARLING ULTIMATE FOOTBALL FACT AND QUIZ BOOK

Quiz 5
WHO THE HELL ARE YOU?

1 Which Leicester City player was born in Winchester on March 29, 1969 and made his name at Wycombe?

2 Which Aston Villa and former Tottenham Hotspur defender was born in Stranraer on January 20, 1965?

3 Which famous defender was born in Newham (London) on September 18, 1974 and given the forenames Sulzeer Jeremiah?

4 Which Liverpool player was born at Barton-on-Sea on June 25, 1973 and has the middle name Frank, after his footballing uncle?

5 Which Premiership player was born at Gassin, near St Tropez, on January 25, 1971?

6 Which Arsenal player was born in L'Arbesle on April 3, 1966?

7 Which Italian in the Premiership was born in Bagnara Calabra on August 14, 1971?

8 Which Premiership player was born in Tobago on November 3, 1971?

9 Which current Liverpool player was born in Lakewood, Ohio (USA)?

10 Which current Tottenham Hotspur defender was born in Dublin on August 29, 1976?

11 Which Leeds United player was born in Setubal on October 22, 1975?

12 Which Chelsea player was born in Oliena (Sardinia) on July 5, 1966?

13 Which famous Premiership striker's middle name is Victor?

14 Which Liverpool player has the middle name Bernard?

15 Which Blackburn Rovers player was born in Stirling on June 25, 1976?

THE CARLING ULTIMATE FOOTBALL FACT AND QUIZ BOOK

Quiz 6
WHO THE HELL ARE YOU?

1 Which goalkeeper was born in Vancouver, Canada, on September 20, 1967 and has the middle name Lorne?

2 Which Premiership player was born at Glodsone on November 18, 1968 and has the middle name Boleslaw?

3 Which Blackburn Rovers striker has the middle name Cyril?

4 Which Leeds United player was born in Drogheda on August 31, 1977?

5 Which Middlesbrough player was born in Cagliari, Sardinia on March 12, 1969?

6 Which current Tottenham Hotspur player was born in St Alban's on February 6, 1969 and joined Watford as a trainee in 1987?

7 Which Newcastle United player was born in Stirling on December 27, 1971?

8 Which Premiership goalkeeper was born in Gouda on December 20, 1966?

9 Which current England defender was born on November 7, 1978 and has the middle name Gavin?

10 Which Italian in the Premiership was born in Sciaffusa, Switzerland, on May 29, 1970?

11 Which Arsenal defender was born in Manchester on March 17, 1964?

12 Which West Ham player was born in Dulwich on March 2, 1973 and joined Blackpool as a trainee?

13 Which Wimbledon player has the middle name Stanley?

14 Which Blackburn Rovers player was born in Ballboden (Scotland) on March 2, 1979?

15 Which Leeds United player announced his retirement from the game in 1999 after a career that had begun at Gillingham in August 1985?

OVERMATTER 30 Which Nigerian Premiership player was born in Manchester on June 8, 1967, has the middle name Goziem and is known as 'Chief'? Efan Ekoku 11   Which Premiership player was born on April 20, 1976 and christened Seamus John? Shay Given

---

Answers

13 *Peter Fear* **14** *Damien Duff* **15** *Mark Beeney*
7 *Duncan Ferguson* **8** *Ed De Goey* **9** *Rio Ferdinand* **10** *Roberto Di Matteo* **11** *Lee Dixon* **12** *Trevor Sinclair*
1 *Craig Forrest* **2** *Peter Schmeichel* **3** *Kevin Davies* **4** *Ian Harte* **5** *Gianluca Festa* **6** *Tim Sherwood*

THE CARLING ULTIMATE FOOTBALL FACT AND QUIZ BOOK

Quiz 1
1998 WORLD CUP

1 Which of his own players nearly beat Jim Leighton with a back header after just under a quarter of an hour of Scotland's opening game against Brazil?

2 Who was the first player to be booked in the tournament?

3 A foul on which Scot led to the award of a penalty in the game against Brazil?

4 Which Brazilian scored his team's first goal and then conceded the penalty?

5 Whose own goal sank the Scots in their opening game against Brazil?

6 Which Brazilian had had a shot saved by Jim Leighton just before the own goal?

7 Which Scot had a clear run on goal towards the end of the match but didn't shoot hard enough to trouble the Brazilian keeper?

8 Who was the Brazilian keeper in this match?

9 With which English Premiership club was he at the time being linked (although he never went there)?

10 Who was the only Norwegian to score in his country's 2-2 draw with Morocco?

11 Who scored both goals for Chile in their 2-2 draw with Italy?

12 Who scored Italy's first goal in their 2-2 draw with Chile?

13 Who equalised with a penalty for Italy?

14 Who scored Cameroon's wonder goal against Austria?

15 Who equalised for Austria in injury time against Cameroon?

THE CARLING ULTIMATE FOOTBALL FACT AND QUIZ BOOK

Quiz 2
1998 WORLD CUP

1 Which Bulgarian played much of his country's 0-0 draw with Paraguay with his head bandaged?

2 Name the free-kick taking Paraguayan goalkeeper.

3 Which South African scored two own goals against France?

4 In the match against France, which England-based South African handled the ball in his own area but didn't give away a penalty because the officials didn't see it?

5 Who scored Nigeria's winner from 25 yards in their 3-2 defeat of Spain?

6 Which South Korean scored and was then sent off in his country's 3-1 defeat by Mexico?

7 Who scored two goals for Mexico in their 3-1 defeat of South Korea?

8 Who played in boots with the same colour scheme as the Mexican national flag?

9 What was the score in the derby game between Holland and Belgium?

10 Which Japanese player dyed his hair orange?

11 Who scored for Argentina in their 1-0 victory over Japan?

12 Who scored Yugoslavia's winner against Iran?

13 Who gave away the free kick that led to Croatia's second goal in their 3-1 victory over Jamaica?

14 Who scored Romania's winner against Colombia?

15 Who scored Scotland's goal against Norway?

Answers

1 Krassimir Balakov **2** Jose Chilavert **3** Pierre Issa **4** Mark Fish **5** Sunday Oliseh **6** Ha Seok-Ju **7** Luis Hernandez **8** Cuauhtemoc Blanco **9** 0-0 **10** Hidetoshi Nakata **11** Gabriel Batistuta **12** Sinisa Mihajlovic **13** Frank Sinclair **14** Adrian Ilie **15** Craig Burley

THE CARLING ULTIMATE FOOTBALL FACT AND QUIZ BOOK

Quiz 3
1998 WORLD CUP

1 Who kept goal for Austria in the 1998 World Cup finals?

2 Which Cameroonian player was sent off for a tackle on Luigi Di Biagio?

3 Name any of the three players who were sent off in Denmark's 1-1 draw with South Africa.

4 Who put Denmark ahead in their game against South Africa?

5 Who equalised for South Africa against Denmark?

6 Who scored twice for France in their 4-0 defeat of Saudi Arabia?

7 Who scored both Belgium's goals against Mexico, the first direct from a corner?

8 Which Belgian was sent off after conceding a penalty against Mexico?

9 Who refereed Mexico's 2-2 draw with Belgium?

10 Who was credited with Yugoslavia's first goal against Germany even though television replays showed he never touched the ball on its way into the goal?

11 Which Jamaican was sent off just before half time in his country's 5-0 defeat by Argentina?

12 Who was captain of the USA team at the 1998 World Cup finals?

13 Who scored the USA's goal in their 2-1 defeat by Iran?

14 Who came on as substitute and scored the winner for Colombia against Tunisia?

15 Who did he replace?

THE CARLING ULTIMATE FOOTBALL FACT AND QUIZ BOOK

Quiz 4 — 1998 WORLD CUP

1 Who came off in England's match against Romania to be replaced by David Beckham?

2 Who scored Romania's first goal against England?

3 Who equalised for England against Romania?

4 Who scored for Chile in their 1-1 draw with Cameroon?

5 How many Cameroon players ended their game against Chile?

6 Who scored Brazil's goal in their game against Norway?

7 Who equalised for Norway and then won the penalty from which they scored the winner against Brazil?

8 Who scored from the penalty spot for Norway against Brazil?

9 Who scored his first ever goal for France in the 2-1 defeat of Denmark?

10 Who beat Bulgaria 6-1 on the day both countries went out of the competition?

11 Name either of Holland's scorers in their 2-2 draw with Mexico.

12 Which Mexican was sent off for protesting against the decision to disallow Blanco's goal against Holland?

13 Who scored for South Korea in their 1-1 draw with Belgium?

14 Who scored Yugoslavia's winner against the USA?

15 Who scored Argentina's winner against Croatia?

1998 WORLD CUP

1 Which Croatian had the number 10 shaved on the back of his head?

2 Who scored both goals for Jamaica in their 2-1 victory over Japan?

3 Who scored Italy's winner in their second round game against Norway?

4 Which Chilean dyed his hair red for his country's second round match against Brazil?

5 Who scored Brazil's first two goals in their 4-1 victory over Chile?

6 Which Frenchman scored the golden goal that put Paraguay out of the 1998 World Cup?

7 Which Dutch defender was described by David Pleat as being 'like Steve Bould on roller-skates'?

8 Who scored the winner for Holland in their second round game against Yugoslavia?

9 Which two Dutch players appeared to have a punch-up as the team celebrated its 2-1 victory over Yugoslavia?

10 Who fell over to win the decisive penalty in the Croatia v Romania match?

11 Why was Croatia's first penalty attempt ordered to be retaken?

12 In the second round game against England, which Argentine handled the ball in his own penalty area – an infringement which escaped the referee but not the cameras?

13 In the second round game against Argentina, which England player handled the ball in his own penalty area but escaped detection?

14 Who did Beckham kick in the game against Argentina?

15 What, according to Beckham, did England manager Glenn Hoddle say to him after he had been sent off – a) 'Bad luck, mate' b) 'By rights, you'll be reincarnated as a weevil' or c) Nothing?

Answers

1 Zvonimir Boban 2 Theodore Whitmore 3 Christian Vieri 4 Javier Margas 5 Cesar Sampaio 6 Laurent Blanc 7 Jaap Stam 8 Edgar Davids 9 Winston Bogarde and Edwin van der Sar 10 Aljosa Asanovic 11 Encroaching in the box 12 Jose Chamot 13 Tony Adams 14 Diego Simeone 15 c) Nothing

THE CARLING ULTIMATE FOOTBALL FACT AND QUIZ BOOK

Quiz 6
1998 WORLD CUP

1 Who scored the opening goal in the quarter final between Holland and Argentina?

2 Who equalised in the quarter final between Holland and Argentina?

3 Which Dutchman was sent off for a tackle on Diego Simeone?

4 Which Argentine was sent off in the quarter final against Holland?

5 Who scored Holland's winner against Argentina?

6 In the quarter finals, which German was sent off for taking a hack at Croatia's Davor Suker?

7 Which Dutchman seemed to be held in the penalty area at the end of extra time in the semi-final against Brazil but got booked for diving?

8 Who scored Croatia's goal in the semi-final against France?

9 Who then equalised and scored the winner for France?

10 In the third place play-off, which Dutchman got booked for dissent and thus ensured that he would miss the opening match of Euro 2000, of which his country is co-host?

11 Which Croatian defender was booed throughout the third place play-off, no doubt because of his perceived role in getting Frenchman Laurent Blanc sent off in the semi-final?

12 During the World Cup Final, what number was on the back of the team shirt held up by French President Jacques Chirac?

13 Which Frenchman became the first player to be sent off in a World Cup Final?

14 Who scored two goals for France in the World Cup Final?

15 Who came on as substitute for Stephane Guivarc'h?

SEASON 1998-1999

THE CARLING ULTIMATE FOOTBALL FACT AND QUIZ BOOK

Quiz 1

SEASON 1998-1999

July-August 1998

1 From which club did Rangers buy Andrei Kanchelskis?

2 Who did Tottenham Hotspur buy from Perugia for £3.5 million?

3 Where did Manchester United get Jesper Blomqvist?

4 At which neutral ground did Rangers play Shelburne in the UEFA Cup?

5 Which Irish club held Celtic to a goalless draw at Parkhead in the Champions' League?

6 Who took over from Littlewoods as sponsors of the English FA Cup?

7 Who became the first English club to go out of Europe, after losing to Samsunspor in the Inter Toto Cup?

8 Who joined Everton from Monaco for £2.5 million?

9 Who became the first Peruvian to play in top-flight English football?

10 From which Dutch club did Sheffield Wednesday get Wim Jonk?

11 Who were double-winning Arsenal's opponents in the FA Charity Shield?

12 Who won the 1998 FA Charity Shield?

13 What nationality is Coventry City's new signing Robert Jarni?

14 Which First Division club drew the opening day's largest crowd - 41,008 for the visit of Queen's Park Rangers?

15 Who spent a week at Aston Villa on his way home to Everton?

Answers

1 Fiorentina 2 Marco Tramezzani 3 Parma 4 Tranmere Rovers 5 St Patrick's Athletic 6 AXA Insurance 7 Crystal Palace 8 John Collins 9 Nolberto Solano (Newcastle United) 10 PSV Eindhoven 11 Manchester United 12 Arsenal 13 Croatian 14 Sunderland 15 David Unsworth

THE CARLING ULTIMATE FOOTBALL FACT AND QUIZ BOOK

Quiz 2
SEASON 1998-1999
September 1998

1 Which broadcasting company made a £625 million takeover bid for Manchester United?

2 Which broadcasting company made a bid for Arsenal?

3 In the Premiership, who came from 3-0 down to win at Upton Park?

4 Who came on as a substitute and scored two late goals to give Aston Villa a 3-2 victory at home to Stromsgodset in the UEFA Cup?

5 Who scored for Arsenal in their Champions' League draw at Lens?

6 Which Second Division club knocked West Ham United out of the Worthington Cup?

7 Who scored his first League goal for Derby County in the 2-1 win at Leicester?

8 Who inflicted Oxford United's record League defeat, 7-0?

9 Which Blackburn Rovers player was sent off in the 4-3 home defeat by Chelsea?

10 Which Chelsea player was sent off in the same match?

11 Which Third Division team knocked Premiership Sheffield Wednesday out of the Worthington Cup?

12 Who resigned as manager of Swindon Town?

13 Which Third Division club had three players sent off during their match at Swansea?

14 Who scored a hat trick for Aston Villa in the second leg of their UEFA Cup tie against Stromsgodset?

15 Who scored twice for Arsenal in their 3-0 win at Newcastle?

THE CARLING ULTIMATE FOOTBALL FACT AND QUIZ BOOK

Quiz 3
SEASON 1998-1999
October 1998

1 Who kicked Eyal Berkovic in the face at Chadwell Heath?

2 With which Belgian Second Division club did Manchester United announce a 'feeder' arrangement?

3 Which Finn resigned as manager of Motherwell?

4 Which was the last club in England to win a League match?

5 Which Blackburn Rovers player had his nose broken and got sent off against Arsenal?

6 At whom did Paul Ince make a two-fingered gesture after being sent off in the Sweden v England European Championship game?

7 Which Premiership manager did Leeds United want to approach when George Graham defected to White Hart Lane?

8 Who was sold by Newcastle United to Aston Villa for £4 million?

9 What was the score in the European Champions' League match between Brondby and Manchester United in Denmark?

10 For how many matches was Paolo Di Canio banned for pushing referee Paul Alcock?

11 Who booked 12 players in the Leeds United v Chelsea Premiership match?

12 Which Chelsea player was sent off at the end of their 4-1 defeat of Aston Villa?

13 Who scored the winner for Wales against Denmark?

14 Who equalised for Chelsea in the first leg of their Cup Winners' Cup tie against Copenhagen?

15 Who scored four of Liverpool's five goals against Nottingham Forest?

Answers

1 John Hartson **2** Antwerp **3** Harri Kampmann **4** Wycombe Wanderers **5** Chris Sutton **6** John Gorman **7** Martin O'Neill (Leicester City) **8** Steve Watson **9** Brondby 2 Manchester United 6 **10** Eleven **11** Mike Reed **12** Dennis Wise **13** Craig Bellamy **14** Marcel Desailly **15** Michael Owen

Quiz 4

SEASON 1998-1999

November 1998

1 Which Spanish club knocked Aston Villa out of the UEFA Cup 3-2 on aggregate?

2 Which Italian club knocked Leeds United out of the UEFA Cup?

3 Name either of the Liverpool players sent off in their 2-2 draw at Valencia in the UEFA Cup.

4 Which club did Manchester United beat 5-0 at Old Trafford in the Champions' League?

5 Who scored Chelsea's winner in he Cup Winners' Cup game against Copenhagen and then promptly joined the losers?

6 Who was sacked as manager of Wolverhampton Wanderers?

7 In the 3-3 draw at Southampton, which Middlesbrough player was sent off for calling referee Paul Alcock 'useless'?

8 Who won at Anfield for the first time since 1970?

9 What number shirt did Pierre Van Hooijdonk wear on his return from self-imposed exile to the Nottingham Forest side?

10 Who resigned as General Manager of Celtic?

11 Which Chelsea player's season ended prematurely after a collision with West Ham United goalkeeper Shaka Hislop?

12 Which French international scored twice on his debut as Rangers won 7-0 at St Johnstone?

13 Which rock singer joined forces with Kenny Dalglish to make a takeover bid for Celtic?

14 At Liverpool, who became Gérard Houllier's assistant manager on the departure of Roy Evans?

15 Who scored a hat trick for Aston Villa in their 4-1 win over Southampton at The Dell?

Answers

1 Celta Vigo **2** Roma **3** Steve McManaman and Paul Ince **4** Brondby **5** Brian Laudrup **6** Mark McGhee **7** Phil Stamp **8** Derby County **9** 40 **10** Jock Brown **11** Pierluigi Casiraghi **12** Stephane Guivarc'h **13** Jim Kerr of Simple Minds **14** Phil Thompson **15** Dion Dublin

THE CARLING ULTIMATE FOOTBALL FACT AND QUIZ BOOK

Quiz 5
SEASON 1998-1999

1 Who called Glenn Hoddle 'a coward' and 'a bad communicator'?

2 Who inflicted Aston Villa's first League defeat of the season?

3 Who scored two goals for Villa in this game and also missed a penalty?

4 Who inflicted First Division leaders Sunderland's first League defeat of the season?

5 Which wing-back was sold to Leicester City over the head of West Ham United manager Harry Redknapp?

6 Who said 'The books have to be balanced and Harry [Redknapp] knows that as well as I did. He can like it or lump it'?

7 Who scored the penalty against Newcastle United that gave Everton their first home win since April?

8 Who was reported to have burst into tears on being told that he was leaving Everton for Newcastle?

9 Which Arsenal player was sent off in the Champions' League game against Lens?

10 Which Arsenal defender was accused of feigning injury against Lens in order to get Tony Vareilles sent off?

11 Who won the Scottish Coca-Cola Cup?

12 Who did they beat 2-1 in the Final?

13 Celtic beat Rangers by the biggest margin for 30 years - what was the score?

14 Name the assistant manager of Sheffield United who was arrested at Loftus Road for swearing.

15 Who was sacked as manager of Blackburn Rovers?

Answers

1 Andy Cole 2 Liverpool 3 Dion Dublin 4 Barnsley 5 Andrew Impey 6 Peter Storrie 7 Michael Ball 8 Duncan Ferguson 9 Ray Parlour 10 Lee Dixon 11 Rangers 12 St Johnstone 13 Celtic 5 Rangers 1 14 John Deehan 15 Roy Hodgson

THE CARLING ULTIMATE FOOTBALL FACT AND QUIZ BOOK

Quiz 6
SEASON 1998-1999

1 Who announced that he was going to step down as Everton chairman because of 'health concerns'?

2 Which Premiership manager narrowly avoided hot water when he said that his players had 'a nice few bob' on themselves to win the Worthington Cup?

3 Which West Ham United defender was sent off in his team's 4-0 premiership defeat at Elland Road?

4 Which Chelsea player was sent off for the third time this season during a goalless draw at Goodison Park?

5 Which Spanish club knocked Liverpool out of the UEFA Cup?

6 Which Italian club knocked Rangers out of the UEFA Cup?

7 Where did Celtic find Mark Viduka?

8 What nationality is Mark Viduka?

9 After scoring the winner against Aston Villa at Stamford Bridge, who was described by Chelsea manager Gianluca Vialli as 'a lethal weapon'?

10 The FA announced that they were going to investigate transfer dealings between Tranmere Rovers and which Premiership club?

11 Which Manchester United player was sent off during his side's 2-2 draw at White Hart Lane?

12 Who beat Oxford 7-1 at the Manor?

13 Who was described by Arsène Wenger as 'an aggressive player on the pitch but very kind off it'?

14 Who scored Chelsea's equaliser at Old Trafford?

15 From which First Division club did Coventry City buy John Aloisi for £650,000?

Answers

1 Peter Johnson **2** Joe Kinnear (Wimbledon) **3** Neil Ruddock **4** Dennis Wise **5** Celta Vigo **6** Parma **7** Croatia Zagreb **8** Australian **9** Tore Andre Flo **10** Everton **11** Gary Neville **12** Birmingham City **13** Patrick Viera **14** Gianfranco Zola **15** Portsmouth

THE CARLING ULTIMATE FOOTBALL FACT AND QUIZ BOOK

SEASON 1998-1999

1 Which former England international was appointed coach of Sampdoria?

2 Who stepped down as Portsmouth chairman after receiving death threats from fans?

3 Who beat Manchester United 3-2 at Old Trafford?

4 Against Leeds United at Highbury, which Frenchman became the fifth Arsenal player to be sent off this season and the 17th since Arsène Wenger became manager of Arsenal?

5 At the end of the West Ham United Christmas party, which two players were arrested for climbing over a Mini with the driver inside it?

6 Who went from Leeds United on loan to Sampdoria?

7 Which Aston Villa player was sent off at Blackburn on Boxing Day, a dismissal which was later revoked?

8 Who refereed the Blackburn Rovers v Aston Villa Premiership match on Boxing Day?

9 Who inflicted Sunderland's first away defeat of the season?

10 Which Stenhousemuir player made a record 864th appearance for the club against East Stirlingshire?

11 Which non-League club held Leeds United to a 0-0 draw in the Third Round of the FA Cup?

12 In the FA Cup Third Round tie between Manchester United and Middlesbrough, who gave away a penalty when he was adjudged to have tripped Nicky Butt?

13 Who refereed the FA Cup Third Round tie between Manchester United and Middlesbrough?

14 How many Scotsmen played in the match between Celtic and Rangers on January 3 - 22, 17, 12, eight, five or none?

15 Who scored a penalty for Liverpool in their 3-0 victory over Port Vale in the FA Cup Third Round?

THE CARLING ULTIMATE FOOTBALL FACT AND QUIZ BOOK

SEASON 1998-1999

January 1999

1 Which Preston North End player was flattened by an opposition defender just before Arsenal scored the third goal in their 4-2 victory at Deepdale in the Third Round of the FA Cup?

2 Who was sacked as manager of Nottingham Forest on January 7?

3 Which two clubs were reported to be considering a merger under the new name Manchester North End?

4 Who scored a hat-trick as Coventry City beat Nottingham Forest 4-0?

5 Which Grimsby Town player equalled Terry Paine' record number of League appearances in the outfield in the match against Brentford?

6 Why was Manchester United's Premiership game against West Ham United delayed for an hour?

7 Who took over as manager of Nottingham Forest?

8 Who was sacked as manager of Wycombe Wanderers?

9 Which Third Division club knocked Premiership West Ham United out of the FA Cup in the Third Round?

10 Which Second Division club knocked Premiership Southampton out of the FA Cup in the Third Round?

11 Which Nigerian joined Arsenal from Inter Milan for £4 million?

12 Who had his tracksuit set on fire as part of the hilarious initiation ritual when he joined Wimbledon?

13 Who beat Reading 6-0 after a goalless first half?

14 Which Newcastle United defender was sent off towards the end of their 2-2 draw at Charlton Athletic?

15 Which Everton player was sent off as they lost 3-0 at Aston Villa?

Answers

1 Ryan Kidd **2** Dave Bassett **3** Bury and Rochdale **4** Darren Huckerby **5** Tony Ford **6** Power cut **7** Ron Atkinson **8** Neil Smillie **9** Swansea City **10** Fulham **11** Nwankwo Kanu **12** John Hartson **13** Bristol Rovers **14** Nikos Dabizas **15** Alec Cleland

THE CARLING ULTIMATE FOOTBALL FACT AND QUIZ BOOK

SEASON 1998-1999

1 Who was sacked after 15 years as manager of Port Vale?

2 Who was sacked as manager of Hartlepool United?

3 Who did Blackburn Rovers buy from Crystal Palace for £4 million?

4 Which Tottenham international was charged in January with assaulting a steward as the teams left the pitch after their match at Derby County in October?

5 Who resigned as manager of Colchester United?

6 Who left Brighton and Hove Albion to replace John Rudge at Port Vale?

7 Which Second Division club won 2-0 at Villa Park in the FA Cup Fourth Round?

8 Who opened the scoring for Liverpool after two minutes in the FA Cup Fourth Round tie at Old Trafford?

9 Who became the seventh Arsenal player to be sent off this season after swearing at an assistant referee during the FA Cup Fourth Round tie at Wolverhampton Wanderers?

10 Who refereed the FA Cup Fourth Round tie between Oxford United and Chelsea?

11 Which Oxford United player made the challenge on Gianluca Vialli that led to the award of a penalty to Chelsea?

12 Who was the manager of Oxford United, who was alleged to have threatened Chelsea's Frank Leboeuf?

13 Why did a crowd of 33,517 turn out to watch Sunderland reserves against Liverpool reserves?

14 Which Liverpool player announced that he would be joining Real Madrid at the end of the season in a deal worth £14 million over 5 years?

15 Who quit Scarborough to become manager of Colchester United?

Answers

1 John Rudge **2** Mick Tait **3** Matt Jansen **4** Sol Campbell **5** Steve Wignall **6** Brian Horton **7** Fulham
8 Michael Owen **9** Emmanuel Petit **10** Mike Reed **11** Kevin Francis **12** Malcolm Shotton
13 Admission was free **14** Steve McManaman **15** Mick Wadsworth

THE CARLING ULTIMATE FOOTBALL FACT AND QUIZ BOOK

Quiz 10

SEASON 1998-1999

February 1999

1 Who scored four goals for Manchester United after coming on as a substitute against Nottingham Forest?

2 Who took over from Glenn Hoddle as England manager for the friendly against World Champions France?

3 Who scored both goals for France in their 2-0 defeat of England at Wembley?

4 Who scored Manchester United's winner in their 1-0 FA Cup Fifth Round victory over Fulham?

5 In the FA Cup Fifth Round tie at Highbury, who took the throw-in that led to the controversial Arsenal winner against Sheffield United?

6 Who refereed the FA Cup Fifth Round tie between Arsenal and Sheffield United?

7 Which Arsenal players set up and then scored the 'winning goal' in their first FA Cup tie against Sheffield United?

8 Which bottle blond scored Chelsea's winner at Hillsborough in the FA Cup Fifth Round?

9 Who scored Huddersfield Town's first goal in the 2-2 draw with Derby County in the FA Cup Fifth Round?

10 Who scored a penalty for Derby County in the FA Cup Fifth Round tie at Huddersfield?

11 Who scored a hat-trick for Arsenal in their 5-0 win over Leicester City?

12 Who scored direct from a corner for West Ham United against Liverpool at Anfield?

13 Which Dutchman scored the winner for Leeds United at home to Everton?

14 Where did Charlton Athletic get Jamaican-Swedish striker Martin Pringle?

15 Which Charlton Athletic player had a penalty saved by Nottingham Forest's Mark Crossley?

Answers

1 Ole Gunnar Solskjaer **2** Howard Wilkinson **3** Nicolas Anelka **4** Andy Cole **5** Ray Parlour **6** Peter Jones **7** Nwankwo Kanu and Marc Overmars **8** Roberto Di Matteo **9** Chris Beech **10** Tony Dorigo **11** Nicolas Anelka **12** Marc Keller **13** Willem Korsten **14** Benfica **15** Neil Redfearn

THE CARLING ULTIMATE FOOTBALL FACT AND QUIZ BOOK

Quiz 11
SEASON 1998-1999

1 Which Australian scored twice in Coventry City's first ever League victory at Aston Villa?

2 Which Dutchman scored twice in Coventry City's first ever League victory at Aston Villa?

3 Who scored two goals for the First Division's bottom club Crewe Alexandra in their 3-1 victory at Bolton Wanderers?

4 Which Liverpool player handled the ball in the area to concede a penalty against Chelsea?

5 Which Dane scored Chelsea's second goal in their 2-1 victory over Liverpool at Stamford Bridge?

6 Who took over as England manager?

7 Which Tottenham player was sent off in the 1-1 Premiership draw with Derby County?

8 Which Blackburn player was reportedly asked en passant by Ken Bates if he fancied playing for Chelsea?

9 Who scored his first goal for West Ham United in the 2-0 victory over Blackburn Rovers?

10 Who scored two goals for Sheffield Wednesday in their 3-1 defeat of Middlesbrough?

11 Who scored all Gillingham's goals in their 5-0 defeat of Burnley at Turf Moor?

12 At what time did the Oxford United v Sunderland First Division match - the first ever live televised pay-to-view League game - kick off on Saturday February 27, 1999?

13 What was the score in the historic Oxford United v Sunderland First Division match?

14 How much did it cost to watch Oxford United's game against Sunderland on telly?

15 Which Barnsley player was injured when he slipped in the mess his puppy had made in the kitchen?

THE CARLING ULTIMATE FOOTBALL FACT AND QUIZ BOOK

Quiz 12
SEASON 1998-1999

1 Which building society let it be known that Glenn Hoddle had 'a responsibility to ensure that his personal views [are not] confused with those of the England team, the FA or its sponsors'?

2 Who resigned after only six matches and no victories in charge of Sampdoria?

3 Which 17-year-old Finn scored twice for Chelsea in their 4-2 victory over Oxford United in an FA Cup Fourth Round replay?

4 Which Chelsea player was sent off for two handballs in his team's 4-2 defeat of Oxford United in an FA Cup Fourth Round replay?

5 Which Croatian signed for Newcastle in February, claiming 'my favourite bird is the magpie'?

6 Who succeeded Brian Kidd as assistant to Manchester United manager Alex Ferguson?

7 From which Premiership club did Manchester United sign him?

8 Who was appointed manager of Wycombe Wanderers?

9 Where did Blackburn Rovers score their first Premiership away win of the 1998-99 season?

10 Which Englishman left Turkey after allegedly being racially abused by the Chairman of Trabzonspor?

11 Who did the USA beat 3-0 in a friendly in Florida?

12 How many Arsenal defenders played for England in the friendly international against France?

13 Which Arsenal player was picked for the friendly international against France, his first cap in five years?

14 Who was the French coach at Wembley against England in February?

15 At which ground were four men caught trying to tamper with the floodlights?

Answers

1 The Nationwide Building Society **2** David Platt **3** Mikael Forssell **4** Dennis Wise **5** Silvio Maric **6** Steve McLaren **7** Derby County **8** Lawrie Sanchez **9** Villa Park **10** Kevin Campbell **11** Germany **12** Four **13** Lee Dixon **14** Roger Lemerre **15** Charlton Athletic

THE CARLING ULTIMATE FOOTBALL FACT AND QUIZ BOOK

Quiz 13

SEASON 1998-1999

1 Which referee sent off Liverpool's Jamie Carragher at Charlton?

2 Whose goal for Tottenham Hotspur knocked Wimbledon out of the Worthington Cup semi-final?

3 Who missed a penalty for Manchester United against Arsenal in the Premiership?

4 Which Chelsea player was sent off in the 1-1 Premiership draw with Blackburn Rovers?

5 Which Blackburn Rovers player was sent off in the 1-1 Premiership draw with Chelsea?

6 Which striker scored his third hat trick in four games in Celtic's 7-1 win at Motherwell?

7 Which on-loan Frenchman scored the goal for Newcastle United that knocked Blackburn Rovers out of the FA Cup?

8 Which former Hartlepool United goalkeeper became the club's manager in February?

9 Which Briton took over as caretaker manager of Real Madrid?

10 Which Italian club was reported to have offered £26 million for Michael Owen?

11 For which Spurs player were Lazio and Real Madrid each reported to have bid £15 million?

12 During the 1998-99 season, which Manchester United player's name was chosen most often by fans to go on the back of their replica team shirts?

13 Why was the FA Cup Sixth Round tie between Barnsley and Tottenham Hotspur postponed on the morning of the match?

14 Against which team did Paolo Di Canio score his first goal for West Ham United?

15 During which match did Wimbledon manager Joe Kinnear have a heart attack?

Quiz 14

SEASON 1998-1999

March 1999

1 Name the chief executive of the Scottish FA who was suspended and then sacked over his alleged role in the Cadete Affair..

2 Who was charged by the FA with misconduct after making remarks about the referee in the Charlton v Liverpool Premiership game?

3 Who refereed the Charlton v Liverpool Premiership game?

4 Which two players had a running battle during the Chelsea v Liverpool Premiership match?

5 Who scored both goals for Manchester United in their 2-0 defeat of Inter in the Champions' League quarter final first leg?

6 Which Inter player had a goal disallowed in the Champions' League quarter final first leg against Manchester United?

7 During the 1998-99 season, which Arsenal player's name was chosen most often by fans to go on the back of their replica team shirts?

8 Which Coventry City player was sent off against Charlton Athletic?

9 Against which team did Leicester City record their first Premiership victory since Boxing Day?

10 Which Queen's Park Rangers' player announced his retirement?

11 Which Chelsea player was sent off at Old Trafford in the Premiership?

12 Who scored twice for Newcastle United in their 4-1 defeat of Everton in the FA Cup Sixth Round?

13 Which Villan turned down a move to Nottingham Forest?

14 Who offered to resign as manager of Burnley after his team lost 6-0 at home to Manchester City?

15 Who scored both Manchester United goals in their defeat of Chelsea in the FA Cup Sixth Round?

Answers

1 Jim Farry 2 Gérard Houllier 3 Mike Reed 4 Graeme Le Saux and Robbie Fowler 5 Dwight Yorke 6 Diego Simeone 7 Dennis Bergkamp 8 John Aloisi 9 Wimbledon 10 Vinnie Jones 11 Roberto Di Matteo 12 Temuri Ketsbaia 13 Stan Collymore 14 Stan Ternent 15 Dwight Yorke

THE CARLING ULTIMATE FOOTBALL FACT AND QUIZ BOOK

Quiz 15

SEASON 1998-1999

1 Who moved from Nottingham Forest to Aston Villa for £5 million?

2 To which Coventry City player were Aston Villa accused of making an illegal approach?

3 How much did the English National Stadium Trust (part of the FA) pay for Wembley?

4 Who scored twice for Manchester United in their 2-1 win at Newcastle?

5 Which Gunner was sent off at Goodison?

6 Which Everton player was sent off in the game against Arsenal?

7 Which club inflicted Chelsea's first home Premiership defeat of the season?

8 Who scored Tottenham Hotspur's spectacular winner in the FA Cup Sixth Round tie at Barnsley?

9 Which Barnsley player was sent off in the FA Cup Sixth Round tie against Tottenham Hotspur?

10 Name the manager sacked by York City.

11 Who scored Manchester United's equaliser against Inter at the San Siro Stadium, Milan?

12 Who beat Rangers 1-0 at Ibrox in the Scottish Premiership?

13 Who scored Tottenham Hotspur's Worthington Cup Final winner against Leicester City?

14 Who was sent off in the Worthington Cup Final?

15 Who was dropped from the Leicester City side for turning up late to a team meeting on the day of the Worthington Cup Final?

Answers

1 Steve Stone **2** George Boateng **3** £106 million **4** Andy Cole **5** Emmanuel Petit **6** Don Hutchison **7** West Ham United **8** David Ginola **9** Adrian Moses **10** Alan Little **11** Paul Scholes **12** Dundee United **13** Allan Nielsen **14** Justin Edinburgh **15** Frank Sinclair

THE CARLING ULTIMATE FOOTBALL FACT AND QUIZ BOOK

Quiz 16

SEASON 1998-1999
March-April 1999

1 In the qualifiers for Euro 2000, which nation inflicted Scotland's first home defeat since 1987?

2 Who succeeded Alvin Martin as manager of Southend United?

3 Who sniffed the white line during Liverpool's defeat of Everton?

4 Who scored Charlton Athletic's Easter Monday winner at West Ham?

5 Still on Easter Monday, why did West Bromwich Albion's Fabian de Freitas miss his team's 5-1 defeat of Crewe Alexandra?

6 Who scored Manchester United's equaliser in their 1-1 home draw with Juventus in the Champions League semi-final first leg?

7 Who was sacked as manager of Halifax Town?

8 Who scored Chelsea's equaliser in the first leg of their European Cup Winners' Cup semi-final at home to Mallorca?

9 Who was sacked as manager of Brighton and Hove Albion?

10 Which Scot announced his retirement from international football after taking stick from the crowd during his country's most recent match?

11 Name the Trade Secretary who announced that the government was blocking BSkyB's proposed take-over of Manchester United.

12 For how many matches was Robbie Fowler banned after abusing Graeme Le Saux?

13 For how many matches was Graeme le Saux banned for hitting Robbie Fowler?

14 Which Premiership player walked out of the ground after being substituted? (You can get it without being given the name of the club.)

15 Which Derby County player suffered a broken cheekbone after a close encounter with Pierre Van Hooijdonk?

Answers

1 Czech Republic *2 Alan Little* *3 Robbie Fowler* *4 Graham Stuart* *5 He thought the game was an evening kick-off* *6 Ryan Giggs* *7 Kieran O'Regan* *8 Tore Andre Flo* *9 Jeff Wood* *10 Gary McAllister* *11 Stephen Byers* *12 Six* *13 One* *14 Pierre Van Hooijdonk* *15 Vas Borbokis*

Quiz 17

SEASON 1998-1999

April 1999

1 Which former Sampdoria player scored for First Division Bradford City in their 2-1 victory over Portsmouth?

2 Who did Celtic beat 2-0 in the semi-final of the Scottish FA Cup?

3 In the English FA Cup semi-final, which Newcastle United player's handball in the penalty area went unnoticed by referee Paul Durkin?

4 Who then scored two goals for Newcastle United in extra time of their FA Cup semi-final against Tottenham Hotspur?

5 Who became the record-breaking 10th Arsenal player to be sent off this season during the other FA Cup semi-final against Manchester United?

6 Who was appointed the new manager of Brighton and Hove Albion?

7 Who did Rangers beat 4-0 in the semi-final of the Scottish FA Cup?

8 Who scored four goals as Sunderland clinched promotion with a 5-2 win at Bury?

9 Which Premiership manager likened his club to a Ferrari that was only being driven in fourth gear?

10 Why were all games played on Saturday April 17 preceded by a minute's silence?

11 Which two Second Division clubs contested the Auto Windscreens' Final at Wembley?

12 And which of them won the trophy?

13 Which famous footballing addict fell off the wagon in April?

14 Who was sacked as manager of First Division Barnsley?

15 Which Premiership manager said he'd like Charlton Athletic to stay up because 'it's not very far for us to travel'?

Answers

1 Lee Sharpe **2** Dundee United **3** Nikos Dabizas **4** Alan Shearer **5** Nelson Vivas **6** Micky Adams **7** St Johnstone **8** Kevin Phillips **9** Ruud Gullit (Newcastle United) **10** It was the tenth anniversary of the Hillsborough Disaster **11** Millwall and Wigan Athletic **12** Wigan Athletic **13** Paul Merson **14** John Hendrie **15** George Graham (Tottenham Hotspur)

THE CARLING ULTIMATE FOOTBALL FACT AND QUIZ BOOK

Quiz 18
SEASON 1998-1999

1 Who scored the winner for Manchester United in their 3-2 victory in the Champions' League semi-final second leg at Juventus?

2 Which Chelsea player missed a chance in the last minute of the second leg of their Cup Winners' Cup semi-final against Mallorca?

3 Who assured themselves of promotion from the GM Vauxhall Conference to the Third Division of the Football League by drawing with Yeovil?

4 Who scored two goals for Arsenal as they beat Middlesbrough 6-1 at the Riverside?

5 Which Premiership manager made a double announcement - that his team was pathetic and that he was retiring from the game?

6 Who won both the English PFA's and the Writers' Player of the Year award?

7 Who won the PFA's Young Player of the Year award?

8 Who scored for Scotland as they beat Germany in a friendly in Bremen?

9 According to a report published this month, which Newcastle United player was the highest earner in the Premiership, with £40,000 a week?

10 Which former England manager died at the age of 79?

11 Who scored the winning goal for Southampton against Leicester City?

12 Which referee sent off three West Ham United players in the game against Leeds United?

13 Which three Hammers went west?

14 Which former Celtic player did the club announce would become their 'Technical Director' next season?

15 Who was the referee hit by a missile during the Celtic v Rangers match at Parkhead in which three players were sent off?

Answers

1 Andy Cole **2** Dennis Wise **3** Cheltenham **4** Nwankwo Kanu **5** Ron Atkinson (Nottingham Forest) **6** David Ginola **7** Nicolas Anelka **8** Don Hutchison **9** Duncan Ferguson **10** Sir Alf Ramsey **11** James Beattie **12** Rob Harris **13** Ian Wright, Shaka Hislop and Steve Lomas **14** Kenny Dalglish **15** Hugh Dallas

Quiz 19

SEASON 1998-1999

May 1999

1 In which city was the 1999 UEFA Cup Final between Marseille and Parma played?

2 Which Premiership club won the FA Youth Cup, winning the two-legged Final by the record margin of 9-0?

3 During the 1998-99 season, which Chelsea player's name was chosen most often by fans to go on the back of their replica team shirts?

4 Which Manchester United player was sent off in their 2-2 draw at Anfield?

5 Who scored the winner for Leeds United in their home Premiership game aganst Arsenal?

6 Who put Tottenham Hotspur ahead at Old Trafford on the final day of the Premiership season?

7 Who scored a Premiership hat trick for Everton against West Ham United?

8 Name the goalkeeper who scored the injury time goal that kept Carlisle United in the Football League.

9 From which First Division club was this goalkeeper on loan?

10 Which club was relegated from the Football League after finishing bottom of Division Three?

11 Who scored the winner for Wycombe Wanderers at Lincoln City which kept the visitors up and sent the hosts down?

12 Who scored both goals for Southampton in the 2-0 win over Everton that guaranteed their Premiership survival?

13 What nationality is the above player?

14 What was achieved in the 1998-99 Premiership season only by Geoff Thomas of Nottingham Forest, David Howells of Southampton, Brian Deane of Middlesbrough, Jimmy Floyd Hasselbaink of Leeds United and Carl Cort of Wimbledon?

15 Who directed and managed Brentford to the 1999 Third Division Championship?

Answers

1 Moscow **2** West Ham United **3** Gianfranco Zola **4** Dennis Irwin **5** Jimmy Floyd Hasselbaink **6** Les Ferdinand **7** Kevin Campbell **8** Jimmy Glass **9** Swindon Town **10** Scarborough **11** Neil Emblen **12** Marians Pahars **13** Latvian **14** They are the only players who scored against Arsenal at Highbury **15** Ron Noades

THE CARLING ULTIMATE FOOTBALL FACT AND QUIZ BOOK

Quiz 20

SEASON 1998-1999

1 Which club won the 1999 UEFA Cup?

2 Which club won the English First Division Championship?

3 Which club won automatic promotion by finishing second in the Third Division?

4 Which club won automatic promotion by finishing second in the First Division?

5 Which club won automatic promotion by finishing third in the Third Division?

6 Which Liverpool player scored 18 Premiership goals in the 1998-99 season?

7 Which two Manchester United players scored 17 goals apiece in the 1998-99 Premiership season?

8 Which club went up automatically with Second Division Champions Fulham?

9 Which club came second in the Scottish Third Division, thus securing promotion for the first time in their 114-year history?

10 Of which promoted club is Geoffrey Richmond the chairman?

11 Where was the last European Cup Winners' Cup Final played?

12 Who was the victorious captain of Lazio?

13 Which Italian scored Lazio's first goal in the last European Cup Winners' Cup Final?

14 Which Portuguese scored Real Mallorca's goal in the last European Cup Winners' Cup Final?

15 Which Czech scored Lazio's winner in the last European Cup Winners' Cup Final?

THE CARLING ULTIMATE FOOTBALL FACT AND QUIZ BOOK

SEASON 1998-1999

1 During the 1998-99 season, which West Ham United player's name was chosen most often by fans to go on the back of their replica team shirts? ?

2 Which Croatian got the Golden Boot in 1998 and then the sack from Real Madrid at the end of this season?

3 Who scored the goal at Maine Road that took Manchester City past Wigan Athletic to the Second Division Play-Off Final?

4 Who scored the goal at the Priestfield Stadium that took Gillingham past Preston North End to the Third Division Play-Off Final?

5 Who scored two goals for Ipswich Town in the second leg of their First Division Play-Off Semi-Final against Bolton Wanderers?

6 Who scored two goals for Bolton Wanderers in the second leg of their First Division Play-Off Semi-Final against Ipswich Town?

7 Who scored two goals for Scunthorpe in the second leg of their Third Division Play-Off Semi-Final against Swansea City?

8 Who scored Watford's goal in the first leg of their Second Diviison Play-Off Semi-Final against Birmingham City?

9 Who scored Birmingham City's goal in the second leg of their Second Division Play-Off Semi-Final against Watford?

10 After extra time at the end of the second leg of the above match, Watford beat Birmingham City in a shoot-out - what was the score in penalties?

11 Who resigned as manager of Sheffield United and was almost immediately linked with a job at Huddersfield Town?

12 Who was sued by Sheffield Wednesday Suppporters' Club for losing their Player of the Year Cup?

13 Which star stopped flirting with relegation from the Premiership and announced plans to marry Marilyn from television soap opera Home & Away?

14 Who took over from David Mellor as host of Radio Five Live's 606 phone-in?

15 Which Spanish club reportedly offered West Ham United £12 million for Rio Ferdinand?

Answers

1 Ian Wright **2** Davor Suker **3** Shaun Goater **4** Andy Hessenthaler **5** Matt Holland **6** Bob Taylor **7** Gareth Sheldon **8** Michel Ngonge **9** Ade Adebola **10** Birmingham City **6** Watford **11** Steve Bruce **12** Paolo di Canio **13** Matthew Le Tissier **14** Richard Littlejohn **15** Real Madrid

THE CARLING ULTIMATE FOOTBALL FACT AND QUIZ BOOK

Quiz 22

SEASON 1998-1999

The FA Cup Final

1 What was the final score in the 1999 FA Cup Final?

2 Whose tackle on Roy Keane led to the Manchester United captain being replaced in the eighth minute?

3 Who replaced Roy Keane?

4 Newcastle United appeared in last year's FA Cup Final - but in which year had they last won the trophy?

5 Which was the last team to have lost in two consecutive FA Cup Finals?

6 Who kept goal for Newcastle United?

7 Who started the Final at centre back for Manchester United in place of Jaap Stam?

8 Who provided the pass from which Teddy Sheringham scored Manchester United's first goal in the Final?

9 Who replaced Newcastle United's Dietmar Hamann at half time?

10 Whose poor clearance let in Paul Scholes for Manchester United's second goal?

11 Who replaced Andy Cole after 60 minutes?

12 Which Newcastle United forward hit the Manchester United post in the second half?

13 Who came on as substitute for Nolberto Solano after 68 minutes?

14 Who presented the FA Cup?

15 What did Roy Keane say as he lifted the FA Cup?

Answers

1 Manchester United 2 Newcastle United 0 **2** Gary Speed **3** Teddy Sheringham **4** 1955 **5** Everton in 1985 and 1986 **6** Steve Harper **7** David May **8** Paul Scholes **9** Duncan Ferguson **10** Nikos Dabizas **11** Dwight Yorke **12** Temur Ketsbaia **13** Silvio Maric **14** Prince Charles **15** 'You beauty!'

THE CARLING ULTIMATE FOOTBALL FACT AND QUIZ BOOK

Quiz 23

SEASON 1998-1999

The European Cup Final

1 In which city was the 1999 European Cup Final played?

2 What nationality was the 1999 European Cup Final referee P Collina?

3 Whose foul on Carsten Jancker led to the free kick from which Bayern Munich scored their goal?

4 Who scored for Bayern Munich?

5 Who replaced Lothar Matthaus after 79 minutes?

6 Who replaced Andy Cole after 81 minutes?

7 Who hit the Manchester United upright and saw the ball rebound into the arms of Peter Schmeichel?

8 Whose overhead kick hit the Manchester United crossbar?

9 How many minutes of injury time did the Fourth Official display at the end of the game?

10 Who gave away the corner that led to Manchester United's equaliser?

11 Who took the corner?

12 Who scored the Manchester United equaliser?

13 Who scored Manchester United's winner 43 seconds before the full time whistle?

14 Who was the only player to be shown a yellow card in the match?

15 In which year had Manchester United previously won the European Cup?

THE CARLING ULTIMATE FOOTBALL FACT AND QUIZ BOOK

SEASON 1998-1999
The Scottish FA Cup Final

1 Rangers completed the last part of their treble when they won the Scottish FA Cup, beating Celtic 1-0 in the Final at Hampden Park. In which year had there last been an Old Firm FA Cup Final?

2 Back to the current season: who scored the winner for Rangers in the 49th minute?

3 From which English club had Rangers signed him on a free transfer?

4 Whose cross from the left led to the goal?

5 How many times have Rangers now won the Scottish FA Cup?

6 How many times have Celtic won the Scottish FA Cup?

7 Who refereed the 1999 Scottish FA Cup Final?

8 Who was the captain of Rangers in this match?

9 Who presented the trophy at the end of the match?

10 Who announced after the game that he would remain at Rangers until 2002?

11 What nationality is Celtic midfielder Lubomir Moravcik?

12 Who replaced Enrico Annoni after 60 minutes?

13 Who came on for Sergio Porrini after 77 minutes?

14 Who replaced Stephane Mahe after 78 minutes?

15 Who came on for Gabriel Amato after 88 minutes?

THE CARLING ULTIMATE FOOTBALL FACT AND QUIZ BOOK

Quiz 25
SEASON 1998-1999

1 Which Basque scored Scunthorpe United's winner against Leyton Orient in the Third Division Play-Off Final at Wembley on Saturday May 29?

2 Who supplied the cross from which he scored?

3 Which former French international played for Leyton Orient in this match?

4 Which former Nottingham Forest player was manager of Scunthorpe?

5 Who scored the first goal for Gillingham after 81 minutes of the Second Division Play-Off Final at Wembley?

6 Who loooked as if he'd made it safe for Gillingham by scoring their second after 87 minutes?

7 At the end of the Second Division Play-Off Final between Gillingham and Manchester City, how many minutes did the referee's assistant display on the injury time board?

8 What was the score at the moment he did so?

9 Who scored Manchester City's first goal?

10 Who equalised for Manchester City?

11 Who refereed the Second Division Play-Off Final at Wembley?

12 The Gillingham goalkeeper was with Manchester City's Paul Dickov at Arsenal and had been his best man - name him.

13 Who was the manager of Gillingham?

14 What was the score in the penalty shoot-out which decided the Second Division Play-Off Final at Wembley?

15 Who scored the only goal of the Peace International in Dublin between Ireland and Northern Ireland?

Answers

1 Alexander Calvo-Garcia 2 Gareth Sheldon 3 Amara Simba 4 Brian Laws 5 Carl Asaba 6 Robert Taylor 7 Five 8 Gillingham 2 Manchester City 0 9 Kevin Horlock 10 Paul Dickov 11 Mark Halsey 12 Vince Bartram 13 Tony Pulis 14 Manchester City 3 Gillingham 1 15 Danny Griffin

THE CARLING ULTIMATE FOOTBALL FACT AND QUIZ BOOK

Quiz 26
SEASON 1998-1999

1 Who refereed both the Worthington Cup Final and the First Division Play-Off Final between Bolton Wanderers and Watford at Wembley?

2 For which club did goalkeeper Alec Chamberlain make 90 appearances before joining Watford?

3 Who was the only international in the Watford side?

4 What was the name of Bolton Wanderers' left winger, a Jamaica international?

5 Which distinguished former Watford player was assistant to club manager Graham Taylor?

6 In which year had Watford last been in the top flight of the English Football League?

7 Who scored Watford's first ever goal at Wembley in the 37th minute of the First Division Play-Off Final?

8 Who scored Watford's second goal a minute from time?

9 For which club did both Watford scorers formerly play?

10 Which Bolton Wanderers player missed at least three clear chances during this match?

11 Who was the Welsh captain of Watford?

12 Who replaced Michael Johansen for Bolton Wanderers?

13 What number shirt was worn by Andy Todd, the son of Bolton Wanderers' manager Colin?

14 What nationality is Watford's Michel Ngonge?

15 Who resigned as Vice-Chairman of Rangers after revelations in the Scottish Daily Record?

Answers

1 Terry Heilbron **2** Sunderland **3** Steve Palmer **4** Ricardo Gardner **5** Kenny Jackett **6** 1988 **7** Nick Wright **8** Allan Smart **9** Carlisle United **10** Eidur Gudjohnsen **11** Robert Page **12** Scott Sellars **13** Five **14** Zairean **15** Donald Findlay

FOOTBALL FACTS

FOOTBALL FACTS CONTENTS

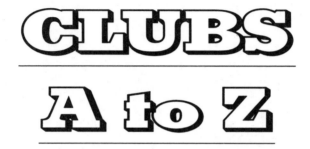

CLUBS
A

THE CARLING ULTIMATE FOOTBALL FACT AND QUIZ BOOK

Clubs – A

Aberdeen

Aberdeen play in an all-red strip with white trim. Their modern nickname is The Dons, although they were formerly known as The Whites and before that as The Wasps.

Aberdeen were originally formed in 1881 and joined the Scottish Football League in 1903.

Since 1899, Aberdeen have played their home games at Pittodrie – the word means dung heap in Gaelic. The stadium is built on ground that was once used to exercise police horses.

Pittodrie has long been the home of innovation – in the 1920s, it was the first ground to have a dug-out built along the touchline so that the management and training staff could watch the players' footwork.

More significantly in historical terms, in 1978, Pittodrie became the first all-seater football venue in the British Isles.

Aberdeen won promotion in their first season in the League but had to wait until 1955 for their first Scottish League Championship. Since then they have won the Premiership title three more times – in 1980, 1984 and 1985.

To date, Aberdeen have won the Scottish FA Cup seven times – in 1947, 1970, 1982, 1983, 1984, 1986 and 1990.

Aberdeen have so far won the Scottish League Cup five times – in 1955-56, 1976-77, 1985-86, 1989-90 and 1995-96.

In 1983, Aberdeen achieved European glory, beating Real Madrid 2-1 after extra time in the Final of the Cup Winners' Cup in Gothenburg, Sweden. Ten days later, they won the Scottish FA Cup to bring off an unprecedented double.

When I was a lad a tiny wee lad
My mother said to me
Go see the Dons the glorious Dons
Away down at Pittodrie
They call them the heavenly dancers
Superb in attack and defence
I'll never forget that wonderful sight
I've been a supporter since

The northern lights of old Aberdeen
Are home sweet home to me
The northern lights of old Aberdeen
Are where I long to b
I've been a wanderer all of my life
And many a sight I've seen
But God speed the day
When I'm on my way
To my home in old Aberdeen

(Tune: The Northern Lights of Old Aberdeen)

THE CARLING ULTIMATE FOOTBALL FACT AND QUIZ BOOK

Clubs – A

Airdrieonians

Airdrieonians play at the Excelsior Stadium, Broomfield Park, Craigneuk Avenue.

The club was formed in 1878 and first took the field as Excelsior. They took their present name in 1881. Airdrieonians joined the Scottish Football League in 1894.

Airdrieonians have never won the Scottish Championship but they finished second in the First Division four years running – 1923, 1924, 1925 and 1926.

Airdrieonians won the Scottish FA Cup for the only time in 1924, when they beat Hibernian 2-0 in the Final at Ibrox.

Airdrieonians are usually nicknamed The Diamonds after their traditional strip of white shirts decorated with a red diamond, white shorts and red socks.

Airdrieonians are also known as The Waysiders, possibly because that is where they have been left standing by their near neighbours Celtic and Rangers.

Airdrie's record victory came in 1886, when they beat Rangers 10-2 (this is also the Gers' record defeat).

Albion Rovers

Nicknamed The Wee Rovers to distinguish them from Raith, Albion play their home matches at the Cliftonville Stadium in Main Street, Coatbridge, which is on the outskirts of Motherwell.

The Albion Rovers home strip consists of yellow shirts with red trim, yellow shorts and black and yellow hooped socks.

Albion Rovers were formed in 1882 and joined the Scottish Football League in 1903.

In 1920, they knocked Rangers out of the Scottish FA Cup in the semi-final, but lost 3-2 to Kilmarnock the Final.

Albion Rovers have twice been Champions of the Scottish Second Division – in 1934 and 1989.

THE CARLING ULTIMATE FOOTBALL FACT AND QUIZ BOOK

Clubs – A

Alloa Athletic

Alloa Athletic play at the Recreation Park in Clackmannan Road. They are nicknamed The Wasps in reference to their home strip, which is black and gold striped shirts, black shorts with gold trim and gold socks with black trim.

Alloa Athletic were formed in 1883 and joined the Scottish League in 1921. In 1922 they became the first team to be promoted to the First Division under the newly launched one-up-one-down system.

Alloa Athletic were Scottish Second Division Champions in 1922 and Third Division Champions in 1998.

Arbroath

Arbroath are nicknamed The Red Lichties (English: Red Lights) after the town's Stephenson-built Bell Rock Lighthouse.

The club was founded in 1878. In 1885 they scored one of the world's most famous victories when they beat Bon Accord of Aberdeen 36-0, a record score in senior football. They joined the Scottish Football League in 1921.

Arbroath play their home games at Gayfield Park. Their strip is maroon shirts with white sleeves, maroon shorts with white trim and maroon socks with white tops.

Arsenal

Although Arsenal's ground is known universally as Highbury, this is strictly the name of the area of London in which they have made their home. The ground itself is correctly known as the Arsenal Stadium, Avenell Road, London N5.

Arsenal play their home games in red shirts with white sleeves, white shorts and red socks with white trim. Their away strip is predominantly yellow with blue areas. Until 1933, they played in all red. In 1895, they experimented briefly with red and light blue stripes.

Arsenal are nicknamed the Gunners or the Gooners, the latter probably being derived from the northern pronunciation of the former.

The club now known as Arsenal was founded in October 1886 in Woolwich, southeast London, and was originally called Dial Square, after the thoroughfare in which stood an army workshop with a sundial over the entrance.

The club's original players included two former Nottingham Forest players, Morris Bates and Fred Beardsley. It is because their old club donated some old shirts that Arsenal came to play in red. Their earliest nickname was The Woolwich Reds.

THE CARLING ULTIMATE FOOTBALL FACT AND QUIZ BOOK

Facts
Clubs – A

Arsenal continued...

In 1886, the club was renamed Royal Arsenal. However, they received no royal patronage and the name may be derived from that of a local pub.

In 1890, the club acquired the Invicta Ground in Plumstead.

In 1891 the club turned professional and changed its name to Woolwich Arsenal, which it remained until it became plain Arsenal in 1914.

In 1893, Woolwich Arsenal were elected to the Second Division of the Football League. Also in that year they bought their own ground, Manor Field, which they had previously leased in the 1888-90 season.

In 1904, Arsenal won promotion to the First Division but they were debt-ridden and went into liquidation in 1910.

Henry Norris, a property developer, stepped into the breach and devised a plan for a merger with Fulham.

In 1913, Woolwich Arsenal finished bottom of the First Division, setting an unwanted record by winning only once at home all season. Relegation exacerbated their financial problems, and the solution was to move to a new stadium at Highbury in north London.

The proposed move was vigorously opposed by the Borough Council of Islington (in which Highbury stands) but their efforts to prevent the club moving there were unsuccessful.

On moving north of the River Thames, Woolwich Arsenal became The Arsenal in 1914. Although the definite article was dropped in 1927, it may still be heard in supporters' chants and people still speak of going 'up the Arsenal'.

When the Football League resumed its normal business after the disruptions caused by the First World War, it proposed to expand the First Division by two clubs. Although Arsenal remained strapped for cash, Henry Norris used his personal wealth to secure a place for his team in the new elite, even though they failed to win promotion after finishing fifth in the Second Division.

Since then, Arsenal have never been out of the top flight of English League football and is the only club to have achieved this distinction.

In 1925, Norris pulled off what turned out to be his master stroke – the appointment as manager of former Huddersfield Town boss Herbert Chapman.

Henry Norris bowed out of football in 1925 after being found guilty of financial irregularities, including the unauthorised use of a chauffeur.

Arsenal won the First Division Championship in 1931, 1933, 1934, 1935, 1938, 1948, 1953, 1971, 1989, 1991 and the Premiership in 1998. In 1971 and 1998, they also won the FA Cup. They have also won the FA Cup in 1930, 1936, 1950, 1979 and 1993. In 1993, they won both the FA and the League Cup, the first time a club had achieved this double.

THE CARLING ULTIMATE FOOTBALL FACT AND QUIZ BOOK

Clubs – A

Arsenal continued...

Arsenal won the European Fairs' Cup in 1970 and the European Cup Winners' Cup in 1994.

Arsenal Managers
1894-97	Sam Hollis
1897-98	Tom Mitchell
1898-99	George Elcoat
1899-1904	Harry Bradshaw
1904-08	Phil Kelso
1908-15	George Morrell
1919-25	Leslie Knighton
1925-34	Herbert Chapman
1934-47	George Allison
1947-56	Tom Whittaker
1956-58	Jack Crayston
1958-62	George Swindin
1962-66	Billy Wright
1966-76	Bertie Mee
1976-83	Terry Neill
1984-86	Don Howe
1986-95	George Graham
1995-96	Bruce Rioch
1996-	Arsène Wenger

Arsenal League Record
1893-1904	Division Two
1904-1913	Division One
1913-1919	Division Two
1919-1992	Division One
1992-	Premiership

Good old Arsenal
We're proud to say that name
While we sing this song
We'll win the game

(tune: Rule Britannia)

We've got Dennis Bergkamp
We've got Dennis Bergkamp
La-la la la, la-la la la

(tune: Let's All Do The Conga)

In the 1998-99 season, the Arsenal player whose replica team shirt sold in the greatest numbers was Dennis Bergkamp.

THE CARLING ULTIMATE FOOTBALL FACT AND QUIZ BOOK

Facts
Clubs – A

Aston Villa

Aston Villa – nicknamed The Villans – are one of only four professional clubs in the United Kingdom to play in claret and blue (the others are Burnley, Scunthorpe United and West Ham United). Villa play their home matches at Villa Park in Trinity Road, Birmingham, a capacious stadium which is one of the traditional neutral venues for the semi-finals of the FA Cup.

The club was founded in 1874, traditionally at an open-air meeting of cricketers held in the light of a street lamp. The club's first home game at the Aston Lower Grounds amusement park was a strange hybrid affair. The opposition were Aston Brook St Mary's rugby club and so one half of the game was rugby, the other soccer.

In 1876, the club moved to Perry Barr, where they remained until 1897, when they moved to their present home.

Aston Villa were among the 12 founder members of the Football League in 1888 and finished the first season as runners-up to Preston North End.

Aston Villa won the League Championship for the first time in 1894 and have since repeated the achievement in 1896, 1897, 1899, 1900, 1910 and 1981.

Aston Villa have won the FA Cup seven times, in 1887, 1895, 1897, 1905, 1913, 1920 and 1957.

In 1897, Aston Villa became the second club – after Preston North End – to win the League and FA Cup double.

Aston Villa were the first winners of the League Cup, in 1961.

The 1970s were the worst years in Villa's history – they spent two years in Division Three. But they revived, returning to the top flight in 1975, and went on to win the League in 1981 and the European Cup the following year.

In 1993, the first year of the Premier League, Aston Villa finished runners-up to Manchester United.

Clubs – A

Aston Villa continued...

Aston Villa Managers

1884-1926	George Ramsay
1926-34	W J Smith
1934-35	Jimmy McMullan
1936-44	Jimmy Hogan
1945-50	Alex Massie
1950-53	George Martin
1953-58	Eric Houghton
1958-64	Joe Mercer
1965-67	Dick Taylor
1967-68	Tommy Cummings
1968-70	Tommy Docherty
1970-74	Vic Crowe
1974-82	Ron Saunders
1982-84	Tony Barton
1984-86	Graham Turner
1986-87	Billy McNeill
1987-90	Graham Taylor
1990-91	Dr Jozef Venglos
1991-94	Ron Atkinson
1994-98	Brian Little
1998-	John Gregory

Aston Villa League Record

1888-1936	Division One
1936-1938	Division Two
1938-1959	Division One
1959-1960	Division Two
1960-1967	Division One
1967-1970	Division Two
1970-1972	Division Three
1972-1975	Division Two
1975-1987	Division One
1987-1988	Division Two
1988-1992	Division One
1992-	Premiership

Villa fans are famous for having nary a song in their hearts.

In the 1998-99 season, the Aston Villa player whose replica team shirt sold in the greatest numbers was Dion Dublin.

THE CARLING ULTIMATE FOOTBALL FACT AND QUIZ BOOK

Clubs – A

Atletico Madrid

Founded in 1903, Atletico Madrid play their home matches in the Vicente Calderon Stadium.

The Atletico Madrid strip consists of red and white striped shirts, blue shorts and red socks with a white trim.

Although generally in the shadow of Spain's big two – Real Madrid and Barcelona – Atletico have won both the domestic League and the Cup nine times to date, as well as the European Cup Winners' Cup in 1962.

In the late 1930s, the club faced bankruptcy and only survived through a merger with the Spanish Air Force Football Club.

In 1959, Atletico Madrid came within a whisker of the European Cup Final but were beaten by Real, the holders of the trophy, in a semi-final play-off.

In the 1960s, Atletico Madrid's owners completed the sale of their old ground to property developers before their new stadium could be completed and thus Atletico had to swallow their pride and play in the Bernabeu Stadium of their great local rivals, Real Madrid.

Atletico Madrid reached their first European Cup Final in 1974, but lost 4-0 to Bayern Munich in a replay after the first match had been drawn 1-1.

For political reasons, Bayern Munich refused to play in the World Club Championship against Independiente of Argentina. Atletico took their place and won the game 1-0.

At the end of the 1980s, Atletico Madrid was taken over by Jesus Gil, a property developer, who bankrolled the club and acquired a reputation for a low tolerance of underachieving managers.

In 1996, Atletico Madrid won the Spanish League and Cup double.

Ayr United

Ayr United are nicknamed The Honest Men – this is a reference to the lines in Tam O'Shanter by Robert Burns:

> *Auld Ayr, wham ne'er a town surpasses,*
> *For honest men and bonnie lasses*

Ayr United were founded in 1910 through the merger of Ayr FC and Ayr Parkhouse. Ayr United play their home games at Somerset Park in Tryfield Place in a strip that consists of white shirts with black trim, black shorts and white socks with black trim.

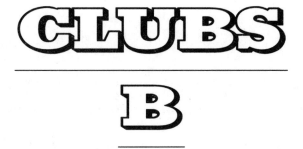

THE CARLING ULTIMATE FOOTBALL FACT AND QUIZ BOOK

Clubs – B

Barcelona

Founded in 1899 by a Swiss man named Joan Gamper, Barcelona play in the magnificent 115,000-seater Nou Camp Stadium on the western outskirts of the city.

Barcelona colours are blue and red striped shirts, blue shorts and blue socks.

The club's first match was against a team of English sailors who were on shore leave in the city.

In addition to being a football club, Barcelona is a focus of Catalan nationalism. The rivalry with Castilian clubs – above all Real Madrid – is particularly intense.

In the 1920s, the ground was closed for a while after supporters had whistled during a royal march played at half time.

These feelings were most keenly expressed during the rule of General Franco (1939-1975), when Catalan nationalism was suppressed in everyday life but expressed itself subversively at football matches.

To date, Barcelona have won the Spanish League 16 times (their most recent title coming in 1999) and the Cup 24 times. They have won the European Cup once, in 1992, and the European Cup Winners' Cup four times – in 1979, 1982, 1989 and 1997. They won the Inter Cities Fairs Cup in 1958, 1960 and 1966.

Among the famous managers of Barcelona have been the Englishmen Bobby Robson and Terry Venables and the Dutchmen Johan Cruyff and Louis Van Gaal.

Pope John Paul II is an honorary member of Barcelona and is therefore widely assumed to be a supporter of the club. .

Barnet

Barnet play their home matches at the Underhill Stadium, Barnet Lane. Their nickname is The Bees.

They play their home games in amber and black striped shirts, black shorts and black socks.

Although Barnet were founded in 1888, they did not join the Football League until 1991 after winning the GM Vauxhall Conference. Their first game in the Fourth Division was a 7-4 home defeat to Crewe Alexandra.

Barnet have had a chequered financial history and were fined for irregularities in 1992. The club Chairman was for many years Stan Flashman.

THE CARLING ULTIMATE FOOTBALL FACT AND QUIZ BOOK

Clubs – B

Barnet continued...

Barnet Managers
1991-1993	Barry Fry
1993-1994	Gary Phillips
1994-1996	Ray Clemence
1996-1997	Alan Mullery
1997	Terry Bullivant
1997-	John Still

Barnet League Record
1991-1992	Division Four
1992-1993	Division Three
1993-1994	Division Four
1994-	Division Three

We're dreaming of a nine-point Christmas
Just like the ones we used to know
Where goal posts glisten
And children listen
To hear the West Bank in full flow

In the 1998-99 season, the Barnetl player whose replica team shirt sold in the greatest numbers was Sean Devine.

Barnsley

Nicknamed the Tykes, the Reds or the Colliers, Barnsley were founded in 1887 as the church team of Barnsley St Peter's by the Reverend Tiverton Preedy. They play their home matches at the Oakwell Ground in Grove Street.

Barnsley joined the League and adopted their present name in 1898, since when they have spent more time in the Second Division than any other team.

Barnsley play their home matches in red shirts, white shorts and red socks.

Barnsley's greatest moment came in 1912, when they won the FA Cup, beating West Bromwich Albion in the Final replay.

This FA Cup-winning team were nicknamed Battling Barnsley because of the particularly hard route they had taken to the Final. They played a total of 12 games en route to the trophy. Six of these games – including the first Final at Crystal Palace – were 0-0 draws; five were 1-0 victories, including the Final replay at Bramall Lane, Sheffield. (The other tie was a 3-1 goal riot against Birmingham City.)

THE CARLING ULTIMATE FOOTBALL FACT AND QUIZ BOOK

Facts
Clubs – B

Barnsley continued...

Harry Tufnell's FA Cup-winning goal for the Tykes came from the penalty spot in the last minute of extra time in the replay.

Barnsley had previously reached the Final in 1910, but lost to Newcastle United.

In 1997, Barnsley won promotion to the Premiership but their first ever taste of life in the top flight of English football was not a happy one and they were relegated at the end of the season.

Barnsley Managers

1898-1901	Arthur Fairclough
1901-1904	John McCartney
1904-1912	Arthur Fairclough
1912-1914	John Hastie
1914-1919	Percy Lewis
1919-1926	Peter Sant
1926-1929	John Commins
1929-1930	Arthur Fairclough
1930-1937	Brough Fletcher
1937-1953	Angus Seed
1953-1960	Tim Ward
1960-1971	Johnny Steele
1971-1972	John McSeveney
1972-1973	Johnny Steele
1973-1978	Jim Iley
1978-1980	Allan Clarke
1980-1984	Norman Hunter
1984-1985	Bobby Collins
1985-1989	Allan Clarke
1989-1993	Mel Machin
1993-1994	Viv Anderson
1994-1998	Danny Wilson
1998-	John Hendrie

Barnsley League Record

1898-1932	Division Two
1932-1934	Division Three (North)
1934-1938	Division Two
1938-1939	Division Three (North)
1946-1953	Division Two
1953-1955	Division Three (North)
1955-1959	Division Two
1959-1965	Division Three
1965-1968	Division Four
1968-1972	Division Three

Clubs – B

Barnsley continued...

1972-1979	Division Four
1979-1981	Division Three
1981-1992	Division Two
1992-1997	Division One
1997-1998	Premiership
1998-	Division One

From the green green grass of Oakwell
To the shores of Sicily
We will fight, fight, fight for Barnsley
Till we win the Football League

(tune: Halls of Montezuma)

In the 1998-99 season, the Barnsley player whose replica team shirt sold in the greatest numbers was Ashley Ward, despite the fact that the player ended the campaign at Blackburn Rovers.

Bayern Munich

Bayern Munich were founded in 1900. They play their home matches in the Olimpiastadion and their strip is all red.

Although Bayern Munich first won the German League in 1932, it was not until the 1960s that they became pre-eminent in West Germany. Indeed, when the Bundesliga replaced the old regional tournaments in 1963, Bayern were not even members. But times changed drastically, and they have now won the League 14 times and the Cup eight times.

Bayern Munich's three European Cup victories came in three consecutive years – 1974, 1975 and 1976.

The three great stars of Bayern's emergence as a major footballing power were goalkeeper Sepp Maier, attacking midfielder-cum-sweeper Franz Beckenbauer and prolific striker Gerd Muller. This trio led Bayern to promotion in 1965, the West German Cup in 1966 and the European Cup Winners' Cup in 1967.

Franz Beckenbauer has now been a player, captain, manager, vice-president and president of the club.

In 1996, Bayern Munich won the UEFA Cup, thus becoming the fourth club to win all three major European trophies.

Clubs – B

Benfica

Benfica have always been the outstanding team in Portugal. Since they were founded in 1904, they have won the Portuguese League 29 times and the Cup 26 times.

They are nicknamed the Eagles and play in red shirts, white shorts and red socks. They play their home games at the Estadio da Luz (Stadium of Light) on the outskirts of Lisbon.

It was Benfica who finally broke Real Madrid's stranglehold on the European Cup, which they won for the first time in 1961 and retained the following year.

The Benfica motto is *E pluribus unum*, the Latin for 'all for one'.

Berwick Rangers

Berwick Rangers are the only football club in England that plays in the Scottish League. They were founded in 1881 and were originally members of the Northumberland FA, but joined the Scottish League in 1951.

Berwick Rangers are nicknamed The Borderers; they play their home matches at Shielfield Park, Shielfield Terrace, Tweedmouth.

Berwick Rangers' strip consists of black and gold striped shirts, black shorts and black and gold socks.

Berwick Rangers' only League honour to date has been the Second Division Championship, which they won in 1979.

In the 1963-64 season, Berwick Rangers reached the semi-final of the Scottish League Cup, losing eventually to Rangers.

In 1967, however, they took unforgettable revenge on Rangers, beating them 1-0 at Shielfield Park in the First Round of the Scottish FA Cup on January 28, 1967. The scorer that day was Sammy Reid. Berwick's other hero was goalkeeper Jock Wallace, who kept out everything the Glasgow club subsequently threw at him.

THE CARLING ULTIMATE FOOTBALL FACT AND QUIZ BOOK

Clubs – B

Birmingham City

Birmingham City are nicknamed the Blues and play their home matches at St Andrews.

Birmingham City play in blue shirts, white shorts and blue and white hooped socks.

The club was founded in 1875 by a group of cricketers who attended Trinity Church, Bordesley. They entered the Second Division of the Football League in 1892 as Small Heath, a name they kept until 1905, when they changed their name to Birmingham; the City was added in 1945.

Birmingham have achieved less success than any other big-city club in Britain. They have never won anything other than the League Cup in 1963, the Leyland Daf Cup in 1991 and the Auto Windscreens Shield in 1995.

Birmingham Managers

1892-1908	Alfred Jones
1908-1910	Alec Watson
1910-1915	Bob McRoberts
1915-1923	Frank Richards
1923-1927	Billy Beer
1928-1933	Leslie Knighton
1933-1939	George Liddell
1945-1948	Harry Storer
1949-1954	Bob Brocklebank
1954-1958	Arthur Turner
1959-1960	Pat Beasley
1960-1964	Gil Merrick
1965	Joe Mallett
1965-1970	Stan Cullis
1970-1975	Fred Goodwin
1975-1977	Willie Bell
1978-1982	Jim Smith
1982-1986	Ron Saunders
1986-1987	John Bond
1987-1989	Garry Pendrey
1989-1991	Dave Mackay
1991	Lou Macari
1991-1993	Terry Cooper
1993-1996	Barry Fry
1996-	Trevor Francis

Birmingham City League Record

1892-1894	Division Two
1894-1896	Division One
1896-1901	Division Two
1901-1902	Division One

THE CARLING ULTIMATE FOOTBALL FACT AND QUIZ BOOK

Clubs – B

Birmingham City continued...

1902-1903	Division Two
1903-1908	Division One
1908-1921	Division Two
1921-1939	Division One
1946-1948	Division Two
1948-1950	Division One
1950-1955	Division Two
1955-1965	Division One
1965-1972	Division Two
1972-1979	Division One
1979-1980	Division Two
1980-1984	Division One
1984-1985	Division Two
1985-1986	Division One
1986-1989	Division Two
1989-1992	Division Three
1992-1994	Division One
1994-1995	Division Two
1995-	Division One

Aston Villa are the most successful club in the Birmingham conurbation, but their supporters are a largely silent lot – the best songs are the Blues'.

> *All through life it's a long long road*
> *There'll be joys and sorrows too*
> *As we journey on we will sing this song*
> *For the boys in royal blue*
> *We're often partisan la la*
> *We will journey on la la*
> *Keep right on to the end of the road*
> *Keep right on to the end*
> *Though the way be long*
> *Let your hearts be strong*
> *Keep right on round the bend*
> *Though you're tired and weary*
> *Still journey on*
> *Til you come to your happy abode*
> *With all your love*
> *We'll be dreaming of*
> *We'll be there – where?*
> *At the end of the road*
> *Birmingham Birmingham*

(tune: Keep Right On To The End of the Road)

THE CARLING ULTIMATE FOOTBALL FACT AND QUIZ BOOK

Facts
Clubs – B

Birmingham City continued...

When Birmingham find themselves in a lower division than they think behoves a club of their standing, and their fans visit grounds that they think are less well-appointed than their own, they sing the following, to the tune When The Saints Go Marching In:

> *My garden shed (My garden shed)*
> *My garden shed (My garden shed)*
> *My garden shed is bigger than this*
> *It's got a door and a window*
> *My garden shed is bigger than this*

In the 1998-99 season, the Birmingham City player whose replica team shirt sold in the greatest numbers was Dele Adebola.

Blackburn Rovers

Blackburn Rovers – nicknamed the Blue and Whites after the colours they wear – were founded in 1875 as the Blackburn Grammar School Old Boys' XI. In their first season they played all their matches away from home.

Blackburn's first permanent ground was at Oozehead (1876); they then moved to Pleasington Cricket Ground (1877), Alexandra Meadows (1878) and Leamington Road (1881). In 1890, they moved into their present home, Ewood Park.

Blackburn Rovers turned professional in 1880 and were founder members of the English Football League. In the first season of the competition (1888-89), they finished fourth.

The Blackburn Rovers motto is Arte et labore, which is Latin for 'Through skill and labour'.

Blackburn play their home matches in blue and white halved shirts, white shorts and white socks.

Blackburn Rovers made the first of their eight FA Cup Final appearances in 1882, when they lost 1-0 to the Old Etonians.

They have since won the FA Cup six times, in 1884, 1885, 1886, 1890, 1891 and 1928.

Blackburn Rovers won the League Championship in 1912 and 1914 and the Premiership in 1995.

THE CARLING ULTIMATE FOOTBALL FACT AND QUIZ BOOK

Facts
Clubs – B

Blackburn Rovers continued...

Blackburn Rovers Managers
1884-1896	Thomas Mitchell
1896-1903	J Walmsley
1903-1925	R B Middleton
1925-1926	Jack Carr
1926-1930	Bob Crompton
1931-1936	Arthur Barritt
1936-1938	Reg Taylor
1938-1941	Bob Crompton
1944-1947	Eddie Hapgood
1947	Will Scott
1947-1949	Jack Bruton
1949-1953	Jackie Bestall
1953-1958	Johnny Carey
1958-1960	Dally Duncan
1960-1967	Jack Marshall
1967-1970	Eddie Quigley
1970-1971	Johnny Carey
1971-1973	Ken Furphy
1974-1975	Gordon Lee
1975-1978	Jim Smith
1978	Jim Iley
1978-1979	John Pickering
1979-1981	Howard Kendall
1981-1986	Bobby Saxton
1987-1991	Don Mackay
1991-1995	Kenny Dalglish
1995-1997	Ray Harford
1997-1998	Roy Hodgson
1998-	Brian Kidd

Blackburn Rovers League Record
1888-1936	Division One
1936-1939	Division Two
1946-1948	Division One
1948-1958	Division Two
1958-1966	Division One
1966-1971	Division Two
1971-1975	Division Three
1975-1979	Division Two
1979-1980	Division Three
1980-1992	Division Two
1992-1999	Premiership

THE CARLING ULTIMATE FOOTBALL FACT AND QUIZ BOOK

Facts
Clubs – B

Blackburn Rovers continued...

Most Blackburn supporters' songs are critical of local rivals Burnley and too rude to be included here.

The recent success of Blackburn has been due in large part to the benefactions of jack Walker, a longtime supporter of the club who sold his business for £365 million and thus had a vast amount of cash to invest in the club.

The club's attendances, however, remain among the smallest in the top flight of English football, with the result that opposition fans sing 'Can't buy supporters, You know you can't buy supporters', to the tune of Juantanamera.

In the 1998-99 season, the Blackburn Rovers player whose replica team shirt sold in the greatest numbers was Kevin Davies.

Blackpool

Founded in 1887, Blackpool play in tangerine shirts with navy blue and white trim, tangerine shorts and tangerine socks with white tops. They are nicknamed The Seasiders.

Blackpool played at Raikes Hall Gardens from 1887 and spent the years 1897 to 1899 at the Blackpool Athletic Grounds before settling at their present home, Bloomfield Road, in 1899. Until they turned professional, they were known as Blackpool St John's because they had been founded by old boys of St John's School in a meeting at the Stanley Arms Hotel.

Also in 1899, the club amalgamated with South Shore FC but retained its own name.

In their first year at Bloomfield Road, Blackpool finished third from bottom of the Second Division and failed to win re-election to the Football League.

The following year they applied successfully for re-election. They spent the next 30 years in the Second Division before winning promotion in 1930.

Blackpool were most successful in the 1940s and 1950s. They appeared in the 1948 and 1951 FA Cup Finals, losing both times. But it was third time lucky – in 1953, the year of Queen Elizabeth II's coronation. Their great game at Wembley is known as the Matthews Final, after Stanley Matthews, the great winger who set up the goals in a stirring 4-3 victory over Bolton Wanderers.

Blackpool's best League season was in 1955-56, when they finished runners-up to Manchester United in the First Division.

In other competitions, Blackpool reached the semi-final of the League Cup in 1962 and won the Anglo-Italian Cup in 1971.

Facts
Clubs – B

Blackpool continued...

Blackpool Managers
1903-1909	Tom Barcroft
1909-1911	John Cox
1911-1919	Tom Barcroft
1919-1923	Bill Norman
1923-1927	Major Frank Buckley
1927-1928	Sid Beaumont
1928-1933	Harry Evans
1933-1935	Alex Macfarlane
1935-1958	Joe Smith
1958-1967	Ronnie Suart
1967-1969	Stan Mortensen
1969-1970	Les Shannon
1970-1972	Bob Stokoe
1972-1976	Harry Potts
1976-1978	Allan Brown
1978-1979	Bob Stokoe
1979-1980	Stan Ternent
1980-1981	Alan Ball
1981-1982	Allan Brown
1982-1989	Stan Ellis
1989-1990	Jimmy Mullen
1990	Graham Carr
1990-1994	Bill Ayre
1994-1996	Sam Allardyce
1996-1997	Gary Megson
1997-	Nigel Worthington

Blackpool League Record
1896-1899	Division Two
1899-1900	Not in Football League
1900-1930	Division Two
1930-1933	Division One
1933-1937	Division Two
1937-1967	Division One
1967-1970	Division Two
1970-1971	Division One
1971-1978	Division Two
1978-1981	Division Three
1981-1985	Division Four
1985-1990	Division Three
1990-1992	Division Four
1992-	Division Two

THE CARLING ULTIMATE FOOTBALL FACT AND QUIZ BOOK

Clubs – B

Blackpool continued...

Blackpool supporters are not great singers themselves, but their team is the inspiration for the songs of others, especially fans of Preston North End and Wigan Athletic, who – needless to say – traditionally hate the Seasiders like poison.

In the 1998-99 season, the Blackpool player whose replica team shirt sold in the greatest numbers was Steve Banks.

Boca Juniors

Boca Juniors play their home games at the Bombonera Stadium in Buenos Aires, Argentina. (Bombonera is Spanish for chocolate box.)

Boca Juniors' home strip consists of dark blue and yellow hooped shirts, dark blue shorts and dark blue socks.

Boca Juniors were founded in 1905 by an Irishman named Patrick MacCarthy and a group of recent immigrants from Italy.

Bolton Wanderers

The club now known as Bolton Wanderers play in white shirts, navy blue shorts and blue socks. But when they were founded, in 1874, they were known as Christ Church Sunday School FC and played in red and white quartered shirts – even today, some supporters may still call them The Reds.

In 1883, Bolton Wanderers played for a while in an experimental strip of white shirts with red spots because it was thought that they made the players who wore them look larger than life.

Bolton are nicknamed The Trotters because for many years they had no fixed home ground. They played at the Park Recreation Ground and Cockle's Field, Bolton before moving to Pike's Lane in 1881. In 1895, they settled at Burnden Park, where they remained until 1997. Since then they have played at the purpose-built Reebok Stadium.

THE CARLING ULTIMATE FOOTBALL FACT AND QUIZ BOOK

Clubs – B

Bolton Wanderers continued...

Bolton were founder members of the English Football League in 1888. In the first season, they finished fifth.

Bolton Wanderers was one of the first clubs to use professional players – this was controversial in the late 19th century, but soon became the accepted norm.

Bolton Wanderers reached the FA Cup Final in 1894 and 1904 but did not win the trophy until 1923, in the first Final to be played at Wembley Stadium.

Bolton won the Cup again in 1926 and 1929. In all three of these Finals, they used only 17 different players.

1946 was the year of the Burnden Park Disaster, which occurred just before the start of Bolton's FA quarter-final against Stoke City. About 85,000 came to see the game and the turnstiles became blocked with people who avoided the jams by climbing over fences around the perimeter of the ground. But then someone left the ground, leaving behind him an open door through which thousands rushed headlong, causing a stampede. Two barriers behind the corner flag at the Railway End collapsed and 33 people were crushed to death. The game went ahead.

In the wake of this disaster, the Moelwyn Hughes Report recommended strict controls over the number of people allowed into a football ground. But it took several more disasters (see Liverpool and Rangers) before anything much was done.

Bolton won the FA Cup for the fourth time in 1958, beating fierce local rivals Manchester United in the Final.

Bolton Wanderers Managers

1874-1885	Tom Rawthorne
1885-1886	J J Bentley
1886-1887	W G Struthers
1887	Fitzroy Norris
1887-1895	J J Bentley
1895-1896	Harry Downs
1896-1898	Frank Brettell
1898-1910	John Somerville
1910-1915	Will Settle
1915-1919	Tom Mather
1919-1944	Charles Foweraker
1944-1950	Walter Rowley
1951-1968	Bill Ridding
1968-1970	Nat Lofthouse
1970	Jimmy McIlroy
1971	Jimmy Meadows
1971	Nat Lofthouse

THE CARLING ULTIMATE FOOTBALL FACT AND QUIZ BOOK

Clubs – B

Bolton Wanderers continued...

1971-1974	Jimmy Armfield
1974-1980	Ian Greaves
1980-1981	Stan Anderson
1981-1982	George Mulhall
1982-1985	John McGovern
1985	Charlie Wright
1985-1992	Phil Neal
1992-1995	Bruce Rioch
1995-1995	Roy McFarland
1996-	Colin Todd

Bolton Wanderers League Record

1888-1899	Division One
1899-1900	Division Two
1900-1903	Division One
1903-1905	Division Two
1905-1908	Division One
1908-1909	Division Two
1909-1910	Division One
1910-1911	Division Two
1911-1933	Division One
1933-1935	Division Two
1935-1964	Division One
1964-1971	Division Two
1971-1973	Division Three
1973-1978	Division Two
1978-1980	Division One
1980-1983	Division Two
1983-1987	Division Three
1987-1988	Division Four
1988-1992	Division Three
1992-1993	Division Two
1993-1995	Division One
1995-1996	Premiership
1996-1997	Division One
1997-1998	Premiership
1998-	Division One

THE CARLING ULTIMATE FOOTBALL FACT AND QUIZ BOOK

Clubs – B

Bolton Wanderers continued...

Fans of Bolton Wanderers vent their worst spleen on Manchester United. Their most positive song is sung to the tune 'Look Who's Coming Up The Hill Boys':

> *Look who's coming up the hill boys*
> *The Wanderers are coming up the hill boys*
> *They all laugh at us*
> *They all mock at us*
> *They say our days are numbered*
> *Born to be a Wanderer*
> *Victorious are we*
> *So you'd better hurry up*
> *Cause we're gonna win the Cup*
> *We're the pride of Division Three – Two – One*
> *Victorious and glorious*
> *We took the Stretford End*
> *Between the four of us*
> *Glory be to God that there ain't no more of us*
> *Coz the Lever End took the lot.*

In the 1998-99 season, the Bolton Wanderers player whose replica team shirt sold in the greatest numbers was Arnar Gunnlaugsson.

AFC Bournemouth

Bournemouth were founded in 1899 and are nicknamed The Cherries after their strip – the shirts are predominantly red with three-inch black stripes and a white pinstripe, white shorts and white socks.

The present club grew out of Boscombe St John's, which was founded in 1890. The present club has played at Dean Court since 1910 and was elected to the Football League in 1923.

Bournemouth remained in the Third Division longer than any other team in history, finally being relegated to Division Four in 1970.

From 1923 they were known as Bournemouth and Boscombe Athletic but changed their name to AFC Bournemouth in 1971.

Bournemouth reached the Sixth Round of the FA Cup in 1957. In the Fourth Round they beat Wolverhampton Wanderers, who won the League that year. The winning goal was scored by Reg Cutler, who also in the same match managed to bring the goal down when he collided with an upright.

AFC Bournemouth won the FA Associate Members' Cup in 1984.

THE CARLING ULTIMATE FOOTBALL FACT AND QUIZ BOOK

Clubs – B

AFC Bournemouth continued…

Bournemouth Managers

1914-1923	Vincent Kitcher
1923-1925	Harry Kinghorn
1925-1928	Leslie Knighton
1928-1930	Frank Richards
1930-1935	Billy Birrell
1935-1936	Bob Crompton
1936-1939	Charlie Bell
1939-1947	Harry Kinghorn
1947-1950	Harry Lowe
1950-1956	Jack Bruton
1956-1958	Fred Cox
1958-1961	Don Welsh
1961-1963	Bill McGarry
1963-1965	Reg Flewin
1965-1970	Fred Cox
1970-1973	John Bond
1974-1978	Trevor Hartley
1975-1978	John Benson
1979-1980	Alec Stock
1980-1982	David Webb
1983	Don Megson
1983-1992	Harry Redknapp
1992-1994	Tony Pulis
1994-	Mel Machin

Bournemouth League Record

1923-1970	Division Three
1970-1971	Division Four
1971-1975	Division Three
1975-1982	Division Four
1982-1987	Division Three
1987-1990	Division Two
1990-1992	Division Three
1992-	Division Two

We're from Bournemouth – sunny, sunny Bournemouth
And if you can't hear us we'll sing a little louder
We're from Bournemouth – sunny, sunny Bournemouth
And if you can't hear us we'll sing a little louder

In the 1998-99 season, the Bournemouth player whose replica team shirt sold in the greatest numbers was Eddie Howe.

THE CARLING ULTIMATE FOOTBALL FACT AND QUIZ BOOK

Clubs – B

Bradford City

Bradford City play in amber shirts with claret strips, black shorts and claret socks. It is from the supposed similarity between this distinctive and unusual colour scheme and the markings of a farmyard fowl that their nickname, The Bantams, is thought to be derived.

Bradford City were founded in 1903. They joined the League before they had even played a game, so great was the football authorities' enthusiasm to carve an enclave of soccer in this predominantly Rugby League-loving area of Yorkshire.

Bradford City play their home matches in The Pulse Stadium at Valley Parade.

Bradford City won the FA Cup in 1911, beating Newcastle United 1-0 in the Final.

The club's best League season was in 1911, when they finished fifth in the First Division.

Bradford City Managers

1903-1905	Robert Campbell
1905-1921	Peter O'Rourke
1921-1926	David Menzies
1926-1928	Colin Veitch
1928-1930	Peter O'Rourke
1930-1935	Jack Peart
1935-1937	Dick Ray
1938-1943	Fred Westgarth
1943-1946	Bob Sharp
1946-1947	Jack Barker
1947-1948	John Milburn
1948-1952	David Steele
1952	Albert Harris
1952-1955	Ivor Powell
1955-1961	Peter Jackson
1961-1964	Bob Brocklebank
1965-1966	Bill Harris
1966-1969	Willie Watson
1969-1971	Jimmy Wheeler
1971-1975	Bryan Edwards
1975-1978	Bobby Kennedy

Clubs – B

Bradford City continued...

1978	John Napier
1978-1981	George Mulhall
1981-1982	Roy McFarland
1982-1987	Trevor Cherry
1987-1989	Terry Dolan
1989-1990	Terry Yorath
1990-1991	John Docherty
1991-1994	Frank Stapleton
1994-1995	Lennie Lawrence
1995-1998	Chris Kamara
1998-	Paul Jewell

Bradford City League Record

1903-1908	Division Two
1908-1922	Division One
1922-1927	Division Two
1927-1929	Division Three (North)
1929-1937	Division Two
1937-1961	Division Three
1961-1969	Division Four
1969-1972	Division Three
1972-1977	Division Four
1977-1978	Division Three
1978-1982	Division Four
1982-1985	Division Three
1985-1990	Division Two
1990-1992	Division Three
1992-1996	Division Two
1996-1999	Division One

Bradford City supporters still sing about local rivals Bradford Park Avenue, even thought the latter dropped out of the Football League in 1970.

Oh we'd go up the Avenue
But we're not all that hard up
We would go up the Avenue
But they've got no beer to sup
So we'll stay with the City

Coz we know they're going up

(Tune: Up The Avenue)

In the 1998-99 season, the Bradford City player whose replica team shirt sold in the greatest numbers was Stuart McCall.

THE CARLING ULTIMATE FOOTBALL FACT AND QUIZ BOOK

Clubs – B

Bradford City continued...

The Bradford Fire Disaster

On May 11, 1985, fifty-six people were burned to death, 70 more detained in hospital with severe burns, and a further 211 supporters and police injured when a timber stand caught fire at Valley Parade during an end-of-season game. The fire broke out just before half time beneath wooden tip-up seats three rows from the back of Block G during the final home League match of the season against Lincoln City. The game was fairly well attended, because Bradford had just ensured promotion from the old English Third Division, and many fans had come to celebrate.

The fire began amid rubbish which had accumulated beneath the stand over a long period and had never been swept up. The felt and wood roof, which was tinder-dry, increased the speed at which flames engulfed the structure. When the fire was first noticed, there were a few tongues of flame licking the base of a row of seats. Within two minutes it had spread the entire length of the stand, moving faster than grown men could run.

Most of the victims were trapped in the stand itself. The first to perish were those who tried to reach the back of the stand; of those who fled onto the pitch, most were saved. At least 15 bodies were found in a walkway 4 ft (1.3 m) wide which ran along the entire length of the back of the stand.

A dozen bodies were found in clusters of two or three lying against six of the exits. They had been crushed to death as they desperately attempted to crawl out under turnstiles which had been locked to prevent latecomers getting in without paying. To make matters worse, there were no fire extinguishers in this part of the ground: they had been removed and stored in a room in the clubhouse because during previous games they been set off and used as missiles by unruly fans. The Chief Fire Officer of West Yorkshire, interviewed in The Times, said that as far as he knew there had never been a fire inspection at the ground because under English law the Fire Brigade was not empowered to carry one out on private property.

Brechin City

Brechin City were founded in 1906 through the amalgamation of Hearts and Harp and joined the Scottish League in 1929.

Brechin in Angus is the smallest settlement in the British Isles to have its own football League team.

Brechin City play at Glebe Park in Trinity Road; they wear red shirts with blue and white striped epaulets, red shorts with blue trim and red socks with white trim.

Brechin City won the Scottish Division C in 1954 and the Second Division in 1983 and 1990.

THE CARLING ULTIMATE FOOTBALL FACT AND QUIZ BOOK

Clubs – B

Brentford

Brentford play in red and white striped shirts, black shorts and black socks and are nicknamed The Bees.

The club was founded in 1889, turned professional in 1899 and settled at their present ground, Griffin Park, in 1904.

Prior to that, the club had played at Clifden Road from 1889 to 1891, Benns Fields, Little Ealing from 1891 to 1895, Shotters Field from 1895 to 1898, Cross Road, South Ealing from 1898 to 1900 and Boston Park from 1900 to 1904.

In 1929, while in the Third Division, Brentford became the only club ever to win every one of its home matches (21 in all). Despite that, they finished only second; the Third Division title in 1930 was taken by Plymouth Argyle.

Between 1935 and 1947, Brentford played in the First Division, finishing fifth in 1936, their best season to date.

In 1949, a record crowd of 38,678 attended Brentford's FA Cup Sixth Round tie at home to Leicester City. It has always been said that Brentford have a much larger catchment area than either of their near neighbours Queen's Park Rangers or Fulham. But, since the present capacity of Griffin Park is presently only 12,763, the truth of this theory is unlikely to be tested.

In the 1960s Brentford fell into financial difficulties and a merger was proposed with Queen's Park Rangers. To the relief of both sets of supporters, nothing came of it.

In 1999, Brentford won the Third Division Championship.

Brentford Managers

1900-1903	Will Lewis
1903-1906	Dick Molyneux
1906-1908	W G Brown
1908-1912	Fred Halliday
1912-1915	Ephraim Rhodes
1921-1922	Archie Mitchell
1926-1949	Harry Curtis
1949-1952	Jackie Gibbons
1952-1953	Jimmy Blain
1953	Tommy Lawton
1953-1957	Bill Dodgin Snr
1957-1965	Malcolm Macdonald
1965-1966	Tommy Cavanagh
1966-1967	Billy Gray
1967-1969	Jimmy Sirrel
1969-1973	Frank Blunstone

THE CARLING ULTIMATE FOOTBALL FACT AND QUIZ BOOK

Clubs – B

Brentford continued...

1973-1975	Mike Everitt
1975-1976	John Docherty
1976-1980	Bill Dodgin Jr
1980-1984	Fred Callaghan
1984-1987	Frank McLintock
1987-1990	Steve Perryman
1990-1993	Phil Holder
1993-1997	David Webb
1997-1998	Micky Adams
1998-	Ron Noades

Brentford League Record

1920-1933	Division Three
1933-1935	Division Two
1935-1947	Division One
1947-1954	Division Two
1954-1962	Division Three
1962-1963	Division Four
1963-1966	Division Three
1966-1972	Division Four
1972-1973	Division Three
1973-1978	Division Four
1978-1992	Division Three
1992-1993	Division One
1993-1999	Division Two

Brentford fans do not often have a great deal of on-field success to sing about and thus their most famous song is discursive to say the least:

Hey Jude don't make it bad
Just take a stilton and make it cheddar

(Tune: Hey Jude by Lennon and McCartney)

When the mood is on them, they may also chant *'We are Bees, We are Bees, We are Bees'* ad nauseam.

In the 1998-99 season, the Brentford player whose replica team shirt sold in the greatest numbers was Lloyd Owusu.

THE CARLING ULTIMATE FOOTBALL FACT AND QUIZ BOOK

Clubs – B

Brighton and Hove Albion

Brighton and Hove Albion play in blue and white striped shirts, blue shorts with red trim and white socks.

They are known mainly as The Seagulls and also as The Shrimps.

The club was founded in 1900 to replace the disbanded Brighton United. They first appeared as Brighton and Hove Rangers but this team folded in 1901 to be replaced by Brighton and Hove United. But Hove FC objected to this name and so it was changed to the present Brighton and Hove Albion before United ever played a game.

Brighton played the 1901 season at the County Ground and then moved to the Goldstone Ground, where they remained until 1997, when the land was sold and the team had to take up lodgings in Gillingham.

Brighton's greatest years were between 1979 and 1983, when they were in the First Division. In 1983 they suffered the double disappointment of finishing as runners-up in the FA Cup and being relegated in the same season.

Brighton and Hove Albion Managers

1901-1905	John Jackson
1905-1908	Frank Scott-Walford
1908-1914	John Robson
1919-1947	Charles Webb
1947	Tommy Cook
1947-1951	Don Welsh
1951-1961	Billy Lane
1961-1963	George Curtis
1963-1968	Archie Macaulay
1968-1970	Fred Goodwin
1970-1973	Pat Saward
1973-1974	Brian Clough
1974-1976	Peter Taylor
1976-1981	Alan Mullery
1981-1982	Mike Bailey
1982-1983	Jimmy Melia
1983-1986	Chris Caitlin
1986-1987	Alan Mullery
1987-1993	Barry Lloyd
1993-1995	Liam Brady
1995-1996	Jimmy Case
1996-1998	Steve Gritt
1998-	Brian Horton

THE CARLING ULTIMATE FOOTBALL FACT AND QUIZ BOOK

Clubs – B

Brighton and Hove Albion continued...

Brighton and Hove Albion League Record

1920-1958	Division Three
1958-1962	Division Two
1962-1963	Division Three
1963-1965	Division Four
1965-1972	Division Three
1972-1973	Division Two
1973-1977	Division Three
1977-1979	Division Two
1979-1983	Division One
1983-1987	Division Two
1987-1988	Division Three
1988-1996	Division Two
1996-	Division Three

Good old Sussex by the sea
Good old Sussex by the sea
For we're going up
And we'll win the Cup
For Sussex by the sea

In the 1998-99 season, the Brighton and Hove Albion player whose replica team shirt sold in the greatest numbers was Gary Hart.

Bristol City

Bristol City are nicknamed The Robins because of their team strip, which is red shirts, white short and red socks. The club was originally formed in 1894 under the name Bristol South End but changed to City in 1897.

In 1901 Bristol City merged with neighbouring Bedminster and joined the Football League. They played at St John's Lane from their foundation to 1904, when they moved to Ashton Gate, where they remain to this day.

In 1907, Bristol City finished runners-up in the First Division; in 1909 they reached the Final of the FA Cup.

In 1976, Bristol City returned to the top flight of English Football, where they remained until 1980. Since then, they have declined drastically and only narrowly avoided liquidation in 1982.

THE CARLING ULTIMATE FOOTBALL FACT AND QUIZ BOOK

Clubs – B

Bristol City continued...

Bristol City Managers
1897-1899	Sam Hollis
1899-1901	Bob Campbell
1901-1905	Sam Hollis
1905-1910	Harry Thickett
1911-1913	Sam Hollis
1913-1915	George Hedley
1915-1919	Jack Hamilton
1919-1921	Joe Palmer
1921-1929	Alex Raisbeck
1929-1932	Joe Bradshaw
1932-1949	Bob Hewison
1949-1950	Bob Wright
1950-1958	Pat Beasley
1958-1960	Peter Doherty
1960-1967	Fred Ford
1967-1980	Alan Dicks
1980-1982	Bobby Houghton
1982	Roy Hodgson
1982-1988	Terry Cooper
1988-1990	Joe Jordan
1990-1992	Jimmy Lumsden
1992-1993	Denis Smith
1993-1994	Russell Osman
1994-1997	Joe Jordan
1997-	John Ward

Bristol City League Record
1901-1906	Division Two
1906-1911	Division One
1911-1922	Division Two
1922-1923	Division Three
1923-1924	Division Two
1924-1927	Division Three
1927-1932	Division Two
1932-1955	Division Three
1955-1960	Division Two
1960-1965	Division Three
1965-1976	Division Two
1976-1980	Division One
1980-1981	Division Two
1981-1982	Division Three
1982-1984	Division Four

Clubs – B

Bristol City continued...

1984-1990	Division Three
1990-1992	Division Two
1992-	Division One

Many of the best Bristol City supporters' songs are hostile to their local rivals, Rovers. Ashton Gate fans are particularly keen to luxuriate in Rovers' forced exile after the sale of their historic stadium to a well-known supermarket chain (see below). One of the best and more repeatable of these has the words:

Tesco's went down the Rovers
To take old Eastville over
And there's no Tote End any more

(Tune: Drink Up Thee Cider by Adge Cutler and the Wurzels – the ones who had a hit with Oi've Got A Brand New Combine Harvester)

In the 1998-99 season, the Bristol City player whose replica team shirt sold in the greatest numbers was Ade Akinbiyi.

Bristol Rovers

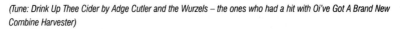

Bristol Rovers were originally known as The Purdown Poachers, then changed their name to The Black Arabs because they played in black shirts. In 1884 they became Eastville Rovers, when they moved to that part of the city, and in 1898 they adopted their present name. They are now nicknamed The Pirates.

Bristol City's strip is now blue and white quartered shirts, white shorts and blue socks.

Bristol City joined the English Football League in 1920 as founder members of Division Three. In 1939, they nearly went out of business through debt and needed to apply for re-election.

Bristol City reached the Sixth Round of the FA Cup in 1951. In 1953 they won the Third Division (South) Championship, which remained their only honour until they won the Third Division title in 1990.

In 1980, Bristol City's Eastville ground was severely damaged by fire and in 1986, they were forced to leave their old ground altogether. They lodged first with Bath City, with whom they shared Twerton Park, and then with Bath Rugby Club at the Memorial Ground.

Clubs – B

Bristol Rovers continued…

Bristol Rovers Managers

1899-1920	Alfred Homer
1920-1921	Ben Hall
1921-1926	Andy Wilson
1926-1929	Joe Palmer
1929-1930	Dave McLean
1930-1936	Albert Prince-Cox
1936-1937	Percy Smith
1938-1949	Brough Fletcher
1950-1968	Bert Tann
1968-1969	Fred Ford
1969-1972	Bill Dodgin Snr
1972-1977	Don Megson
1978-1979	Bobby Campbell
1979-1980	Harold Jarman
1980-1981	Terry Cooper
1981-1983	Bobby Gould
1983-1985	David Williams
1985-1987	Bobby Gould
1987-1991	Gerry Francis
1991	Martin Dobson
1992	Dennis Rofe
1992-1993	Malcolm Allison
1993-1996	John Ward
1996-	Ian Holloway

Bristol Rovers League Record

1920-1953	Division Three
1953-1962	Division Two
1962-1974	Division Three
1974-1981	Division Two
1981-1990	Division Three
1990-1992	Division Two
1992-1993	Division One
1993-	Division Two

Irene goodnight Irene goodnight
Goodnight Irene goodnight Irene
I'll see you in my dreams

In the 1998-99 season, the Bristol Rovers player whose replica team shirt sold in the greatest numbers was Jamie Cureton.

THE CARLING ULTIMATE FOOTBALL FACT AND QUIZ BOOK

Facts
Clubs – B

Burnley

Burnley were one of the founder members of the English Football League. In 1888-89, the first season of the competition, they finished ninth out of 12 clubs.

Nicknamed The Clarets, Burnley play in claret shirts with sky blue sleeves, white shorts and white socks.

Burnley play their home matches at Turf Moor.

Burnley were founded in 1881 by members of Burnley Rovers rugby team, which had just been disbanded. They originally played in green.

Burnley won the FA Cup for the only time in their history in 1914.

Burnley have won the League Championship twice – in 1921 and 1960.

In the 1946-47 season, Burnley let in only 31 goals in 51 games – they finished second in the Second Division.

Since 1960, Burnley have been in long-term decline. The lowest point in their history came in 1987, when they finished only one point above Lincoln City at the bottom of the Fourth Division.

Burnley Managers

1893-1896	Arthur F Sutcliffe
1896-1899	Harry Bradshaw
1899-1903	Ernest Magnall
1903-1910	Spen Whittaker
1910-1911	R H Wadge
1911-1925	John Haworth
1925-1932	Albert Pickles
1932-1935	Tom Bromilow
1935-1939	Alf Boland
1945-1948	Cliff Britton
1948-1954	Frank Hill
1954-1957	Alan Brown
1957-1958	Billy Dougall
1958-1970	Harry Potts
1970-1976	Jimmy Adamson
1976-1977	Joe Brown
1977-1979	Harry Potts
1979-1983	Brian Miller
1983-1984	John Bond
1984-1985	John Benson
1985	Martin Buchan
1985-1986	Tommy Cavanagh

THE CARLING ULTIMATE FOOTBALL FACT AND QUIZ BOOK

Clubs – B

Burnley continued…

1986-1989	Brian Miller
1989-1991	Frank Casper
1991-1996	Jimmy Mullen
1996-1997	Adrian Heath
1997-1998	Chris Waddle
1998-	Stan Ternent

Burnley League Record

1888-1897	Division One
1897-1898	Division Two
1898-1900	Division One
1900-1913	Division Two
1913-1930	Division One
1930-1947	Division Two
1947-1971	Division One
1971-1973	Division Two
1973-1976	Division One
1976-1980	Division Two
1980-1982	Division Three
1982-1983	Division Two
1983-1985	Division Three
1985-1992	Division Four
1992-1994	Division Two
1994-1995	Division One
1995-	Division Two

The most heartfelt songs on the terraces at Turf Moor are those which express the supporters' loathing of nearby Blackburn Rovers. This animus has been greater than usual since Jack Walker financed a resurgence at Ewood Park which Burnley – without a sugar daddy – have been unable to emulate.

> *There once was an alehouse I used to frequent*
> *I saw Kenny Dalglish his money was spent*
> *He asked me a question I answered him nay*
> *I said rubbish like you we can beat any day*

(Tune: The Wild Rover)

In the 1998-99 season, the Burnley player whose replica team shirt sold in the greatest numbers was Andy Payton.

THE CARLING ULTIMATE FOOTBALL FACT AND QUIZ BOOK

Facts
Clubs – B

Bury

Bury play in white shirts, navy blue shorts and navy blue socks and are nicknamed The Shakers.

Bury were formed at the Old White Horse Hotel in the town in 1885 as successors to Bury Unitarians and Bury Wesleyans.

Bury have played since their foundation at Gigg Lane.

Bury won the FA Cup in 1900 and 1903. On the second occasion, they beat Derby County 6-0 – this remains the record margin for the Final of the competition.

In 1971, it was suggested that the club's name be changed to Manchester North End, but the plan was hugely unpopular with the fans and was never implemented.

Bury Managers

1887	T Hargreaves
1887-1907	H S Hamer
1907-1915	Archie Montgomery
1919-1923	William Cameron
1923-1927	James Hunter Thompson
1927-1930	Percy Smith
1930-1934	Arthur Paine
1934-1938	Norman Bullock
1944-1945	Jim Porter
1945-1949	Norman Bullock
1950-1953	John McNeil
1953-1961	Dave Russell
1961-1965	Bob Stokoe
1965-1966	Bert Head
1966-1969	Les Shannon
1969	Jack Marshall
1970	Les Hart
1970-1972	Tommy McAnearney
1972-1973	Alan Brown
1973-1977	Bobby Smith
1977-1978	Bob Stokoe
1978-1979	David Hatton
1979-1980	Dave Connor
1980-1984	Jim Iley
1984-1989	Martin Dobson
1989-1990	Sam Ellis
1990-1995	Mike Walsh
1995-1998	Stan Ternent
1998-	Neil Warnock

In the 1998-99 season, the Bury player whose replica team shirt sold in the greatest numbers was Nigel Jemson.

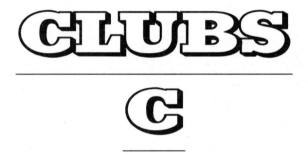

THE CARLING ULTIMATE FOOTBALL FACT AND QUIZ BOOK

Clubs – C

Cambridge United

Cambridge United play their home games at the Abbey Stadium on Newmarket Road. Their strip is amber and black quartered shirts, black shorts, and black and amber hooped socks.

From its foundation in 1919, the club was known as Abbey United but adopted its present name in 1949.

Cambridge United entered the Fourth Division of the English Football League on August 15, 1970. They took the place of Bradford Park Avenue.

Cambridge United Managers

1949-1955	Bill Whittaker
1955	Gerald Williams
1955-1959	Bert Johnson
1959-1960	Bill Craig
1960-1963	Alan Moore
1964-1966	Roy Kirk
1967-1974	Bill Leivers
1974-1978	Ron Atkinson
1978-1983	John Docherty
1984-1985	John Ryan
1985	Ken Shellito
1985-1990	Chris Turner
1990-1992	John Beck
1992-1993	Ian Atkins
1993-1995	Gary Johnson
1995-1996	Tommy Taylor
1996-	Roy McFarland

Cambridge United League Record

1970-1973	Division Four
1973-1974	Division Three
1974-1977	Division Four
1977-1978	Division Three
1978-1984	Division Two
1984-1985	Division Three
1985-1990	Division Four
1990-1991	Division Three
1991-1992	Division Two
1992-1993	Division One
1993-1995	Division Two
1995-1999	Division Three

THE CARLING ULTIMATE FOOTBALL FACT AND QUIZ BOOK

Clubs – C

Cambridge United continued...

The Cambridge United mascot is a moose, which explains the strange spelling of one of the words in the following supporters' anthem, sung to the tune Lord of the Dance:

> *We beat the Aston Villa and we drew at Coventry*
> *We even drew at home against Manchester City*
> *And when we beat the Swansea we won Division Three*
> *And we've never lost at Wembley*
> *Win, win, wherever we may be*
> *We are the famoose CUFC*
> *And we'll see you all wherever you may be*
> *And we'll see you all in the Premier League*

In the 1998-99 season, the Cambridge United player whose replica team shirt sold in the greatest numbers was John Taylor.

Cardiff City

Nicknamed the Bluebirds because of their strip – blue shirts, white shorts and white socks – Cardiff City play their home games at Ninian Park, the ground to which they moved in 1910 after spells at Riverside, Sophia Gardens, Old Park and Fir Gardens.

Cardiff City joined the Football League in 1920 and this was the dawn of their finest era – in 1924, they came second in the First Division, missing the Championship only by having a slightly inferior goal average to that of the title-winners, Huddersfield Town.

1923-1924 Season
First Division Final Table

	P	W	D	L	F	A	Pts
Huddersfield Town	42	23	11	8	60	33	57
Cardiff City	42	22	13	7	61	34	57

This gave Huddersfield a goal average of 1.8181, which was 0.024 of a goal better than that of Cardiff City, whose final goal average was 1.7941. This is the closest English League Championship in history.

In 1927, Cardiff City won the FA Cup, beating Arsenal 1-0 in the Final. This is the only time the trophy has left England.

In 1929, Cardiff City conceded only 29 goals in a 42-match season – a record – but were nevertheless relegated form the First Division.

THE CARLING ULTIMATE FOOTBALL FACT AND QUIZ BOOK

Clubs – C

Cardiff City continued...

To date, Cardiff City have won the Welsh Cup a record 21 times.

Cardiff City Managers
1910-1911	Davy McDougall
1911-1933	Fred Stewart
1933-1934	Bartley Wilson
1934-1937	B Watts-Jones
1937-1939	Bill Jennings
1939-1946	Cyril Spiers
1946-1948	Billy McCandless
1948-1954	Cyril Spiers
1954-1958	Trevor Morris
1958-1962	Bill Jones
1962-1964	George Swindin
1964-1973	Jimmy Scoular
1973-1974	Frank O'Farrell
1974-1978	Jimmy Andrews
1978-1982	Richie Morgan
1982-1984	Len Ashurst
1984	Jimmy Goodfellow
1984-1986	Alan Durban
1986-1989	Frank Burrows
1989-1991	Len Ashurst
1991-1994	Eddie May
1994-1995	Terry Yorath
1995	Eddie May
1995	Kenny Hibbitt
1996	Phil Neal
1996	Russell Osman
1996-1998	Kenny Hibbitt
1998-	Frank Burrows

Cardiff City League Record
1920-1921	Division Two
1921-1929	Division One
1929-1931	Division Two
1931-1947	Division Three (South)
1947-1952	Division Two
1952-1957	Division One
1957-1960	Division Two
1960-1962	Division One
1962-1975	Division Two
1975-1976	Division Three

THE CARLING ULTIMATE FOOTBALL FACT AND QUIZ BOOK

Clubs – C

Cardiff City continued...

1976-1982	Division Two
1982-1983	Division Three
1983-1985	Division Two
1985-1986	Division Three
1986-1988	Division Four
1988-1990	Division Three
1990-1992	Division Four
1992-1993	Division Three
1993-1995	Division Two
1995-	Division Three

Although Arsenal still get sung about at Ninian Park, as Cardiff supporters continue to gloat over their most recent major trophy, the 1927 FA Cup, most of the fans' vitriol is reserved for Swansea, whom they'll naturally hate evermore.

In the 1998-99 season, the Cardiff City player whose replica team shirt sold in the greatest numbers was Kevin Nugent.

Carlisle United

Carlisle is in the old county of Cumberland and the team is thus nicknamed The Cumbrians.

Carlisle United play in blue shirts, white shorts and white socks. Their home ground is Brunton Park, to which they moved in 1909. Previously, they had played at Milholme Bank (1903-1905) and Devonshire Park (1905-1909).

Carlisle United were formed in 1903 through the amalgamation of Shaddongate United and Carlisle Red Rose. They joined the Football League in 1928.

In 1970, Carlisle United reached the semi-final of the League Cup, eventually going out to West Bromwich Albion.

Carlisle entered the First Division in 1974 and briefly led the table, but they finished bottom and were relegated.

Carlisle United Managers

1904-1905	Harry Kirkbride
1905-1906	McCumiskey
1906-1908	Jack Houston
1908-1910	Bert Stansfield
1910-1912	Jack Houston

THE CARLING ULTIMATE FOOTBALL FACT AND QUIZ BOOK

Clubs – C

Carlisle United continued...

1912-1913	Davie Graham
1913-1930	George Bristow
1930-1933	Billy Hampson
1933-1935	Bill Clarke
1935-1936	Robert Kelly
1936-1938	Fred Westgarth
1938-1940	David Taylor
1940-1945	Howard Harkness
1945-1946	Bill Clark
1946-1949	Ivor Broadis
1949-1951	Bill Shankly
1951-1958	Fred Emery
1958-1960	Andy Beattie
1960-1963	Ivor Powell
1963-1967	Alan Ashman
1967-1968	Tim Ward
1968-1970	Bob Stokoe
1970-1972	Ian MacFarlane
1972-1975	Alan Ashman
1975-1976	Dick Young
1976-1980	Bobby Moncur
1980	Martin Harvey
1980-1985	Bob Stokoe
1985	Bryan 'Pop' Robson
1985-1986	Bob Stokoe
1986-1987	Harry Gregg
1987-1991	Cliff Middlemass
1991-1992	Aidan McCaffery
1992-1993	David McCreery
1993-1996	Mick Wadsworth
1996-1997	Mervyn Day
1997-	David Wilkes, John Halpin and chairman Michael Knighton

Carlisle United League Record

1928-1958	Division Three (North)
1958-1962	Division Four
1962-1963	Division Three
1963-1964	Division Four
1964-1965	Division Three
1965-1974	Division Two
1974-1975	Division One
1975-1977	Division Two
1977-1982	Division Three

THE CARLING ULTIMATE FOOTBALL FACT AND QUIZ BOOK

Facts
Clubs – C

Carlisle United continued...

1982-1986	Division Two
1986-1987	Division Three
1987-1992	Division Four
1992-1995	Division Three
1995-1996	Division Two
1996-1997	Division Three
1997-1998	Division Two
1998-	Division Three

Carlisle United fans have no noteworthy songs, no doubt because they have little to sing about.

In the 1998-99 season, the Carlisle United player whose replica team shirt sold in the greatest numbers was Ian Stevens.

Celtic

Nicknamed The Bhoys, Celtic play their home matches in the 60,000-capacity Celtic Park at 95 Kerrydale Street, Glasgow. Their strip is green and white hooped shirts, white shorts and white socks.

Since their foundation in 1888, Celtic have had strong links with the Irish Catholic community in Glasgow's East End.

Celtic have won the Scottish League 35 times, the Scottish FA Cup 30 times and the Scottish League Cup nine times. Their greatest achievement, however, came in 1967, when they became the first British club to win the European Cup.

Some Celtic songs are anti-monarchy and pro-IRA. One of the best of the purely footballing ones concerns Jimmy McGrory, the forward who scored nearly 400 goals for the Bhoys between 1922 and 1939:

Sure you boast of your famous inventors
And you sing of the land of the free
But my song it concerns a centre
Who plays for the Celtic FC
Though he doesn't seem tall
At chasing the ball
And at playing the game
He's ahead of them all

James McGrory my boy
Your own pride and joy
Your opponents you make them look sad
For with eight of the best
McColl's record goes west
Clever lad from old Garnard

THE CARLING ULTIMATE FOOTBALL FACT AND QUIZ BOOK

Clubs – C

Charlton Athletic

Nicknamed The Addicks, the Robins or The Valiants, Charlton Athletic play in red shirts, white shorts and white socks.

Charlton Athletic were founded in 1905 and entered the Football League in 1921.

Charlton Athletic are based at The Valley in Floyd Road, London SE7. Although this has been their home since 1920, they have had various periods of enforced absence. In 1923, they played at The Mount in nearby Catford, from 1985 to 1991 they played at Crystal Palace's Selhurst Park Stadium, and in 1991 they played at Upton Park, the home of West Ham United.

In 1992, Charlton Athletic returned to the new all-seater stadium at The Valley.

In 1937, Charlton Athletic were runners-up to Manchester City in the First Division – this was their best season to date.

Charlton Athletic were beaten finalists in the 1946 FA Cup but returned to take the trophy in the following year.

Charlton Athletic Managers

1920-1925	Bill Rayner
1925-1927	Alex McFarlane
1928	Albert Lindon
1928-1932	Alex McFarlane
1933-1956	Jimmy Seed
1956-1961	Jimmy Trotter
1961-1965	Frank Hill
1965-1967	Bob Stokoe
1967-1970	Eddie Firmani
1970-1974	Theo Foley
1974-1979	Andy Nelson
1979-1981	Mike Bailey
1981-1982	Alan Mullery
1982	Ken Craggs
1982-1991	Lennie Lawrence
1991-1995	Alan Curbishley and Steve Gritt
1995-	Alan Curbishley

Charlton Athletic League Record

1921-1929	Division Three (South)
1929-1933	Division Two
1933-1935	Division Three (South)
1935-1936	Division Two
1936-1957	Division One
1957-1972	Division Two

Clubs – C

Charlton Athletic continued…

1972-1975	Division Three
1975-1980	Division Two
1980-1981	Division Three
1981-1986	Division Two
1986-1990	Division One
1990-1992	Division Two
1992-1998	Division One
1998-1999	Premiership

Charlton Athletic's most famous song is about their ground – a stadium their fans feel unusually strongly about because they've come so close to losing it.

Miles have I travelled
Many games have I seen
Following Charlton
My only team
Many hours have I spent
In the covered end choir
Singing Valley Floyd Road
Valley Floyd Road
Mist rolling in from the Thames
My desire is always to be there
At Valley Floyd Road

(Tune: Mull of Kintyre)

In the 1998-99 season, the Charlton Athletic player whose replica team shirt sold in the greatest numbers was Clive Mendonca.

Chelsea

Chelsea play their home games at Stamford Bridge in London SW6.

Chelsea's home strip consists of royal blue shirts with white and yellow trim, royal blue shorts with white and yellow trim and white socks with blue and yellow trim. They are consequently nicknamed The Blues, although they are also sometimes known as The Pensioners.

Chelsea were founded in 1905 after Fulham FC had turned down an approach to use Stamford Bridge. The owner of the Stadium, H A Mears, was adamant that football should be played there and so he founded his own team.

THE CARLING ULTIMATE FOOTBALL FACT AND QUIZ BOOK

Facts
Clubs – C

Chelsea continued...

Chelsea entered the Football League in 1905 after their application for membership of the Southern League had been rejected.

Throughout their history, Chelsea have had a reputation for hiring established stars to achieve success quickly; the stars themselves, however, have sometimes been past their best and have displayed a tendency to be seduced by the bright lights of the nearby West End.

Chelsea are thus widely perceived as a flash club, with more style than substance. Nevertheless, they do have several substantial achievements to their credit, having won the League Championship in 1955, the FA Cup in 1970 and 1997, the League Cup in 1965 and 1998 and the European Cup Winners' Cup in 1971 and 1998.

Chelsea Managers
1905-1907	John Tait Robertson
1907-1933	David Calderhead
1933-1939	Leslie Knighton
1939-1952	Billy Birrell
1952-1961	Ted Drake
1961-1967	Tommy Docherty
1967-1974	Dave Sexton
1974-1975	Ron Suart
1975-1977	Eddie McCreadie
1977-1978	Ken Shellito
1978-1979	Danny Blanchflower
1979-1981	Geoff Hurst
1981-1985	John Neal
1985-1988	John Hollins
1988-1991	Bobby Campbell
1991-1993	Ian Porterfield
1993	Dave Webb
1993-1996	Glenn Hoddle
1996-1998	Ruud Gullit
1998-	Gianluca Vialli

Chelsea League Record
1905-1907	Division Two
1907-1910	Division One
1910-1912	Division Two
1912-1924	Division One
1924-1930	Division Two
1930-1962	Division One
1962-1963	Division Two
1964-1975	Division One
1975-1977	Division Two

Clubs – C

Chelsea continued...

1977-1979	Division One
1979-1984	Division Two
1984-1988	Division One
1988-1989	Division Two
1989-1992	Division One
1992-	Premiership

Chelsea fans who are hate-minded traditionally hate Tottenham most; Millwall have come a close second since 1988, when they took Chelsea's place in the old First Division; latterly, West Ham United and their supporters have come in for some stick at Stamford Bridge, not all of it verbal.

Flying high up in the sky
We'll keep the blue flag flying high
From Stamford Bridge to Wembley
We'll keep the blue flag flying high

(Tune: The Internationale)

Blue is the colour
Football is the game
We're all together
And winning is our aim
So cheer us on through the sun and rain
Coz Chelsea Chelsea is our name

In the 1998-99 season, the Chelsea player whose replica team shirt sold in the greatest numbers was Gianfranco Zola.

Chester City

Founded in 1884, Chester City – nicknamed The Cestrians or The Blues – entered the Football League in 1931.

After short periods between 1904 and 1906 at Faulkner Street, the Old Showground and Whipcord Lane, Chester City played all their home games from 1906 to 1990 at Sealand Road. The following season, they shared the Moss Rose Ground with then non-League Macclesfield Town before settling at their own Deva Stadium in Bumpers Lane in 1992.

Chester City's home strip consists of blue and white striped shirts, blue shorts and blue socks.

Chester City have won the Welsh Cup three times, in 1908, 1933 and 1947.

Clubs – C

Chester City continued...

In 1975, Chester City reached the semi-final of the League Cup, going out narrowly (5-4 on aggregate) to the eventual winners, Aston Villa.

Chester City Managers
1930-1936	Charlie Hewitt
1936-1938	Alex Raisbeck
1938-1953	Frank Brown
1953-1956	Louis Page
1956-1959	John Harris
1959-1961	Stan Pearson
1962-1963	Bill Lambton
1963-1968	Peter Hauser
1968-1976	Ken Roberts
1976-1982	Alan Oakes
1982	Cliff Sear
1982-1983	John Sainty
1984	John McGrath
1985-1992	Harry McNally
1992-1994	Graham Barrow
1994-1995	Mike Pejic
1995	Derek Mann
1995-	Kevin Ratcliffe

Chester City League Record
1931-1958	Third Division (North)
1958-1975	Division Four
1975-1982	Division Three
1982-1986	Division Four
1986-1992	Division Three
1992-1993	Division Two
1993-1994	Division Three
1994-1995	Division Two
1995-	Division Three

Although Chester City do not make replica shirts, an informed insider at the club reported that, in the 1998-99 season, the most popular player was Nick Richardson.

THE CARLING ULTIMATE FOOTBALL FACT AND QUIZ BOOK

Facts
Clubs – C

Chesterfield

Nicknamed The Spireites, Chesterfield play in blue shirts, white shorts and blue socks.

Chesterfield play their home matches at the Recreation Ground.

The fourth oldest club in England – their seniors are Stoke, Notts County and Nottingham Forest – Chesterfield were founded in 1866 and joined the Football League in 1899.

Chesterfield's honours to date have been the Third Division Championship in 1931 and 1936, the Fourth Division Championship in 1970 and 1985, and the Anglo-Scottish Cup in 1981. In 1997, they reached the semi-final of the FA Cup and but for a bad decision would have gone on to Wembley.

Chesterfield Managers

1891-1895	E Russell Timmeus
1895-1901	Gilbert Gillies
1901-1902	E F Hind
1902-1906	Jack Hoskin
1906-1907	W Furness
1907-1910	George Swift
1911-1913	G H Jones
1913-1917	R L Weston
1919	T Callaghan
1920-1922	J J Caffrey
1922	Harry Hadley
1922-1927	Harry Parkes
1927	Alec Campbell
1927-1932	Ted Davison
1932-1938	Bill Harvey
1938-1945	Norman Bullock
1945-1948	Bob Brocklebank
1948-1952	Bobby Marshall
1952-1958	Ted Davison
1958-1962	Duggie Livingstone
1962-1967	Tony McShane
1967-1973	Jimmy McGuigan
1973-1976	Joe Shaw
1976-1980	Arthur Cox
1980-1983	Frank Barlow
1983-1987	John Duncan
1987-1988	Kevin Randall
1988-1991	Paul Hart
1991-1993	Chris McMenemy
1993-	John Duncan

THE CARLING ULTIMATE FOOTBALL FACT AND QUIZ BOOK

Clubs – C

Chesterfield continued...

Chesterfield League Record
1899-1909	Division Two
1909	Failed to gain re-election – went out of League
1921-1931	Division Three (North)
1931-1933	Division Two
1933-1936	Division Three (North)
1936-1951	Division Two
1951-1958	Division Three (North)
1958-1961	Division Three
1961-1970	Division Four
1970-1983	Division Three
1983-1985	Division Four
1985-1989	Division Three
1989-1992	Division Four
1992-1995	Division Three
1995-	Division Two

In the 1998-99 season, the Chesterfield player whose replica team shirt sold in the greatest numbers was Jon Howard.

Clyde

Clyde are nicknamed The Bully Wee after their most famous forward line who made up in toughness what they lacked in inches.

The club was founded in 1878 and played for many years at Shawfield on the banks of the River Clyde. But in 1986 they moved controversially to share Partick Thistle's ground at Firhill Park. in 1991, they went to Douglas Park in Hamilton but then finally in 1994 they settled in their permanent new home, The Broadwood Stadium in Cumbernauld.

Clyde play their home matches in white shirts with black and red trim, black shorts with white and red trim, and white socks with two red bands.

To date, Clyde have won the Scottish FA Cup three times – in 1939, 1955 and 1958.

Clydebank

Clydebank play at Boghead Park in Miller Street, Dumbarton. They are nicknamed The Bankies.

Clydebank play in red and white striped shirts, black shorts and black socks.

Clubs – C

Clydebank continued...

Clydebank were founded in 1965 and joined the Scottish League the following year.

In 1976, Clydebank won the Scottish Second Division Championship; in 1977, they finished second in the First Division and thus became the first club in Scottish league history to win promotion in consecutive seasons. (Sadly, the bubble burst in '78, when the Bankies finished bottom of the Premier.)

In 1990, Clydebank reached the semi-final of the Scottish FA Cup, losing 2-0 to Celtic.

Colchester United

Colchester United play in blue and white striped shirts, white shorts and white socks. Their home games are held at the Layer Road Ground.

The club was founded in 1937 to replace the area's old amateur club, Colchester Town. They joined the Football League in 1950.

The highlight of Colchester United's fairly undistinguished history is the great and famous 3-2 victory over First Division leaders Leeds United in the Fifth Round of the 1971 FA Cup. The team became known in the press as Grandad's Army because they had seven players over the age of 30.

Colchester United Managers

1946-1948	Ted Fenton
1948-1953	Jimmy Allen
1953-1955	Jack Butler
1955-1963	Benny Fenton
1963-1968	Neil Franklin
1968-1972	Dick Graham
1972-1975	Jim Smith
1975-1982	Bobby Roberts
1982-1983	Allan Hunter
1983-1986	Cyril Lea
1986-1987	Mike Walker
1987-1988	Roger Brown
1989	Jock Wallace
1990	Mick Mills
1990-1991	Ian Atkins
1991-1994	Roy McDonough
1994	George Burley
1995-	Steve Wignall

THE CARLING ULTIMATE FOOTBALL FACT AND QUIZ BOOK

Facts
Clubs – C

Colchester United continued...

Colchester United League Record

1950-1958	Division Three (South)
1958-1961	Division Three
1961-1962	Division Four
1962-1965	Division Three
1965-1966	Division Four
1966-1968	Division Three
1968-1974	Division Four
1974-1976	Division Three
1976-1977	Division Four
1977-1981	Division Three
1981-1990	Division Four
1990-1992	GM Vauxhall Conference
1992-	Division Three

Colchester United songs are mainly abusive towards supporters of other East Anglian clubs, especially Southend United, Ipswich Town, Cambridge United and Norwich City.

In the 1998-99 season, the Colchester United player whose replica team shirt sold in the greatest numbers was Paul Abrahams.

Colo Colo

One of the leading clubs in Chile, Colo Colo – the name is Spanish for a South American wildcat – play in the capital, Santiago.

Colo Colo's strip is white shirts, black shorts and white socks.

Colo Colo was founded in 1925 by five players who left the old Magellanes Football Club after a dispute about the appointment of a captain. One of the five, David Orellano, became the first captain of the new club.

Colo Colo have always had a reputation for innovation – in 1927, they sent a team on a tour of Spain and Portugal; in 1933 they were founder members of the Chilean Football League; in 1941 they became one of the first clubs to appoint a foreign coach when they hired Ferenc Platko, a Hungarian; in 1948, they organised a South American tour which was the forerunner of the Copa Libertadores, the South American equivalent of the European Cup.

Colo Colo have won the Chilean League title more often than any other club (19 times to date). In 1991, they became the first Chilean club ever to win the Copa Libertadores, beating the holders, Olimpia of Paraguay, in the Final.

Clubs – C

Coventry City

Coventry City are nicknamed The Sky Blues after their strip, which consists of sky blue and navy striped shirts, navy blue shorts and navy blue socks.

Coventry City play their home matches at the Highfield Road Stadium in King Richard Street.

Coventry City were founded in 1883 as Singers FC, the works team of the sewing machine factory. They adopted their present name in 1898.

From 1883 to 1887, Coventry City played at Binley Road, then spent the next two years at Stoke Road before moving to their present home in 1899.

Coventry City joined the Second Division of the Football League in 1919 – their first game was a 5-0 home defeat by Tottenham Hotspur.

In 1967, Coventry City won promotion to the First Division. They have remained in the top flight of English football ever since, despite many flirtations with the drop and being among the bookies' and pundits' perennial favourites for relegation.

In 1987, Coventry City won the FA Cup, beating Tottenham Hotspur 3-2 in the Final.

Coventry City Managers

1909-1910	H R Buckle
1910-1913	Robert Wallace
1913-1915	Frank Scott-Walford
1917-1919	William Clayton
1919-1920	H Pollitt
1920-1924	Albert Evans
1924-1928	Jimmy Kerr
1928-1931	James McIntyre
1931-1945	Harry Storer
1945-1947	Dick Bayliss
1947-1948	Billy Frith
1948-1953	Harry Storer
1953-1954	Jack Fairbrother
1954-1955	Charlie Elliott
1955-1956	Jesse Carver
1956-1957	Harry Warren
1957-1961	Billy Frith
1961-1967	Jimmy Hill
1967-1972	Noel Cantwell
1972	Bob Dennison
1972-1975	Joe Mercer
1975-1981	Gordon Milne
1981-1983	Dave Sexton

THE CARLING ULTIMATE FOOTBALL FACT AND QUIZ BOOK

Facts
Clubs – C

Coventry City continued...

1983-1984	Bobby Gould
1985-1986	Don Mackay
1986-1987	George Curtis
1987-1990	John Sillett
1990-1992	Terry Butcher
1992	Don Howe
1992-1993	Bobby Gould
1993-1995	Phil Neal
1995-1996	Ron Atkinson
1996-	Gordon Strachan

Coventry City League Record

1919-1925	Division Two
1925-1926	Division Three (North)
1926-1936	Division Three (South)
1936-1952	Division Two
1952-1958	Division Three (South)
1958-1959	Division Four
1959-1964	Division Three
1964-1967	Division Two
1967-1992	Division One
1992-	Premiership

Coventry supporters are usually too busy biting their fingernails to sing, but they sometimes come out with the following, to the tune of the Eton Boating Song:

Let's all sing together
Play up the Sky Blues
While we sing together
We will never lose
Tottenham or Chelsea
United or anyone
They can't defeat us
We'll fight till the game is won

In the 1998-99 season, the Coventry City player whose replica team shirt sold in the greatest numbers was Darren Huckerby.

THE CARLING ULTIMATE FOOTBALL FACT AND QUIZ BOOK

Clubs – C

Cowdenbeath

Cowdenbeath's home strip is royal blue and white shirts, royal blue and white shorts and blue socks. Their main away strip – yellow shirts with green piping, blue shorts and white socks – has given rise to the club's nickname, The Blue Brazil.

Cowdenbeath were formed in 1881 and joined the Scottish Second Division in 1905.

Cowdenbeath play their home games at Central Park in Cowdenbeath High Street.

Although generally unaccustomed to success, Cowdenbeath spent some of the 1930s in the Scottish First Division and reached the quarter-finals of the Scottish FA Cup in the same decade.

Cowdenbeath have twice reached the semi-finals of the Scottish League Cup – in 1959-60 and 1970-71.

Crewe Alexandra

Based at Gresty Road and nicknamed The Railwaymen, Crewe Alexandra play in red shirts, white shorts and white socks.

The club was founded in 1877 and joined the Second Division of the Football League in 1892. They named themselves after Princess Alexandra.

Twice winners of the Welsh Cup (1936 and 1937), Crewe Alexandra reached the semi-final of the English FA Cup in 1888.

Although never a great club, Crewe has a tradition of developing outstanding players who are then sold on to finance the nursery. Among the recent stars who began here are David Platt and Rob Jones.

Crewe Alexandra Managers

1892-1894	W C McNeill
1895-1896	J G Hall
1897	R Roberts
1898-1925	J B Bromerley
1925-1938	Tom Bailey
1938-1944	George Lillicrop
1944-1948	Frank Hill
1948-1951	Arthur Turner
1951-1953	Harry Catterick
1953-1955	Ralph Ward
1955-1958	Maurice Lindley

Clubs – C

Crewe Alexandra continued...

1958-1960	Harry Ware
1960-1964	Jimmy McGuigan
1964-1971	Ernie Tagg
1971	Dennis Viollet
1972-1973	Jimmy Melia
1974	Ernie Tagg
1975-1978	Harry Gregg
1978-1979	Warwick Rimmer
1979-1981	Tony Waddington
1981-1982	Arfon Griffiths
1982-1983	Peter Morris
1983-	Dario Gradi

Crewe Alexandra League Record

1892-1896	Division Two
1896-1921	Failed to gain re-election – went out of the League
1921-1958	Division Three (North)
1958-1963	Division Four
1963-1964	Division Three
1964-1968	Division Four
1968-1969	Division Three
1969-1989	Division Four
1989-1991	Division Three
1991-1992	Division Three
1991-1992	Division Four
1992-1994	Division Three
1994-1997	Division Two
1997-	Division One

We're riding along on the Alexandra Special
Woo woo woo woo
Just riding along singing our song
The Alexandra, the Alexandra

In the 1998-99 season, the Crewe Alexandra player whose replica team shirt sold in the greatest numbers was Seth Johnson.

Clubs – C

Crystal Palace

The original Crystal Palace Football Club dates back to 1861 and reached the semi-final of the first FA Cup in 1871.

The present Crystal Palace FC was founded in 1905 and joined the Football League in 1920.

The club played at Crystal Palace itself from 1905 to 1915, at Herne Hill from 1915 to 1918, and then at The Nest from 1918 to 1924.

Since 1924, Crystal Palace have played at Selhurst Park, London SE25.

Palace are nicknamed The Eagles or The Glaziers. Their home strip is red and blue shirts, red shorts and red socks.

Crystal Palace first came into the First Division in 1969.

At the end of the 1970s, manager Terry Venables described Crystal Palace as 'the team of the Eighties'. As the League Record below shows, the club spent most of that decade in the Second Division.

Crystal Palace have won no major honours but were runners-up to Manchester United in the 1990 FA Cup Final, which went to a replay.

Crystal Palace Managers

1905-1907	John T Robson
1907-1925	Edmund Goodman
1925-1927	Alec Maley
1927-1930	Fred Mavin
1930-1935	Jack Tresadern
1935-1936	Tom Bromilow
1936	R S Moyes
1936-1939	Tom Bromilow
1939-1947	George Irwin
1947-1949	Jack Butler
1949-1950	Ronnie Rooke
1950-1951	Fred Dawes and Charlie Slade
1951-1954	Laurie Scott
1954-1958	Cyril Spiers
1958-1960	George Smith
1960-1962	Arthur Rowe
1962-1966	Dick Graham
1966-1972	Bert Head
1973-1976	Malcolm Allison
1976-1980	Terry Venables
1980	Ernie Walley
1980-1981	Malcolm Allison

THE CARLING ULTIMATE FOOTBALL FACT AND QUIZ BOOK

Facts
Clubs – C

Crystal Palace continued...

1981	Dario Gradi
1981-1982	Steve Kember
1982-1984	Alan Mullery
1984-1993	Steve Coppell
1993-1995	Alan Smith
1995-1996	Steve Coppell
1996-1997	Dave Bassett
1997-1998	Steve Coppell
1998	Attilio Lombardo
1998	Terry Venables

Crystal Palace League Record

1920-1921	Division Three
1921-1925	Division Two
1925-1958	Division Three (South)
1958-1961	Division Four
1961-1964	Division Three
1964-1969	Division Two
1969-1973	Division One
1973-1974	Division Two
1974-1977	Division Three
1977-1979	Division Two
1979-1981	Division One
1981-1989	Division Two
1989-1992	Division One
1992-1993	Premiership
1993-1994	Division One
1994-1995	Premiership
1995-1997	Division One
1997-1998	Premiership
1998-	Division One

The Crystal Palace supporters' song is Glad All Over, originally a No 1 hit in 1963 for The Dave Clark Five:

> *You say that you love me*
> *All of the time*
> *You say that you need me*
> *You'll always be mine*
> *I'm feeling glad all over*

In the 1998-99 season, the Crystal Palace player whose replica team shirt sold in the greatest numbers was Matt Jansen, even though he ended the campaign at Blackburn Rovers.

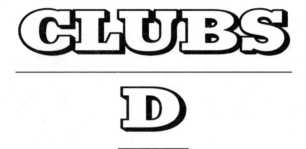

THE CARLING ULTIMATE FOOTBALL FACT AND QUIZ BOOK

Clubs – D

Darlington

The Quakers play in black and white shirts, black shorts and black socks. Their home ground is called Feethams.

Darlington were founded in 1883 and became a leading amateur side before joining the Football League in 1921.

In 1958, Darlington reached the Fifth Round of the FA Cup – their best-ever run in the competition.

Darlington finished bottom of the Fourth Division in 1989 and spent the following season in the GM Vauxhall Conference, but they recaptured their League status in 1990 and celebrated their return by winning the Fourth Division title in 1991, their first year back.

Darlington's only other trophy is the Championship of the Third Division (North), which they won in 1925.

Darlington Managers

1902-1911	Tom McIntosh
1911-1912	W L Lane
1912-1919	Dick Jackson
1919-1928	Jack English
1928-1933	Jack Fairless
1933-1936	George Collins
1936-1938	George Brown
1938-1942	Jackie Carr
1942	Jack Surtees
1945-1946	Jack English
1946-1950	Bill Forrest
1950-1952	George Irwin
1952-1957	Bob Gurney
1957-1960	Dick Duckworth
1960-1964	Eddie Carr
1964-1966	Lol Morgan
1966-1968	Jimmy Greenhalgh
1968-1970	Ray Yeoman
1970-1971	Len Richley
1971	Frank Brennan
1971-1972	Ken Hale
1972	Allan Jones
1972-1973	Ralph Brand
1973-1974	Dick Conner
1974-1976	Billy Horner
1976-1978	Peter Madden
1978-1979	Len Walker

Clubs – D

Darlington continued...

1979-1983	Billy Elliott
1983-1987	Cyril Knowles
1987-1989	Dave Booth
1989-1991	Brian Little
1991-1992	Frank Gray
1992	Ray Hankin
1992-1993	Billy McEwan
1993-1995	Alan Murray
1995	Paul Futcher
1995	David Hodgson and Jim Platt
1995-1996	Jim Platt
1996-	David Hodgson

Darlington League Record

1921-1925	Division Three (North)
1925-1927	Division Two
1927-1958	Division Three (North)
1958-1966	Division Four
1966-1967	Division Three
1967-1985	Division Four
1985-1987	Division Three
1987-1989	Division Four
1989-1990	GM Vauxhall Conference
1990-1991	Division Four
1991-	Division Three*

* In the 1991-92 season, Fourth Division Champions Darlington finished bottom of the Third Division, but they stayed nominally in the same division the following year because at the end of the 1992 season the League was restructured into the Premiership and Divisions One, Two and Three.

> *Come on the Quaker men the boys in black and white*
> *We cheer them every morning every afternoon and night*
> *Feethams is our home ground where we score goals galore*
> *And now we shout for more more more*
> *We'll sing Darlington forever*
> *We'll sing Darlington forever*
> *We'll sing Darlington forever*
> *As the Quakers go marching on on on*
>
> *(Tune: John Brown's Body)*

In the 1998-99 season, the Darlington player whose replica team shirt sold in the greatest numbers was Glenn Naylor.

THE CARLING ULTIMATE FOOTBALL FACT AND QUIZ BOOK

Clubs – D

Derby County

Derby County – nicknamed The Rams – were founded in 1884 by members of Derbyshire County Cricket Club and originally played in a strip of amber, chocolate and pale blue based on the cricketer's colours.

Today, Derby County play their home games in white shirts with black trim, black shorts and white socks with black trim.

From 1884 to 1895, they played at The Racecourse Ground; in 1895 they moved to The Baseball Ground, where they remained until 1997, when they moved to the new purpose-built Pride Park Stadium.

Derby County were founder members of the Football League – in the first season of competition (1888-89) they finished 10th out of 12 clubs.

Although Derby County have won the FA Cup only once – in 1946 – they appeared in 13 of the competition's 15 semi-final rounds between 1895 and 1909.

Derby County won the League Championship for the first time in 1972 under the inspirational management of Brian Clough and his assistant Peter Taylor.

The club won a second League title in 1975, this time under Dave Mackay.

Derby County Managers

1896-1906	Harry Newbould
1906-1922	Jimmy Methven
1922-1925	Cecil Potter
1925-1941	George Jobey
1944-1946	Ted Magner
1946-1953	Stuart McMillan
1953-1955	Jack Barker
1955-1962	Harry Storer
1962-1967	Tim Ward
1967-1973	Brian Clough
1973-1976	Dave Mackay
1977	Colin Murphy
1977-1979	Tommy Docherty
1979-1982	Colin Addison
1982	Johnny Newman
1982-1984	Peter Taylor
1984	Roy McFarland
1984-1993	Arthur Cox
1993-1995	Roy McFarland
1995-	Jim Smith

Clubs – D

Derby County continued...

Derby County League Record

1888-1907	Division One
1907-1912	Division Two
1912-1914	Division One
1914-1915	Division Two
1915-1921	Division One
1921-1926	Division Two
1926-1953	Division One
1953-1955	Division Two
1955-1957	Division Three (North)
1957-1969	Division Two
1969-1980	Division One
1980-1984	Division Two
1984-1986	Division Three
1986-1987	Division Two
1987-1991	Division One
1991-1992	Division Two
1992-1996	Division One
1996-	Premiership

Derby fans hate fans of local rivals Nottingham Forest – that is almost all anyone needs to know about them. Thus their version of Land of Hope and Glory is sung to the words:

> *We hate Nottingham Forest*
> *We hate Forest too*
> *We hate Nottingham Forest*
> *Forest we hate you*

Brilliant, eh? Now see if you can guess the identity of the team in line four of the following:

> *We are the boys in blue and white*
> *We've come to sing this song for you*
> *We love to sing we love to fight*
> *We hate the boys in red and white*
> *We sing a song in harmony*
> *We sing a song of victory*
> *The Villa fans will never mock*
> *When they remember Bruce Rioch Rioch Rioch*

In the 1998-99 season, the Derby County player whose replica team shirt sold in the greatest numbers was Estonian goalkeeper Mart Poom.

THE CARLING ULTIMATE FOOTBALL FACT AND QUIZ BOOK

Clubs – D

Doncaster Rovers

Doncaster Rovers were founded in 1879 by Albert Jenkins, originally to play a one-off game against the Yorkshire Institute for the Deaf.

From 1880 to 1916, Doncaster Rovers played at the Intake Ground; from 1920 to 1922 they were to be seen at the Benetthorpe Ground; in 1922 they moved to their present home, Belle Vue.

Doncaster Rovers play their home games in all red.

Doncaster Rovers turned professional in 1885 and joined the Football League in 1901.

They have since failed to gain re-election twice – once in 1903 and then again in 1905. On the second occasion, they did not get back in until 1923, but since then they have been in the League continuously.

In the 1946-47 season, Doncaster Rovers – then in the Third Division (North) – won 18 of their 21 away League matches and kept a clean sheet for 20 games.

In 1998, Doncaster Rovers finished bottom of the Third Division of the Nationwide Football League and were thus relegated to the Nationwide Conference.

Doncaster Rovers Managers

1920-1921	Arthur Porter
1921-1922	Harry Tufnell
1922-1923	Arthur Porter
1923-1927	Dick Ray
1928-1936	David Menzies
1936-1940	Fred Emery
1944-1946	Bill Marsden
1946-1949	Jackie Bestall
1949-1958	Peter Doherty
1958	Jack Hodgson and Syd Bycroft
1958-1959	Jack Crayston
1959-1960	Jackie Bestall
1960-1961	Norman Curtis
1961-1962	Danny Malloy
1962-1964	Oscar Hold
1964-1966	Bill Leivers
1966-1967	Keith Kettleborough
1967-1968	George Raynor
1968-1971	Lawrie McMenemy
1971-1974	Maurice Setters

Clubs – D

Doncaster Rovers continued...

1975-1978	Stan Anderson
1978-1985	Billy Bremner
1985-1987	Dave Cusack
1987-1989	Dave Mackay
1989-1991	Billy Bremner
1991-1993	Steve Beaglehole
1994	Ian Atkins
1994-1996	Sammy Chung
1996-1997	Kerry Dixon
1997	Dave Cowling
1997-	Mark Weaver

Doncaster Rovers League Record

1901-1903	Division Two
1903-1904	Failed to gain re-election – out of League
1904-1905	Division Two
1905-1923	Failed to gain re-election – out of League
1923-1935	Division Three (North)
1935-1937	Division Two
1937-1947	Division Three (North)
1947-1948	Division Two
1948-1950	Division Three (North)
1950-1958	Division Two
1958-1959	Division Three
1959-1966	Division Four
1966-1967	Division Three
1967-1969	Division Four
1969-1971	Division Three
1971-1981	Division Four
1981-1983	Division Three
1983-1984	Division Four
1984-1988	Division Three
1988-1992	Division Four
1992-1998	Division Three
1998-	Conference

On a visit to Turf Moor in 1991, the Doncaster supporters came up with the following deathless song:

And so this is Burnley
And what have we done
We've lost here already
Would you like a cream bun?

(Tune: Happy Xmas War Is Over by John Lennon)

THE CARLING ULTIMATE FOOTBALL FACT AND QUIZ BOOK

Clubs – D

Dumbarton

Nicknamed The Sons, Dumbarton were founded in 1872 and were a founder member of the Scottish Football League.

Dumbarton play their home matches at Boghead Park in Miller Street.

Dumbarton play in white shirts with a yellow band around the midriff and blue piping, white shorts with black piping and white socks with black piping.

In 1891, Dumbarton shared the Scottish League Championship with Rangers – the only time the title has been shared.

Scottish League Division One: Season 1890-91
Final Table (Top)

	P	W	D	L	F	A	Pts
Dumbarton	18	13	3	2	61	21	29
Rangers	18	13	3	2	58	25	29

In 1892, Dumbarton won the title outright – their only Scottish Championship.

Dumbarton won the Scottish FA Cup in 1883 and were runners-up in 1881, 1882, 1887, 1891 and 1897.

Dundee

Dundee are sometimes called The Dee but are more commonly nicknamed The Dark Blues, after the colour of their shirts. Their shorts are white and their socks blue with red piping.

Dundee were founded in 1893 through the amalgamation of the Our Boys and East End teams. They play at the Dens Park Stadium in Sandeman Street.

Dundee first won the Scottish FA Cup in 1910, after two replays against Clyde.

Dundee won the Scottish League Cup in 1952 and 1953 and then again in 1974.

In 1962, Dundee won their only Scottish Championship with a team containing Alan Gilzean and Ian Ure, who both moved on to even greater fame south of the border.

THE CARLING ULTIMATE FOOTBALL FACT AND QUIZ BOOK

Clubs – D

Dundee United

Nicknamed The Terrors, Dundee United play in tangerine shirts, black shorts and tangerine socks.

Founded in 1909, the club was originally known as Dundee Hibernian - it adopted its present name in 1923.

Dundee United play their home matches at Tannadice Park in Tannadice Street.

Dundee United's golden age began when manager Jim McLean led them to the Scottish League Cup in 1980 and 1981 and then to the 1983 League Championship. In 1984, they reached the semi-finals of the European Cup and in 1987 the UEFA Cup Final.

In 1994, Dundee United won the Scottish FA Cup for the first time in their history.

Dunfermline Athletic

Dunfermline Athletic was founded in 1885 by members of a local cricket club. They joined the Scottish Football League in 1912.

Dunfermline Athletic play their home games at East End Park in Halbeath Road. They wear black and white striped shirts, black shorts and black socks with white piping.

The first major trophy in Dunfermline Athletic's history did not come until 1961, when they won the Scottish FA Cup. They won the trophy again in 1968, but since then nothing.

Dynamo Kiev

Founded in 1927, the leading football club in Ukraine plays in an all white strip with a blue trim. Dynamo Kiev first won the Football League Championship of the USSR, of which Ukraine was then a part, in 1961.

Dynamo Kiev went on to win the title a further 11 times before the break-up of the Soviet Union in 1989. Dynamo Kiev also won the Soviet Union's FA Cup nine times from 1954.

Dynamo Kiev won the European Cup Winners' Cup in 1975 and 1986.

THE CARLING ULTIMATE FOOTBALL FACT AND QUIZ BOOK

Clubs – D

Dynamo Moscow

Dynamo Moscow were founded in 1887 by two Englishmen, Clement and Harry Charnock, while they were building a mill outside the Russian capital. They advertised in The London Times newspaper for 'engineers, mechanics and clerks capable of playing football well'. The club was originally named Orekhovo.

During the Soviet period (1917-1989), the club was adopted by the Electrical Trades' Union (hence the new name) but became associated principally with the secret police, the KGB.

At the end of the Second World War in 1945, Dynamo Moscow made a historic and unforgettable tour of Britain – in their first game, they drew 3-3 with Chelsea; they then beat Cardiff City 10-1 and Arsenal 4-3 before drawing 2-2 in their final game with Rangers.

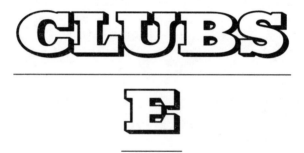

Clubs – E

East Fife

East Fife – nicknamed The Fifers – were founded in 1903 as East of Fife and joined the Scottish Football League in 1921.

East Fife historically play in black and gold striped shirts, black shorts and black socks with gold piping. The stripes have recently been substituted by diamonds of the same colours.

East Fife play their home games at Bayview Stadium, South Street, Methil.

East Fife won the Scottish FA Cup in 1938 – the only Second Division club ever to have achieved this feat.

East Fife won the Scottish League Cup in 1948, 1950 and 1954.

Their crowds may not be large, but those who do attend East Fife games have a strong line in abuse for supporters of neighbouring Cowdenbeath:

> *They come from near Lochgelly*
> *They have nae got a telly*
> *They're dirty and they're smelly*
> *The Cowden family*
>
> *(Tune: The Addams Family)*
>
> *No soap in Cowden*
> *You know there's no soap in Cowden*
>
> *(Tune: Juantanamera)*

East Stirlingshire

East Stirlingshire – nicknamed The Shire – were founded in 1881 and entered the Scottish Football League in 1900.

East Stirlingshire play their home games at Firs Park in Firs Street, Falkirk.

The Shire's home strip is black and white hooped shirts, black shorts and black socks with white piping.

To date, East Stirlingshire have won only one trophy – the Scottish Second Division Championship in 1932.

THE CARLING ULTIMATE FOOTBALL FACT AND QUIZ BOOK

Facts
Clubs – E

Everton

Everton were founded in 1878. They were originally known as St Domingo FC.

Since 1892, Everton have played their home matches at Goodison Park, Liverpool. They previously played at Stanley Park (1878-1882), Priory Road (1882-1884) and Anfield Road (1884-1892).

The Everton strip is royal blue shirts with black and white trim, white shorts with black and blue trim, and blue stockings with black piping. These colours were adopted in 1901 – prior to that, Everton had appeared in black shirts with a white sash, a colour scheme that earned them the nickname The Black Watch, after the Highland Regiment with a similar-looking uniform.

Everton are now generally known as The Toffees – or, at least, any football fan would know who you meant if you called them that. They are also sometimes known as The Moonlight Dribblers, a nickname taken from the legend that in their early days they were so keen to hone their skills that they trained at night.

Everton were founder members of the Football League and finished the 1888-89 season in fifth position.

In all their history, Everton have spent only four seasons outside the top flight of English football.

Everton won the first of their nine League Championships in 1891. Their other titles came in 1915, 1928, 1932, 1939, 1963, 1970, 1985 and 1987.

Everton have won the FA Cup five times – in 1906, 1933, 1966, 1984 and 1995.

In 1985, Everton won the European Cup Winners' Cup. This triumph may have been soured a little by the fact that Everton had only got into the competition as runners- up in the FA Cup – 1984 was the year in which Merseyside rivals Liverpool did the double.

Everton Managers

1888-1889	W E Barclay
1889-1901	Dick Molyneux
1901-1918	William C Cuff
1918-1919	W J Sawyer
1919-1935	Thomas H McIntosh
1936-1948	Theo Kelly
1948-1956	Cliff Britton
1956-1958	Ian Buchan
1958-1961	Johnny Carey
1961-1973	Harry Catterick
1973-1977	Billy Bingham
1977-1981	Gordon Lee
1981-1987	Howard Kendall

THE CARLING ULTIMATE FOOTBALL FACT AND QUIZ BOOK

Clubs – E

Everton continued...

1987-1990	Colin Harvey
1990-1993	Howard Kendall
1994	Mike Walker
1994-1997	Joe Royle
1997-1998	Howard Kendall
1998-	Walter Smith

Everton League Record

1888-1930	Division One
1930-1931	Division Two
1931-1951	Division One
1951-1954	Division Two
1954-1992	Division One
1992-	Premiership

O we hate Bill Shankly and we hate St John
But most of all we hate Big Ron
And we'll hang the Koppites one by one
On the banks of the royal blue Mersey

So to hell with Liverpool and Rangers too
We'll drown them all in the Mersey
And we'll fight fight till our balls turn white
For the boys in the royal blue jersey

(Tune: The Halls of Montezuma)

In the 1998-99 season, the Everton player whose replica team shirt sold in the greatest numbers was John Collins.

Exeter City

Exeter City were founded in 1904 through the amalgamation of St Sidwell's United and Exeter United. After a meeting at the Red Lion Hotel in the city, the club turned professional in 1908. They joined the Football League in 1920.

Exeter City play their home games at St James Park. Their strip consists of red and white striped shirts, black shorts and red socks.

Exeter City are nicknamed The Grecians – this is a reference to the local Greek community, which is traditionally concentrated around the ground in St Sidwell's.

Exeter City's outstanding achievement to date has been the Fourth Division Championship, which they won in 1990.

THE CARLING ULTIMATE FOOTBALL FACT AND QUIZ BOOK

Facts
Clubs – E

Exeter City continued...

Exeter City Managers
1910-1922	Arthur Chadwick
1923-1927	Fred Mavin
1928-1929	Dave Wilson
1929-1935	Billy McDevitt
1935-1939	Jack English
1945-1952	George Roughton
1952-1953	Norman Kirkman
1953-1957	Norman Dodgin
1957-1958	Bill Thompson
1958-1960	Frank Broome
1960-1962	Glen Wilson
1962-1963	Cyril Spiers
1963-1965	Jack Edwards
1965-1966	Ellis Stuttard
1966-1967	Jock Basford
1967-1969	Frank Broome
1969-1976	Johnny Newman
1977-1979	Bobby Saxton
1979-1983	Brian Godfrey
1983-1984	Gerry Francis
1984-1985	Jim Iley
1985-1987	Colin Appleton
1988-1991	Terry Cooper
1991-1994	Alan Ball
1994-1995	Terry Cooper
1995-	Peter Fox

Exeter City League Record
1920-1921	Division Three
1921-1958	Division Three (South)
1958-1964	Division Four
1964-1966	Division Three
1966-1977	Division Four
1977-1984	Division Three
1984-1990	Division Four
1990-1992	Division Three
1992-1994	Division Two
1994-	Division Three

In the 1998-99 season, the Exeter City player whose replica team shirt sold in the greatest numbers was Barry McConnell.

THE CARLING ULTIMATE FOOTBALL FACT AND QUIZ BOOK

Clubs – F

Falkirk

Falkirk are nicknamed The Bairns, after the Burns line: 'Better meddle wi' the Devil than the Bairns o' Falkirk'.

The club was founded in 1876 and joined the Scottish League in 1902.

Since 1883, Falkirk's home ground has been Brockville Park in Hope Street. Before that, they played at Blinkbonny (1881-1883) and Randyford (1876-1881).

Falkirk play in black and white shirts with red piping, black and white shorts with red piping and white socks with a black band at the top.

In 1907, Falkirk became the first Scottish League club to score 100 goals (102, to be exact) in a season.

In 1907-08, their best-ever League season, Falkirk finished runners-up to Celtic in the Scottish First Division.

Falkirk have twice won the Scottish FA Cup – in 1913 and 1957. They also won the Scottish B&Q Cup in 1994.

In 1922, Falkirk became the first British club to pay more than £5,000 for a player when they bought goalkeeper Syd Puddefoot from West Ham United for £5,500.

Ferencvaros

One of the leading teams in Hungary, Ferencvaros are based in Budapest and play in green and white striped shirts with white shorts and white socks.

Since they were founded in 1899, Ferencvaros have dominated the Hungarian domestic League and Cup competitions and won the Inter-City Fairs Cup in 1965.

The Hungarian team that finished runners-up in the 1938 World Cup contained four Ferencvaros players.

THE CARLING ULTIMATE FOOTBALL FACT AND QUIZ BOOK

Clubs – F

Feyenoord

One of the leading Dutch clubs, Feyenoord play at the 52,000-capacity De Kuyp Stadium in Rotterdam, their home since 1937.

The club was founded in 1908 with money provided by a mining tycoon named C R J Kieboom.

Feyenoord play their home games in red and white halved shirts, black shorts and black socks.

To date, Feyenoord have won the Dutch League Championship 13 times and the Dutch FA Cup 10 times. They did the League and Cup double in 1965 and 1969.

In 1970, Feyenoord became the first Dutch club to win the European Cup – this is particularly galling to supporters of Ajax Amsterdam.

In 1974, Feyenoord won the UEFA Cup, beating Tottenham Hotspur 4-2 on aggregate in the two-legged Final.

Flamengo

Flamengo was formed in 1911 when a group of disaffected players walked out on Fluminese (q v) and opened their own football club within a pre-existent sailing club in Rio de Janeiro, Brazil.

Flamengo play in red and black hooped shirts, white shirts and red and black socks. They are sometimes described as The People's Club (cf Fluminese, reputedly the club for toffs).

Flamengo are normally based at the 20,000-capacity Gavea Stadium, but for big matches they transfer to either the Alvaro Chaves Stadium or the 130,000 Maracana.

One of Flamengo's most outstanding players has been Leonidas da Silva, star of the 1938 World Cup, who played for the club from 1936 to 1942, during which period they twice won the Rio State League Championship.

THE CARLING ULTIMATE FOOTBALL FACT AND QUIZ BOOK

Clubs – F

Fluminese

Fluminese were founded in 1902 by Arthur Cox, a British immigrant to Rio de Janeiro, Brazil. Many of their earliest players were English.

Today, Fluminese play their routine home games at the Laranjeira but, like Flamengo, transfer their biggest matches to the Maracana.

Supporters of Fluminese may arrive at games with faces dabbed with white powder – po de arroz, in Portuguese. This cosmetic was a sign of aristocracy at the beginning of the 20th century.

Fluminese have won the Rio State League Championship nearly 30 times.

Fluminese play in red, green and white striped shirts, white shorts and white socks.

The Rio local derby between Fluminese and Flamengo was first played in 1912. The 1963 meeting between them drew an all-time world record crowd of 177,656 to the Maracana Stadium, the second home of both clubs.

Forfar Athletic

Nicknamed The Loons, Forfar Athletic were founded in 1885 and joined the Scottish League in 1921.

Forfar Athletic have always played at Station Park in Carseview Road. Their home strip is sky blue shirts, navy blue shorts and navy blue socks with white piping.

Forfar Athletic won their first honour – the Scottish Second Division Championship – in 1984, the year of their centenary.

Fulham

Founded in 1879 as Fulham St Andrew's Sunday School FC, Fulham adopted their present name and turned professional in 1898.

Fulham joined the Football League in 1907.

Fulham play their home games at Craven Cottage – hence their nickname, The Cottagers.

Fulham's strip is white shirts with red and black trim, black shorts and white socks with red and black trim.

THE CARLING ULTIMATE FOOTBALL FACT AND QUIZ BOOK

Facts
Clubs – F

Fulham continued...

Fulham's greatest on-field achievement came in 1975, when – as a Second Division club – they reached the Final of the FA Cup. They lost – a little unluckily – to First Division West Ham United in what was only the second all-London FA Cup Final in history (the first had been Tottenham Hotspur v Chelsea in 1967).

In 1987, Fulham nearly merged with Queen's Park Rangers but television pundit Jimmy Hill, a former player, averted this catastrophe by buying the club's name and all its players' contracts.

Fulham are now owned by Mohamed Al Fayed, the Chairman of Harrods, and managed by Kevin Keegan, who was also appointed England team coach in 1999. Their plan is to put Fulham back in to the top flight of English football by the millennium.

Fulham Managers
1904-1909	Harry Bradshaw
1909-1924	Phil Kelso
1924-1926	Andy Ducat
1926-1929	Joe Bradshaw
1929-1931	Ned Liddell
1931-1934	Jim MacIntyre
1934-1935	Jimmy Hogan
1935-1948	Jack Peart
1948-1949	Frank Osborne
1949-1953	Bill Dodgin Snr
1953-1956	Frank Osborne
1956-1958	Duggie Livingstone
1958-1964	Bedford Jezzard
1965-1968	Vic Buckingham
1968	Bobby Robson
1969-1972	Bill Dodgin Jnr
1972-1976	Alec Stock
1976-1980	Bobby Campbell
1980-1984	Malcolm Macdonald
1984-1986	Ray Harford
1986-1990	Ray Lewington
1990-1991	Alan Dicks
1991-1994	Don Mackay
1994-1996	Ian Branfoot
1996-1997	Micky Adams
1997-1998	Ray Wilkins
1998-1999	Kevin Keegan

Fulham League Record
1907-1928	Division Two
1928-1932	Division Three (South)

Clubs – F

Fulham continued...

1932-1949	Division Two
1949-1952	Division One
1952-1959	Division One
1959-1968	Division One
1968-1969	Division Two
1969-1971	Division Three
1971-1980	Division Two
1980-1982	Division Three
1982-1986	Division Two
1986-1992	Division Three
1992-1994	Division Two
1994-1997	Division Three
1997-1999	Division Two

When you're born in Fulham you'll never walk alone
Hike a hundred highways to win away from home
Still all in all I'm happy the reason is you see
That I'll keep on following the great Fulham FC

In the 1998-99 season, the Fulham player whose replica team shirt sold in the greatest numbers was Paul Peschisolido.

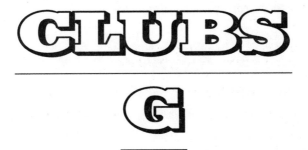

THE CARLING ULTIMATE FOOTBALL FACT AND QUIZ BOOK

Clubs – G

Gillingham

Gillingham – nicknamed The Gills – play their home games at the Priestfield Stadium, a ground they presently sublet to Brighton and Hove Albion (q v).

Gillingham play in royal blue shirts with white trim, white shorts with blue trim and white socks.

Gillingham were founded in 1893. Their original name was Excelsior.

In 1894 they turned professional and changed their name to New Brompton. They took up their present name in 1913.

Gillingham joined the Football League in 1920.

At the end of the 1938 season, Gillingham failed to win re-election and dropped out of the Football League until 1950.

In 1964, Gillingham won the Fourth Division Championship after putting together a run of 52 home games without defeat. This was a record until 1981, when Liverpool went 85 games at Anfield without losing.

Gillingham Managers

1896-1906	W Ironside Groombridge
1906-1908	Steve Smith
1908-1919	W Ironside Groombridge
1919-1920	George Collins
1920-1923	John McMillan
1923-1926	Harry Curtis
1926-1929	Albert Hoskins
1929-1931	Dick Hendrie
1932-1937	Fred Mavin
1937-1938	Alan Ure
1938-1939	Bill Harvey
1939-1958	Archie Clark
1958-1962	Harry Barratt
1962-1965	Freddie Cox
1966-1971	Basil Hayward
1971-1974	Andy Nelson
1974-1975	Len Ashurst
1975-1981	Gerry Summers
1981-1987	Keith Peacock
1988	Paul Taylor
1988-1989	Keith Burkinshaw
1989-1993	Damien Richardson
1993-1995	Mike Flanagan
1995	Neil Smillie
1995-	Tony Pulis

THE CARLING ULTIMATE FOOTBALL FACT AND QUIZ BOOK

Facts
Clubs – G

Gillingham continued...

Gillingham League Record

1920-1921	Division Three
1921-1938	Division Three (South)
1938-1950	Failed to gain re-election; went out of Football League
1950-1958	Division Three (South)
1958-1964	Division Four
1964-1971	Division Three
1971-1974	Division Four
1974-1989	Division Three
1989-1992	Division Four
1992-1996	Division Three
1996-	Division Two

We ain't Jack and Jill
And we ain't Bill and Ben
We ain't Ken Dodd
Or his Diddy Men
We ain't Looby Loo
With all her toys
We are the Gillingham boot boys

(Tune: Just One Of Those Songs)

In the 1998-99 season, the Gillingham player whose replica team shirt sold in the greatest numbers was Carl Asaba.

Greenock Morton

Nicknamed The Ton, Greenock Morton were founded in 1874 and joined the Scottish League in 1893.

In 1896, Greenock Morton became the first football club in Scotland to register itself as a limited company.

Since 1883, Greenock Morton have played at Cappielow Park in Sinclair Street. before that, they played at Grant Street in 1874, Garvel Park in 1875 and Ladyburn Park in 1882.

The Greenock Morton home strip consists of blue and white hooped shirts, white shirts and blue socks.

Greenock Morton's only honour to date is the Scottish FA Cup, which they won in 1922, beating Rangers in the Final. The only goal of the match was scored by Morton legend Jimmy Gourlay.

THE CARLING ULTIMATE FOOTBALL FACT AND QUIZ BOOK

Clubs – G

Grimsby Town

Grimsby Town are nicknamed The Mariners. They do not actually play in Grimsby itself but at Blundell Park which is just across the boundary in neighbouring Cleethorpes.

Grimsby Town was founded in 1878 as Grimsby Pelham FC (Pelham is the family names of the Earls of Yarborough, leading local landowners).

The club adopted its present name in 1879 and joined the Football League in 1892 as founder members of the Second Division.

Grimsby Town play in black and white striped shirts, black shorts with red trim and white socks with red trim.

Grimsby Town's best season to date was in 1934-35, when they finished fifth in Division One.

Grimsby Town have twice reached the semi-finals of the FA Cup – in 1936 and 1939.

Grimsby Town Managers

1902-1920	H N Hickson
1920	Haydn Price
1921-1924	George Fraser
1924-1932	Wilf Gillow
1932-1936	Frank Womack
1937-1951	Charles Spencer
1951-1953	Bill Shankly
1954-1955	Billy Walsh
1955-1959	Allenby Chilton
1960-1962	Tim Ward
1962-1964	Tom Johnson
1964-1967	Jimmy McGuigan
1967-1968	Don McEvoy
1968-1969	Bill Harvey
1969-1971	Bobby Kennedy
1971-1973	Lawrie McMenemy
1973-1975	Ron Ashman

THE CARLING ULTIMATE FOOTBALL FACT AND QUIZ BOOK

Facts
Clubs – G

Grimsby Town continued...

1975-1976	Tom Casey
1976-1979	Johnny Newman
1979-1982	George Kerr
1982-1985	David Booth
1985-1987	Mike Lyons
1987-1988	Bobby Roberts
1988-1994	Alan Buckley
1994-1996	Brian Laws
1997	Kenny Swain
1997-	Alan Buckley

Grimsby Town League Record

1892-1901	Division Two
1901-1903	Division One
1903-1910	Division Two
1910-1911	Failed to gain re-election; dropped out of League
1911-1920	Division Two
1920-1921	Division Three
1921-1926	Division Three (North)
1926-1929	Division Two
1929-1932	Division One
1932-1934	Division Two
1934-1948	Division One
1948-1951	Division Two
1951-1956	Division Three (North)
1956-1959	Division Two
1959-1962	Division Three
1962-1964	Division Two
1964-1968	Division Three
1968-1972	Division Four
1972-1977	Division Three
1977-1979	Division Four
1979-1980	Division Three
1980-1987	Division Two
1987-1988	Division Three
1988-1990	Division Four
1990-1991	Division Three
1991-1992	Division Two
1992-1997	Division One
1997-	Division Two

THE CARLING ULTIMATE FOOTBALL FACT AND QUIZ BOOK

Clubs – G

Grimsby Town continued…

> *Sing when we're fishing*
> *We only sing when we're fishing*
>
> *(Tune: Juantanamera)*
>
> *God rest ye merry Mariners*
> *Let nothing you dismay*
> *A Cup defeat at Blackpool*
> *Is just another day*
> *We save ourselves up for the League*
> *And never lose away*
> *Oh tidings to Al* and the boys*
> *Al and the boys*
> *Oh tidings to Al and the boys*
>
> *(Tune: God Rest Ye Merry Gentlemen)*

* 'Al' is manager Alan Buckley

In the 1998-99 season, the Grimsby Town player whose replica team shirt sold in the greatest numbers was Jack Lester.

THE CARLING ULTIMATE FOOTBALL FACT AND QUIZ BOOK

Clubs – H

Hamburg

Hamburg were founded in 1887 through the amalgamation of the Falke, Germania and Hamburger clubs.

Hamburg play their home games at the Volksparkstadion; their colours are white shirts with red trim, red shorts and red socks.

Hamburg might have won their first German Championship in 1922 – in the play-off final, their opponents, Nuremburg, were reduced by injuries to seven men and Hamburg declined to accept the title.

This sporting gesture was rewarded in the following year (1923), when Hamburg won the first of their six League titles to date.

Hamburg have also won the German Cup three times, the European Cup Winners' Cup in 1977 and the European Cup in 1983.

The greatest player in the club's history is centre forward Uwe Seeler, the West German captain in the 1966 and 1970 World Cup finals.

Hamilton Academical

Nicknamed The Accies, Hamilton Academical were founded in 1874. They are the only first-class football club in the British Isles to be named after a school (Hamilton Academy).

Hamilton Academical play in red and white hooped shirts, red shorts and white socks with red piping.

In 1993, Hamilton moved from Douglas Park – their home since 1875 – to share Partick Thistle's Firhill Stadium at 80 Firhill Road, Glasgow.

Hamilton Academical have never won the Scottish FA Cup but have twice appeared in the Final of the competition – in 1911 and 1935.

Hamilton Academical were the Champions of Scottish League Division Two in 1904 and won the First Division title in 1986 and 1988.

Hamilton Academical won the Scottish B & Q Cup in 1992 and 1993.

THE CARLING ULTIMATE FOOTBALL FACT AND QUIZ BOOK

Facts
Clubs – H

Hartlepool United

Hartlepool United – nicknamed The Pool – were formed in 1908 and joined the Football League in 1921.

Hartlepool have applied for re-election more than any other club in the English Football League.

The club were known as Hartlepools United until 1968, then shortened their name to Hartlepool in the same year as they made a one-season appearance in Division Three. They adopted their present name in 1977.

Hartlepool United play in sky blue shirts, navy blue and white shorts and sky blue socks.

Hartlepool United's home ground is Victoria Park in Clarence Road.

Hartlepool Managers

1908-1912	Alfred Priest
1912-1913	Percy Humphreys
1913-1920	Jack Manners
1920-1922	Cecil Potter
1922-1924	David Gordon
1924-1927	Jack Manners
1927-1931	Bill Norman
1932-1935	Jack Carr
1935-1943	Jimmy Hamilton
1943-1957	Fred Westgarth
1957-1959	Ray Middleton
1959-1962	Bill Robinson
1962-1963	Allenby Chilton
1963-1964	Bob Gurney
1964-1965	Alvan Williams
1965	Geoff Twentyman
1965-1967	Brian Clough
1967-1970	Angus McLean
1970-1971	John Simpson
1971-1974	Len Ashurst
1974-1976	Ken Hale
1976-1983	Billy Horner
1983	Johnny Duncan
1983	Mike Docherty
1984-1986	Billy Horner
1986-1988	John Bird
1988-1989	Bobby Moncur
1989-1991	Cyril Knowles
1991-1993	Alan Murray

Clubs – H

Hartlepool United continued...

1993	Viv Busby
1993-1994	John McPhail
1994-1995	David McCreery
1995-1996	Keith Houchen
1996-	Mick Tait

Hartlepool League Record

1921-1958	Division Three (North)
1958-1968	Division Four
1968-1969	Division Three
1969-1991	Division Four
1991-1992	Division Three
1992-1994	Division Two
1994-	Division Three

In the 1998-99 season, the Hartlepool player whose replica team shirt sold in the greatest numbers was Steve Howard.

Heart of Midlothian

The only football club in the British Isles – or possibly anywhere – to have taken its name from the title of a novel, the work in question being The Heart of Midlothian by Sir Walter Scott, which was published in 1818. The heart referred to in this book was a prison in Edinburgh.

The football club took this name in the year of its formation, 1874, at the suggestion of the captain, Tom Purdie.

Hearts were founder members of the Scottish First Division in 1890. They finished the first season in sixth place, out of 10 clubs.

Heart of Midlothian are nicknamed the Jam Tarts – this is rhyming slang for Hearts.

Hearts play their home games at the Tynecastle Stadium in Gorgie Road, Edinburgh.

Heart of Midlothian play their home games in maroon shirts, white shorts and maroon socks with white trim.

THE CARLING ULTIMATE FOOTBALL FACT AND QUIZ BOOK

Clubs – H

Heart of Midlothian continued...

Heart of Midlothian have had a great deal of success in their long history – they have won the Scottish League Championship five times, in 1895, 1897, 1958, 1960 and 1980.

To date, Hearts have won the Scottish FA Cup five times – in 1891, 1896, 1901, 1906 and 1956.

Hearts have won the Scottish League Cup four times – in 1955, 1959, 1960 and 1963.

> *Away up in Gorgie at Tynecastle Park*
> *There's a wee footba' team that'll aye make its mark*
> *They've won all the honours in footballing arts*
> *And there's nae other team to compare with the Hearts*

CHORUS
> *H-E-A-R-T-S*
> *If ye cannae spell it then here's what it says*
> *Hearts, Hearts, glorious Hearts*
> *It's down at Tynecastle they bide*
> *The talk of the toon are the boys in maroon*
> *And Aluld Reekie supports them with pride*
>
> *For national caps we can always supply*
> *Like Massie and Walker and Bauld and Mackay*
> *If I had the time I could name dozens more*
> *Who've helped in producing the old Hampden Roar*

CHORUS
> *This is our story this is our song*
> *Follow the Hearts and you cannae go wrong*
> *Some say that the Rangers and Celtic are grand*
> *But the boys in maroon are the best in the land*
>
> *We've won the League flag and we've won the League Cup*
> *Though sometimes we go down we'll aye come back up*
> *Our forwards can score and it's no idle talk*
> *Our defence is as strong as the Auld Castle Rock*

THE CARLING ULTIMATE FOOTBALL FACT AND QUIZ BOOK

Clubs – H

Hibernian

Nicknamed The Hibs or The Hibees, Hibernian play their home games at Easter Road Stadium at 12 Albion Place, Edinburgh.

Hibernian were founded in 1875 by Irish immigrants and joined the Scottish Football League in 1893.

To date, Hibernian have won the Scottish League Championship four times – in 1903, 1948, 1951 and 1952.

During the 1950s, Hibernian's outstanding forward line of Peter Johnstone, Willie Ormond, Lawrie Reilly, Gordon Smith and Eddie Turnbull were known collectively as The Famous Five, a name derived from the main characters in a series of children's books by Enid Blyton.

Hibernian have won the Scottish FA Cup twice – in 1887 and 1902.

Up to the end of the 20th century, Hibernian had won the Scottish League Cup twice – in 1972-73 and 1991-92.

The Hibernian home strip consists of green shirts with white sleeves, white shorts with green trim and green socks with white trim. This general design was adopted in 1938 in imitation of Arsenal, although the Hibernian green was still preferred to the Gunners' red in order to keep sight of Hibs' traditional links with Ireland (the Emerald Isle).

Hibernian's fortunes have declined in recent years and the club's financial difficulties have led to talk of a merger with fierce local rivals Heart of Midlothian. The club were relegated from the Bank of Scotland Premier League in 1998 but won the 1999 First Division Championship by 23 points.

Huddersfield Town

Once a great team, Huddersfield Town have sadly declined into relative obscurity since their heyday in the 1920s, when they won the English League Championship three years running – in 1924, 1925 and 1926.

Huddersfield are nicknamed The Terriers. In 1994 they moved from their old Leeds Road ground to the nearby purpose-built Alfred McAlpine Stadium.

Huddersfield Town play in blue and white striped shirts, white shorts and white socks with a single navy blue hoop.

Huddersfield were formed in 1908 and joined the Football League in 1910.

THE CARLING ULTIMATE FOOTBALL FACT AND QUIZ BOOK

Clubs – H

Huddersfield Town continued…

The turning point in the history of Huddersfield Town came in 1921, when the club appointed as manager the now legendary Herbert Chapman, who led them to their first two League titles. (They won their third under Cecil Potter; Chapman had gone on to Arsenal, where he achieved even greater success.)

But first, Chapman masterminded Huddersfield's 1922 FA Cup victory – the only time that they have won the trophy.

Huddersfield remained in the First Division without a break until 1952. Although they subsequently returned to the top flight in 1953 and 1970, these were both only brief appearances.

Huddersfield Town Managers

1908-1910	Fred Walker
1910-1912	Richard Pudan
1912-1919	Arthur Fairclough
1919-1921	Ambrose Langley
1921-1925	Herbert Chapman
1925-1926	Cecil Potter
1926-1929	Jack Chaplin
1929-1942	Clem Stephenson
1943-1947	David Steele
1947-1952	George Stephenson
1952-1956	Andy Beattie
1956-1959	Bill Shankly
1960-1964	Eddie Boot
1964-1968	Tom Johnson
1968-1974	Ian Greaves
1974	Bobby Collins
1975-1978	Tom Johnson
1978-1986	Mike Buxton
1986-1987	Steve Smith
1987-1988	Malcolm Macdonald
1988-1992	Eoin Hand
1992-1993	Ian Ross
1993-1995	Neil Warnock
1995-1997	Brian Horton
1997-	Peter Jackson

Huddersfield Town League Record

1910-1920	Division Two
1920-1952	Division One
1952-1953	Division Two
1953-1956	Division One
1956-1970	Division Two

Clubs – H

Huddersfield Town continued...

1970-1972	Division One
1972-1973	Division Two
1973-1975	Division Three
1975-1980	Division Four
1980-1983	Division Three
1983-1988	Division Two
1988-1992	Division Three
1992-1995	Division Two
1995-	Division One

Those were the days my friend
We thought they'd never end
We won the League three times in a row
We won the FA Cup
And now we're going up
We are the Town
Oh yes we are the Town

(Tune: Those Were The Days)

In the 1998-99 season, the Hudersfield Town player whose replica team shirt sold in the greatest numbers was Ben Thornley.

Hull City

Hull City – nicknamed The Tigers – have played their home games at Boothferry Park since 1946.

Prior to that, they played at Hull Rugby Club's Boulevard Ground from 1904 to 1905 and from 1944 to 1945, and at Hull Cricket Club's Analby Road from 1905 to 1944.

Hull City play in black and amber striped shirts with amber sleeves, black shorts and amber or black and amber socks.

The club was founded in 1904 and joined the Football League in the following year.

Hull City have won the Third Division title in 1933, 1949 and 1966 but have never played in the top flight of English football.

The club's outstanding achievement to date came in 1930, when – as a struggling and subsequently relegated Second Division club – they reached the semi-final of the FA Cup, going out in a replay to the eventual winners, Arsenal.

THE CARLING ULTIMATE FOOTBALL FACT AND QUIZ BOOK

Clubs – H

Hull City continued…

Hull City Managers
1904-1905	James Ramster
1905-1913	Ambrose Langley
1913-1914	Harry Chapman
1914-1916	Fred Stringer
1916-1921	David Menzies
1921-1923	Percy Lewis
1923-1931	Bill McCracken
1931-1934	Haydn Green
1934-1936	John Hill
1936	David Menzies
1936-1946	Ernest Blackburn
1946-1948	Major Frank Buckley
1948-1951	Raich Carter
1952-1955	Bob Jackson
1955-1961	Bob Brocklebank
1961-1970	Cliff Britton
1970-1974	Terry Neill
1974-1977	John Kaye
1977-1978	Bobby Collins
1978-1979	Ken Houghton
1979-1982	Mike Smith
1982	Bobby Brown
1982-1984	Colin Appleton
1984-1988	Brian Horton
1988-1989	Eddie Gray
1989	Colin Appleton
1989-1991	Stan Ternent
1991-1997	Terry Dolan
1997-1998	Mark Hateley
1998-	Warren Joyce

Hull City League Record
1905-1930	Division Two
1930-1933	Division Three (North)
1933-1936	Division Two
1936-1949	Division Three (North)
1949-1956	Division Two
1956-1958	Division Three (North)
1958-1959	Division Three
1959-1960	Division Two
1960-1966	Division Three
1966-1978	Division Two

Clubs – H

Hull City continued...

1978-1981	Division Three
1981-1983	Division Four
1983-1985	Division Three
1985-1991	Division Two
1991-1992	Division Three
1992-1996	Division Two
1996-	Division Three

I took my wife to a football match to see Hull City play
We waited for a trolley bus for nearly half a day
And when we got to Boothferry Park the crowds were rolling in
The bus conductor said to me do you think that they will win
Shoot City shoot! Shoot City shoot!
The grass is green the ball is brown
Shoot City shoot! Shoot City shoot!
There ain't no guy as sly as our goalie Billie Bly

(Tune: Sioux City Sue)

In the 1998-99 season, the Hull City player whose replica team shirt sold in the greatest numbers was David Brown.

THE CARLING ULTIMATE FOOTBALL FACT AND QUIZ BOOK

Clubs – I

Internazionale

Internazionale play at the Giuseppe Meazza Stadium in Milan, Italy. Their home strip consists of black and blue striped shirts, black shorts and black socks.

The club was founded in 1908 by a group of 45 footballers led by Giovanni Paramithiotti who disapproved of the way AC Milan (q v) was run.

After the Second World War, Inter were managed by Alfredo Foni and then by Helenio Herrera, an Argentine-born Frenchman. Under these men the club won many titles but few admirers with a defensive system known as catenaccio (the Italian for door bolt).

The aim of catenaccio was to defend nearly all the time in the greatest possible depth and then score with a rapid – and often a single – counter-attack.

Under Herrera in the 1960s, Internazionale won two Italian League titles, two European Cups and two World Club Championships.

In the 1930s, the cosmopolitan – and thus supposedly subversive – overtones of the word Internazionale aroused the disapproval of Italy's Fascist government. The club was therefore forced to change its name to Ambrosiana-Inter. (St Ambrose was the patron saint of Milan and the new style was thought to demonstrate greater national and regional pride.) The club reverted to its proper name as soon as Benito Mussolini fell.

Internazionale have also won the UEFA Cup twice, in 1991 and 1994.

Inverness Caledonian Thistle

Formed in 1994 and known until 1996 as Caledonian Thistle, Inverness Caledonian Thistle play their homes matches at the Caledonian Stadium in East Longman.

The Inverness Caledonian Thistle home strip consists of royal blue and white striped shirts with a red pinstripe, royal blue shorts and red socks with black and white bands.

In 1997, Inverness Caledonian Thistle won the Scottish Third Division Championship; in 1999, they won promotion from the Second Division after finishing as runners-up to Livingston.

THE CARLING ULTIMATE FOOTBALL FACT AND QUIZ BOOK

Facts
Clubs – I

Ipswich Town

Although Ipswich Town entered the Football League as recently as 1938, the club was formed in 1878.

Ipswich Town play in blue shirts, white shorts and white socks; their home ground is at Portman Road.

Ipswich Town won the League Championship in 1962, under the management of Alf Ramsey, who went on to lead England to victory in the 1966 World Cup Final.

Ipswich Town won the FA Cup in 1978. Their manager then was Bobby Robson – another who went on to lead England.

Again under Robson, Ipswich Town won the UEFA Cup in 1981. They also finished second in the First Division two years running – in 1981 and 1982.

Ipswich Town Managers

1936-1937	Mick O'Brien
1937-1955	Scott Duncan
1955-1963	Alf Ramsey
1963-1964	Jackie Milburn
1964-1968	Bill McGarry
1969-1982	Bobby Robson
1982-1987	Bobby Ferguson
1987-1990	John Duncan
1990-1994	John Lyall
1994-	George Burley

Ipswich Town League Record

1938-1954	Division Three (South)
1954-1955	Division Two
1955-1957	Division Three (South)
1957-1961	Division Two
1961-1964	Division One
1964-1968	Division Two
1968-1986	Division One
1986-1992	Division Two
1992-1995	Premiership
1995-	Division One

Clubs – I

Ipswich Town continued...

> *My name is Edward Ebenezer Jeremiah Brown*
> *I'm a football supporter of Ipswich Town*
> *Wherever they play you'll find me*
> *I haven't missed a game since I was three*
> *With my scarf and rattle and big rosette*
> *Singing Where was the goalie when the ball went in the net?*
> *Follow the Town up or down*
> *My name is Edward Ebenezer Jeremiah Brown*
> *But everyone calls me Ted*

In the 1998-99 season, the Ipswich Town player whose replica team shirt sold in the greatest numbers was Matt Holland.

THE CARLING ULTIMATE FOOTBALL FACT AND QUIZ BOOK

Clubs – J

Juventus

Juventus were founded in 1897 by a group of Italian students – the name means 'youth' – who adopted red as the team's colours.

Juventus play their home games at the Stadio delle Alpi in Turin.

In 1903, a member of the club committee saw a Notts County game in England. He was so excited by their style of play that he persuaded Juventus to adopt the black and white striped shirts for which they are now more famous than the team from which they got them!

In the 1930s, Juventus won the Italian League Championship five times running. They have now won the Championship 24 times, the Italian FA Cup 10 times, the European Cup twice (in 1985 and 1996), the European Cup Winners' Cup in 1984 and the UEFA Cup in 1977, 1990 and 1993.

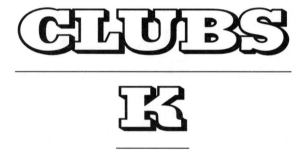

THE CARLING ULTIMATE FOOTBALL FACT AND QUIZ BOOK

Clubs – K

Kilmarnock

Kilmarnock are nickanamed The Killie. They are the second oldest club in Scotland, having been founded in 1869.

Kilmarnock joined the Scottish Football League in 1899, since when they have played their home games at Rugby Park in Rugby Road.

The Kilmarnock strip is blue and white striped shirts, white shorts with blue trim and maroon socks with white tops.

Kilmarnock's one Scottish League Championship to date came in 1965, when they won the title by virtue of a goal average that was 0.04 better than that of runners-up Heart of Midlothian:

Scottish League Division One 1964-65
Final Table

	P	W	D	L	F	A	Pts
Kilmarnock	34	22	6	6	62	33	50
Heart of Midlothian	34	22	6	6	90	49	50

Kilmarnock have won the Scottish FA Cup three times – in 1920, 1929 and 1997.

> *As he lay on the battlefield dying*
> *With the blood pouring out of his head*
> *As he lay on the battlefield dying*
> *These are the last words he said*
> *Kilmarnock Kilmarnock*
> *We are the Champions*

> *(Tune: Poor Scouser Tommy/Red River Valley)*

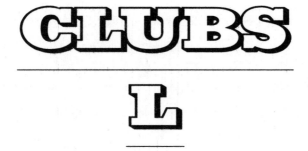

THE CARLING ULTIMATE FOOTBALL FACT AND QUIZ BOOK

Clubs – L

Leeds United

Leeds United are nicknamed The Peacocks because they used to play in blue. Their strip was changed to all white in the 1960s by manager Don Revie, who wanted his team to look and play like the great Real Madrid sides of the late 1950s and early 1960s. (Real play in all white.)

Leeds United came into being in 1919, after Leeds City were expelled from the League because of irregularities in payments to players during the First World War.

During the First World War, 35 guests had played for Leeds City, including seven internationals. This was not a problem in itself, because it was permitted under wartime rules, but when the club refused to render accounts for the 1917-18 and 1918-19 seasons, the League threw them out.

In the aftermath of the Leeds scandal, four of its directors and two of its former managers were banned for life from involvement in football and were forbidden even to attend matches.

One of Leeds City's former managers was George Cripps; the other was Herbert Chapman (see Arsenal and Huddersfield Town).

Leeds United took over Leeds City's Elland Road, a ground which had formerly belonged to the Holbeck club in 1904.

Leeds United joined the Football League in 1920 as members of Division Two.

Don Revie became manager of Leeds United in 1961 and the club soon entered their golden period. They won the Second Division in 1964 and then went on to win the first League Championship in their history in 1969.

Leeds United won the League again in 1974 and 1992 – the latter triumph made them the last ever winners of the old First Division Championship. (The First Division thereafter became the FA Premiership.)

Leeds United won the FA Cup in 1972, the League Cup in 1968 and the European Fairs Cup in 1971.

Despite their great achievements, Leeds United are generally remembered as a nearly club. This was particularly true under Revie – during his time as manager, the club were runners-up in the League in 1965, 1966, 1970, 1971 and 1972. They were losing FA Cup finalists in 1965, 1970 and 1973.

The low point of their golden period was in 1970, when they came close to winning a unique treble of the English League, the FA Cup and the European Cup and ended up with nothing.

After Revie left to take over as England manager, Leeds entered a long period of trying unsuccessfully to find a worthy successor. They hired Brian Clough, and the choice was a disaster – he lasted only 44 days. Then they appointed Jock Stein, who had managed Celtic when they won the European Cup in 1967.

THE CARLING ULTIMATE FOOTBALL FACT AND QUIZ BOOK

Facts
Clubs – L

Leeds United continued…

Even Stein could not recapture the '70s' glory, and the Leeds board then turned to former players. They tried three – Allan Clarke, Eddie Gray and Billy Bremner – but none was a success.

It was not until the arrival of Howard Wilkinson that the club recaptured anything like its old power.

Leeds United Managers

1919-1920	Dick Ray
1920-1927	Arthur Fairclough
1927-1935	Dick Ray
1935-1947	Bill Hampson
1947-1948	Willis Edwards
1948-1953	Major Frank Buckley
1953-1958	Raich Carter
1958-1959	Bill Lambton
1959-1961	Jack Taylor
1961-1974	Don Revie
1974	Brian Clough
1974-1978	Jimmy Armfield
1978	Jock Stein
1978-1980	Jimmy Armfield
1980-1982	Allan Clarke
1982-1985	Eddie Gray
1985-1988	Billy Bremner
1988-1996	Howard Wilkinson
1996-1998	George Graham
1998 -	David O'Leary

Leeds United League Record

1920-1924	Division Two
1924-1927	Division One
1927-1928	Division Two
1928-1931	Division One
1931-1932	Division Two
1932-1947	Division One
1947-1956	Division Two
1956-1960	Division One
1960-1964	Division Two
1964-1982	Division One
1982-1990	Division Two
1990-1992	Division One
1992-	Premiership

Clubs – L

Leeds United continued...

> *Here we go with Leeds United*
> *We're gonna give the boys a hand*
> *Stand up and sing for Leeds United*
> *They are the greatest in the land*
> *Marching on together*
> *We're gonna see you win*
> *La la la la la la*
> *We are so proud*
> *We shout it out loud*
> *We love you Leeds Leeds Leeds*
>
> *(Tune: Old Nell)*

In the 1998-99 season, the Leeds United player whose replica team shirt sold in the greatest numbers was Jimmy Floyd Hasselbaink.

Leicester City

In 1884, a group of old boys from Wyggeston School met at a house on the Roman Fosse Way and formed Leicester Fosse FC.

Leicester Fosse joined the Football League in 1894.

Leicester Fosse adopted their present name, Leicester City, in 1919.

Leicester City are nicknamed The Filberts or – more commonly – The Foxes. They play in royal blue shirts, white shorts and royal blue socks.

Leicester won the League Cup in 1964 and 1997. In 1964 they beat Stoke City 3-2 on aggregate in the two-leg Final.

In 1997 they beat Middlesbrough 1-0 in the Final replay at Hillsborough with a goal by Steve Claridge; the first game at Wembley had been a 1-1 draw (scorers: Emil Heskey for Leicester City; Fabrizio Ravanelli for Middlesbrough).

In the senior knockout competition, by contrast, Leicester have acquired a reputation for their ill-fortune: they have been runners-up in the FA Cup four times, in 1949, 1961, 1963 and 1969.

THE CARLING ULTIMATE FOOTBALL FACT AND QUIZ BOOK

Facts
Clubs – L

Leicester City continued...

Leicester City Managers
1896-1897	William Clark
1898-1907	George Johnson
1907-1909	James Blessington
1909-1911	Andy Aitken
1912-1914	John William Bartlett
1919-1926	Peter Hodge
1926-1932	William Orr
1932-1934	Peter Hodge
1934-1936	Andy Lochhead
1936-1939	Frank Womack
1939-1945	Tom Bromilow
1945-1946	Tom Mather
1946-1949	Johnny Duncan
1949-1955	Norman Bullock
1955-1958	David Halliday
1959-1968	Matt Gillies
1968-1971	Frank O'Farrell
1971-1977	Jimmy Bloomfield
1977-1978	Frank McLintock
1978-1982	Jock Wallace
1982-1986	Gordon Milne
1986-1987	Bryan Hamilton
1987-1991	David Pleat
1991-1994	Brian Little
1994-1995	Mark McGhee
1995-	Martin O'Neill

Leicester City League Record
1894-1908	Division Two
1908-1909	Division One
1909-1925	Division Two
1925-1935	Division One
1935-1937	Division Two
1937-1939	Division One
1946-1954	Division Two
1954-1955	Division One
1955-1957	Division Two
1957-1969	Division One
1969-1971	Division Two
1971-1978	Division One
1978-1980	Division Two
1980-1981	Division One

THE CARLING ULTIMATE FOOTBALL FACT AND QUIZ BOOK

Clubs – L

Leicester City continued...

1981-1983	Division Two
1983-1987	Division One
1987-1992	Division Two
1992-1994	Division One
1994-1995	Premiership
1995-1996	Division One
1996-	Premiership

One of the biggest bogeymen in the Leicester fans' pandemonium is a former manager who left the club quickly and – many thought – disloyally to move to what he then thought were the richer pastures of Wolverhampton Wanderers. Thus almost whenever Leicester have any success you may hear:

> *Are you watching*
> *Are you watching*
> *Are you watching Mark McGhee?*
>
> *(Tune: Bread of Heaven)*

In the 1998-99 season, the Leicester City player whose replica team shirt sold in the greatest numbers was Muzzy Izzet.

Leyton Orient

Leyton Orient were founded in 1881, turned professional in 1903 and joined the Football League in 1905.

From 1881 to 1886, they were known as the Glyn Cricket and Football Club; from 1886 to 1888 they were the Eagle Football Club; from 1888 to 1898 they were Orient FC; from 1898 to 1946 they were Clapton Orient; from 1946 to 1966 they were Leyton Orient; from 1966 to 1987 they were plain Orient; since 1987, they have reverted to one of their old names, Leyton Orient.

Since 1937, Leyton Orient have played their home games at the Leyton Stadium in Brisbane Road, London E10. They previously played at Glyn Road (1884-1896), Whittle Athletic Ground (1896-1900), Millfields Road (1900-1930) and Lea Bridge Road (1930-1937).

In 1962, Leyton Orient won promotion from the old Second Division but their period at the top was brief and inauspicious – they finished bottom of Division One in 1963.

The greatest highlights in the FA Cup history of Leyton Orient came in 1971, when they reached the Sixth Round and 1978, when they lost 3-0 to Arsenal in the semi-final.

THE CARLING ULTIMATE FOOTBALL FACT AND QUIZ BOOK

Facts
Clubs – L

Leyton Orient continued...

Leyton Orient Managers
1905-1906	Sam Ormerod
1906	Ike Ivenson
1907-1922	Billy Holmes
1922-1929	Peter Proudfoot
1929-1930	Arthur Grimsdell
1930-1931	Peter Proudfoot
1931-1933	Jimmy Seed
1933-1934	David Pratt
1935-1939	Peter Proudfoot
1939	Tom Halsey
1939-1945	Bill Wright
1945	Willie Hall
1945-1946	Bill Wright
1946-1948	Charlie Hewitt
1948-1949	Neil McBain
1949-1959	Alec Stock
1961-1963	Johnny Carey
1963-1964	Benny Fenton
1965	Dave Sexton
1966-1968	Dick Graham
1968-1971	Jimmy Bloomfield
1971-1977	George Petchey
1977-1981	Jimmy Bloomfield
1981	Paul Went
1981	Ken Knighton
1982-1991	Frank Clark
1991-1994	Peter Eustace
1994-1995	John Sitton and Chris Turner
1995-1996	Pat Holland
1996-	Tommy Taylor

Leyton Orient League Record
1905-1929	Division Two
1929-1956	Division Three (South)
1956-1962	Division Two
1962-1963	Division One
1963-1966	Division Two
1966-1970	Division Three
1970-1982	Division Two
1982-1985	Division Three
1985-1989	Division Four
1989-1992	Division Three

THE CARLING ULTIMATE FOOTBALL FACT AND QUIZ BOOK

Clubs – L

Leyton Orient continued...

| 1992-1995 | Division Two |
| 1995- | Division Three |

We're not going up and we're not going down
We won't win the League and we won't win the Cup
We're not good in fact we're bad
We are the Orient we're mad.

In the 1998-99 season, the Leyton Orient player whose replica team shirt sold in the greatest numbers was Amara Simba.

Lincoln City

The Imps – so named after one of the gargoyles on the city's cathedral – play their home games at Sincil Bank.

Lincoln City play in red and white striped shirts, white shorts and white socks with red trim.

Lincoln City were founded in 1883 and first joined the Football League in 1892.

Since then, Lincoln have failed to secure re-election to or been relegated from the Football League four times. In 1987, they became the first club ever to suffer automatic relegation to the Conference.

Lincoln City Managers

1900-1907	David Calderhead
1907-1914	John Henry Strawson
1919-1921	George Fraser
1921-1924	David Calderhead Jnr
1924-1927	Horace Henshall
1927-1936	Harry Parkes
1936-1946	Joe McClelland
1946-1965	Bill Anderson
1965-1966	Roy Chapman
1966-1970	Ron Gray
1970-1971	Bert Loxley
1971-1972	David Herd
1972-1977	Graham Taylor
1977-1978	George Kerr and Willie Bell
1978-1985	Colin Murphy
1985	John Pickering
1985-1987	George Kerr

THE CARLING ULTIMATE FOOTBALL FACT AND QUIZ BOOK

Clubs – L

Lincoln City continued...

1987	Peter Daniel
1987-1990	Colin Murphy
1990	Allan Clarke
1990-1993	Steve Thompson
1993-1994	Keith Alexander
1994-1995	Sam Ellis
1995	Steve Wicks
1995-1998	John Beck
1998-	Shane Westley

Lincoln City League Record

1892-1908	Division Two
1908-1909	Failed to gain re-election; dropped out of League
1910-1911	Division Two
1911-1912	Failed to gain re-election; dropped out of League
1912-1920	Division Two
1920-1921	Failed to gain re-election; dropped out of League
1921-1932	Division Three (North)
1932-1934	Division Two
1934-1948	Division Three (North)
1948-1949	Division Two
1949-1952	Division Three (North)
1952-1961	Division Two
1961-1962	Division Three
1962-1976	Division Four
1976-1979	Division Three
1979-1981	Division Four
1981-1986	Division Three
1986-1987	Division Four
1987-1988	GM Vauxhall Conference
1988-1992	Division Four
1992-1998	Division Three
1998-1999	Division Two

In the 1998-99 season, the Lincoln City player whose replica team shirt sold in the greatest numbers was Kevin Austin.

THE CARLING ULTIMATE FOOTBALL FACT AND QUIZ BOOK

Clubs – L

Liverpool

Liverpool are the most successful club in English football history.

Liverpool have a record number of League Championship wins – 18 times to date.

Liverpool have won the FA Cup five times, although they were late developers in this competition, lifting the trophy for the first time as recently as 1965.

They have also won the League Cup five times – in 1981, 1982, 1983, 1984 and 1995.

Liverpool have been England's outstanding club in European competition – they have won the European Cup four times – in 1977, 1978, 1981 and 1984 – and the UEFA Cup twice – in 1973 and 1976.

Liverpool were formed in 1892 and joined the Football League in the following year.

They play at Anfield in an all red strip with a white trim. They are nicknamed The Reds.

Liverpool's golden era began soon after the appointment of Bill Shankly as their manager in 1959.

The otherwise glorious history of Liverpool has been marred by two great crowd disasters. The first occurred on May 29, 1985, when Liverpool played Juventus in the European Cup Final at the Heysel Stadium in Brussels, Belgium.

Liverpool fans charged Italian supporters who had ended up in Block Z, a part of the ground supposedly reserved for neutral spectators. In the ensuing panic, 39 people – most of them Italian – were crushed or suffocated to death. More than 400 others were injured, many of them after a concrete wall in the rather decrepit Stadium collapsed under the weight of people leaning against it.

As a result of the Heysel Disaster, all English clubs were banned from European competition until 1990 (Liverpool were readmitted a year after the others, in 1991).

Worse was to come. On 15 April 1989, 96 people were killed and another 170 were seriously injured at Hillsborough at the start of Liverpool's FA Cup semi-final against Nottingham Forest.

As kick-off time approached, large numbers of Liverpool supporters swarmed into the Leppings Lane End of the ground. This caused severe overcrowding. Spectators closest to the pitch were crushed and had no way of escape because of the perimeter fences which barred their access to the pitch.

The Hillsborough Disaster led to the Taylor Report in which Lord Justice Peter Taylor called for – and got – a wide range of improvements to the facilities at English football grounds. Thus the most significant outcome of the Hillsborough Disaster was the advent of the all-seater stadium.

Liverpool Managers
1892-1896	W E Barclay
1896-1915	Tom Watson
1920-1922	David Ashworth
1923-1928	Matt McQueen
1928-1936	George Patterson

THE CARLING ULTIMATE FOOTBALL FACT AND QUIZ BOOK

Clubs – L

Liverpool continued...

1936-1951	George Kay
1951-1956	Don Welsh
1956-1959	Phil Taylor
1959-1974	Bill Shankly
1974-1983	Bob Paisley
1983-1985	Joe Fagan
1985-1991	Kenny Dalglish
1991-1994	Graeme Souness
1994-1998	Roy Evans
1998-	Gerard Houllier

Liverpool League Record

1893-1894	Division Two
1894-1895	Division One
1895-1896	Division Two
1896-1904	Division One
1904-1905	Division Two
1905-1954	Division One
1954-1962	Division Two
1962-1992	Division One
1992-	Premiership

The Liverpool anthem is 'You'll Never Walk Alone'. It was adopted by the fans on the Kop in 1963, when it was a No 1 UK hit for the Mersey-sound group Gerry and the Pacemakers. The song was in fact originally written for the musical Carousel.

When you walk through the storm
Hold your head up high
And don't be afraid of the dark
At the end of the storm
There's a golden sky
And the sweet silver song of the lark
Walk on through the wind
Walk on through the rain
Though your dreams be tossed and blown
Walk on walk on
With hope in your hearts
And you'll never walk alone
You'll never walk alone

In the 1998-99 season, the Liverpool player whose replica team shirt sold in the greatest numbers was Michael Owen.

THE CARLING ULTIMATE FOOTBALL FACT AND QUIZ BOOK

Facts
Clubs – L

Livingston

Livingston – Livvy's Lions, as they are nicknamed – play their home games at the Almondvale Stadium in Livingston, West Lothian.

The club motto is Fortiter Omnia Vincit – Latin for Strongly Conquers Everything.

Livingston's home strip consists of amber shirts with black trim, amber shorts with black trim and black socks with amber trim.

The club started out as Ferranti Thistle, the works team of that company's Edinburgh plant. When they joined the Scottish League in 1974, they were allowed to do so only on the conditions that they found a ground away from the factory and changed their name. Thus were born Meadowbank Thistle, the name used by the club until 1995, when they left the Meadowbank Stadium in Edinburgh, moved into their new home and became Livingston FC.

Under the name Meadowbank Thistle, the club won the Scottish Second Division Championship in 1987 and reached the semi-final of the 1984-85 Scottish League Cup, going out to the eventual winners, Rangers.

As Livingston, the club won the Scottish Third Division Championship in 1996.

> *Fisul, Fisul!*
> *I want a Fisul and I want one now*
> *Not one not two but three goals in it*
> *I want a Fisul and I want one now*
>
> *(Tune: The Banana Boat Song)*

Luton Town

The first professional football team south of Birmingham, Luton Town are usually nicknamed The Hatters but are sometimes known as The Strawplaiters.

The club was founded in 1885 through the amalgamation of two local clubs named Excelsior and Wanderers.

Luton Town joined the Football League in 1897.

Since 1905, the club have played their home games at the Kenilworth Road Stadium in Maple Road, Luton. Their two previous homes were at Excelsior's old ground in Dallow Lane (1885-1897) and in Dunstable Road (1897-1905).

THE CARLING ULTIMATE FOOTBALL FACT AND QUIZ BOOK

Clubs – L

Luton Town continued...

Luton Town play in white shirts with navy blue and orange trim, nay blue shorts and white socks.

Luton Town's biggest honour to date was their 1988 League Cup victory, in which they beat Arsenal 3-2 in the Final.

The other main highlight of Luton's history has been finishing seventh in the old First Division in 1987.

In the hooligan-plagued 1980s, Luton Town under Chairman David Evans, a right-wing Tory MP, banned away supporters from their ground. This led to Luton being excluded from the 1986 League Cup.

Luton Town Managers
1901-1925	Charlie Green
1925	George Thomson
1926-1927	Charlie Green
1927-1929	John McCartney
1929-1931	George Kay
1931-1935	Harold Wightman
1936-1938	Ted Liddell
1938-1939	Neil McBain
1939-1947	George Martin
1947-1958	Dally Duncan
1959-1960	Syd Owen
1960-1962	Sam Bartram
1962-1964	Bill Harvey
1965-1966	George Martin
1966-1968	Allan Brown
1968-1972	Alec Stock
1972-1978	Harry Haslam
1978-1986	David Pleat
1986-1987	John Moore
1987-1989	Ray Harford
1990-1991	Jim Ryan
1991-1995	David Pleat
1995	Terry Westley
1995-	Lennie Lawrence

Luton Town League Record
1897-1900	Division Two
1900-1920	Failed to win re-election; dropped out of League
1920-1921	Division Three
1921-1937	Division Three (South)
1937-1955	Division Two

Clubs – L

Luton Town continued...

1955-1960	Division One
1960-1963	Division Two
1963-1965	Division Three
1965-1968	Division Four
1968-1970	Division Three
1970-1974	Division Two
1974-1975	Division One
1975-1982	Division Two
1982-1996	Division One
1996-	Division Two

In the 1998-99 season, the Luton Town player whose replica team shirt sold in the greatest numbers was Kelvin Davis.

THE CARLING ULTIMATE FOOTBALL FACT AND QUIZ BOOK

Clubs – M

Macclesfield Town

Macclesfield Town play their home games at the Moss Rose Ground in London Road.

Macclesfield Town are nicknamed The Silkmen and play in royal blue shirts, white shorts and blue socks.

The club was formed in 1874 but came into the Football League only in 1997 after finishing as Champions of the GM Vauxhall Conference.

Macclesfield Town Managers
1997-   Sammy McIlroy

Macclesfield Town League Record
1997-1998   Division Three
1998-1999   Division Two

In the 1998-99 season, the Macclesfield Town player whose replica team shirt sold in the greatest numbers was Efetobar Sodje.

Manchester City

Nicknamed The Citizens, Manchester City play their home games at Maine Road in Moss Side.

Manchester City were founded in 1887 as Ardwick FC, which was itself an amalgamation of two even older clubs – West Gorton and Gorton Athletic. The present name was adopted in 1894.

Manchester City had five grounds before moving to Maine Road: Clowes Street (1880-81); Kirkmanshulme Cricket Ground (1881-82); Queens Road (1882-84); Pink Bank Lane (1884-1897) and Hyde Road (1894-1923).

Manchester City play at home in sky blue shirts, white shorts and navy blue socks.

For many years, City were the leading club in Manchester – they won the Second Division Championship in 1899 and 1903; in 1904 they won the FA Cup for the first time and finished second in the First Division.

City were punished severely by the FA for illegal payments and this allowed local rivals Newton Heath (later to become better known as Manchester United) to steal more and more of the Blues' limelight.

Manchester City won the Second Division Championship again in 1910 and 1928, and then the FA Cup for the second time in 1934. The team captain who raised the Cup at Wembley was Matt Busby (see Manchester United).

THE CARLING ULTIMATE FOOTBALL FACT AND QUIZ BOOK

Clubs – M

Manchester City continued…

City's consistent progress eventually culminated in the biggest prize of all – the League Championship, which they won for the first time in 1937.

In 1947, City won the Second Division Championship again and followed it in 1956 with their third FA Cup triumph.

In the 1957-58 season, Manchester City became the first and only First Division club to both score and concede more than 100 goals in a 42-match season. They finished fifth.

Manchester City's most recent golden era came in the late 1960s under manager Joe Mercer and his assistant Malcolm Allison.

Manchester City won the Second Division Championship in 1966, the League Championship in 1968 and the FA Cup for the fourth and last time in 1969. In 1970 they did a unique double of the domestic League Cup and the European Cup Winners' Cup.

Manchester City won the League Cup again in 1976 and were founder members of the Premiership in 1992. But since then they have declined alarmingly, and they spent the 1998-99 season in the new Second Division, the lowest ebb in their history.

Manchester City Managers

1893-1895	Joshua Parlby
1895-1902	Sam Ormerod
1902-1906	Tom Maley
1906-1912	Harry Newbould
1912-1924	Ernest Magnall
1924-1925	David Ashworth
1926-1932	Peter Hodge
1932-1946	Wilf Wild
1946-1947	Sam Cowan
1947-1950	Jock Thomson
1950-1963	Leslie McDowall
1963-1965	George Poyser
1965-1971	Joe Mercer
1972-1973	Malcolm Allison
1973	Johnny Hart
1973-1974	Ron Saunders
1974-1979	Tony Book
1979-1980	Malcolm Allison
1980-1983	John Bond
1983	John Benson
1983-1986	Billy McNeill
1986-1987	Jimmy Frizzell
1987-1989	Mel Machin

Clubs – M

Manchester City continued...

1990	Howard Kendall
1990-1993	Peter Reid
1993-1995	Brian Horton
1995-1996	Alan Ball
1996	Steve Coppell
1996-1998	Frank Clark
1998-	Joe Royle

Manchester City League Record

1892-1899	Division Two
1899-1902	Division One
1902-1903	Division Two
1903-1909	Division One
1909-1910	Division Two
1910-1926	Division One
1926-1928	Division Two
1928-1938	Division One
1938-1947	Division Two
1947-1950	Division One
1950-1951	Division Two
1951-1963	Division One
1963-1966	Division Two
1966-1983	Division One
1983-1985	Division Two
1985-1987	Division One
1987-1989	Division Two
1989-1992	Division One
1992-1996	Premiership
1996-1998	Division One
1998-	Division Two

In 1962 we fell into Division Two
The Stretford End cried out aloud
It's the end of the Sky Blues
Joe Mercer came we played the game
We went to Rotherham we won 1-0
And we were back into Division One.

Since then we've won the league
We've won the Cup
And played in Europe too (and won)
And when we win the League this year
We'll sing this song for you.

In the 1998-99 season, the Manchester City player whose replica team shirt sold in the greatest numbers was Jamie Pollock.

THE CARLING ULTIMATE FOOTBALL FACT AND QUIZ BOOK

Clubs – M

Manchester United

Manchester United are nicknamed The Red Devils and normally play in red shirts, white shorts and black socks. In 1934, however, in a desperate attempt to escape relegation from the Second Division, they played against Millwall in cherry and white hooped shirts. They won 2-0 and avoided the drop but they did not persist with the experiment.

The present club was formed in 1902 after their predecessors, Newton Heath, went bankrupt.

Newton Heath – which had been formed by workers on the Lancashire and Yorkshire Railway – joined the Football League in 1892.

Manchester United now play their home games at Old Trafford in Sir Matt Busby Way. They went to this ground in 1910; before that, United and Newton Heath had played at North Road/Monsall Road (1880-93) and in Bank Street (1893-1910).

Because of bomb damage to Old Trafford during the Second World War, from 1941 to 1949 Manchester United were forced to pay their home games at Maine Road, the home of deadly local rivals Manchester City.

Manchester United won their first major honour – the League Championship – in 1908. Much of the credit for this success went to the great Welsh winger Billy Meredith.

In 1909, United won the FA Cup for the first time and then took the League again in 1911.

But thereafter the club achieved little until Matt Busby, the former Manchester City captain, became manager at Old Trafford in 1945.

Busby built a team around captain Johnny Carey that included Stan Pearson and Jack Rowley. United won the FA Cup in 1948 and the league in 1952.

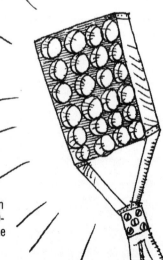

The manager then brought on a new generation of young stars – the Busby Babes as the press knew them. These included Bobby Charlton, Duncan Edwards, Tommy Taylor and Roger Byrne.

The second Busby team dominated English football, and United won the League Championship in 1956 and 1957.

In 1956-57, Manchester United became England's first entrants to the European Cup. They started well, defeating Belgian champions Anderlecht 2-0 in the first leg in Brussels and then 10-0 in the second leg, which was played at Maine Road because the floodlights at Old Trafford were not yet ready.

THE CARLING ULTIMATE FOOTBALL FACT AND QUIZ BOOK

Clubs – M

Manchester United continued...

United went on to beat Athletic Bilbao and then reached the semi-final, the first leg of which was their first game under floodlights. They lost this 2-0 and went out 5-3 on aggregate to Real Madrid, the holders, who went on to retain the trophy.

Within less than a week of their elimination, Manchester United clinched the Championship and thus had the consolation of knowing that they would be back in the European Cup the following season. They finished eight points ahead of their nearest challengers, Tottenham Hotspur.

United's 13-man championship-winning squad featured the following: Johnny Berry, Jackie Blanchflower, Roger Byrne (captain), Bobby Charlton, Eddie Colman, Duncan Edwards, Bill Foulkes, Mark Jones, David Pegg, Tommy Taylor, Dennis Viollet , Liam 'Billy' Whelan and Ray Wood (goalkeeper).

At 3.04 pm on February 6, 1958, the season was overshadowed by the terrible Munich air disaster, in which the cream of the Busby Babes were killed.

United were returning from Yugoslavia, where they had just drawn 3-3 in their European Cup quarter final against Red Star Belgrade. After a refuelling stop en route, the Elizabethan airliner of British European Airways (BEA) made two attempts to take off from Munich Airport but each time aborted the attempt at the last minute because of snow.

The pilot made a third effort to take off, reached the point of no return, but failed to get the plane airborne, probably because of the slush on the runway, although some people have attributed the crash to ice on the wings. The plane ploughed through the airport perimeter fence and split in half; the port wing and part of the tail section hit a house.

Of the 43 passengers, 23 lost their lives. Among the dead were eight Manchester United players – captain Roger Byrne, reserve left back Geoff Bent, right half Eddie Colman, left half Duncan Edwards, centre half Mark Jones, outside left David Pegg, centre forward Tommy Taylor and inside right Billy Whelan.

Among those seriously injured were manager Matt Busby together with Johnny Berry and Jackie Blanchflower, who never played again. Of those who escaped with relatively minor injuries were Bobby Charlton, Bill Foulkes, Harry Gregg, Ken Morgans and Dennis Viollet.

Despite the tragedy, Manchester United fulfilled their remaining fixture commitments. Although – not surprisingly – they lost the second the second leg of their match with Red Star, UEFA offered the team a place in Europe the following season. The English FA and Football League, however, banned them from participating on this basis.

Three months later, on May 3, 1958, Manchester United played in the Final of the FA Cup. Four of the Busby Babes had recovered sufficiently to play – Bobby Charlton, Harry Gregg, Bill Foulkes and Dennis Viollet. Bolton Wanderers beat them 2-0 at Wembley.

Matt Busby then built a third Manchester United team, which won the FA Cup in 1963, the First Division title in 1965 and 1967 and then, in 1968, became the first English club to win the European Cup.

THE CARLING ULTIMATE FOOTBALL FACT AND QUIZ BOOK

Clubs – M

Manchester United continued...

In the 1968 European Cup Final, played at Wembley, Manchester United beat Benfica, the champions of Portugal, 4-1. The goals were scored by Bobby Charlton (2), George Best and Brian Kidd.

The stars of the great Manchester United team of the 1960s were Alex Stepney, Denis Law, Bobby Charlton and George Best.

The break-up of the European Cup-winning team and the retirement of Busby imposed a great strain on their successors and United spent a season in Division Two.

But they returned to dominate the Premiership, which they won in 1993, 1994, 1996, 1997 and 1999 and were runners-up in the other two years.

Manchester United Managers

1900-1912	Ernest Magnall
1914-1921	John Robson
1921-1926	John Chapman
1926-1927	Clarence Hildrith
1927-1931	Herbert Bamlett
1931-1932	Walter Crickmer
1932-1937	Scott Duncan
1938-1944	Jimmy Porte
1944-1945	Walter Crickmer
1945-1969	Matt Busby
1969-1970	Wilf McGuinness
1971-1972	Frank O'Farrell
1972-1977	Tommy Docherty
1977-1981	Dave Sexton
1981-1986	Ron Atkinson
1986-	Alex Ferguson

Manchester United League Record

1892-1894	Division One
1894-1906	Division Two
1906-1922	Division One
1922-1925	Division Two
1925-1931	Division One
1931-1936	Division Two
1936-1937	Division One
1937-1938	Division Two
1938-1974	Division One
1974-1975	Division Two
1975-1992	Division One
1992-	Premiership

THE CARLING ULTIMATE FOOTBALL FACT AND QUIZ BOOK

Clubs – M

Manchester United continued...

The following words are sometimes sung at Old Trafford to the tune of The Wild Rover:

From the dark snows of Munich back in '58
I remember those players who once were so great
Their memory it still lingers on in my mind
So I'll follow United till the end of my time

CHORUS
And it's Man United, Man United FC
We're by far the greatest team
The world has ever seen

We went down to Wembley one sweet night in May
The crowd were all happy and singing away
And when it was over and when it was done
We'd beaten Benfica by four goals to one

CHORUS
And it's Man United, Man United FC
We're by far the greatest team
The world has ever seen

The first came from Bobby he outjumped the rest
The second it came from wee Georgie Best
The crowd were all cheering they roared United
And the third goal it followed from young Brian Kidd

CHORUS
And it's Man United, Man United FC
We're by far the greatest team
The world has ever seen

The crowd were all calling and shouting for more
So Bobby obliged by making it four
That night I'll remember when I do recall
Manchester United – the greatest of all

CHORUS
And it's Man United, Man United FC
We're by far the greatest team
The world has ever seen

In the 1998-99 season, the Manchester United player whose replica team shirt sold in the greatest numbers was Dwight Yorke.

THE CARLING ULTIMATE FOOTBALL FACT AND QUIZ BOOK

Clubs – M

Mansfield Town

Founded in 1910 and previously known as Mansfield Wesleyans, Mansfield Town are nicknamed The Stags.

After seven unsuccessful applications, Mansfield Town joined the Football League in 1931. They play their home games at the Field Mill Ground in Quarry Lane.

The Mansfield Town strip consists of amber shirts with a royal blue strip down the side and a royal blue collar, amber shorts with a royal blue stripe down the side, and royal blue socks with amber trim.

Mansfield Town have won three honours – the Third Division Championship in 1977, the Fourth Division Championship in 1975 and the Freight Rover Trophy in 1987.

In 1969, Mansfield Town – then in the Third Division – reached the sixth round of the FA Cup; their victims included First Division West Ham United.

Mansfield Town Managers

1922-1925	John Baynes
1926-1928	Ted Davison
1928-1933	Jack Hickling
1933-1935	Henry Martin
1935	Charlie Bell
1936	Harold Wightman
1936-1938	Harold Parkes
1938-1944	Jack Poole
1944-1945	Lloyd Barke
1945-1949	Roy Goodall
1949-1951	Freddie Steele
1952-1953	George Jobey
1953-1955	Stan Mercer
1956-1958	Charlie Mitten
1958-1960	Sam Weaver
1960-1963	Raich Carter
1963-1967	Tommy Cummings
1967-1970	Tommy Eggleston
1970-1971	Jock Basford
1971-1974	Danny Williams
1974-1976	Dave Smith
1976-1978	Peter Morris
1978-1979	Billy Bingham
1979-1981	Mick Jones
1981-1983	Stuart Boam
1983-1989	Ian Greaves

THE CARLING ULTIMATE FOOTBALL FACT AND QUIZ BOOK

Clubs – M

Mansfield Town continued...

1989-1993	George Foster
1993-1996	Andy King
1996-	Steve Parkin

Mansfield Town League Record

1931-1932	Division Three (South)
1932-1937	Division Three (North)
1937-1947	Division Three (South)
1947-1958	Division Three (North)
1958-1960	Division Three
1960-1963	Division Four
1963-1972	Division Three
1972-1975	Division Four
1975-1977	Division Three
1977-1978	Division Two
1978-1980	Division Three
1980-1986	Division Four
1986-1991	Division Three
1991-1992	Division Four
1992-1993	Division Two
1993-	Division Three

The most unusual chant at Mansfield Town must be derived from the local brewery, for many years the town's biggest employer:

Oh when I die (Oh when I die)
Don't bury me alone (Don't bury me alone)
Just lay my bones in alcohol (Just lay my bones in alcohol)
And on my chest (And on my chest)
Lay a barrel of the best (Lay a barrel of the best)
And tell my friend (And tell my friend)
I've gone to rest (I've gone to rest)

In the 1998-99 season, the Mansfield Town player whose replica team shirt sold in the greatest numbers was Iyseden Christie.

THE CARLING ULTIMATE FOOTBALL FACT AND QUIZ BOOK

Clubs – M

Marseille

Founded in 1898, Olympique Marseille play their home games at the 46,000-seater Vélodrome. Their home strip is all white with a blue trim.

Olympique Marseille won the French League Championship in 1937, 1948, 1971 but the club became even more prominent in the domestic game after it was taken over by multi-millionaire Bernard Tapie in 1985.

Under Tapie, Marseille won further titles in 1989 and 1990, as well as their tenth victory in the French FA Cup in 1989.

After losing to Red Star Belgrade on penalties in the European Cup Final of 1991, Olympique Marseille became the first French club to take the trophy in 1993 with a 1-0 victory over Milan.

But shortly after their triumph it was revealed that some of Tapie's money had been used to fix French domestic matches.

It was subsequently proved that Marseille midfielder Jean-Jacques Eydelie had given cash to three Valenciennes players to 'go easy' on Marseille in a League game a week before the European Cup Final.

As a result, Olympique Marseille were stripped of the European Cup, their League title and relegated. Bankruptcy followed shortly afterwards.

Middlesbrough

Middlesbrough were formed in 1876 and joined the Football League in 1899.

They are nicknamed The Boro and play in red shirts, white shorts and red socks.

The club has played its home matches at five different grounds: from 1877 to 1879 at the Old Archery Ground in Albert Park; from 1879 to 1882 at Breckon Hill; from 1882 to 1903 at the Linthorpe Road Ground; from 1903 to 1995 at Ayresome Park; from 1995 at the Cellnet Riverside Stadium.

Middlesbrough won the old Second Division Championship three times – in 1927, 1929 and 1974 (the last time by a record 15-point margin).

On September 18, 1996, against Hereford United in the League Cup, Middlesbrough became the first British football team to field three Brazilians – Branco, Emerson and Juninho.

In 1997, Boro reached the Finals of the FA and the League Cups but lost in both; they were also relegated from the FA Carling Premiership.

THE CARLING ULTIMATE FOOTBALL FACT AND QUIZ BOOK

Clubs – M

Middlesbrough continued...

Middlesbrough would have avoided the drop in 1997 if they had not had three points deducted by the FA as a punishment for their failure to turn up to their away game at Blackburn Rovers because they considered they did not have enough fit players.

In the following season (1997-98), Middlesbrough were again runners-up in the League Cup, but this time they had the consolation of regaining their Premiership place after only a season in the First Division.

Middlesbrough Managers

1899-1905	John Robson
1905-1906	Alex Mackie
1906-1909	Andy Aitken
1909-1910	J Gunter
1910-1911	Andy Walker
1911-1919	Tom McIntosh
1920-1923	Jimmy Howie
1923-1926	Herbert Bamlett
1927-1934	Peter McWilliam
1934-1944	Wilf Gillow
1944-1952	David Jack
1952-1954	Walter Rowley
1954-1963	Bob Dennison
1963-1966	Raich Carter
1966-1973	Stan Anderson
1973-1977	Jack Charlton
1977-1981	John Neal
1981-1982	Bobby Murdoch
1982-1984	Malcolm Allison
1984-1986	Willie Maddren
1986-1990	Bruce Rioch
1990-1991	Colin Todd
1991-1994	Lennie Lawrence
1994-	Bryan Robson

Middlesbrough League Record

1899-1902	Division Two
1902-1924	Division One
1924-1927	Division Two
1927-1928	Division One
1928-1929	Division Two
1929-1954	Division One
1954-1966	Division Two
1966-1967	Division Three
1967-1974	Division Two

Clubs – M

Middlesbrough continued...

1974-1982	Division One
1982-1986	Division Two
1986-1987	Division Three
1987-1988	Division Two
1988-1989	Division One
1989-1992	Division Two
1992-1993	Premiership
1993-1995	Division One
1995-1997	Premiership
1997-1998	Division One
1998-	Premiership

Sunderland don't bother me
Sunderland don't bother me
Go away come back another day
Don't bother me

(Tune: Hey Girl Don't Bother Me)

In the 1998-99 season, the Middlesbrough player whose replica team shirt sold in the greatest numbers was Paul Gascoigne.

AC Milan

AC Milan were founded as Milan Cricket and Football Club in 1899 by an exiled Englishman, Alfred Edwards. That is why they are called Milan – the English name for their city – rather than the Italian Milano.

AC Milan play in red and black striped shirts, white shorts and white socks.

AC Milan's home ground is what for many years was known as the San Siro Stadium but was renamed the Meazza Stadium in 1979 after Giuseppe Meazza (1910-1979).

Nicknamed Peppino, Meazza was a star of AC Milan, Inter Milan, Juventus and also of Italy in two World Cup triumphs (1934 and 1938).

AC Milan won their first Italian League Championship in 1901, only two years after they were established. In 1999 they won their 16th Serie A title.

AC Milan have won the Italian Cup four times – in 1967, 1972, 1973 and 1977 – the European Cup Winners' Cup twice – in 1968 and 1973 – and the European Cup five times – in 1963, 1969, 1989, 1990 and 1994.

THE CARLING ULTIMATE FOOTBALL FACT AND QUIZ BOOK

Facts
Clubs – M

AC Milan continued...

AC Milan owe much of their current eminence to the immense wealth of their President, media mogul and former Italian prime minister Silvio Berlusconi, who has been president of the club since 1986.

Berlusconi invested £20 million in the club for starters and then provided further funds which enabled the club to buy great stars of the period such as the Liberian George Weah and Dutchmen Frank Rijkaard, Ruud Gullit and Marco Van Basten.

Millwall

Nicknamed The Lions, Millwall play their home games in blue shirts, white shorts and blue socks.

Millwall were founded in 1885 and were originally the works team of Morton's jam and marmalade company in West Ferry Road. Most of the early players were Scots.

The club were originally known as Millwall Rovers; in 1889 they changed their name to Millwall Athletic before becoming plain Millwall.

Millwall have had six grounds: from 1885 to 1886, they played at Glengall Road; from 1886 to 1890 they were to be seen playing 'at the back of the Lord Nelson'; from 1890 to 1901 they were in East Ferry Road; from 1901 to 1910 they played at North Woolwich.

In 1910, Millwall moved to The Den in Cold Blow Lane. Here they remained until 1993, when they moved down the road to The New Den in Zampa Road, Bermondsey, London SE16.

Millwall joined the Football League in 1920. The high point of their history to date came in 1988, when they won the old Second Division Championship and began a two-year sojourn in the top flight of English football.

In their first year in Division One, Millwall finished tenth, but the following year they came bottom and were relegated.

Millwall have thrice reached the semi-finals of the FA Cup – in 1900, 1903 and in 1937, when they became the first Third Division club to reach that stage of the competition.

The Den has long been regarded as an unwelcoming venue for visiting teams and their supporters – Millwall fans have a reputation for toughness and this explains their version of Rod Stewart's 'Sailing' (see below).

THE CARLING ULTIMATE FOOTBALL FACT AND QUIZ BOOK

Clubs – M

Millwall continued...

Millwall Managers
1894-1899	William Henderson
1899-1900	E R Stopher
1900-1911	George Saunders
1911-1919	Herbert Lipsham
1919-1933	Robert Hunter
1933-1936	Bill McCracken
1936-1940	Charlie Hewitt
1940-1944	Bill Voisey
1944-1948	Jack Cock
1948-1956	Charlie Hewitt
1956-1957	Ron Gray
1958-1959	Jimmy Seed
1959-1961	Reg Smith
1961-1963	Ron Gray
1963-1966	Billy Gray
1966-1974	Benny Fenton
1974-1977	Gordon Jago
1978-1980	George Petchey
1980-1982	Peter Anderson
1982-1986	George Graham
1986-1990	John Docherty
1990	Bob Pearson
1990-1992	Bruce Rioch
1992-1996	Mick McCarthy
1996-1997	Jimmy Nicholl
1997	John Docherty
1997-1998	Billy Bonds
1998-	Keith Stevens

Millwall League Record
1920-1921	Division Three
1921-1928	Division Three (South)
1928-1934	Division Two
1934-1938	Division Three (South)
1938-1948	Division Two
1948-1958	Division Three (South)
1958-1962	Division Four
1962-1964	Division Three
1964-1965	Division Four
1965-1966	Division Three
1966-1975	Division Two
1975-1976	Division Three

Clubs – M

Millwall continued…

1976-1979	Division Two
1979-1985	Division Three
1985-1988	Division Two
1988-1990	Division One
1990-1992	Division Two
1992-1996	Division One
1996-	Division Two

*We are Millwall we are Millwall
We are Millwall from The Den
We are Millwall super Millwall
We are Millwall from The Den
No one likes us no one likes us
No one likes us we don't care
We are Millwall super Millwall
We are Millwall from The Den*

(Tune: Sailing by Rod Stewart)

*It's Saturday in Cold Blow Lane
We've all come down to cheer
We've had our jellied eels
And our glass of beer
Come rain or shine all the time
Our families we'll bring
And as the Lions run out on the pitch
Everyone will sing loud and clear
Let 'em come let 'em come
We'll only have to beat them again
We're the best team in London
No the best team of all
Everybody knows us we're called Millwall
Let 'em come let 'em come let 'em come
Let 'em all come down to The Den*

In the 1998-99 season, the Millwall player whose replica team shirt sold in the greatest numbers was Lucas Neill.

Clubs – M

Montrose

Montrose were founded in 1879 and are known as The Gable Endies.

They play in blue shirts with white sleeves, white shorts with blue trim and blue socks with white trim.

Montrose first played on a pitch known as Metally because it stood next to a metal bridge. They now play at the Links Park Stadium in Wellington Street.

In 1975-76, Montrose reached the semi-final of the Scottish League Cup.

In 1985, Montrose won the Scottish Second Division Championship – this was their first trophy in 106 years.

Motherwell

Motherwell – The Well for short – play their home games at Fir Park.

Motherwell were founded in 1886 and joined the Scottish Second Division in 1893.

Motherwell play in amber shirts with a claret midriff hoop and white trim, white socks with claret trim and claret socks with amber trim.

Motherwell won their only Scottish League Championship in 1932. They have won the Scottish FA Cup twice – in 1952 and 1991 – and the Scottish League Cup once, in 1950-51.

THE CARLING ULTIMATE FOOTBALL FACT AND QUIZ BOOK

Clubs – N

Newcastle United

Newcastle United play in black and white striped shirts, black shorts and black socks. They are nicknamed The Magpies.

The club was founded in 1881 and played for a season as Stanley FC. From October 1882 they were known as Newcastle East End, before adopting their present name in 1892.

Newcastle United have played at St James' Park since 1892. Before then, they played at South Byker (1881-1886) and Chillingham Road, Heaton (1886-1892).

Newcastle United won the League Championship in 1905, 1907, 1909 and 1927.

Newcastle United have won the FA Cup six times – in 1910, 1924, 1932, 1951, 1952 and 1955.

Newcastle United won the European Fairs Cup in 1969.

Newcastle United Managers

1895-1930	Frank Watt
1930-1935	Andy Cunningham
1935-1939	Tom Mather
1939-1947	Stan Seymour
1947-1950	George Martin
1950-1954	Stan Seymour
1954-1956	Duggie Livingstone
1956-1958	Stan Seymour
1958-1961	Charlie Mitten
1961-1962	Norman Smith
1962-1975	Joe Harvey
1975-1977	Gordon Lee
1977	Richard Dinnis
1977-1980	Bill McGarry
1980-1984	Arthur Cox
1984	Jack Charlton
1985-1988	Willie McFaul
1988-1991	Jim Smith
1991-1992	Osvaldo Ardiles
1992-1997	Kevin Keegan
1997-1998	Kenny Dalglish
1998-	Ruud Gullit

Newcastle United League Record

1893-1898	Division Two
1898-1934	Division One
1934-1948	Division Two
1948-1961	Division One

Clubs – N

Newcastle United continued...

1961-1965	Division Two
1965-1978	Division One
1978-1984	Division Two
1984-1989	Division One
1989-1992	Division Two
1992-1993	Division One
1993-	Premiership

We went to Blaydon Races
'Twas on the ninth of June
Eighteen hundred and sixty-two
On a summer's afternoon
We took the bus from Bamburghs
And she was heavy laden
Away we went along Collingwood Road
That's on the road to Blaydon
Oh me lads you should have seen us gannin'
Passing the folks along the road
Just as they were standin'
All the lads and lassies there
All with smiling faces
Gannin' along the Scotswood Road
To see the Blaydon Races

In the 1998-99 season, the Newcastle United player whose replica team shirt sold in the greatest numbers was Alan Shearer.

Northampton Town

Northampton Town are nicknamed The Cobblers, after the traditional local trade of shoemaking. They have played in all four divisions of the Football League.

The club was founded in 1897 by elementary school teachers and joined the Football League in 1920.

Northampton Town play their home matches in claret and white shirts, white shorts and claret socks.

From 1920 to 1994, Northampton Town played at the County Ground which they shared with Northamptonshire County Cricket Club.

In 1994, Northampton Town moved to the new Sixfields Stadium in Upton Way.

THE CARLING ULTIMATE FOOTBALL FACT AND QUIZ BOOK

Facts
Clubs – N

Northamprton Town continued...

Northampton Town Managers
1897-1907	Arthur Jones
1907-1912	Herbert Chapman
1912-1913	Walter Bull
1913-1919	Fred Lessons
1920-1925	Bob Hewison
1925-1930	Jack Tresadern
1931-1935	Jack English
1935-1937	Syd Puddefoot
1937-1939	Warney Cresswell
1939-1949	Tom Smith
1949-1954	Bob Dennison
1954-1959	Dave Smith
1959-1967	David Bowen
1967-1968	Tony Marchi
1968-1969	Ron Flowers
1969-1972	Dave Bowen
1972-1973	Billy Baxter
1973-1976	Bill Dodgin Jnr
1976-1977	Pat Crerand
1977	Bill Dodgin Jnr
1977-1978	John Petts
1978-1979	Mike Keen
1979-1980	Clive Walker
1980-1982	Bill Dodgin Jnr
1982-1984	Clive Walker
1984-1985	Tony Barton
1985-1990	Graham Carr
1990-1992	Theo Foley
1992-1993	Phil Chard
1993-1995	John Barnwell
1995-	Ian Atkins

Northampton Town League Record
1920-1921	Division Three
1921-1958	Division Three (South)
1958-1961	Division Four
1961-1963	Division Three
1963-1965	Division Two
1965-1966	Division One
1966-1967	Division Two
1967-1969	Division Three
1969-1976	Division Four

THE CARLING ULTIMATE FOOTBALL FACT AND QUIZ BOOK

Clubs – N

Northampton Town continued...

1976-1977	Division Three
1977-1987	Division Four
1987-1990	Division Three
1990-1992	Division Four
1992-1997	Division Three
1997-1999	Division Two

In the 1998-99 season, the Northampton Town player whose replica team shirt sold in the greatest numbers was Ali Gibb.

Norwich City

Norwich City play in yellow shirts, green shorts and yellow socks and are consequently nicknamed The Canaries.

Norwich City's ground is at Carrow Road, where they have played their home games since 1935. Before that, their grounds were Newmarket Road (1902-1908) and The Nest in Rosary Road (1908-1935).

Norwich City were formed in 1902 by two local schoolmasters at a meeting in The Criterion Cafe. In 1904, the FA declared the club professional and unceremoniously threw them out of the Amateur Cup. In response to this slur, the club turned fully and unequivocally professional in 1905. They joined the Football League in 1920.

Norwich City have won the League Cup twice – in 1962 and 1985. The second time they won the trophy, they were also relegated from the First Division in the same season.

Norwich City first reached the First Division in 1975. Their best season in the League was 1992-93, when they came third in the Premiership.

Norwich City Managers

1905-1907	John Bowman
1907-1908	James McEwen
1909-1910	Arthur Turner
1910-1915	Bert Stansfield
1919-1920	Major Frank Buckley
1920-1921	Charles O'Hagan
1921-1926	Albert Gosnell
1926	Bert Stansfield
1926-1929	Cecil Potter
1929-1933	James Kerr

THE CARLING ULTIMATE FOOTBALL FACT AND QUIZ BOOK

Clubs – N

Norwich City continued...

1933-1937	Tom Parker
1937-1939	Bob Young
1939	Jimmy Jewell
1939-1945	Bob Young
1946-1947	Cyril Spiers
1947-1950	Duggie Lochhead
1950-1955	Norman Low
1955-1957	Tom Parker
1957-1961	Archie Macaulay
1961-1962	Willie Reid
1962	George Swindin
1962-1966	Ron Ashman
1966-1969	Lol Morgan
1969-1973	Ron Saunders
1973-1980	John Bond
1980-1987	Ken Brown
1987-1992	Dave Stringer
1992-1994	Mike Walker
1994-1995	John Deehan
1995	Martin O'Neill
1995-1996	Gary Megson
1996-1998	Mike Walker
1998-	Bruce Rioch

Norwich City League Record

1920-1921	Division Three
1921-1934	Division Three (South)
1934-1939	Division Two
1946-1958	Division Three (South)
1958-1960	Division Three
1960-1972	Division Two
1972-1974	Division One
1974-1975	Division Two
1975-1981	Division One
1981-1982	Division Two
1982-1985	Division One
1985-1986	Division Two
1986-1992	Division One
1992-1995	Premiership
1995-	Division One

THE CARLING ULTIMATE FOOTBALL FACT AND QUIZ BOOK

Clubs – N

Norwich City continued…

> *On the ball City never mind the danger*
> *Steady on now's your chance*
> *Hurrah! We've scored a goal*
>
> *In the days to call which we have left behind*
> *Our boyhood's glorious game*
> *And our youthful vigour has declined*
> *With its mirth and its lonesome end*
> *You will think of the time the happy time*
> *Its memories fond recall*
> *When in the bloom of our youthful prime*
> *We've kept upon the ball*
>
> *Kick off throw it have a little scrimmage*
> *Keep it low a splendid rush bravo win or die*
> *On the ball City never mind the danger*
> *Steady on now's your chance*
> *Hurrah! We've scored a goal*
>
> *Let all tonight then drink with me*
> *To the football game we love*
> *And wish it may successful be*
> *As other games of old*
> *And in one grand united toast*
> *Join player game and song*
> *And fondly ledge your pride and toast*
> *Success to the City club.*

In the 1998-99 season, the Norwich City player whose replica team shirt sold in the greatest numbers was Craig Bellamy.

Nottingham Forest

Nottingham Forest are the only team to have won the European Cup more often than their own domestic League Championship.

Forest won the First Division title for the only time in 1978; they won the European Cup the following year and then retained the trophy in 1980.

THE CARLING ULTIMATE FOOTBALL FACT AND QUIZ BOOK

Facts
Clubs – N

Nottingham Forest continued…

Forest are one of the oldest football clubs in the world, having been founded in 1865 at a meeting held in the Clinton Arms, a Nottingham pub.

Nottingham Forest play their home games in red shirts with black shoulders, white shorts and red socks.

Since 1890, Nottingham Forest have played their home games at The City Ground on the banks of the River Trent.

Before moving to The City Ground, Forest had six previous homes: from 1865 to 1879 at The Forest Racecourse (from which they took their name); from 1879 to 1880 at The Meadows; from 1880 to 1882 at Trent Bridge Cricket Ground, the home of Nottinghamshire C C C; from 1882 to 1885 at Parkside in Lenton; from 1885 to 1890 at Gregory in Lenton; and from 1890 to 1898 at The Town Ground, Nottingham.

Nottingham Forest played their first Football League game on September 3, 1892. It was a 2-2 draw with Everton in Division One.

Until the 1970s, Nottingham Forest's only major honour had been the FA Cup, which they had won twice – in 1898 and 1959.

The fortunes of Nottingham Forest changed dramatically when the club appointed as their manager Brian Clough and his assistant Peter Taylor in 1975.

The management duo had won the League with Derby County in 1972, and they set about repeating the trick at Forest.

When Clough and Taylor arrived, Forest were in the middle of the Second Division capturing no one's imagination.

But with some judicious purchases of other clubs' bad boys and those branded no hopers, the team was transformed. They scraped promotion from the Second Division in 1977 but then took the top flight at a gallop.

Nottingham Forest have made the League Cup a bit of a speciality – they have won the trophy four times to date – in 1978, 1979, 1989 and 1990.

Nottingham Forest Managers

1889-1997	Harry Radford
1897-1909	Harry Haslam
1909-1912	Fred Earp
1912-1925	Bob Masters
1925-1929	John Baynes

THE CARLING ULTIMATE FOOTBALL FACT AND QUIZ BOOK

Clubs – N

Nottingham Forest continued...

1930-1931	Stan Hardy
1931-1936	Noel Watson
1936-1939	Harold Wightman
1939-1960	Billy Walker
1960-1963	Andy Beattie
1963-1968	Johnny Carey
1969-1972	Matt Gillies
1972	Dave Mackay
1973-1975	Allan Brown
1975-1993	Brian Clough
1993-1996	Frank Clark
1996-1997	Stuart Pearce
1997-1998	Dave Bassett
1998-1999	Ron Atkinson

Nottingham Forest League Record

1892-1906	Division One
1906-1907	Division Two
1907-1911	Division One
1911-1922	Division Two
1922-1925	Division One
1925-1949	Division Two
1949-1951	Division Three (South)
1951-1957	Division Two
1957-1972	Division One
1972-1977	Division Two
1977-1992	Division One
1992-1993	Premiership
1993-1994	Division One
1994-1997	Premiership
1997-1998	Division One
1998-1999	Premiership

Oh City Ground
The mist rolling in from the Trent
My desire is always to be there
Oh City Ground

(Tune: Mull of Kintyre)

In the 1998-99 season, the Nottingham Forest player whose replica team shirt sold in the greatest numbers was Steve Stone.

Clubs – N

Notts County

The oldest club in the English Football League, Notts County play in black and white striped shirts with amber sleeves and trim, black shorts with white trim and black socks with white and amber trim.

Their strip is similar to that of Newcastle United and, like the Geordies, they are nicknamed The Magpies. Their colours were adopted by Juventus (q v) of Turin, Italy.

Notts County – originally known as Notts FC – claim to have been founded in 1862, although they did not become properly organised until after a meeting at the George IV Hotel in Nottingham in 1864.

Notts County were founder members of the Football League in 1888. They finished that inaugural season in 11th place – the only team below them was Stoke.

The most glorious moment in Notts County's history to date came when they won the FA Cup in 1894. They thus became the first Second Division team to take the trophy.

Notts County's only other honour to date was victory in the Anglo-Italian Cup in 1995.

Notts County first played at The Park (1862-64), then moved to The Meadows (1864-1877); this was followed by three years at Beeston Cricket Ground (1877-1880). Later they played at The Castle Ground from 1880 to 1883 and then at Trent Bridge until 1910, when they finally settled at The County Ground in Meadow Lane, their present home.

Notts County Managers

1883-1893	Edwin Browne
1893	Tom Featherstone
1893-1913	Tom Harris
1913-1927	Albert Fisher
1927-1934	Horace Henshall
1934-1935	Charlie Jones
1935	David Pratt
1935-1936	Percy Smith
1936-1937	Jimmy McMullan
1938-1939	Harry Parkes
1939-1942	Tony Towers
1942-1943	Frank Womack
1944-1946	Major Frank Buckley
1946-1949	Arthur Stollery
1949-1953	Eric Houghton
1953-1957	George Poyser
1957-1958	Tommy Lawton
1958-1961	Frank Hill
1961-1963	Tim Coleman

THE CARLING ULTIMATE FOOTBALL FACT AND QUIZ BOOK

Clubs – N

Notts County continued...

1963-1965	Eddie Lowe
1965-1966	Tim Coleman
1966-1967	Jack Burkitt
1967-1968	Billy Gray
1969-1975	Jimmy Sirrel
1975-1977	Ron Fenton
1978-1982	Jimmy Sirrel
1982-1983	Howard Wilkinson
1983-1984	Larry Lloyd
1984-1985	Richie Barker
1985-1987	Jimmy Sirrel
1987-1988	John Barnwell
1989-1993	Neil Warnock
1993-1994	Mick Walker
1994-1995	Russell Slade
1995	Howard Kendall
1995	Colin Murphy
1996	Steve Thompson
1997-	Sam Allardyce

Notts County League Record

1888-1893	Division One
1893-1897	Division Two
1897-1913	Division One
1913-1914	Division Two
1914-1920	Division One
1920-1923	Division Two
1923-1926	Division One
1926-1930	Division Two
1930-1931	Division Three (South)
1931-1935	Division Two
1935-1950	Division Three (South)
1950-1958	Division Two
1958-1959	Division Three
1959-1960	Division Four
1960-1964	Division Three
1964-1971	Division Four
1971-1973	Division Three
1973-1981	Division Two
1981-1984	Division One
1984-1985	Division Two
1985-1990	Division Three
1990-1991	Division Two

Clubs – N

Notts County continued...

1991-1995	Division One
1995-1997	Division Two
1997-	Division Three

Meadow Lane lies within the metropolitan borough of Nottingham; Forest's City Ground is on the south bank of the River Trent and does not. Hence the following (to the tune of Chicory Tip's Son of My Father) is popular on the County terraces:

Oh-oh Notts County
The only football team to come from Nottingham

In the 1998-99 season, the Notts County player whose replica team shirt sold in the greatest numbers was Darren Ward.

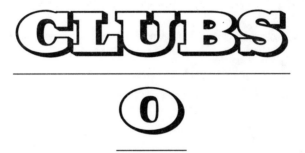

Clubs – O

Oldham Athletic

Oldham Athletic – nicknamed Latics – play in red and blue shirts, white shorts and red and blue hooped socks.

The club was founded in 1895 as Pine Villa and first played at Sheepfoot Lane. The prime mover in the establishment of the club was John Garland, landlord of the Featherstall and Junction Hotel.

In 1899 they changed their name to Oldham Athletic, in 1905 they moved to their present ground, Boundary Park, and in 1907 they joined the Football League.

In 1915, Oldham Athletic were runners-up in the First Division, finishing only one point behind the champions, Everton. This has been their high water mark to date.

In 1913, 1990 and 1994 Oldham Athletic reached the semi-finals of the FA Cup. In 1990, they were runners-up in the League Cup, losing 1-0 to Nottingham Forest in the Final at Wembley.

Oldham Athletic Managers

1906-1914	David Ashworth
1914-1921	Herbert Bamlett
1921-1922	Charlie Roberts
1923-1924	David Ashworth
1924-1927	Bob Mellor
1927-1932	Andy Wilson
1933-1934	Jimmy McMullan
1934-1945	Bob Mellor
1945-1947	Frank Womack
1947-1950	Billy Wootton
1950-1956	George Hardwick
1956-1958	Ted Goodier
1958-1960	Norman Dodgin
1960-1963	Jack Rowley
1963-1965	Les McDowall
1965-1966	Gordon Hurst

THE CARLING ULTIMATE FOOTBALL FACT AND QUIZ BOOK

Clubs – O

Oldham Athletic continued…

1966-1968	Jimmy McIlroy
1968-1969	Jack Rowley
1970-1982	Jimmy Frizzell
1982-1994	Joe Royle
1994-1997	Graeme Sharp
1997-1998	Neil Warnock
1998-	Andy Ritchie

Oldham Athletic League Record

1907-1910	Division Two
1910-1923	Division One
1923-1935	Division Two
1935-1953	Division Three (North)
1953-1954	Division Two
1954-1958	Division Three (North)
1958-1963	Division Four
1963-1969	Division Three
1969-1971	Division Four
1971-1974	Division Three
1974-1991	Division Two
1991-1992	Division One
1992-1994	Premiership
1994-1997	Division One
1997-	Division Two

The best Oldham song – to the tune of A Scottish Soldier – extols one of their erstwhile defenders:

> *There was a half back a Scottish half back*
> *And Lawson was his name and clogging was his game*
> *He came to Oldham when Celtic sold him*
> *And Alan Lawson was his name*
>
> *For on the green fields down at Boundary*
> *There's a melée there with bodies everywhere*
> *For on those green fields down at Boundary*
> *Alan Lawson reigns supreme*
>
> *And Barry Stobart and Jimmy Fryat*
> *He sent them far away to the infirmary*
> *He clogged victorious he clogged so glorious*
> *And Alan Lawson was his name*

In the 1998-99 season, the Oldham Athletic player whose replica team shirt sold in the greatest numbers was Andy Ritchie.

THE CARLING ULTIMATE FOOTBALL FACT AND QUIZ BOOK

Clubs – O

Oxford United

Oxford United play in yellow shirts with navy blue trim, navy blue shorts and navy blue socks.

Oxford play their home games at The Manor Ground in Headington on the eastern edge of the city. A move is planned to a new, purpose-built stadium at Minchery Farm outside the city but this is being held up by lack of funds.

Founded in 1893, the club was originally known as Headington. The following year they became Headington United and kept that name until they became Oxford United in 1960.

Oxford United joined the Football League in 1962 to fill the vacancy created by the departure of Accrington Stanley.

In 1964, Oxford United reached the Sixth Round of the FA Cup – further than any Fourth Division club had ever got in the competition.

In 1984, Oxford won the Third Division Championship. They followed this with the Second Division title in 1985 and thereafter spent three years in the top flight of English football.

In 1986 Oxford United won the League Cup, beating Queen's Park Rangers 3-0 in the Final at Wembley.

During the 1980s, Oxford United were rather overshadowed by their chairman, publishing tycoon Robert Maxwell, whose plans for the club did not meet the approval of the supporters. One of his most hated schemes was the proposed amalgamation of the club with Reading (q v) under the name Thames Valley Royals.

Oxford United Managers

1949-1958	Harry Thompson
1959-1969	Arthur Turner
1969	Ron Saunders
1969-1975	George Summers
1975-1979	Mike Brown
1979-1980	Bill Asprey
1980-1982	Ian Greaves
1982-1985	Jim Smith
1985-1988	Maurice Evans
1988	Mark Lawrenson
1988-1993	Brian Horton
1993-1997	Denis Smith
1997	Malcolm Crosby
1998-	Malcolm Shotton

Clubs – O

Oxford United continued...

Oxford United League Record

1962-1965	Division Four
1965-1968	Division Three
1968-1976	Division Two
1976-1984	Division Three
1984-1985	Division Two
1985-1988	Division One
1988-1992	Division Two
1992-1994	Division One
1994-1996	Division Two
1996-1999	Division One

In the 1998-99 season, the Oxford United player whose replica team shirt sold in the greatest numbers was Joey Beauchamp.

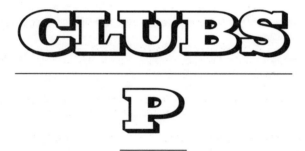

THE CARLING ULTIMATE FOOTBALL FACT AND QUIZ BOOK

Clubs – P

Partick Thistle

Partick Thistle were founded in 1876 and joined the Scottish Football League in 1893. They are nicknamed The Jags ('jag' being Scottish for 'thistle').

Partick Thistle play in red and yellow hooped shirts, black shorts with red and amber trim and red and yellow hooped socks.

Since 1909, Partick Thistle have played their home games at the Firhill Stadium at 80 Firhill Road, Glasgow.

Partick Thistle's previous grounds were Jordanvale Park, Muirpark, Inchview and Meadowside Park.

The Jags have won the Scottish FA Cup once – in 1921, when they beat Rangers 1-0 in the Final at Celtic Park. They were also runners-up in the competition in 1930, when Rangers got their revenge.

In 1971-72, Partick Thistle won the Scottish League Cup, beating Celtic 4-1 in the Final at Hampden Park. They had previously lost in three League Cup Finals – in 1953-54 to East Fife, in 1956-57 to Celtic and in 1958-59 to Heart of Midlothian.

Partick Thistle's achievements to date in the Scottish League have been as follows: the First Division title in 1976 and the Second Division Championship in 1897, 1900 and 1971.

Partick Thistle's most famous player is also the man who made most appearances for the club – goalkeeper Alan Rough turned out 410 times for them between 1969 and 1982. He also won 53 caps for Scotland.

Peñarol

The most successful club in Uruguay, Peñarol were founded in 1891 by British immigrants as the Central Uruguayan Railway Cricket Club.

They adopted their present name – that of the Montevideo district in which they are based – in 1913.

Peñarol play their routine matches at Las Acacias Stadium but move for their big games to Centenario, the national stadium.

Peñarol have won the Uruguayan League title more than 40 times and they were the first club to win the World Club Championship three times – in 1961, 1966 and 1982.

Peñarol play in black and yellow striped shirts, black shorts and black socks. The club provided most of the players in both Uruguay's World Cup winning sides – 1930 and 1950.

Clubs – P

Peterborough United

Peterborough United are nicknamed The Posh and play their home games at London Road.

Peterborough United were founded in 1934 in succession to Peterborough and Fletton FC and turned professional in the same year.

Peterborough United lost only one of 105 Midland League matches between 1955 and 1960, when they were admitted to Division Four. This was their 20th application to join the Football League.

In 1960-61, Peterborough United became the first club to win the Fourth Division in their first season in the League. While doing so, they scored a record number of goals – 134 – in 46 games.

Peterborough United Managers

1934-1936	Jock Porter
1936-1937	Fred Taylor
1937-1938	Vic Poulter
1938-1948	Sam Madden
1948-1950	Jack Blood
1950-1952	Bob Gurney
1952-1954	Jack Fairbrother
1954-1958	George Swindin
1958-1962	Jimmy Hagan
1962-1964	Jack Fairbrother
1964-1967	Gordon Clark
1967-1969	Norman Rigby
1969-1972	Jim Iley
1972-1977	Noel Cantwell
1977-1978	John Barnwell
1978-1979	Billy Hails
1979-1982	Peter Morris
1982-1983	Martin Wilkinson
1983-1986	John Wile
1986-1988	Noel Cantwell
1988-1989	Mick Jones
1989-1990	Mark Lawrenson
1991-1992	Chris Turner
1992-1993	Lil Fuccillo
1994-1995	John Still
1995-1996	Mick Halsall
1996-	Barry Fry

THE CARLING ULTIMATE FOOTBALL FACT AND QUIZ BOOK

Clubs – P

Peterborough United continued...

Peterborough United League Record
1960-1961	Division Four
1961-1968	Division Three
1968-1974	Division Four
1974-1979	Division Three
1979-1991	Division Four
1991-1992	Division Three
1992-1994	Division One
1994-1997	Division Two
1997-	Division Three

Peterborough's best song dates back to their non-League days, and particularly to their FA Cup run of 1956-57.

> *It's a non-League team called Posh*
> *That we are going to see*
> *At London Road we've watched them*
> *Storm on to victory*
> *They beat their Midland League mates*
> *Divisions Two and Three*
> *A darn good FA Cup run*
> *We're sure you'll all agree*
>
> *(Tune: The Yellow Rose of Texas)*

In the 1998-99 season, the Peterborough United player whose replica team shirt sold in the greatest numbers was Leon McKenzie.

Plymouth Argyle

Nicknamed The Pilgrims, Plymouth Argyle wear green and white striped shirts, black shorts and white socks with a green trim.

Plymouth Argyle play at Home Park, where they have been based since their formation in 1886.

Plymouth Argyle joined the Football League in 1920.

Although Plymouth Argyle have never been in the top flight of English football, they have had some great moments, the finest of which was probably their appearance in the 1984 FA Cup semi-final, in which they lost 1-0 to Watford.

THE CARLING ULTIMATE FOOTBALL FACT AND QUIZ BOOK

Clubs – P

Plymouth Argyle continued...

Plymouth Argyle have twice reached the semi-finals of the League Cup – first in 1965, when they lost to Leicester City, and again in 1974, when they went out to Manchester City.

From 1922 to 1927, Plymouth Argyle came second in the Third Division (South) six years running – a record.

Plymouth Argyle Managers
1903-1905	Frank Brettell
1905-1906	Bob Jack
1906-1907	Bill Fullerton
1910-1938	Bob Jack
1938-1947	Jack Tresadern
1948-1955	Jimmy Rae
1955-1960	Jack Rowley
1961	Neil Dougall
1961-1963	Ellis Stuttard
1963-1964	Andy Beattie
1964-1965	Malcolm Allison
1965-1968	Derek Ufton
1968-1970	Billy Bingham
1970-1972	Ellis Stuttard
1972-1977	Tony Waiters
1977-1978	Mike Kelly
1978-1979	Malcolm Allison
1979-1981	Bobby Saxton
1981-1983	Bobby Moncur
1983-1984	Johnny Hore
1984-1988	Dave Smith
1988-1990	Ken Brown
1990-1992	David Kemp
1992-1995	Peter Shilton
1995	Steve McCall
1995-1997	Neil Warnock
1997-1998	Mick Jones
1998-	Kevin Hodges

Plymouth Argyle League Record
1920-1921	Division Three
1921-1930	Division Three (South)
1930-1950	Division Two
1950-1952	Division Three (South)
1952-1956	Division Two
1956-1958	Division Three (South)
1958-1959	Division Three

Clubs – P

Plymouth Argyle continued...

1959-1968	Division Two
1968-1975	Division Three
1975-1977	Division Two
1977-1986	Division Three
1986-1995	Division Two
1995-1996	Division Three
1996-1997	Division Two
1997-	Division Three

As might be expected, the Plymouth Argyle supporters' songbook contains a lot of rude stuff, particularly about local(ish) rivals Exeter City.

But the words of their best song were written by John Bunyan:

> *He who would valiant be*
> *'Gainst all disaster*
> *Let him in constancy*
> *Follow the master*
> *There's no discouragement*
> *Shall make him once relent*
> *His first avowed intent*
> *To be a Pilgrim*

In the 1998-99 season, the Plymouth Argyle player whose replica team shirt sold in the greatest numbers was Paul Gibbs.

Port Vale

Since 1950, Port Vale have played at Vale Park, Burslem, Stoke-on-Trent. Before moving there they had five grounds: Limekin Lane, Longport (1876-1881); Westport (1881-1884); Moorland Park, Burslem (1884-1886); The Athletic Ground, Cobridge (1886-1913); and The Recreation Ground, Hanley (1913-1950).

The Port Vale strip is white shirts, black shorts and white socks.

Like Charlton Athletic (q v), Port Vale are nicknamed The Valiants.

Port Vale were founded in 1876. They became Burslem Port Vale when they moved to that part of the city in 1884 but reverted to their original name in 1909. Port Vale was the name of the house in which the founders met to establish the club.

THE CARLING ULTIMATE FOOTBALL FACT AND QUIZ BOOK

Clubs – P

Port Vale continued...

Port Vale joined the Football League in 1892. They failed to win re-election in 1896 and went out of the League until 1898. They dropped out again in 1907 because of financial problems and did not rejoin until 1919, when they took the place of Leeds City (see Leeds United).

In 1954, Port Vale – at that time in the Third Division – reached the semi-finals of the FA Cup. They were eventually knocked out by West Bromwich Albion, whose winner was scored by ex-Valiant Ronnie Allen.

Also in 1954, on their way to the Third Division (North) title, Port Vale established a record by going 30 League matches without conceding a goal.

Port Vale were expelled from the Football League in 1968 because of a scandal over allegedly illegal payments, but they were quickly re-elected and did not miss even a game, never mind a season.

In 1993, Port Vale were winners of the Autoglass Trophy.

Port Vale Managers

1896-1905	Sam Gleaves	
1905-1911	Tom Clare	
1911-1912	A S Walker	
1912-1914	H Myatt	
1919-1924	Tom Holford	
1924-1930	Joe Schofield	
1930-1932	Tom Morgan	
1932-1935	Tom Holford	
1936-1937	Warney Cresswell	
1937-1938	Tom Morgan	
1945-1946	Billy Frith	
1946-1951	Gordon Hodgson	
1951	Ivor Powell	
1951-1957	Freddie Steele	
1957-1962	Norman Low	
1962-1965	Freddie Steele	
1965-1967	Jackie Mudie	1965-1968 General Manager Sir Stanley Matthews
1968-1974	Gordon Lee	
1974-1977	Roy Sproson	
1977	Colin Harper	
1977-1978	Bobby Smith	
1978-1979	Dennis Butler	
1979	Alan Bloor	
1980-1983	John McGrath	
1984-1999	John Rudge	

Clubs – P

Port Vale continued...

Port Vale League Record
1892-1896	Division Two
1896-1898	Failed to gain re-election; dropped out of League
1898-1907	Division Two
1907-1919	Resigned from League
1919-1929	Division Two
1929-1930	Division Three (North)
1930-1936	Division Two
1936-1938	Division Three (North)
1938-1952	Division Three (South)
1952-1954	Division Three (North)
1954-1957	Division Two
1957-1958	Division Three (South)
1958-1959	Division Four
1959-1965	Division Three
1965-1970	Division Four
1970-1978	Division Three
1978-1983	Division Four
1983-1984	Division Three
1984-1986	Division Four
1986-1989	Division Three
1989-1994	Division Two
1994-	Division One

Port Vale's best song has nothing to do with football but celebrates the local brewing traditions:

On the twelfth day of Christmas
My true love sent to me
Twelve pints of Bass
Eleven pints of Bass
Ten pints of Bass
Nine pints of Bass
Eight pints of Bass
Seven pints of Bass

Six pints of Bass
Five Pedigrees
Four pints of Bass
Three pints of Bass
Two pints of Bass
And a pint of Bass in a straight glass – ooh aah!

(Tune: The Twelve Days of Christmas)

In the 1998-99 season, the Port Vale player whose replica team shirt sold in the greatest numbers was Ian Bogie.

THE CARLING ULTIMATE FOOTBALL FACT AND QUIZ BOOK

Clubs – P

Porto

The only Portuguese club to seriously challenge the footballing supremacy of the capital, Lisbon, FC Porto were founded in 1906 and are nicknamed The Dragons.

Before the Second World War, FC Porto's home ground was the Campo da Constituição but they now play at the 76,000-capacity Estadio Das Antas.

For home games, FC Porto wear blue and white striped shirts, blue shorts and white socks.

FC Porto won the European Cup for the first time in 1987 with an exciting 2-1 victory over the favourites, Bayern Munich, in the Final.

FC Porto's 1999 League Championship was their fifth Portuguese title in a row.

Portsmouth

Portsmouth were the first club from the Third Division (South) to go on to win the English League Championship.

Portsmouth play in blue shirts, white shorts and red socks and are nicknamed Pompey.

Portsmouth were founded in 1898 by Alderman J E Pink, a local solicitor who bought a plot of land in Frogmore Road on which was built the ground that has been the club's home throughout its history – Fratton Park.

Portsmouth are a one of the few clubs to have won the English League Championship in consecutive years – 1949 and 1950. These are their only League successes to date.

The club have won the FA Cup only once but they have held it longest – after their 4-1 victory over Wolverhampton Wanderers at Wembley in 1939, the outbreak of the Second World War and the suspension of normal football meant that they did not have to hand over the trophy until 1946.

The superstitious attributed Portsmouth's FA Cup triumph to the lucky white spats worn by their manager, Jack Tinn.

Portsmouth Managers

1898-1901	Frank Brettell
1901-1904	Bob Blyth
1905-1908	Richard Bonney
1911-1920	Bob Brown
1920-1927	John McCartney
1927-1947	Jack Tinn

THE CARLING ULTIMATE FOOTBALL FACT AND QUIZ BOOK

Facts
Clubs – P

Portsmouth continued...

1947-1952	Bob Jackson
1952-1958	Eddie Iever
1958-1961	Freddie Cox
1961-1970	George Smith
1970-1973	Ron Tindall
1973-1974	John Mortimore
1974-1977	Ian St John
1977-1979	Jimmy Dickinson
1979-1982	Frank Burrows
1982-1984	Bobby Campbell
1984-1989	Alan Ball
1989-1990	John Gregory
1990-1991	Frank Burrows
1991-1995	Jim Smith
1995-1998	Terry Fenwick
1998-	Alan Ball

Portsmouth League Record

1920-1921	Division Three
1921-1924	Division Three (South)
1924-1927	Division Two
1927-1959	Division One
1959-1961	Division Two
1961-1962	Division Three
1962-1976	Division Two
1976-1978	Division Three
1978-1980	Division Four
1980-1983	Division Three
1983-1987	Division Two
1987-1988	Division One
1988-1992	Division Two
1992-	Division One

Portsmouth supporters are famous for The Pompey Chimes, a chant in which they imitate a striking clock as they endlessly repeat:

Play up Pompey, Pompey play up

In the 1998-99 season, the Portsmouth player whose replica team shirt sold in the greatest numbers was John Aloisi, even though he ended the campaign at Coventry City.

THE CARLING ULTIMATE FOOTBALL FACT AND QUIZ BOOK

Clubs – P

Preston North End

Preston North End are nicknamed The Lilywhites. They play in white and navy blue shirts, navy blue shorts and navy blue socks. The initials PP on the club badge stand for Proud Preston.

Preston North End play their home matches at Deepdale.

Preston North End have their deepest roots in the North End Cricket and Rugby Club which was founded in 1863 and dabbled in most sports before becoming serious about soccer in 1879.

Preston North End were founder members of the Football League in 1888 and its first Champions in 1889. They were undefeated throughout the season.

The First English Football League Final Table, Season 1888-89

		P	W	D	L	F	A	Pts
1	Preston North End	22	18	4	0	74	15	40
2	Aston Villa	22	12	5	5	61	43	29
3	Wolverhampton Wanderers	22	12	4	6	50	37	28
4	Blackburn Rovers	22	10	6	6	66	45	26
5	Bolton Wanderers	22	10	2	10	63	59	22
6	West Bromwich Albion	22	10	2	10	40	46	22
7	Accrington	22	6	8	8	48	48	20
8	Everton	22	9	2	11	35	46	20
9	Burnley	22	7	3	12	42	62	17
10	Derby County	22	7	2	13	41	61	16
11	Notts County	22	5	2	15	40	73	12
12	Stoke	22	4	4	14	26	51	12

In 1889, Preston North End also won the FA Cup, thus achieving the first ever Double.

Preston North End won the League for the second time and last time in the following year, 1890.

Preston won the FA Cup for the second and last time in 1938.

In 1953, Preston North End missed their third League title by the narrowest of margins:

1952-53 Top of the First Division Final Table

	P	W	D	L	F	A	Pts
Arsenal	42	21	12	9	97	64	54
Preston North End	42	21	12	9	85	60	54

Arsenal and Preston North End were separated only by goal average – 1.51 against 1.41.

Clubs – P

Preston North End continued…

Preston North End were runners-up once more in 1958, but this time finished five points behind Wolverhampton Wanderers.

The most celebrated and quite possibly the greatest player in the long and distinguished history of Preston North End is the winger Tom Finney, who later became president of the club. Finney played 76 times for England between 1946 and 1958, scoring 30 international goals and playing in every position in the forward line.

Finney is sometimes known as The Preston Plumber because of the trade he practised outside the game.

Preston North End Managers

1906-1915	Charlie Parker
1919-1923	Vincent Hayes
1923-1925	Jim Lawrence
1925-1927	Frank Richards
1927-1931	Alex Gibson
1931-1932	Lincoln Hayes
1932-1936	Committee
1936-1937	Tommy Muirhead
1937-1949	Committee
1949-1953	Will Scott
1953-1954	Scot Symon
1954-1956	Frank Hill
1956-1961	Cliff Britton
1961-1968	Jimmy Milne
1968-1970	Bobby Seith
1970-1973	Alan Ball Snr
1973-1975	Bobby Charlton
1975-1977	Harry Catterick
1977-1981	Nobby Stiles
1981	Tommy Docherty
1981-1983	Gordon Lee
1983-1985	Alan Kelly
1985-1986	Tommy Booth
1986	Brian Kidd
1986-1990	John McGrath
1990-1992	Les Chapman
1992-1994	John Beck
1994-1998	Gary Peters
1998-	David Moyes

THE CARLING ULTIMATE FOOTBALL FACT AND QUIZ BOOK

Clubs – P

Preston North End continued...

Preston North End League Record

1888-1901	Division One
1901-1904	Division Two
1904-1912	Division One
1912-1913	Division Two
1913-1914	Division One
1914-1915	Division Two
1919-1925	Division One
1925-1934	Division Two
1934-1949	Division One
1949-1951	Division Two
1951-1961	Division One
1961-1970	Division Two
1970-1971	Division Three
1971-1974	Division Two
1974-1978	Division Three
1978-1981	Division Two
1981-1985	Division Three
1985-1987	Division Four
1987-1992	Division Three
1992-1993	Division Two
1993-1996	Division Three
1996-	Division Two

In the 1998-99 season, the Preston North End player whose replica team shirt sold in the greatest numbers was Sean Gregan.

PSV Eindhoven

One of the leading clubs in the Netherlands, PSV Eindhoven play in red shirts, white shorts and red socks.

The club was founded in 1913 as the sports club of the Philips, the massive Dutch-based electronics corporation.

PSV won their first Dutch League title in 1929. They were Champions again in 1935, 1951, 1963, 1975, 1976, 1978, 1986, 1987, 1988, 1989 and 1990.

In 1978, PSV Eindhoven won the UEFA Cup.

In 1988, PSV Eindhoven became only the third club in Europe to do the treble of domestic League and Cup and the European Cup in the same season. The other two clubs to have achieved this feat were Celtic (q v) in 1967 and Ajax Amsterdam (q v) in 1972.

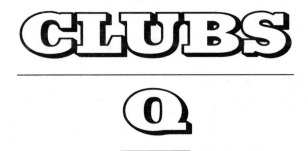

THE CARLING ULTIMATE FOOTBALL FACT AND QUIZ BOOK

Clubs – Q

Queen of the South

Queen of the South are so called after the traditional nickname of Dumfries, the town in which they play.

Queen of the South are nicknamed The Doonhamers; they play at Palmerston Park in Terregles Street.

The Doonhamers' strip is royal blue and white shirts, royal blue shorts and royal blue socks with a broad white band in the middle.

Queen of the South were founded in 1919 through the merger of three teams named Arrol-Johnson, Dumfries and K O S B. They joined the Scottish Football League in 1923.

Queen of the South's only honour is the Scottish League Second Division Championship, which they won in 1951.

Queen's Park

Nicknamed The Spiders, Queen's Park play in black and white hooped shirts, white socks and black socks with two thin white bands around the middle.

Queen's Park were founded in 1807 and have played their home matches at Hampden Park on Mount Florida, Glasgow since 1903.

Queen's Park have won the Scottish FA Cup 10 times – in 1874, 1875, 1876, 1880, 1881, 1882, 1884, 1886, 1890 and 1893.

The 20th century has seen Queen's Park win nothing other than the the championship of Division Two in 1923 and 1981 and Division B in 1956.

Queen's Park Rangers

Queen's Park Rangers – the name is usually shortened to QPR and they are known to their supporters as The Rs – have played their home games in 18 different locations.

QPR were formed in 1885 or 1886 through the amalgamation of Christchurch Rangers and St Jude's Institute. They were originally known as St Jude's but adopted their present name in 1887 because most of the players at the time lived in the Queen's Park district of northwest London.

THE CARLING ULTIMATE FOOTBALL FACT AND QUIZ BOOK

Clubs – Q

Queen's Park Rangers continued...

QPR have had four different home colours in their time but they presently play in blue and white hoops, white shorts and white socks.

In chronological order, QPR's most long-lasting previous home grounds have been as follows: Welford's Fields (1885-1888); London Scottish Ground, Brondesbury, Home Farm, Kensal Rise Green, Gun Club, Wormwood Scrubs, Kilburn Cricket Ground (1888-1899); Kensal Rise Athletic Ground (1899-1901); Latimer Road, Notting Hill (1901-1904); Agricultural Society, Park Royal (1904-1907); Park Royal Ground (1907-1917); Loftus Road (1917-1931); White City (1931-1933); Loftus Road (1933-1962); White City (1962-1963); Loftus Road (1963-).

Queen's Park Rangers joined the Football League in 1920.

Queen's Park Rangers' first major impact on the history of the game came in 1967, when – as a Third Division club – they won the League Cup, beating the holders, West Bromwich Albion of Division One, in the first Final of the competition to be held at Wembley.

In the same year (1967) Queen's Park Rangers also won the Third Division Championship to pull off a unique double.

The following season (1967-68), QPR were denied the League Cup winners' place in the Fairs Cup because they were not in the top flight of domestic football.

This at least ensured that they were not distracted from the League – they finished second in the Second Division and thus in 1968 they entered Division One for the first time in their history.

Since then Queen's Park Rangers have been runners-up in the League (1976) and the FA Cup (1982).

In the glorious August of 1975, QPR beat the reigning champions of three countries – England (QPR 5 Derby County 1); West Germany (QPR 4 Borussia Moenchengladbach 1); and Portugal (QPR 4 Benfica 2).

Queen's Park Rangers Managers

1906-1913	James Cowan
1913-1920	Jimmy Howie
1920-1924	Ted Liddell
1924-1925	Will Wood
1925-1930	Bob Hewison
1930-1931	John Bowman
1931-1933	Archie Mitchell
1933-1935	Mick O'Brien
1935-1939	Billy Birrell
1939-1944	Ted Vizard
1944-1952	Dave Mangnall
1952-1959	Jack Taylor

Clubs – Q

Queen's Park Rangers continued...

1959-1968	Alec Stock
1968	Bill Dodgin Jnr
1968	Tommy Docherty
1968-1971	Les Allen
1971-1974	Gordon Jago
1974-1977	Dave Sexton
1977-1978	Frank Sibley
1978-1979	Steve Burtenshaw
1979-1980	Tommy Docherty
1980-1984	Terry Venables
1984	Gordon Jago
1984	Alan Mullery
1984-1985	Frank Sibley
1985-1988	Jim Smith
1988-1990	Trevor Francis
1990-1991	Don Howe
1991-1994	Gerry Francis
1994-1996	Ray Wilkins
1996-1997	Stewart Houston
1997-1998	Ray Harford
1998-	Gerry Francis

Queen's Park Rangers League Record

1920-1921	Division Three
1921-1948	Division Three (South)
1948-1952	Division Two
1952-1958	Division Three (South)
1958-1967	Division Three
1967-1968	Division Two
1968-1969	Division One
1969-1973	Division Two
1973-1979	Division One
1979-1983	Division Two
1983-1992	Division One
1992-1996	Premiership
1996-	Division One

In the 1998-99 season, the Queen's Park Rangers player whose replica team shirt sold in the greatest numbers was Kevin Gallen.

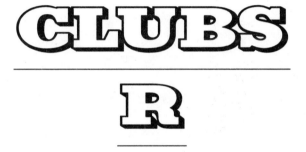

Clubs – R

Raith Rovers

Raith Rovers – Rovers for short – are based in Kirkcaldy, Fife. They play in royal blue shirts with white trim, white shots with royal blue trim and white socks with blue trim.

They were founded in 1883 and take their name from that of the Laird of Raith and Novar, who leased to them part of Robbie's Park, the land in Kirkcaldy on which they first played their home games.

Since 1891, Raith Rovers have played their home games at Stark's Park in Pratt Street.

Raith Rovers became members of the Scottish Football League in 1902. They won the Second Division title outright in 1908, 1910 (shared with Leith), 1938 and 1949.

Raith Rovers were runners-up in the Scottish FA Cup in 1913 and the League Cup in 1949.

While winning the 1938 Scottish Second Division Championship, Raith scored 142 goals in a 34-game season – an all-time record for a British league football club.

Raith Rovers' proudest moment came on November 27, 1994, when they finally won the Scottish League Cup. They beat Celtic 6-5 on penalties in the Final at Ibrox after the match had finished 2-2 at the end of extra time.

Raith's goalscorers on this great day were Crawford and Dalziel.

Rangers

Rangers are nicknamed The Gers; the club motto is: Ready.

Rangers' home strip consists of royal blue shirts with red and white trim, white shorts with red and blue trim and red socks with black trim.

Rangers were founded in 1873 by a group of rowing enthusiasts from Grarelock in western Scotland. They first played on Flesher's Haugh and then at Kinning Park before settling at the Ibrox Stadium in Edminston Drive, Glasgow.

Rangers have won the Scottish FA Cup 27 times (Check at end of this season!!!- if they win this year it'll be 28) – this is a poor success rate when compared to their performance in the Scottish League, of which they have been Champions 48 times between 1891 (when they shared it with Dumbarton, q v) and the end of the 20th century.

They have also won the Scottish League Cup 20 times (unless they won it in 1998, in which case it's 21).

THE CARLING ULTIMATE FOOTBALL FACT AND QUIZ BOOK

Clubs – R

Rangers continued…

In European competition, however, Rangers have failed to dominate – their only trophy is the 1972 Cup Winners' Cup.

In their 1898-99 Championship-winning season, Rangers won every one of their 18 League matches.

The history of Rangers has been darkened by two great disasters at their stadium. Rangers themselves were not involved in the first, which occurred on April 5, 1902 during Scotland's Home International match against England. The newly extended Western Stand collapsed and hundreds of spectators fell through a hole – 26 of them were killed and more than 500 injured.

The second Ibrox Stadium disaster happened on January 2, 1971 during Rangers' Old Firm game against Celtic. As crowds were making their way towards the exits just before the end of the game, people slipped on the stairs, tripping those immediately behind them and causing a human avalanche in which 66 people were killed, all crushed to death; some of the bodies were found in an upright position. The scene of the tragedy – Staircase 13 – had already claimed two lives in 1961 and there had been further serious but non-fatal incidents there in 1967 and 1969, in which more than 30 people had been injured.

Just as Celtic (q v) derive much of their support from Glasgow's Irish Roman Catholic community, so Rangers are a focal point of Scottish Protestantism. The complex and hate-riddled relationship between the two religious groups comes out in many of the terrace songs, some of the lyrics of which refer to historical events in Ireland.

> *Sure I'm an Orange Ulsterman from Erin's Isle I came*
> *To see my British brethren all of honour and of fame*
> *And they tell them of my forefathers who fought in days of yore*
> *That I might have the right to wear the sash my father wore*
>
> *It is old but it is beautiful and its colours they are fine*
> *It was worn at Derry, Aughrim, Enniskillen and the Boyne*
> *My father wore it as a youth in bygone days of yore*
> *And it's on the Twelfth* I love to wear the sash my father wore*

* July 12, the anniversary of William III's victory over the deposed Roman Catholic King James II at the Battle of the Boyne near Drogheda, Ireland in 1690.

To end this entry on a happier note, here is a non-sectarian Rangers song:

> *As I was walking down Copland Road I met a crowd of strangers*
> *They said to me where can we see the famous Glasgow Rangers*
> *So I took them off to Ibrox Park to see a great eleven*
> *Said I it isn't paradise but man it's my blue heaven*

(Tune: We're No Awa' To Bide Awa'')

THE CARLING ULTIMATE FOOTBALL FACT AND QUIZ BOOK

Clubs – R

Rapid Vienna

Rapid Vienna were founded in 1873 under the name of First Workers' Football Club. They play their home games in the Hanappi Stadium, which is known locally as the Wiener. Their colours are all white with green trim.

In the early years of the 20th century, Rapid developed a short passing style which became known as The Vienna School and with which they won the Austrian League Championship eight times in the 12 years between 1912 and 1923.

There were four Rapid Vienna players in the so-called Wunderteam, the Austrian national side which finished fourth in the 1934 World Cup.

In 1938 Hitler's Germany annexed Austria in the Anschluss. Although the country in which it had previously played had now ceased to exist, Rapid Vienna were apparently undeterred and went on to win the German Cup in that year and the German League Championship in 1941.

Among Rapid's most distinguished former players are Franz 'Bimbo' Binder, who scored 1,006 goals in his career, and Gerhard Hanappi, the wing-half architect who designed the club's stadium.

Reading

Reading are nicknamed The Royals, because they are in Royal Berkshire, or The Biscuitmen, after one of the town's major industries. They were founded in 1871 and are thus the oldest League club south of the River Trent.

The Reading home strip is royal blue and white hoped shirts, white shorts and white and blue hooped socks.

From 1871 to 1882, Reading played at the town's Recreation and Cricket Ground; from 1882 to 1889, they played at Coley Park and then from 1889 to 1896 they were at Caversham Cricket Ground.

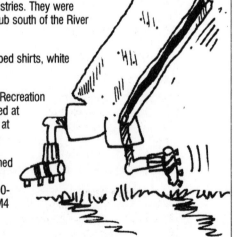

In 1896, Reading settled at Elm Park, which remained their home until the end of the 1998 season, when they moved to the brand new, purpose-built, 15,000-capacity Madejski Stadium at Junction 11 on the M4 motorway.

Reading joined the Football League in 1920.

THE CARLING ULTIMATE FOOTBALL FACT AND QUIZ BOOK

Clubs – R

Reading continued...

In 1927, the Biscuitmen – who were then, as so often, in the Third Division (South) – reached the semi-finals of the FA Cup, where they lost to the eventual winners, Cardiff City. Reading had eliminated Manchester United and Portsmouth on the way.

Between April 1933 and January 1936, Reading went 55 home games without defeat.

Although Reading were never owned by Robert Maxwell, the publishing magnate did try to involve himself in their affairs in the 1980s when he proposed a merger with Oxford United (q v) under the name Thames Valley Royals.

In the 1985-86 season, Reading won all their first 13 League matches, an all-time record.

Reading Managers

1897-1901	Thomas Sefton
1901-1902	James Sharp
1902-1920	Harry Matthews
1920-1922	Harry Marshall
1923-1925	Arthur Chadwick
1925-1926	H S Bray
1926-1931	Andrew Wylie
1931-1935	Joe Smith
1935-1939	Billy Butler
1939	John Cochrane
1939-1947	Joe Edelston
1947-1952	Ted Drake
1952-1955	Jack Smith
1955-1963	Harry Johnston
1963-1969	Roy Bentley
1969-1971	Jack Mansell
1972-1977	Charlie Hurley
1977-1984	Maurice Evans
1984-1989	Ian Branfoot
1989-1991	Ian Porterfield
1991-1994	Mark McGhee
1994-1997	Mick Gooding and Jimmy Quinn
1997-1998	Terry Bullivant
1998-	Tommy Burns

Reading League Record

1920-1921	Division Three
1921-1926	Division Three (South)
1926-1931	Division Two
1931-1958	Division Three (South)
1958-1971	Division Three

THE CARLING ULTIMATE FOOTBALL FACT AND QUIZ BOOK

Clubs – R

Reading continued...

1971-1976	Division Four
1976-1977	Division Three
1977-1979	Division Four
1979-1983	Division Three
1983-1984	Division Four
1984-1986	Division Three
1986-1988	Division Two
1988-1992	Division Three
1992-1994	Division Two
1994-	Division One

Chim chiminee chim chiminee
Chim chim cheroo
We've got a kit that's more yellow than blue

(Tune: Chim-Chim-Cheree from the film of Mary Poppins)

In the 1998-99 season, the Reading player whose replica team shirt sold in the greatest numbers was Martin Williams.

Real Madrid

Founded as plain Madrid in 1902, the Spanish capital's leading football club was given the prefix Real (meaning 'Royal') by King Alfonso XIII in 1920.

Real Madrid play in white shirts with blue trim, white shorts and white socks. This strip was adopted by Leeds United (q v) under Don Revie in the 1960s. This was partly a tribute to the Spaniards, partly an attempt to make some of their magic rub off on Yorkshire.

Real announced themselves as the top club in Castile if not the whole of Spain by winning the League Championship twice in the 1930s.

The Spanish Civil War (1936-39) left Real's original Chamartin Stadium in ruins. It was rebuilt with money collected from an appeal organised by club president Santiago Bernabeu, a lawyer who had been a Real player and later their team manager. Fittingly, Real Madrid's present 105,000-capacity home is named the Bernabeu Stadium in his memory.

Real Madrid won the Spanish League 23 times and the FA Cup nine times between 1946 and 1990.

Real Madrid were undefeated at home for 114 games between February 1957 and March 1965.

THE CARLING ULTIMATE FOOTBALL FACT AND QUIZ BOOK

Clubs – R

Real Madrid continued...

Real Madrid's greatest achievement was their early domination of the European Cup, which they won in each of the first five years of its existence. They have now won the trophy seven times altogether.

Real Madrid's European Cup Final Victories

1956	Real Madrid 4	Reims 3
1957	Real Madrid 2	Fiorentina 0
1958	Real Madrid 3	AC Milan 2 (after extra time)
1959	Real Madrid 2	Reims 0
1960	Real Madrid 7	Eintracht Frankfurt 3
1966	Real Madrid 2	Partizan Belgrade 1
1998	Real Madrid 1	Juventus 0

Among the greatest players in the Real Madrid team of the 1950s were Didi, Raymond Kopa, Ferenc Puskas and Alfredo di Stefano.

Real Madrid have also won the UEFA Cup twice, in 1985 and 1986.

Red Star Belgrade

Red Star were founded in 1945 by students at the University of Belgrade. The club quickly became a major power in Yugoslav football. Since the break-up of Yugoslavia in the early 1990s, Red Star have become the dominant team in Serbia.

Red Star Belgrade's home strip consists of red and white striped shirts, red shorts and red socks.

Their Stadium is officially called Crvena Zvezda – Serbian for Red Star – and nicknamed Maracana, in homage to the arena of the same name in Rio de Janeiro, Brazil.

Red Star Belgrade's crowning glory came in 1991 when they won the European Cup, beating Marseille on penalties after the Final ended 0-0.

Red Star then went on to win the World Club Championship in the same year, beating South American Champions Colo Colo (q v), again on penalties.

Clubs – R

River Plate

River Plate were founded in 1901 by English expatriates and now play at the Estadio Monumental in Buenos Aires, Argentina.

River Plate play in white shirts with a red diagonal sash, black shorts and white socks.

The great River Plate side of the late 1940s was nicknamed La Maquina (The Machine) because of its efficiency.

Rochdale

Rochdale play in blue shirts with white trim, blue shorts and blue socks with a white hoop on the turnover. They are nicknamed The Dale.

The club was founded in 1907, when it succeeded Rochdale Town. They joined the Football League in 1921.

The greatest moment in the generally undistinguished history of Rochdale came in 1962, when – as a Fourth Division side – they reached the Final of the League Cup.

Rochdale Managers

1922-1923	Tom Wilson
1923-1930	Jack Peart
1930-1931	Will Cameron
1932-1934	Herbert Hopkinson
1934-1935	Billy Smith
1935-1937	Ernest Nixon
1937-1938	Sam Jennings
1938-1952	Ted Goodier
1952-1953	Jack Warner
1953-1958	Harry Catterick
1958-1960	Jack Marshall
1960-1967	Tony Collins
1967-1968	Bob Stokoe
1968-1970	Len Richley
1970-1973	Dick Conner
1973-1976	Walter Joyce
1976-1977	Brian Green
1977-1978	Mike Ferguson
1979	Doug Collins
1979-1980	Bob Stokoe
1980-1983	Peter Madden

THE CARLING ULTIMATE FOOTBALL FACT AND QUIZ BOOK

Clubs – R

Rochdale continued...

1983-1984	Jimmy Greenhoff
1984-1986	Vic Halom
1986-1988	Eddie Gray
1988-1989	Danny Bergara
1989-1991	Terry Dolan
1991-1994	Dave Sutton
1995-1996	Mick Docherty
1996-	Graham Barrow

Rochdale League Record

1921-1958	Division Three (North)
1958-1959	Division Three
1959-1969	Division Four
1969-1974	Division Three
1974-1992	Division Four
1992-	Division Three

In the 1998-99 season, the Rochdale player whose replica team shirt sold in the greatest numbers was Robbie Painter.

AS Roma

AS Roma are nicknamed I Giallorossi after their home strip, which is red shirts with yellow trim, red shorts and red socks.

The club was founded in 1927 and is based at the Olympic Stadium. They won their first Italian League Championship in 1942 and their first Cup in 1964. They reached the Final of the European Cup in 1984, but lost on penalties to Liverpool.

Ross County

Ross County – The County for short – play at Victoria Park, Jubilee Park Road, Dingwall, Ross-shire. They are the most northerly football league club in the British Isles.

The Ross County home strip consists of dark blue shirts with white trim, white shorts and dark blue socks with red and white trim.

Ross County were founded in 1929 and joined the Scottish Football League in 1994. In 1999, they won the Scottish Third Division Championship – their first honour.

THE CARLING ULTIMATE FOOTBALL FACT AND QUIZ BOOK

Facts
Clubs – R

Rotherham United

Rotherham United – nicknamed The Merry Millers – were founded in 1870 and joined the Football League in 1893. They were previously known as Thornhill United (1877-1905) and Rotherham County (1905-1925).

In 1925, Rotherham County amalgamated with Rotherham Town to become Rotherham United.

Since 1907, Rotherham United have had their home at Millmoor. Before that, they played at The Red House Ground.

Rotherham United play in red shirts, white shorts and red socks.

Although Rotherham have never been in the top flight of English football, in 1955 they missed promotion to the First Division only on goal average:

1955 League Division Two (Top) Final Table

	P	W	D	L	F	A	Pts
Birmingham City	42	22	10	10	92	47	54
Luton Town	42	23	8	11	88	53	54
Rotherham United	42	25	4	13	94	64	54

(In those days, there were only two points for a win and only two clubs went up.)

The disappointment of this near miss was great – the following year, they finished fourth from bottom of Division Two

In 1961, Rotherham United – then a Second Division side – were finalists in the first League Cup.

Rotherham United Managers

1925-1929	Billy Heald
1929-1930	Stanley Davies
1930-1933	Billy Heald
1934-1952	Reg Freeman
1952-1958	Andy Smailes
1958-1962	Tom Johnston
1962-1965	Danny Williams
1965-1967	Jack Mansell
1967-1968	Tommy Docherty
1968-1973	Jimmy McAnearney
1973-1979	Jimmy McGuigan
1979-1981	Ian Porterfield
1981-1983	Emlyn Hughes
1983-1985	George Kerr

THE CARLING ULTIMATE FOOTBALL FACT AND QUIZ BOOK

Clubs – R

Rotherham United continued...

1985-1987	Norman Hunter
1987-1988	Dave Cusack
1988-1991	Billy McEwan
1991-1994	Phil Henson
1994-1996	Archie Gemmill and John McGovern
1996-1997	Danny Bergara
1997	Ronnie Moore

Rotherham United League Record

1893-1896	Division Two
1896-1919	Failed to win re-election; dropped out of League
1919-1923	Division Two
1923-1951	Division Three (North)
1951-1968	Division Two
1968-1973	Division Three
1973-1975	Division Four
1975-1981	Division Three
1981-1983	Division Two
1983-1988	Division Three
1988-1989	Division Four
1989-1991	Division Three
1991-1992	Division Four
1992-1997	Division Two
1997-	Division Three

When I was young my father said
Son I have something to say
And what he told me I'll never forget
Until my dying day

He said son you are a Rotherham fan
And that's the way to stay
Happy to be a Rotherham fan
Until your dying day

(Tune: Bachelor Boy)

In the 1998-99 season, the Rotherham United player whose replica team shirt sold in the greatest numbers was Lee Glover.

THE CARLING ULTIMATE FOOTBALL FACT AND QUIZ BOOK

Clubs – S

St Etienne

Nicknamed Les Verts, St Etienne play in green shirts, white shorts and green socks. The club was founded in 1920 and play their home games at the Geoffroy Guichard Stadium in the city of St Etienne.

Between 1962 and 1977, St Etienne won the French League and Cup double four times.

In 1976, St Etienne were runners-up in the European Cup, losing 2-0 to Bayern Munich in the Final.

In 1982, St Etienne were implicated in an illegal payments scandal and the club was relegated to the Second Division in 1984.

St Johnstone

St Johnstone come from Perth, Scotland and their name is derived from that city's traditional associations with John the Baptist – the area in which the club's ground stands was formerly known as St John's Toun of Perth.

St Johnstone now play their home games at McDiarmid Park in Crieff Road. They were previously based at Muirton Park.

St Johnstone are nicknamed The Saints and play in royal blue and white shirts, white and royal blue shorts and royal blue socks with white trim.

St Mirren

St Mirren play at St Mirren Park in Love Street, Paisley, Scotland. They are nicknamed The Buddies.

The club was founded in 1877 by local cricket and rugby players and joined the Scottish Football League in 1890. They were nomadic at first but settled in Love Street in 1895.

St Mirren's home strip is black and white striped shirts, black and white shorts and white socks.

To date, St Mirren have won the Scottish FA Cup three times – in 1926, 1959 and 1987.

THE CARLING ULTIMATE FOOTBALL FACT AND QUIZ BOOK

Clubs – S

Santos

Santos play their home games at the Vila Belmiro Stadium in Santos, Brazil. Their colours are all white.

They were founded in 1912, according to legend, after British sailors on shore leave in the port had demonstrated football to the fascinated natives.

Santos have won their domestic League Championship 15 times; in 1962 and 1963 they won both the South American Cup and the World Club Championship two years running.

No matter how great or numerous their achievements on the field, Santos – more than any other club – is overshadowed by one of its former players. That player was born Edson Arantes do Nascimento and is known everywhere as Pele.

While Pele was at his peak, Santos capitalised on his fame by touring the world performing exhibition matches – they were a footballing equivalent of the Harlem Globetrotters in basketball.

Scarborough

Scarborough's home strip is red and black shirts, white shorts and red socks.

Scarborough were founded in 1879 as Scarborough Cricketers' FC. They turned professional in 1926 and joined the Football League in 1987.

Scarborough play their home games at the McCain Stadium in Seamer Road.

At the end of the 1998-99 season, Scarborough were relegated to the Conference after finishing bottom of Division Three.

Scarborough Managers

1945-1946	B Chapman
1946-1947	George Hall
1947-1948	Harold Taylor
1948-1950	Frank Taylor
1950-1953	A C Bell
1953-1954	Reg Halton
1954-1957	Charles Robson
1957-1958	George Higgins
1959-1961	Andy Smailes
1961-1964	Eddie Brown
1964-1965	Albert Franks
1965-1966	Stuart Myers

THE CARLING ULTIMATE FOOTBALL FACT AND QUIZ BOOK

Facts
Clubs – S

Scarborough continued...

1968-1969	Graham Shaw
1969-1973	Colin Appleton
1974-1975	Ken Houghton
1975-1981	Colin Appleton
1981-1982	Jimmy McAnearney
1982-1984	John Cottam
1984-1986	Harry Dunn
1986-1988	Neil Warnock
1989	Colin Morris
1989-1993	Ray McHale
1993	Phil Chambers
1993-1994	Steve Wicks
1994	Billy Ayre
1994-1996	Ray McHale
1996	Mitch Cook
1996-	Mick Wadsworth

Scarborough League Record

| 1987-1992 | Division Four |
| 1992-1999 | Division Three |

In the 1998-99 season, the Scarborough player whose replica team shirt sold in the greatest numbers was Gareth Williams.

Scunthorpe United

Nicknamed The Iron, Scunthorpe United play in claret and blue shirts, blue shorts and blue socks with claret trim.

Scunthorpe United were founded in 1899; from 1910 to 1958 they were known as Scunthorpe and Lindsey United.

Scunthorpe United joined the Football League in 1950. Since 1988, they have played at Glanford Park; before they moved there, they had played their home games at The Old Showground.

Three England captains have played for Scunthorpe United – they are Ray Clemence, Kevin Keegan and cricketer Ian Botham.

Scunthorpe United continued...

Clubs – S

Scunthorpe United Managers

1915-1936	Harry Allcock
1936-1937	Tom Crilly
1937-1946	Harry Allcock
1946-1948	Bernard Harper
1948-1950	Harry Allcock
1950-1951	Leslie Jones
1952-1956	Bill Corkhill
1956-1958	Ron Suart
1959	Tony McShane
1959	Bill Lambton
1959-1960	Frank Soo
1960-1964	Dick Duckworth
1964-1966	Fred Goodwin
1967-1973	Ron Ashman
1973-1974	Ron Bradley
1974-1976	Dick Rooks
1976-1981	Ron Ashman
1981-1983	John Duncan
1983-1984	Allan Clarke
1984-1987	Frank Barlow
1987-1991	Mick Buxton
1991-1993	Bill Green
1993-1994	Richard Money
1994-1996	David Moore
1996-1997	Mick Buxton
1997-	Brian Laws

Scunthorpe United League Record

1950-1958	Division Three (North)
1958-1964	Division Two
1964-1968	Division Three
1968-1972	Division Four
1972-1973	Division Three
1973-1983	Division Four
1983-1984	Division Three
1984-1992	Division Four
1992-	Division Three

Scunthorpe United continued...

THE CARLING ULTIMATE FOOTBALL FACT AND QUIZ BOOK

Clubs – S

Although Scunthorpe United were originally and now are again claret and blue, the club played for nearly a quarter of a century in red and white and experimented in the 1960s and '70s with a white, amber and blue strip. Thus when they reverted to their traditional strip this came as a surprise to young Scunny fans with an incomplete knowledge of the club's history, hence the following words to the tune Que Sera Sera:

> When I was just a little boy
> Scunny were red and white oh what joy
> Now we are claret now we are blue
> Why we ain't got a clue
> Tell me mam, me mam
> They've dressed us up like West Ham
> We look like blue paint and Spam
> We look like West Ham

In the 1998-99 season, the Scunthorpe United player whose replica team shirt sold in the greatest numbers was Jamie Forrester.

Sheffield United

Nicknamed The Blades, Sheffield United play their home games at Bramall Lane.

Sheffield United were formed in 1889 by Yorkshire County Cricket Club, who saw soccer as a way of raising money and of keeping fit during the winter – J B Wostinholm, United's first manager, was for a time secretary of both clubs.

Sheffield United's strip is red and white striped shirts with black trim, black shorts and black socks with red trim.

Sheffield United's most successful period came at the end of the 19th century – they won their only League Championship in 1898. They were also runners-up in 1897 and 1900.

Sheffield United have won the FA Cup four times – in 1899, 1902, 1915 and 1925.

Sheffield United Managers

1889-1899	J B Wostinholm
1899-1932	John Nicholson
1932-1952	Ted Davison
1952-1955	Reg Freeman
1955-1958	Joe Mercer
1959-1968	Johnny Harris
1968-1969	Arthur Rowley

THE CARLING ULTIMATE FOOTBALL FACT AND QUIZ BOOK

Sheffield United continued...

1969-1973	Johnny Harris
1973-1975	Ken Furphy
1975-1977	Jimmy Sirrel
1978-1981	Harry Haslam
1981	Martin Peters
1981-1986	Ian Porterfield
1986-1988	Billy McEwan
1988-1995	Dave Bassett
1995-1997	Howard Kendall
1997-1998	Nigel Spackman
1998-1999	Steve Bruce

Sheffield United League Record

1892-1893	Division Two
1893-1934	Division One
1934-1939	Division Two
1946-1949	Division One
1949-1953	Division Two
1953-1956	Division One
1956-1961	Division Two
1961-1968	Division One
1968-1971	Division Two
1971-1976	Division One
1976-1979	Division Two
1979-1981	Division Three
1981-1982	Division Four
1982-1984	Division Three
1984-1988	Division Two
1988-1989	Division Three
1989-1990	Division Two
1990-1992	Division One
1992-1994	Premiership
1994-	Division One

You light up my senses
Like a gallon of Magnet
Like a packet of Woodbine
Like a good pinch of snuff
Like a night out in Sheffield

Like a greasy chip butty
Oh Sheffield United
Come thrill me again

(Tune: Annie's Song by John Denver)

In the 1998-99 season, the Sheffield United player whose replica team shirt sold in the greatest numbers was Wayne Quinn.

THE CARLING ULTIMATE FOOTBALL FACT AND QUIZ BOOK

Clubs – S

Sheffield Wednesday

Sheffield Wednesday are nicknamed the Owls because they come from the Owlerton district of the city.

The full name itself comes is taken from that of Sheffield Wednesday Cricket Club, which met on the weekday afternoon when there was half-day closing.

The fifth oldest League club in England, Sheffield Wednesday FC were formed in 1867 at a meeting in the Adelphi Hotel.

From the year in which they entered the League (1892) until 1929, the club was known simply as The Wednesday.

Wednesday's first ground was Highfield, where they played from 1867 to 1869; after that they were at Myrtlr Road until 1877, then spent a decade at Sheaf House. From 1887 to 1899 they played at Olive Grove before moving to a stadium in Owlerton which, from 1912 onwards, became known as Hillsborough.

Sheffield Wednesday play in blue and white striped shirts, blue shorts and blue socks.

Sheffield Wednesday have won the Football League Championship four times – in 1903, 1904, 1929 and 1930.

The Owls have won the FA Cup on three occasions – in 1896, 1907 and 1935 – and the League Cup in 1991.

Sheffield Wednesday Managers

1891-1920	Arthur Dickinson
1920-1933	Robert Brown
1933-1937	Billy Walker
1937-1942	Jimmy McMullan
1942-1958	Eric Taylor
1958-1961	Harry Catterick
1961-1964	Vic Buckingham
1964-1968	Alan Brown
1968-1969	Jack Marshall
1969-1971	Danny Williams
1971-1973	Derek Dooley
1974-1975	Steve Burtenshaw
1975-1977	Len Ashurst
1977-1983	Jack Charlton
1983-1988	Howard Wilkinson
1988-1989	Peter Eustace
1989-1991	Ron Atkinson
1991-1995	Trevor Francis

Clubs – S

Sheffield Wednesday continued...

1995-1997	David Pleat
1997-1998	Ron Atkinson
1998-	Danny Wilson

Sheffield Wednesday League Record

1892-1899	Division One
1899-1900	Division Two
1900-1920	Division One
1920-1926	Division Two
1926-1937	Division One
1937-1950	Division Two
1950-1951	Division One
1951-1952	Division Two
1952-1955	Division One
1955-1956	Division Two
1956-1958	Division One
1958-1959	Division Two
1959-1970	Division One
1970-1975	Division Two
1975-1980	Division Three
1980-1984	Division Two
1984-1990	Division One
1990-1991	Division Two
1991-1992	Division One
1992-	Premiership

We've travelled far and wide
We've been to Merseyside
But there is only one place I want to be
And that is Hillsborough
Where it is magnifique
And all the Blades lay down on their faces

(Tune: Milord by Frankie Vaughan)

In the 1998-99 season, the Sheffield Wednesday player whose replica team shirt sold in the greatest numbers was Benito Carbone.

THE CARLING ULTIMATE FOOTBAL

Clubs -

Shrewsbury To

Shrewsbury Town are nicknamed The Shrews. They were founde
League in 1950.

Shrewsbury's home strip consists of blue shirts with white trim, b
white trim.

Shrewsbury Town first played at Old Shrewsbury Racecourse but
Meadow.

Shrewsbury Town's greatest League honour to date is the Third Divi
won in 1979 and 1994.

The club has won the Welsh Cup six times – in 1891, 1938, 1977, 1

Shrewsbury Town reached the Sixth Round of the FA Cup in 1979 an
League Cup in 1961.

Shrewsbury Town Managers

1905-1912	W Adams
1912-1934	A Weston
1934-1935	Jack Roscamp
1935-1936	Sam Ramsey
1936-1940	Ted Bousted
1945-1949	Leslie Knighton
1949-1950	Harry Chapman
1950-1954	Sammy Crooks
1955-1957	Walter Rowley
1957-1958	Harry Potts
1958	Johnny Spuhler
1958-1968	Arthur Rowley
1968-1972	Harry Gregg
1972-1973	Maurice Evans
1974-1978	Alan Durban
1978	Richie Barker
1978-1984	Graham Turner
1984-1987	Chic Bates
1987-1990	Ian McNeill
1990-1991	Asa Hartford
1991-1993	John Bond
1994-1997	Fred Davies
1997-	Jake King

Clubs – S

...own continued...

...rewsbury Town League Record
...50-1951	Division Three (North)
...51-1958	Division Three (South)
...58-1959	Division Four
...59-1974	Division Three
...74-1975	Division Four
...75-1979	Division Three
...979-1989	Division Two
...989-1994	Division Three
...994-	Division Two

...98-99 season, the Shrewsbury Town player whose replica team shirt sold in the greatest ...was Austin Berkeley.

Southampton

...mpton play their home games in red and white striped shirts, black shorts and white socks ...trim.

...b was founded in 1885 and first played under the name of the local church, Southampton St ...– it is from this that their current nickname, The Saints, is derived.

...mpton played first at the Antelope Ground (1885-1897) and then spent a year at Hampshire ...Cricket Ground before settling at The Dell in Milton Road in 1898.

...ampton reached the FA Cup Final in 1900 and 1902 but did not join the Football League until

...ampton first won promotion to Division One in 1966. They were relegated again in 1974, but ...ur years they spent in Division Two were alleviated by victory in the 1976 FA Cup, when they ...ot favourites Manchester United 1-0 in the Final.

...ampton returned to the top flight in 1978 and have remained there ever since. In 1984, they ...ed second in the First Division but generally they have been closer to the bottom of the table ...ave had numerous – almost annual – close encounters of the undesirable kind with relegation.

Southampton Managers
1894-1895	Cecil Knight
1895-1897	Charles Robson
1897-1911	E Arnfield
1911-1912	George Swift

THE CARLING ULTIMATE FOOTBALL FACT AND QUIZ BOOK

Clubs – S

Southampton continued...

1912-1919	Ernest Arnfield
1919-1924	Jimmy McIntyre
1925-1931	Arthur Chadwick
1931-1936	George Kay
1936-1937	George Gross
1937-1943	Tom Parker
1943-1946	Arthur Dominy
1946-1949	Bill Dodgin Snr
1949-1951	Sid Cann
1952-1955	George Roughton
1955-1973	Ted Bates
1973-1985	Lawrie McMenemy
1985-1991	Chris Nicholl
1991-1994	Ian Branfoot
1994-1995	Alan Ball
1995-1996	Dave Merrington
1996-1997	Graeme Souness
1997-	Dave Jones

Southampton League Record

1920-1921	Division Three
1921-1922	Division Three (South)
1922-1953	Division Two
1953-1958	Division Three (South)
1958-1960	Division Three
1960-1966	Division Two
1966-1974	Division One
1974-1978	Division Two
1978-1992	Division One
1992-	Premiership

O when the Saints go marching in
O when the Saints go marching in
I want to be in that number
When the Saints go marching in

In the 1998-99 season, the Southampton player whose replica team shirt sold in the greatest numbers was Matthew Le Tissier.

Clubs – S

Southend United

Southend United – nicknamed The Shrimpers – play their home matches in blue shirts with yellow trim, blue shorts with blue trim and blue socks.

The club was formed in 1906 and joined the Football League in 1920.

Since 1955, Southend United have played their home matches at Roots Hall in Victoria Avenue. Before that they were based at an old Roots Hall in Prittlewell (1906-1920), Kursaal (1920-1934) and Southend Stadium (1934 to 1955).

Southend United's only honour to date is the Fourth Division Championship, which they won in 1981. On their way to this title, they won 30 of their 46 matches and went 985 minutes without conceding a goal (both club records).

Southend United Managers

1906-1910	Bob Jack
1910-1911	George Molyneux
1911-1912	O M Howard
1912-1919	Joe Bradshaw
1919-1920	Ned Liddell
1920-1921	Tom Mather
1921-1934	Ted Birnie
1934-1940	David Jack
1945-1956	Harry Warren
1956-1960	Eddie Perry
1960	Frank Broome
1961-1965	Ted Fenton
1965-1967	Alvan Williams
1967-1969	Ernie Shepherd
1969-1970	Geoff Hudson
1970-1976	Arthur Rowley
1976-1983	Dave Smith
1983-1984	Peter Morris
1984-1986	Bobby Moore
1986-1987	Dave Webb
1987	Dick Bate
1987-1988	Paul Clark
1988-1992	Dave Webb
1992-1993	Colin Murphy
1993	Barry Fry
1993-1995	Peter Taylor
1995	Steve Thompson
1995-1997	Ronnie Whelan
1997-1999	Alvin Martin

THE CARLING ULTIMATE FOOTBALL FACT AND QUIZ BOOK

Clubs – S

Southend United continued...

Southend United League Record

1920-1921	Division Three
1921-1958	Division Three (South)
1958-1966	Division Three
1966-1972	Division Four
1972-1976	Division Three
1976-1978	Division Four
1978-1980	Division Three
1980-1981	Division Four
1981-1984	Division Three
1984-1987	Division Four
1987-1989	Division Three
1989-1990	Division Four
1990-1991	Division Three
1991-1992	Division Two
1992-1997	Division One
1997-1998	Division Two
1998-	Division Three

Oh Southend Pier oh Southend Pier
Oh Southend Pier is longer than yours
It's got some shops and a railway
Oh Southend Pier is longer than yours

(Tune: When The Saints Go Marching In)

In the 1998-99 season, the Southend United player whose replica team shirt sold in the greatest numbers was Scott Houghton.

Sporting Lisbon

Sporting Clube do Portugal were founded in 1906 and play at the José Alvalade Stadium in Lisbon, barely a mile from Benfica (q v). They are nicknamed The Lions.

The Sporting strip is green and white hooped shirts, black shorts and green and white socks.

Sporting Lisbon won the European Cup Winners' Cup in 1964, beating MTK Budapest in a replayed Final.

In the 1981-82 season, Sporting Lisbon did the League and Cup double under the management of an Englishman, Malcolm Allison.

In 1992, the club turned once again to England for inspiration, this time to former England manager Bobby Robson.

THE CARLING ULTIMATE FOOTBALL FACT AND QUIZ BOOK

Clubs – S

Stenhousemuir

At the end of the 1999 season Stenhousemuir finished second in the Scottish League Division Three and thereby won promotion for the first time in their 115-year history.

Stenhousemuir were founded in 1884 and are based at Ochilview Park in Gladstone Road. They are nicknamed The Warriors.

Stenhousemuir's home strip consists of maroon shirts, white shorts and black socks.

Stirling Albion

Stirling Albion are nicknamed The Binos. They were founded in 1945 to replace King's Park, which was disbanded after bombs dropped by the German Luftwaffe had caused irreparable damage their ground during World War Two.

Stirling Albion play at the Forthbank Stadium, Springkerse. Their home colours are red shirts with white sleeves, white shorts and red socks.

Stirling Albion joined the Scottish Football League in 1947.

In 1984, Stirling Albion set a record for the greatest victory in the Scottish FA Cup with a 20-0 defeat of the amateur club Selkirk.

Stockport County

Stockport County are generally known as County but are also sometimes nicknamed The Hatters, after one of the town's old industries – millinery.

Stockport County were founded in 1883 as Heaton Norris Rovers. They dropped the Rovers in 1888 and then adopted their present name in 1890.

Stockport County joined the Football League in 1900.

County's home strip consists of blue and white striped shirts, blue shorts and blue socks with white trim.

Since 1902, Stockport County have played their home matches at Edgeley Park in Hardcastle Road.

THE CARLING ULTIMATE FOOTBALL FACT AND QUIZ BOOK

Clubs – S

Stockport County continued...

They previously played at Heaton Norris Recreation Ground (1883-1884); Heaton Norris Wanderers Cricket Ground (1884-1885); Chorlton's Farm, Chorlton's Lane (1885-1886); Heaton Norris Cricket Ground (1886-1887); Wilkes' Field, Belmont Street (1887-1889); and Nursery Inn, Green Lane (1889-1902).

In 1997, Stockport County reached the semi-final of the League Cup – this is the best Cup run in their history.

Stockport County Managers

1894-1911	Fred Stewart
1911-1914	Harry Lewis
1914-1919	David Ashworth
1919-1924	Albert Williams
1924-1926	Fred Scotchbrook
1926-1931	Lincoln Hyde
1932-1933	Andrew Wilson
1934-1936	Fred Westgarth
1936-1938	Bob Kelly
1938-1939	George Hunt
1939-1949	Bob Marshall
1949-1952	Andy Beattie
1952-1956	Dick Duckworth
1956-1960	Billy Moir
1960-1963	Reg Flewin
1963-1965	Trevor Porteous
1965-1966	Eddie Quigley
1966-1969	Jimmy Meadows
1969-1970	Wally Galbraith
1970-1971	Matt Woods
1972-1974	Brian Doyle
1974-1975	Jimmy Meadows
1975-1976	Roy Chapman
1976-1977	Eddie Quigley
1977-1978	Alan Thompson
1978-1979	Mike Summerbee
1979-1982	Jimmy McGuigan
1982-1985	Eric Webster
1985	Colin Murphy
1985-1986	Les Chapman
1986	Jimmy Melia
1986-1987	Colin Murphy
1987-1989	Asa Hartford
1989-1995	Danny Bergara

THE CARLING ULTIMATE FOOTBALL FACT AND QUIZ BOOK

Clubs – S

Stockport County continued...

1995-1997	Dave Jones
1997-	Gary Megson

Stockport County League Record

1900-1904	Division Two
1904-1905	Failed to gain re-election; dropped out of League
1905-1921	Division Two
1921-1922	Division Three (North)
1922-1926	Division Two
1926-1937	Division Three (North)
1937-1938	Division Two
1938-1958	Division Three (North)
1958-1959	Division Three
1959-1967	Division Four
1967-1970	Division Three
1970-1991	Division Four
1991-1992	Division Three
1992-1997	Division Two
1997-	Division One

At the turn of the century
In the clear blue skies over Edgeley
Came a roar and a thunder like you never heard
On the pitch the boys in blue
They beat the Palace and West Ham too (thank you)
And their fans cried
And their fans died
And we buried them together on the Popular Side
We used our hands and we used our feet
And they ran like hell down Castle Street

(Tune: something between The Red Baron and Standing On The Bridge At Midnight)

In the 1998-99 season, the Stockport County player whose replica team shirt sold in the greatest numbers was Brett Angell.

THE CARLING ULTIMATE FOOTBALL FACT AND QUIZ BOOK

Clubs – S

Stoke City

Stoke City are one of the 12 founder members of the English Football League. They finished the first season of competition (1888-89) in last place.

Nicknamed The Potters, Stoke City now play their home matches at the Britannia Stadium. Between 1878 and 1998 they played at the Victoria Ground.

Stoke City were founded in about 1863; from 1875 their first permanent ground was Sweeting's Fields.

Stoke City's home strip is red and white striped shirts, white shorts and white socks.

In 1890, Stoke City dropped out of the League for a season, and then went bankrupt in 1907. The club later re-formed and rejoined the League in 1919.

Stoke City's first – and to date still their only – trophy in a major competition came in 1972, when they won the League Cup.

Stoke City Managers

1874-1883	Tom Slaney
1883-1884	Walter Cox
1884-1990	Harry Lockett
1890-1892	Joseph Bradshaw
1892-1895	Arthur Reeves
1895-1897	William Rowley
1897-1908	H D Austerberry
1908-1914	A J Barker
1914-1915	Peter Hodge
1915-1919	Joe Schofield
1919-1923	Arthur Shallcross
1923	Jock Rutherford
1923-1935	Tom Mather
1935-1952	Bob McGrory
1952-1960	Frank Taylor
1960-1977	Tony Waddington
1977-1978	George Eastham
1978	Alan A'Court
1978-1981	Alan Durban
1981-1983	Richie Barker
1984-1985	Bill Asprey
1985-1989	Mick Mills
1989-1991	Alan Ball
1991-1993	Lou Macari
1993-1994	Joe Jordan

Clubs – S

Stoke City continued...

1994-1997	Lou Macari
1997-1998	Chic Bates
1998	Chris Kamara
1998-	Brian Little

Stoke City League Record

1888-1890	Division One
1890-1891	Failed to be re-elected; went out of the League
1891-1907	Division One
1907-1908	Division Two
1908-1919	Resigned from Football League
1919-1922	Division Two
1922-1923	Division One
1923-1926	Division Two
1926-1927	Division Three (North)
1927-1933	Division Two
1933-1953	Division One
1953-1963	Division Two
1963-1977	Division One
1977-1979	Division Two
1979-1985	Division One
1985-1990	Division Two
1990-1992	Division Three
1992-1993	Division Two
1993-1998	Division One
1998-	Division Two

In the 1998-99 season, the Stoke City player whose replica team shirt sold in the greatest numbers was Dean Crowe.

Stranraer

Stranraer are nicknamed The Blues after the colour of their shirts; the rest of their home strip consists of white shorts and blue socks with red tops.

The third oldest club in Scotland, Stranraer were founded in 1870 but did not join the League until 1949. From then until 1998, they had never been higher than the Second Division. They spent the 1998-99 season in the First Division but finished bottom.

Stranraer play their home games at Stair Park in London Road.

Clubs – S

Sunderland

Sunderland are nicknamed The Rokermen after their old ground, Roker Park, which they finally vacated at the end of the 1997 season.

Sunderland now play their home games at The Stadium of Light. Their strip is red and white striped shirts, black shorts and red socks with white trim.

Sunderland were founded in 1879 as Sunderland and District Teachers' Association Football Club. They joined the Football League in 1890.

Sunderland were one of the first clubs to dominate English football, winning the League Championship three times in the 1890s – in 1892, 1893 and 1895.

Sunderland won a further three League titles in 1902, 1913 and 1936, making a total of six Championships to date.

Sunderland have won the FA Cup twice – in 1937 and then again, as a Second Division side, in 1973.

In the 1973 FA Cup Final at Wembley, they beat Leeds United 1-0 with a goal by Ian Porterfield and a heroic performance by Jim Montgomery, the Sunderland keeper who holds the record number of League appearances for the club – 537 between 1962 and 1977.

Sunderland Managers

1888-1896	Tom Watson
1896-1899	Bob Campbell
1899-1905	Alex Mackie
1905-1928	Bob Kyle
1928-1939	Johnny Cochrane
1939-1957	Bill Murray
1957-1964	Alan Brown
1964-1965	George Hardwick
1965-1968	Ian McColl
1968-1972	Alan brown
1972-1976	Bob Stokoe
1976-1978	Jimmy Adamson
1979-1981	Ken Knighton
1981-1984	Alan Durban
1984-1985	Len Ashurst
1985-1987	Lawrie McMenemy
1987-1991	Denis Smith
1992-1993	Malcolm Crosby
1993	Terry Butcher
1993-1995	Mick Buxton
1995-	Peter Reid

Clubs – S

Sunderland continued...

Sunderland League Record

1890-1958	Division One
1958-1964	Division Two
1964-1970	Division One
1970-1976	Division Two
1976-1977	Division One
1977-1980	Division Two
1980-1985	Division One
1985-1987	Division Two
1987-1988	Division Three
1988-1990	Division Two
1990-1991	Division One
1991-1992	Division Two
1992-1996	Division One
1996-1997	Premiership
1997-1999	Division One

Oh I could fly without wings
On the back of Reidy's kings
At three o'clock I'm happy as can be
Coz the good times they are here
And the Premiership is near
So watch out world as all of Roker sings

CHORUS
Cheer up Peter Reid
O what can it mean
To be a Sunderland supporter
To be top of the League

We once thought of you
As a Scouser dressed in blue
Now you're red and white through and through
We had all dreamt of the day
When a saviour'd come our way
And now we know our dreams are coming true...

CHORUS

(Tune: Daydream Believer by Neil Diamond – originally a hit for The Monkees in 1967 and then – with the above words – for the Sunderland-supporting Simply Red and White in 1996)

In the 1998-99 season, the Sunderland player whose replica team shirt sold in the greatest numbers was Kevin Phillips.

THE CARLING ULTIMATE FOOTBALL FACT AND QUIZ BOOK

Clubs – S

Swansea City

Founded in 1912, this club was originally known as Swansea Town but became City in February 1970.

Swansea City play their home games at the Vetch Field. The team is nicknamed The Swans and their supporters – indeed, people from the city in general – are known as Swansea Jacks.

Swansea joined the Football League in 1920 and have since spent most of their time in the lower divisions. Their most glorious season was 1981-82, when they finished sixth in the old First Division, but they were relegated the following year.

Swansea have reached the semi-finals of the FA Cup twice – in 1926 and 1964.

Swansea have won the Welsh Cup nine times and through that have qualified eight times for the European Cup Winners' Cup.

Swansea City play in white shirts with maroon and black facing, white shorts with maroon and black trim and maroon socks with a white band.

Swansea City Managers

1912-1914	Walter Whittaker
1914-1915	William Bartlett
1919-1926	Joe Bradshaw
1927-1931	Jimmy Thomson
1934-1939	Neil Harris
1939-1947	Haydn Green
1947-1955	Bill McCandless
1955-1958	Ron Burgess
1958-1965	Trevor Morris
1965-1966	Glyn Davies
1967-1969	Billy Lucas
1969-1972	Roy Bentley
1972-1975	Harry Gregg
1975-1977	Harry Griffiths
1978-1984	John Toshack
1984	Colin Appleton
1984-1985	John Bond
1985-1986	Tommy Hutchison
1986-1989	Terry Yorath
1989-1990	Ian Evans
1990-1991	Terry Yorath
1991-1995	Frank Burrows
1996	Kevin Cullis
1996-1997	Jan Molby

Clubs – S

Swansea City continued...

1997	Micky Adams
1997-1998	Alan Cork
1998-	John Hollins

Swansea City League Record

1920-1921	Division Three
1921-1925	Division Three (South)
1925-1947	Division Two
1947-1949	Division Three (South)
1949-1965	Division Two
1965-1967	Division Three
1967-1970	Division Four
1970-1973	Division Three
1973-1978	Division Four
1978-1979	Division Three
1979-1981	Division Two
1981-1983	Division One
1983-1984	Division Two
1984-1986	Division Three
1986-1988	Division Four
1988-1992	Division Three
1992-1996	Division Two
1996-	Division Three

Swansea City fans sometimes sing Bread of Heaven with the proper words! They may also sing this:

Swansea O Swansea
O City said I
I'll stand there on the North Bank
Until the day I die
Take me to the Vetch Field
Way down by the sea
Where I will follow Swansea
Swansea City

In the 1998-99 season, the Swansea City player whose replica team shirt sold in the greatest numbers was Roger Freestone.

Clubs – S

Swindon Town

Swindon Town are nicknamed The Robins because of their all-red home strip.

The club was founded as The Spartans in 1881 but changed to its present name when it amalgamated with St Mark's Young Men's Friendly Society in 1883.

From 1881 to 1896 Swindon Town played at The Croft but then moved to The County Ground, which has been their home ever since.

Swindon Town reached the semi-finals of the FA Cup twice – in 1910 and 1912 – before joining the Football League in 1920. Their first ever League match was a 9-1 home win over Luton Town.

Swindon Town's greatest moment came in 1969, when they won the League Cup, beating Arsenal 3-1 in the Final. They also won promotion that season.

At the time of their Wembley victory, Swindon were in the Third Division, members of which were not allowed to take the place in the Fairs Cup that was normally reserved for the English League Cup winners. So instead they entered the new Anglo-Italian Cup, which they won in both the next two seasons.

In 1990, Swindon Town won promotion through the play-offs to the top flight of English football but their place was taken from them because of financial irregularities under the management of Lou Macari. In addition to being denied promotion, they were at first demoted by a division as well, but on appeal were allowed to remain in Division Two.

Swindon Town finally made it to the Premiership in 1993, but lasted there only for one season.

Swindon Town Managers

1902-1933	Sam Allen
1933-1939	Ted Vizard
1939-1941	Neil Harris
1945-1953	Louis page
1953-1955	Maurice Lindley
1956-1965	Bert Head
1965-1969	Danny Williams
1969-1971	Fred Ford
1971-1972	Dave Mackay
1972-1974	Les Allen
1974-1978	Danny Williams
1978-1980	Bobby Smith
1980-1983	John Trollope
1983-1984	Ken Beamish
1984-1989	Lou Macari
1989-1991	Osvaldo Ardiles
1991-1993	Glenn Hoddle

Clubs – S

Swindon Town continued...

1993-1994	John Gorman
1994-1998	Steve McMahon

Swindon Town League Record

1920-1921	Division Three
1921-1958	Division Three (South)
1958-1963	Division Three
1963-1965	Division Two
1965-1969	Division Three
1969-1974	Division Two
1974-1982	Division Three
1982-1986	Division Four
1986-1987	Division Three
1987-1992	Division Two
1992-1993	Division One
1993-1994	Premiership
1994-1995	Division One
1995-1996	Division Two
1996-	Division One

In the 1998-99 season, the Swindon Town player whose replica team shirt sold in the greatest numbers was Mark Walters.

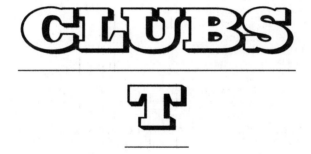

CLUBS

T

Clubs – T

Torquay United

Nicknamed The Gulls, Torquay United play their home games at Plainmoor. Their strip is yellow and navy blue striped shirts, navy blue shorts and yellow socks.

The club was founded in 1898 by former students of Torquay and Torbay colleges. From 1910 they played under the name Torquay Town but became United in 1921.

Torquay have never won a divisional championship and have never gone beyond the Fourth Round of the FA Cup or the Third Round of the League Cup. They have, however, twice won promotion and in 1989 were runners-up in the Sherpa Van Trophy.

In 1987, Torquay United were languishing near the bottom of the Fourth Division and on the last day of the season found themselves needing a point to avoid becoming the first team to suffer automatic relegation from the Football League. They were 2-1 down to Crewe Alexandra and looking beaten when a police dog named Bryn ran onto the pitch and bit Gulls' scorer, Jim McNichol, on the leg, causing a gash that required 17 stitches. It was in time added on for treatment to this injury that Torquay equalised through Paul Dobson and sent Lincoln City down to the GM Vauxhall Conference. After the match, Torquay chairman Lew Pope bought Bryn a steak.

Torquay United Managers

1927-1929	Percy Mackrill
1929	A H Hoskins
1929-1932	Frank Womack
1932-1938	Frank Brown
1938-1940	Alf Steward
1946-1946	Billy Butler
1946-1947	Jack Butler
1947-1950	John McNeil
1950	Bob John
1950-1951	Alex Massie
1951-1965	Eric Webber
1965-1968	Frank O'Farrell
1969-1971	Alan Brown
1971-1973	Jack Edwards
1973-1976	Malcolm Musgrove
1977-1981	Mike Green
1981-1982	Frank O'Farrell

THE CARLING ULTIMATE FOOTBALL FACT AND QUIZ BOOK

Clubs – T

Torquay United continued...

1982-1984	Bruce Rioch
1984-1985	Dave Webb
1985	John Sims
1985-1987	Stuart Morgan
1987-1989	Cyril Knowles
1989-1991	Dave Smith
1991-1992	John Impey
1992	Ivan Golac
1992-1993	Paul Compton
1993-1995	Don O'Riordan
1995-1996	Eddie May
1996-1998	Kevin Hodges
1998-	Wes Saunders

Torquay United League Record

1927-1958	Division Three (South)
1958-1960	Division Four
1960-1962	Division Three
1962-1966	Division Four
1966-1972	Division Three
1972-1991	Division Four
1991-	Division Three

In the 1998-99 season, the Torquay United player whose replica team shirt sold in the greatest numbers was Scott Partridge.

Tottenham Hotspur

The original Hotspur FC was founded in 1882 by cricketing old boys of St John's Presbyterian School and Tottenham Grammar. The name was taken from that of Harry Hotspur, the most famous member of the aristocratic Percy family who own much land in this area of North London. The word Tottenham was added in 1885 so that people might have a better idea of where to find them.

The Spurs first played on Tottenham Marshes and then at Northumberland Park. They moved to their present home, White Hart Lane, in 1898.

Tottenham Hotspur play in white shirts, navy blue shorts and navy blue socks with white trim.

In 1901, Tottenham Hotspur became the only non-League club of the 20th century to win the FA Cup. They have now won the trophy eight times altogether – in 1901, 1921, 1961, 1962, 1967, 1981, 1981 and 1991.

THE CARLING ULTIMATE FOOTBALL FACT AND QUIZ BOOK

Clubs – T

Tottenham Hotspur continued...

Tottenham Hotspur joined the Second Division of the Football League in 1908 and won promotion in their first season.

Tottenham Hotspur won their first League Championship in 1951. In 1961, they did the League and Cup double – a feat which had only been achieved twice before, by Preston North End and Aston Villa (q q v) in the previous century, and which many people thought was no longer possible because of the number of games needed to perform it.

Tottenham Hotspur have also won the League Cup twice – in 1971 and 1973.

In 1963, Tottenham Hotspur became the first British team to win a European trophy when they beat Atletico Madrid 5-1 in the Final of the Cup Winners' Cup.

Tottenham Hotspur won the UEFA Cup in 1972.

Spurs have always had a reputation as a clean, footballing side. When Frank Saul was sent off against Burnley on December 4, 1965, he became the first Tottenham Hotspur player to be ordered from the field of play since 1928.

Tottenham Hotspur Managers

1898-1899	Frank Brettell
1899-1906	John Cameron
1907-1908	Fred Kirkham
1912-1927	Peter McWilliam
1927-1929	Billy Minter
1930-1935	Percy Smith
1935-1938	Jack Tresadern
1938-1942	Peter McWilliam
1942-1946	Arthur Turner
1946-1949	Joe Hulme
1949-1955	Arthur Rowe
1955-1958	Jimmy Anderson
1958-1974	Bill Nicholson
1974-1976	Terry Neill
1976-1984	Keith Burkinshaw
1984-1986	Peter Shreeves
1986-1987	David Pleat
1987-1991	Terry Venables
1991-1992	Peter Shreeves
1993-1994	Osvaldo Ardiles
1994-1997	Gerry Francis
1997-1998	Christian Gross
1998-	George Graham

Clubs – T

Tottenham Hotspur continued...

Tottenham Hotspur League Record

1908-1909	Division Two
1909-1915	Division One
1919-1920	Division Two
1920-1928	Division One
1928-1933	Division Two
1933-1935	Division One
1935-1950	Division Two
1950-1977	Division One
1977-1978	Division Two
1978-1992	Division One
1992-	Premiership

Glory glory Tottenham Hotspur
Glory glory Tottenham Hotspur
Glory glory Tottenham Hotspur
And the Spurs go marching on on on

(Tune: Glory Glory Hallelujah)

In the 1998-99 season, the Tottenham Hotspur player whose replica team shirt sold in the greatest numbers was David Ginola.

Tranmere Rovers

A Merseyside but not a Liverpool club, Tranmere Rovers were founded in 1884 and joined the Football League in 1921. They were originally known as Belmont but adopted their present name in 1885.

Tranmere Rovers play in white shirts, blue shorts and white socks. Since 1912, they have played at Prenton Park in Prenton Road West, Birkenhead. Before then, they played on Steeles Field (1884-1887) and Ravenshaws Field/Old Prenton Park (1887-1912).

Tranmere Rovers were Champions of Division Three (North) in 1938 – this is their only League honour to date.

Tranmere Rovers won the Welsh Cup in 1935 and the Leyland Daf Cup in 1990. Although they have never gone beyond the Fifth Round of the FA Cup, they reached the League Cup semi-final in 1994, when they lost to Aston Villa on penalties.

Clubs – T

Tranmere Rovers continued...

Tranmere Rovers Managers
1912-1935	Bert Cooke
1935-1936	Jackie Carr
1936-1939	Jim Knowles
1939-1945	Bill Ridding
1946-1955	Ernie Blackburn
1955-1957	Noel Kelly
1957-1960	Peter Farrell
1961	Walter Galbraith
1961-1969	Dave Russell
1969-1972	Jackie Wright
1972-1975	Ron Yeats
1975-1980	John King
1980-1985	Bryan Hamilton
1985-1987	Frank Worthington
1987	Ronnie Moore
1987-1996	John King
1996-	John Aldridge

Tranmere Rovers League Record
1921-1938	Division Three (North)
1938-1939	Division Two
1946-1958	Division Three (North)
1958-1961	Division Three
1961-1967	Division Four
1967-1975	Division Three
1975-1976	Division Four
1976-1979	Division Three
1979-1989	Division Four
1989-1991	Division Three
1991-1992	Division Two
1992-	Division One

Don't be mistaken
Don't be misled
We're not Scousers
We're from Birkenhead

In the 1998-99 season, the Tranmere Rovers player whose replica team shirt sold in the greatest numbers was Kenny Irons.

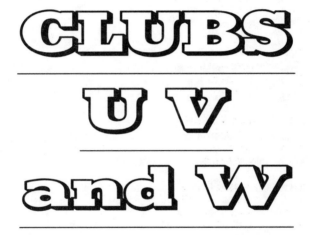

THE CARLING ULTIMATE FOOTBALL FACT AND QUIZ BOOK

Clubs – W

Walsall

Walsall are nicknamed The Saddlers. They play their home games at the Bescot Stadium in Bescot Crescent (until 1990, their home ground was Fellows Park).

For home games, Walsall wear red shirts with black trim, red shorts with black trim and red socks with black turnover.

Walsall were founded in 1878 when Walsall Swifts merged with Walsall Town. The club went under the name Walsall Town Swifts until 1895 when it shortened itself to its present moniker.

Walsall joined the Football League in 1892 but dropped out again in 1895, only to return a year later. They went out again in 1901 and this time did not return until the Third Division was started in 1921.

Walsall's only honour to date is the Fourth Division Championship, which they won in 1960. The club gained promotion in 1999, finishing second to Fulham in the Second Division.

Walsall have never progressed beyond the Fifth Round of the FA Cup, but in 1933 they pulled off one of the biggest and most celebrated shocks in the history of the competition when they knocked Arsenal out in the Third Round. Walsall's first goal against Arsenal was scored after an hour's play by centre forward Gilbert Alsop, who headed home from a corner. Five minutes later, Bill Sheppard scored the second from the penalty spot. Black, the defender who committed the foul in the area, was immediately transfer-listed and never played for Arsenal again.

In 1984 – as a Third Division side – Walsall reached the League Cup semi-final, losing 4-2 over two legs to the eventual winners, Liverpool.

Walsall Managers
1888-1891	H Smallwood
1891-1893	A G Burton
1893-1895	J H Robinson
1895-1896	C H Ailso
1896-1897	A E Parsloe
1897-1898	L Ford
1898-1899	G Hughes
1899-1901	L Ford
1908-1913	J E Shutt
1914-1920	Haydn price
1920-1926	Joe Burchell

Clubs – W

Walsall continued...

1926-1927	David Ashworth
1927-1928	Jack Torrance
1928-1929	James Kerr
1929-1930	Sid Scholey
1930-1932	Peter O'Rourke
1932-1934	Bill Slade
1934-1937	Andy Wilson
1937-1944	Tommy Lowes
1944-1951	Harry Hibbs
1951	Tony McPhee
1952-1953	Brough Fletcher
1953-1955	Major Frank Buckley
1955-1957	John Love
1957-1964	Billy Moore
1964	Alf Wood
1964-1968	Reg Shaw
1968	Dick Graham
1968-1969	Ron Lewin
1969-1972	Billy Moore
1972-1973	John Smith
1973-1977	Doug Fraser
1977-1978	Dave Mackay
1978	Alan Ashman
1979	Frank Sibley
1979-1986	Alan Buckley
1986-1988	Tommy Coakley
1989-1990	John Barnwell
1990-1994	Kenny Hibbitt
1994-1997	Chris Nicholl
1997-1998	Jan Sorensen
1998-	Ray Graydon

Walsall League Record

1892-1895	Division Two
1895-1896	Failed to be re-elected; dropped out of League
1896-1901	Division Two
1901-1921	Failed to be re-elected; dropped out of League
1921-1927	Division Three (North)
1927-1931	Division Three (South)
1931-1936	Division Three (North)
1936-1958	Division Three (South)
1958-1960	Division Four
1960-1961	Division Three

Clubs – W

Walsall continued...

1961-1963	Division Two
1963-1979	Division Three
1979-1980	Division Four
1980-1988	Division Three
1988-1989	Division Two
1989-1990	Division Three
1990-1992	Division Four
1992-1995	Division Three
1995-1999	Division Two

In the 1998-99 season, the Walsall player whose replica team shirt sold in the greatest numbers was Andy Rammell.

Watford

Watford play in yellow shirts with red sleeves and black collar and cuffs, red shorts and red socks with yellow tops and two black hoops. They are thus nicknamed The Hornets.

The club was founded in 1881 as Watford Rovers. In 1893, its name was changed to West Herts. It became Watford in 1898, when the club assimilated Watford St Mary's FC.

Watford joined the Football League in 1920. At that time they still played their home games at Cassio Road, but since 1922 they have been settled in the Vicarage Road Stadium.

Watford were a small-time club with few prospects until the late 1970s, when Elton John decided to sink some of the millions he'd earned as a pop singer into the club he'd supported since childhood.

From then on, Watford quickly raised both its profile and its League position. The club became famous for crowd-pulling marketing initiatives such as the Family Enclosure and the 1983 Tour of China. In 1982, Watford reached the First Division, where they remained until 1988.

In 1984 Watford reached the FA Cup Final, losing 2-0 to Everton at Wembley.

Watford Managers

1903-1910	John Goodall
1910-1926	Harry Kent
1926-1929	Fred Pagnam
1929-1937	Neil McBain
1938-1947	Bill Findlay
1947-1948	Jack Bray
1948-1950	Eddie Hapgood

THE CARLING ULTIMATE FOOTBALL FACT AND QUIZ BOOK

Facts
Clubs – W

Watford continued...

1950-1951	Ron Gray
1951-1952	Haydn Green
1952-1955	Len Goulden
1955-1956	Johnny Paton
1956-1959	Neil McBain
1959-1963	Ron Burgess
1963-1964	Bill McGarry
1964-1971	Ken Furphy
1971-1973	George Kirby
1973-1977	Mike Keen
1977-1987	Graham Taylor
1987-1988	Dave Bassett
1988-1990	Steve Harrison
1990	Colin Lee
1990-1993	Steve Perryman
1993-1996	Glenn Roeder
1996-1997	Kenny Jackett
1997-	Graham Taylor

Watford League Record

1920-1921	Division Two
1921-1958	Division Three (South)
1958-1960	Division Four
1960-1969	Division Three
1969-1972	Division Two
1972-1975	Division Three
1975-1978	Division Four
1978-1979	Division Three
1979-1982	Division Two
1982-1988	Division One
1988-1992	Division Two
1992-1996	Division One
1996-1998	Division Two
1998-	Division One

In London's fair city
Where the girls are so pretty
I first set my eyes on sweet Molly
Malone
As she wheeled her wheelbarrow
From Watford to Harrow

Singing...
(Clap clap
Clap clap clap
Clap clap clap clap)
... Watford

In the 1998-99 season, the Watford player whose replica team shirt sold in the greatest numbers was Peter Kennedy.

THE CARLING ULTIMATE FOOTBALL FACT AND QUIZ BOOK

Clubs – W

West Bromwich Albion

West Bromwich Albion are one of the 12 founder members of the English Football League. In the inaugural season of competition – 1888-89 – they finished in sixth position.

At the time the Football League began, West Bromwich Albion were the holders of the FA Cup – they had won the trophy for the first time in 1888.

West Bromwich Albion were the first club ever to win the FA Cup with an all-English team.

To date, West Bromwich Albion have won the FA Cup five times – in 1888, 1892, 1931, 1954 and 1968.

West Bromwich Albion won their only League Championship to date in 1920. They were runners-up in 1925 and 1954.

In their Championship-winning season, West Bromwich Albion became the first English League team to score more than 100 goals in a season – 104, to be exact.

West Bromwich Albion won the League Cup in 1966 and were runners-up in the same competition in 1967 and 1970.

West Bromwich Albion play in navy blue and white striped shirts, white shorts and white socks. They are nicknamed The Baggies, The Throstles or The Albion.

The club was founded in 1879 by employees of Salter's Spring Works and was originally known as West Bromwich Strollers. They adopted their present name in 1881.

From 1879 to 1880, West Bromwich Albion played their home games at Dartmouth Park. They spent 1881 at Bunns Field in Walsall Street, and then moved to the Four Acres Ground of Dartmouth Cricket Club from 1882 to 1885. They then spent fifteen years at Stoney Lane before moving in 1900 to their present ground, The Hawthorns.

West Bromwich Albion have spent all but one of their years in the Football League in either the top or the second division. The one slip came in 1991-92, which they spent in Division Three.

West Bromwich Albion Managers

1890-1892	Louis Ford
1892-1894	Henry Jackson
1894-1895	Edward Stephenson
1895-1896	Clement Keys
1896-1902	Frank Heaven
1902-1948	Fred Everiss
1948-1952	Jack Smith
1952	Jesse Carver
1953-1959	Vic Buckingham
1959-1961	Gordon Clark
1961-1963	Archie Macaulay
1963-1967	Jimmy Hagan

Facts
Clubs – W

West Bromwich Albion continued...

1967-1971	Alan Ashman
1971-1975	Don Howe
1975-1977	Johnny Giles
1977	Ronnie Allen
1978-1981	Ron Atkinson
1981-1982	Ronnie Allen
1982-1984	Ron Wylie
1984-1985	Johnny Giles
1986-1987	Ron Saunders
1987-1988	Ron Atkinson
1988-1991	Brian Talbot
1991-1992	Bobby Gould
1992-1993	Osvaldo Ardiles
1993-1994	Keith Burkinshaw
1994-1997	Alan Buckley
1997	Ray Harford
1997-	Denis Smith

West Bromwich Albion League Record

1888-1901	Division One
1901-1902	Division Two
1902-1904	Division One
1904-1911	Division Two
1911-1927	Division One
1927-1931	Division Two
1931-1938	Division One
1938-1949	Division Two
1949-1973	Division One
1973-1976	Division Two
1976-1986	Division One
1986-1991	Division Two
1991-1992	Division Three
1992-1993	Division Two
1993-	Division One

If you like kick and rush
Played by fat gorillas
Don't waste your time at the Albion
Shove off down the Villa

(Tune: One Man Went To Mow)

In the 1998-99 season, the West Bromwich Albion player whose replica team shirt sold in the greatest numbers was Lee Hughes

THE CARLING ULTIMATE FOOTBALL FACT AND QUIZ BOOK

Facts
Clubs – W

West Ham United

West Ham United are nicknamed The Hammers. During matches their supporters encourage them with cries of 'C'mon you Irons' . This is a reference to the club's original name – Thames Ironworks FC.

Thames Ironworks were formed in 1895 by workers at a shipyard of that name in the East End of London. The idea of their works team is thought to have been that of Arnold F Hills, the factory's owner.

Thames Ironworks played their home games at the Memorial Recreation Ground in Canning Town. In 1900, however, they were disbanded and replaced by a professional limited company which took the name of West Ham United.

In 1904, the club moved from Canning Town to their current location – The Boleyn Ground in Green Street, Upton Park, London E13.

West Ham United play their home games in claret shirts with blue sleeves, white shorts and claret and blue hooped socks.

West Ham United were elected to the Football League in 1919; since then they have never been out of the top two divisions.

West Ham United took part in the first Wembley FA Cup Final, losing 2-0 to Bolton Wanderers in 1923.

West Ham United's first taste of glory came in 1964, when they won the FA Cup, beating Preston North End 3-2 in the Final.

The following year, West Ham United went on to win the European Cup Winners' Cup, beating Munich 1860 2-0 in the Final at Wembley.

To date, West Ham United have won the FA Cup three times – in 1964, 1975 and 1980.

In 1976, West Ham United were runners-up in the European Cup Winners' Cup, losing 4-2 to Anderlecht in the Final which was held in Brussels.

West Ham United were a Second Division club when they beat hot favourites Arsenal 1-0 in the 1980 FA Cup Final.

Clubs – W

West Ham United continued...

West Ham United Managers
1902-1932	Syd King
1932-1950	Charlie Paynter
1950-1961	Ted Fenton
1961-1974	Ron Greenwood
1974-1989	John Lyall
1989-1990	Lou Macari
1990-1994	Billy Bonds
1994-	Harry Redknapp

West Ham United League Record
1919-1923	Division Two
1923-1932	Division One
1932-1958	Division Two
1958-1978	Division One
1978-1981	Division Two
1981-1989	Division One
1989-1991	Division Two
1991-1993	Division One
1993-	Premiership

I'm forever blowing bubbles
Pretty bubbles in the air
They fly so high
Nearly reach the sky
Then like my dreams
They fade and die
Fortune's always hiding
I've looked everywhere
I'm forever blowing bubbles
Pretty bubbles in the air

In the 1998-99 season, the West Ham United player whose replica team shirt sold in the greatest numbers was Ian Wright.

Clubs – W

Wigan Athletic

Wigan Athletic play their home games in blue shirts with white side panels, blue shorts and blue socks. They are nicknamed Latics.

Wigan Athletic were founded in 1932 after the collapse of Wigan Borough FC and their resignation from the Football League in the previous year. Before Wigan Borough there had been Wigan Town, Wigan United and Wigan County – none survived.

Almost as soon as they were inaugurated, Wigan Athletic purchased their present ground at Springfield Park in order to add weight to their application to join the Football League. Unfortunately, the Football league were not impressed and the club had to wait until the demise of Southport in 1978 before gaining election to the Fourth Division.

Wigan Athletic were the last English football club to be elected to the League before the advent of the new automatic promotion and relegation between the lowest division and the Conference.

In 1982, Wigan were promoted from the Fourth Division. The manager who led them there, Larry Lloyd, was sacked the folllowing season.

In 1985, Wigan Athletic won the Freight Rover Trophy.

In 1993, Wigan Athletic were relegated for the first time in their history.

Wigan Athletic won the Third Division Championship in 1997.

Wigan Athletic Managers
1932-1937	Charlie Spencer
1946-1947	Jimmy Milne
1949-1952	Bob Pryde
1952-1954	Ted Goodier
1954-1955	Walter crook
1955-1956	Ron Suart
1956	Billy Cooke
1957	Sam Barkas
1957-1958	Trevor Hitchen
1958-1959	Malcolm Barrass
1959	Jimmy Shirley
1959-1960	Pat Murphy
1960	Allenby Chilton
1961-1963	Johnny Ball
1963-1966	Allan Brown
1966-1967	Alf Craig
1967-1968	Harry Leyland
1968	Alan Saunders
1968-1970	Ian McNeill

THE CARLING ULTIMATE FOOTBALL FACT AND QUIZ BOOK

Wigan Athletic continued...

1970-1972	Gordon Milne
1972-1974	Les Rigby
1974-1976	Brian Tiler
1976-1981	Ian McNeill
1981-1983	Larry Lloyd
1983-1985	Harry McNally
1985-1986	Bryan Hamilton
1986-1989	Ray Mathias
1989-1993	Bryan Hamilton
1993	Dave Philpotts
1993-1994	Kenny Swain
1994-1995	Graham Barrow
1995-1998	John Deehan
1998-	Ray Mathias

In the 1998-99 season, the Wigan Athletic player whose replica team shirt sold in the greatest numbers was Roy Carroll.

Wimbledon

Wimbledon – nicknamed The Dons – play in an all navy blue strip with yellow trim.

The club was founded in 1889 by old boys of the Central School in southwest London and was thus originally known as Wimbledon Old Centrals.

Wimbledon first attracted widespread attention in 1975 when, though still a non-League side, they beat one First Division side, Burnley, in the Third Round of the FA Cup and held another, Leeds United, to a replay in the Fourth.

Wimbledon were elected to the Fourth Division in 1977, when they took the place of Workington Town.

Wimbledon proceeded to rise through the divisions, reaching the old First Division in 1986.

In 1988, Wimbledon won the FA Cup, beating Liverpool 1-0 in the Final at Wembley.

Wimbledon have been forced to move from their quaint but inadequate Plough Lane ground to a stadium-share with Crystal Palace at Selhurst Park on the other side of London. Although this has distanced the club from its core supporters, and its home attendances are the smallest in the Premiership, the team has had little difficulty in maintaining the pace at the highest level.

Clubs – W

Wimbledon continued...

Wimbledon Managers

1955-1971	Les Henley
1971-1973	Mike Everitt
1973-1974	Dick Graham
1974-1978	Allen Batsford
1978-1981	Dario Gradi
1981-1987	Dave Bassett
1987-1990	Bobby Gould
1990-1991	Ray Harford
1991	Peter Withe
1992-	Joe Kinnear

Wimbledon League Record

1977-1979	Division Four
1979-1980	Division Three
1980-1981	Division Four
1981-1982	Division Three
1982-1983	Division Four
1983-1984	Division Three
1984-1986	Division Two
1986-1992	Division One
1992-	Premiership

In the 1998-99 season, the Wimbledon player whose replica team shirt sold in the greatest numbers was Neil Sullivan.

Wolverhampton Wanderers

Wolverhampton Wanderers – nicknamed The Wolves – play their home games at Molineux and wear old gold shirts, black shorts and old gold socks.

Wolves sprang originally in 1879 from two local teams called St Luke's and Wanderers. The club turned professional in 1888 and in the same year became founder members of the Football League.

In that first season of League football (1888-89), Wolverhampton Wanderers finished third of 12 clubs, behind Preston North End and Aston Villa.

Clubs – W

Wolverhampton Wanderers continued...

During the late 1950s, Wolves dominated English football with their effective if not universally admired 'kick and rush' style. The club won the League Championship three times – in 1954, 1958 and 1959.

In 1954, Wolves beat Moscow Spartak and Honved in exhibition matches at Molineux. The latter victory was particularly impressive because the opposition contained six of the Hungarian internationals who had beaten the full English side 6-3 at Wembley in November 1953.

Wolves' title-winning manager, Stan Cullis, boasted that his team were 'Champions of the World'. This contentious statement is often seen as the seed from which grew the European Cup competition, which was inaugurated two years later in 1956.

Wolverhampton Wanderers won their first FA Cup in 1893, when they beat Everton 1-0 in the Final. Since then, they have won the Cup a further three times – in 1908, 1949 and 1960.

Wolves have won the League Cup twice – in 1974 and 1980.

Wolverhampton Wanderers have also won the Texaco Cup (1971) and the Sherpa Van Trophy (1988).

Wolverhampton Wanderers Managers

1877-1885	George Worrall
1885-1922	John Addenbrooke
1922-1924	George Jobey
1924-1926	Albert Hoskins
1926-1927	Fred Scotchbrook
1927-1944	Major Frank Buckley
1944-1948	Ted Vizard
1948-1964	Stan Cullis
1964-1965	Andy Beattie
1966-1968	Ronnie Allen
1968-1976	Bill McGarry
1976-1978	Sammy Chung
1978-1981	John Barnwell
1982	Ian Greaves
1982-1984	Graham Hawkins
1984-1985	Tommy Docherty
1985	Bill McGarry
1985-1986	Sammy Chapman
1986	Brian Little
1986-1994	Graham Turner
1994-1995	Graham Taylor
1995-1998	Mark McGhee
1998-	??

Clubs – W

Wolverhampton Wanderers continued...

I was born under a Wanderers scarf
I was born under a Wanderers scarf
Do you know where hell is?
Hell is at West Brom
Heaven is at Molineux
And that's where we come from
I was born under a Wanderers scarf
A Wanderers, Wanderers scarf

(Tune: Wand'rin' Star from Paint Your Wagon)

In the 1998-99 season, the Wolverhampton Wanderers player whose replica team shirt sold in the greatest numbers was Steve Bull.

Wrexham

Wrexham play in red shirts, white shorts and red socks and are nicknamed The Robins.

Founded in 1873, Wrexham is the oldest surviving football club in Wales.

Wrexham joined the Football League in 1921.

Wrexham won the Third Division Championship in 1978 – this is their sole English honour to date. They have, however, won the Welsh Cup a record 23 times.

Wrexham Managers

1912-1925	Ted Robinson
1925-1929	Charlie Hewitt
1929-1931	Jack Baynes
1932-1936	Ernest Blackburn
1937-1938	Jimmy Logan
1938	Arthur Cowell
1938-1940	Tom Morgan
1940-1949	Tom Williams
1949-1950	Les McDowall
1951-1954	Peter Jackson
1954-1957	Cliff Lloyd
1957-1959	John Love
1960-1961	Billy Morris
1961-1965	Ken Barnes
1965	Billy Morris

Clubs – W

Wrexham continued...

1966-1967	Jack Rowley
1967-1968	Alvan Williams
1968-1977	John Neal
1977-1981	Arfon Griffiths
1981-1982	Mel Sutton
1982-1985	Bobby Roberts
1985-1989	Dixie McNeil
1989-	Brian Flynn

Wrexham League Record

1921-1958	Division Three (North)
1958-1960	Division Three
1960-1962	Division Four
1962-1964	Division Three
1964-1970	Division Four
1970-1978	Division Three
1978-1982	Division Two
1982-1983	Division Three
1983-1992	Division Four
1992-1993	Division Three
1993-	Division Two

Here they come our mighty champions
Raise your voices to the anthem
Marching like a mighty army
Wrexham is the name

See the reds who fight together
Speak their names with pride for ever
Marching like a mighty army
Wrexham is the name

Fearless in devotion
Rising to promotion
To the ranks of mighty heroes
Fighting foes in every land
History only tells a story

We are here to see your glory
Stand aside the reds are coming
Wrexham is the name

We have made the mighty humble
We have made the mountains tumble
Falling to our mighty army
Wrexham is the name

Down the wings the reds are roaring
To the greatest goal we're soaring
Destiny we hear you calling
Wrexham is the name

(Tune: Men of Harlech)

In the 1998-99 season, the Wrexham player whose replica team shirt sold in the greatest numbers was Ian Rush.

THE CARLING ULTIMATE FOOTBALL FACT AND QUIZ BOOK

Clubs – W

Wycombe Wanderers

Wycombe Wanderers are nicknamed The Chairboys after the local furniture manufacturing industry.

Wycombe Wanderers play their home games in light blue and dark blue quartered shirts, light blue shorts and light blue socks.

Wycombe Wanderers were founded in 1884 . They played first on The Rye, then spent two years at Spring Park before their first spell at Loakes Park began in 1895. They moved away to Daws Hill Park in 1899 but came back to Loakes Park in 1901 and remained there until 1990.

In 1990, Wycombe Wanderers moved to Adams Park, a new purpose-built stadium in Hillbottom Road, Sands.

Wycombe Wanderers won the GM Vauxhall Conference and joined the Football League in 1993. They won promotion through the play-offs in their first season in Division Three.

Wycombe Wanderers Managers

1951-1952	James McCormack
1952-1961	Sid Cann
1961-1962	Graham Adams
1962-1964	Don Welsh
1964-1968	Barry Darvill
1969-1976	Brian Lee
1976-1977	Ted Powell
1977-1978	John Reardon
1978-1980	Andy Williams
1980-1984	Mike Keen
1984-1986	Paul Bence
1986-1987	Alan Gane
1987-1988	Peter Suddaby
1988-1990	Jim Kelman
1990-1995	Martin O'Neill
1995-1996	Alan Smith
1996-1998	John Gregory
1998-1999	Neil Smillie
1999-	Lawrie Sanchez

Wycombe Wanderers League Record

1993-1994	Division Three
1994-	Division Two

In the 1998-99 season, the Wycombe Wanderers player whose replica team shirt sold in the greatest numbers was Steve Brown.

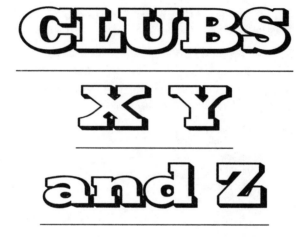

Clubs – Y

York City

York City are nicknamed The Minstermen. They have played at Bootham Crescent since 1932 but were originally at Fulfordgate.

The York City home strip is red shirts and shorts with white and navy blue contoured lines and red socks with four blue bands.

The present York City was founded in 1922 to replace a previous club of the same name which had been disbanded during the First World War.

York City joined the Football League in 1929. They won the Fourth Division Championship in 1984.

In 1955, while in the Third Division, York City reached the semi-final of the FA Cup, knocking out First Division Blackpool on the way. York went out to Newcastle United, the eventual winners of that year's competition.

York City Managers

1924-1929	Bill Sherrington
1929-1936	John Collier
1936-1950	Tom Mitchell
1950-1952	Dick Duckworth
1952-1953	Charlie Spencer
1953-1954	Jimmy McCormick
1956-1960	Sam Bartram
1960-1967	Tom Lockie
1967-1968	Joe Shaw
1968-1975	Tom Johnston
1975-1977	Wilf McGuinness
1977-1980	Charlie Wright
1980-1981	Barry Lyons
1982-1987	Denis Smith
1987-1988	Bobby Saxton
1988-1991	John Bird
1991-1993	John Ward
1993-1999	Alan Little
1999-	Neil Thompson

York City League Record

1929-1958	Division Three (North)
1958-1959	Division Four
1959-1960	Division Three
1960-1965	Division Four
1965-1966	Division Three
1966-1971	Division Four

Clubs – Y

York City continued...

1971-1974	Division Three
1974-1976	Division Two
1976-1977	Division Three
1977-1984	Division Four
1984-1988	Division Three
1988-1992	Division Four
1992-1993	Division Three
1993-	Division Two

From the banks of the River Ouse
To the shores of Sicily
We will fight fight fight for the City
Till we win the Football League
To hell with Donny Rovers
To hell with Scarborough
We will fight fight fight for the City
Till we win the Football League

(Tune: Halls of Montezuma)

In the 1998-99 season, the York City player whose replica team shirt sold in the greatest numbers was Richard Cresswell.

Behave!

Hearts director, Douglas Park, was infuriated with what he considered some of the worst refereeing he had ever seen, he locked the referee in the dressing room after the game and left with the key! Not to be taken lightly by the Scottish FA. They fined him £1,000.

With an injury crisis at the club, non-league Tring Town were forced to name their 37-year-old chairman, David Lane, as one of the substitutes for the game against Berkhamsted in the 1990-91 season. Lane was put on, but was sent-off before kicking the ball.

Bognor's Paul Pullen became involved in a difference of opinion with the referee during a Diadora League match. The referee, however, called twin brother Mick over to him and sent him off. Despite protesting his innocence Mick, Bognor's player-manager at the time, was ordered off, with his brother laughing loudly in the background.

When two teams of referees met for a friendly game in Spain it should have boasted 22 of the best-behaved players. But when the match official sent off one of the players he was approached and hit by the player's father, who also happened to be a referee.

One wit placed an advert in the Portsmouth press which read: 'approximately five acres of grazing land for sale, currently housing eleven donkeys'. Portsmouth FC's telephone number was left.

It's not only players that can score world-class goals, one referee also got in on the act. In a Sunday League fixture in Southampton, the referee told the two teams that he would abandon the match if the persistent fouling continued in the second period. With the message not seeming to get through to the players the ref had had enough. With the ball in play on the edge of the penalty area, he produced an unstoppable shot that flew into the net. 'That is how you are supposed to play the game,' he said as he handed his whistle to his linesman and walked off the pitch.

THE CARLING ULTIMATE FOOTBALL FACT AND QUIZ BOOK

Life in the highlands can be tough. Because of bad weather Inverness Thistle's Scottish Cup tie against Falkirk in 1979 was postponed a record 29 times. The game was not exactly worth the wait – Thistle lost the match 4-0.

When Scottish club Greenock Morton won their first game with their new mascot, Toby the sheep, the celebrations were cut short when Toby was left in the changing room and drowned in the players' bath.

In 1924, Cardiff City had the opportunity to become the first, and only, Welsh club to win the Football League Championship. Needing a victory to take the title, City were awarded a penalty in the final game of the season against Birmingham. But Len Davies missed the kick and Huddersfield won the title on goal average.

Sometimes things go well... and sometimes...

Chelsea defender John Sillett when, hearing a whistle, caught the ball in his penalty area thinking the referee had blown the end of the game. Unfortunately the whistle came from a spectator and Chelsea's opponents, Sheffield Wednesday, were awarded one of the bizarre penalties in history.

Derby County's Andy Comyn made an immediate impact when he came on as a substitute against Bristol City in September 1992. The defender arrived onto the field to face a City free-kick. He rose to head the ball away but only succeeded in putting the ball past stand-in goalkeeper, Paul Williams, to give Bristol City a goal - all within 10 seconds of coming on.

Peruvian broadcaster Mario Sanchez received a terrible shock when he asked the striker Corina why he had missed three easy heading chances and how could that part of his game be improved. Corina answer was a swift head-butt to Sanchez, who was knocked unconscious by the blow. Corina was later arrested by the police.

Brazilian Roberto Rivelino scored some fantastic goals for club and country, but surely the one he scored against Rio Preto will remain one of the strangest. Rio Preto goalkeeper, Isadore Irandir, always prayed in his goalmouth before every game. When Corinthians kicked off, Irandir took up his praying position only to look up and see Rivelino's half-way line shot sail past him en route to the net.

THE CARLING ULTIMATE FOOTBALL FACT AND QUIZ BOOK

Going down?

In a desperate bid to stave off relegation a French team laced the opposing team's drink with knock-out drops. The scenes were hilarious as players started to collapse during the match. The authorities became aware, and when they unearthed the reason for the bizarre behaviour they condemned the offending club to relegation.

Despite losing 10-0 to Liverpool in the 1986 League Cup first round, first leg, Fulham still printed details of what would happen if the tie should finish as a draw. Unfortunately they managed only two goals, with Liverpool scoring three.

Leicester Fosse were already relegated from the First Division in 1909 before playing Nottingham Forest in a match that Forest needed to win to stay up. The day before the game one of the Leicester players was getting married so his team-mates decided to celebrate in style. They lost the game 12-0 and a Football League inquiry was launched to find out the secret for the then-Football League record victory. They found that the large defeat was due to the fact that the Leicester players were still hung over from their wedding celebrations.

Kidderminster were ecstatic when their protest of their 3-1 FA Cup defeat to Darwen was approved and the match was to be replayed. Joy quickly turned to tragedy when Darwen beat them 13-0 to record the highest score in the competition.

Despite losing all their 26 matches in the 1992-93 Darlington and District League, Barton Athletic still managed to pick up a trophy - the League's fair-play award. A club official said: 'We've always been a very popular club - particularly with our opponents.'

THE CARLING ULTIMATE FOOTBALL FACT AND QUIZ BOOK

Lucky, lucky Reds

Reaching your local Cup Final is a dream for thousands of footballers across the country, but for one team their success back-fired. After winning their semi-final, Lags XI, a prison team from Stockton, Cleveland, were thrown out of the competition because they could only play home matches.

Raith Rovers' first overseas tour was not a happy one. Travelling to the Canary Islands in 1930, the Scottish club found themselves ship-wrecked after their boat had capsized. Fortunately all players and officials were rescued, but a decision to play friendlies closer to home was quickly announced.

Cardiff City received a bumper pay-out when they entertained QPR in a third round FA Cup tie in 1990. Record receipts of £50,000 were taken, but it was soon discovered that thieves had stolen the money.

When Exeter City were beaten 5-1 at Millwall in 1982 manager Brian Godfrey decided to keep the team in London and play Millwall reserves the next day. It didn't get any better for Godfrey, Millwall reserves won 1-0.

It was the proudest moment in West Ham's Jimmy Barrett's career when he was picked to make his England debut against Northern Ireland on October 19, 1929. But after only eight minutes he was injured and carried off. He never played for England again and holds the record for shortest England career.

Stephen Gould thought he could play in goal for his strugling works side, Little Aston in Staffordshire. As he began his warm-up on his debut he jumped up to touch the crossbar, only for the bar to fall on his head. He was carried back to the dressing room before the start of the match.

THE CARLING ULTIMATE FOOTBALL FACT AND QUIZ BOOK

Miss-kicked!

One of the easiest spot-the-ball competition's came in Welsh newspaper The Western Mail in January 1993. Instead of publishing that week's competition the newspaper showed the previous week's answer. One thousand copies of the paper were run off before the mistake was realised.

When they entered their first Scottish Cup in 1873 Kilmarnock were more accustomed to playing rugby than football. As they tried to brush up on their football knowledge, opponents Renton were constantly awarded free-kicks after the Kilmarnock players had used their hands rather than their feet. To no-one's surprise Renton won the match 3-0.

After watching their side lose 2-0 in a Uefa Cup tie in September 1992, two Celtic fans were drowning their sorrows in a bar in Cologne. When they hailed a taxi to take them to their hotel they could not remember the name of the digs, or even what town it was located. After consulting each other they decided on Dortmund which was 90 miles away. After the £70 fare they remembered it was Dusseldorf, which was another 70 miles away.

QPR chairman was so anxious to find out the latest news on his club that he rang the Clubcall line on his carphone. Unfortunately he did not replace the handset correctly and only discovered his mistake the next morning when he was hit with a £335 phone bill.

With his Brazilian side San Lorenzo 2-1 up over Estudiantes in the final minutes, defender Siminiota picked up the ball thinking it had already gone out of play. To his amazement the referee, Humberto Dellacasa, awarded a penalty. The spot-kick was converted and two players were sent-off for manhandling the referee who had to be escorted from the pitch by riot police.

Denis Law could even injure himself watching a match on the substitutes bench. In Manchester United's 1968 European Cup semi-final against Real Madrid, Law got so carried away when Bill Foulkes scored that he went to punch the air but smashed his fist through the roof of the dug-out and suffered a broken bone in his hand.

THE CARLING ULTIMATE FOOTBALL FACT AND QUIZ BOOK

THE CARLING ULTIMATE FOOTBALL FACT AND QUIZ BOOK

THE CARLING ULTIMATE FOOTBALL FACT AND QUIZ BOOK

Score Sheet

THE CARLING ULTIMATE FOOTBALL FACT AND QUIZ BOOK

THE CARLING ULTIMATE FOOTBALL FACT AND QUIZ BOOK